How OTTAWA SPENDS
1993 - 1994
A More Democratic Canada...?

Edited by Susan D. Phillips

HOW OTTAWA SPENDS

A More Democratic Canada...?

1993 - 1994

Edited by Susan D. Phillips

Carleton University Press
Ottawa, Canada
1993

©Carleton University Press, Inc. 1993

ISBN 0-88629-201-8 (paperback)

Carleton Public Policy Series #13
Printed and bound in Canada

Canadian Cataloguing in Publication Data

The National Library of Canada has catalogued this
publication as follows:

How Ottawa Spends

1983-
Annual.
1993-94 ed.: A More Democratic Canada...?
Each vol. also has a distinctive title.
Prepared at the School of Public Administration
        Carleton University
Includes bibliographical references.
ISSN 0822-6482
ISBN 0-88629-201-8

1. Canada—Appropriations and expenditures—Periodicals.
I. Carleton University. School of Public Administration.

HJ7663.S6   354.710072'2   C84-030303-3

Distributed by: Oxford University Press
                           70 Wynford Drive
                           Don Mills, Ontario
                           Canada M3C 1J9
                           (416) 441-2941

Cover design: Y Graphic Design

Acknowledgements

Carleton University Press gratefully acknowledges the support extended
to its publishing program by the Canada Council and the Ontario Arts
Council.

The Press would also like to thank the Department of Communications,
Government of Canada, and the Government of Ontario through the
Ministry of Culture, Tourism and Recreation, for their assistance.

The School of Public Administration gratefully acknowledges the support
of the Federal Provincial Relations Branch, Intergovernmental Affairs,
Government of Ontario.

Contents

Preface

The purpose of the *How Ottawa Spends* series is to provide informed analysis and to stimulate debate about federal government policies and practices. In this fourteenth edition, a fundamental question about the process of governing is addressed: How can we make Canada a more democratic nation? The relationship between citizens and their governments is at a critical juncture in the 1990s and—in order to maintain its legitimacy and credibility with Canadians—the federal government needs to examine ways of enhancing democratic practices. In this election year, the authors explore some of the key election issues and consider a number of different routes for extending democratic governance.

How Ottawa Spends is produced by the School of Public Administration at Carleton University. It is truly a collaborative effort that depends on the co-operation and contributions of many people. The authors and staff work under impossible deadlines and I thank all of them for their good cheer and scholarly integrity. On behalf of the authors, I would like to thank the many government officials and representatives of non-governmental organizations who have given generously of their time and their knowledge. As a peer-reviewed publication, *How Ottawa Spends* relies on the assistance of many academic colleagues who provide comments, criticism and advice to the editor. This year, thanks are due to Frances Abele, Amy Bartholomew, Calum Carmichael, Bruce Doern, Katherine Graham, Allan Maslove, Leslie Pal, Philip Ryan, Leslie Seidle, Donald Swartz, Gene Swimmer and Stan Winer, as well as the many individuals who provided constructive criticism directly to the contributors. Special appreciation is expressed to Jane Jenson for her editorial assistance and advice which were offered graciously and which extended well beyond the call of collegial duty. Carolyn Chisholm and Gordon Quaiattini provided expert research assistance. Under the direction of Allan Maslove, Carolyn Chisholm also produced the tables and charts that appear as the appendix, *Fiscal Facts and Trends*.

The School's superb Administrator and bilingual in-house copy editor, Martha Clark, managed the production; our technical wizard and constructive critic, Amanda Begbie, caught our mistakes and industriously converted the manuscripts into an accurate and pleasing text. Shelley Henderson provided extraordinarily efficient copy editing. Invaluable professional service and support was provided by the Carleton University Press staff, Michael Gnarowski, Steven Uriarte and Anne Winship; and by our French translator, Françoise L'heureux. Finally, I would like to thank my friend and husband, Brian Little, for his unfailing personal and intellectual support in this project.

Susan Phillips
Ottawa
April 1993

The opinions expressed by the contributors to this volume are the personal views of the authors of the individual chapters, and do not reflect the views of the editor or the School of Public Administration of Carleton University.

CHAPTER 1

A More Democratic Canada ...?

Susan D. Phillips

Résumé : Les Canadiens demandent instamment que les gouvernements renoncent à l'élitisme et optent pour une administration plus ouverte et démocratique. Le *statu quo* est devenu inacceptable; il est temps d'entrer dans le vif du débat et de faire ce qu'il faut pour améliorer les pratiques qui ont cours au sein de la structure d'administration démocratique. Les modifications qui s'imposent supposent des changements fondamentaux et non simplement un «rafistolage» de la structure gouvernementale. Dans ce chapitre, l'auteur expose des mesures visant à améliorer la structure de l'autorité démocratique à l'échelon fédéral. Une série de réformes démocratiques cohérentes supposent des changements à quatre points de vue : 1) au niveau du régime, y compris la réforme des partis et des systèmes électoraux, du Parlement et du régime constitutionnel; 2) au niveau des rapports entre le gouvernement fédéral et les citoyens, à la fois en tant que particuliers et membres de groupes; 3) sur le plan administratif, ce qui suppose des changements à la structure des institutions et aux pratiques de gestion; 4) au regard des rapports avec d'autres gouvernements, particulièrement les gouvernements autochtones et les autorités municipales. Même si les Conservateurs se sont déjà engagés à tâtons dans cette voie, ils n'ont pas profité de belles occasions qui se sont présentées dans le courant de la dernière année et, d'une manière générale, ils n'ont pas fait cas des Canadiens qui leur font savoir que la démocratie doit être améliorée.

Abstract: Increasingly, Canadians are demanding that their governments become less élitist, more open and more democratic. The status quo is no longer acceptable and we need to engage the debates seriously and take steps to enhance the practices of democratic governance. The modifications required involve fundamental change, rather than mere tinkering with our system of government. This chapter lays out an agenda for enhancing democratic governance at the federal level. A coherent package of democratic reforms will necessitate changes in four areas: 1) the macro or regime level, including reforms to the party and electoral systems, Parliament and the constitutional framework; 2) the relationships between the federal government and citizens, both as individuals and as members of groups; 3) the administrative level, involving changes to institutional structures and management practices; and 4) the relationships with other governments, notably Aboriginal and municipal governments. While the Tories have taken some tentative steps in the right direction, they have missed some

important opportunities over the past year and, in general, have not yet responded
seriously what Canadians are telling them about the need to improve democracy.

The 1990s are a time for rethinking government. During the last
decade, the initial response by many (especially neo-conservative)
governments to burdensome and growing public debts and the
public's concern was to shrink the size of the State, attack the
public service for its incompetency and blame "special interest
groups" for paralysing government. However, the unrelenting
nature of the economic and political pressures generated by the
fiscal crisis gave way to a more significant set of reforms, intended
not simply to create a smaller state through downsizing and
privatization, but to "reinvent" government as a more entrepreneurial and efficient institution.[1] The focus of the "New Public
Management" that has swept Western democracies—which in
Canada is embodied as the package of managerial reforms known
as Public Service 2000—has been an emphasis on forging a
cultural revolution of management and producing a more market-
based, output-focused and service-oriented public service.[2]

   Governments are increasingly recognizing, however, that
the creation of smaller, more entrepreneurial and efficient bureaucracies is not a sufficient response to meet the pressures of the
1990s. Indeed, there have been many signs of a different set of
demands and challenges that governments have to address. For
example, the traditional model of executive federalism followed in
the Meech Lake round of constitutional renewal was vilified by
many Canadians as illegitimate because it was limited to closed-
door negotiations by "11 white men in suits." In the past several
years, the credibility of most of our democratic institutions and
political processes has been under attack, and there is a general
malaise among Canadians who feel that they are overtaxed by
governments that are out of touch and out of control. A national
opinion poll in January 1992 revealed "an electorate deeply
disenchanted with traditional politics and political institutions—
and of a people eager for radical change to both."[3] Ironically,
politicians as different as Kim Campbell, Bob Rae and Preston
Manning have articulated a similar promise as part of their
electoral rhetoric: to give government back to the people.

On February 24, 1993, Prime Minister Brian Mulroney, who had become one of the most unpopular leaders in Canadian history, announced his resignation. His two terms as Prime Minister were unenviable times for any leader. He pursued some very courageous, albeit immensely disliked, policies that included Free Trade, the GST, downsizing and restraint of government, and cuts to social programs. In spite of the continuing hardships of the economic recession and unresolved constitutional issues, there is now a sense that exciting new times are about to unfold—because either a fresh face will lead the Tories or a different political party will form the government in 1993. The candidates vying for the Tory leadership have promised publicly to play by a new set of rules and to conduct "the most democratic and healthy political race yet seen in Canada."[4]

The chapters in this volume of *How Ottawa Spends* argue that the status quo is no longer acceptable to Canadians. If reforms are not undertaken and people continue to feel alienated and distrustful of their leaders and governments, it is very likely that there will be a serious disintegration of a sense of political community and an inability of governments of any political persuasion to maintain sufficient legitimacy and credibility to attain their policy goals. While enhanced democracy *is* on the political agenda, there is no single interpretation of what that means and no one "correct" method for achieving it. Rather, there are a number of fundamental debates to be engaged and this volume is one opportunity to address them. This introduction provides an overview of the nature and range of reforms that are being—or should be—undertaken in Canada. It also offers a synopsis of each of the chapters of the book and relates government spending priorities, as announced in the December 1992 and the April 1993 federal budgets, to a democratic agenda.

The changes required to make the institutions and policy processes of the federal government more democratic do not entail mere tinkering, they necessitate a range of fundamental and interconnected reforms. Democratic governance will not be enhanced merely by giving more control to the elected representatives, by sprinkling the policy process with more "multistakeholder" consultations (although public consultation is an important part of democratic practice) or by rejigging the federal-provincial division of powers to match more appropriately jurisdictional responsibility with policy exigencies. Nor will the demands for extended democratic practices be met simply by throwing the Conservative Party out of office. Rather, the issues are ones that any resident of 24 Sussex Drive in the next decade and her or his government will have to address.

Enhancing democratic governance involves two related and interdependent tasks.[5] On the one hand, *democratic* governance connotes extending the opportunities for representation of citizen views and active participation in the policy process. Participation in policy making not only extends the fairness and social justice dimension of policy, but contributes to the development of political communities and the education of individuals as citizens.[6] It helps transform citizens from being merely passive subjects to being active agents possessing responsibilities, as well as rights.[7] However, there is no single model of decision making involved in democracy; rather there are many different vehicles for organizing representation and participation. Democratic *governance*, on the other hand, involves enabling collective choice in the pursuit of the common welfare.[8] The pragmatic task of governing is to balance citizen interests, channel a multitude of views into policy, make strategic choices and act upon them; in other words, to provide policy unity out of diversity through accountable procedures. This is inherently a political, as well as a democratic, process for which the models of management borrowed from the private sector are inadequate and inappropriate guides because they cannot address this essential duality of public life.

Over the course of its two terms in office, the Conservative government has indicated in several ways that it is responding to the challenge of enhancing democratic governance. In many departments, as well as in the last round of constitutional negotiations, there have been more—and more innovative— mechanisms for public consultation than ever before. The entire electoral process has been reviewed by a royal commission and there have been some genuine attempts, such as the Labour Force Development Strategy and the Healthy Cities program, to develop community-based policy initiatives.[9] But there have also been many serious contradictions and inconsistencies. For instance (to mention only those of recent memory), the Government's intention, leaked to the media in February 1993, to shift the Canadian International Development Agency (CIDA) away from its traditional focus on the world's poorest countries to business promotion in eastern Europe came without consultation with the non-governmental organizations (NGOs) working in development. The merger of the Canada Council and the Social Sciences and Humanities Research Council (SSHRC) was undertaken with little input from the research and arts communities or the councils themselves. Finally, the changes announced to the Unemployment Insurance program in the December 1992 mini-budget (and the subsequent public outcry) were indicative of a government working in isolation from most of its constituencies.[10]

It is evident that, to date, the changes in democratic practice that have occurred at the federal level in Canada have been sporadic and do not yet represent a coherent trend or a planned project of the Government, as the managerial reforms aimed at improving efficiency have been. In fact, the problem the federal government faces in enhancing democratic practice is more akin to herding cats—the task of setting what so far has been a diversity of independent and isolated changes towards a common goal without straying off-track at the first distraction or impediment.[11] One goal of this edition of *How Ottawa Spends* is to identify as part of a broader trend, and to articulate as part of an agenda for enhanced democracy, what at the present time may seem like random encounters with stray cats.

As is evident from the range of topics covered in the following 12 chapters, the recommended modifications are not narrow in their scope. A coherent package of democratic reforms will necessitate changes in four areas: 1) the macro or regime level, including reforms to political and electoral processes and the constitutional framework; 2) the relationships with citizens, both as individuals and as members of interest groups; 3) the administrative level, involving changes to institutional structures and management practices within the federal government; and 4) the relationships with other governments, notably Aboriginal and municipal governments. While this agenda implies primarily political changes to the processes of governing, the underlying impetus for change has both economic and political causes, and the results of reform will have both economic and political consequences. Moreover, these democratizing reforms are extant as Canada grapples with two fundamental challenges—seeking a balance domestically between individual and collective rights, and acting as a participant/observer as global change occurs in the world order. Naturally, this volume cannot address all of the reforms that are, or might be, under way in each of these areas. But each author examines a different key issue and, as a collection, the chapters cover the full spectrum of reforms that we believe should be considered. Because 1993 is an election year, several chapters address issues that are likely to be at the centre of public debate in the coming months.

PRESSURES FOR ENHANCING DEMOCRATIC GOVERNANCE

The pressures for enhancing democracy stem from a number of different sources, both inside and outside the Government. First, the past two decades have witnessed the rise of a multiplicity of social movements, such as the women's, environmental, gay and disabled persons movements, that are engaged in the politics of identity and are interested in the democratization of both everyday life and governance.[12] Although these movements have been portrayed by the political right as narrowly focused "special interest groups," they are, in fact, broadly based inclusive movements that value citizen participation and struggle to empower marginalized people and change social institutions, including the family, the workplace, school and the church, as well as the State. The concept of citizenship emphasized by these popular movements is one in which all citizens should have more or less equal opportunities to exercise the consumption of collective goods and services, and to enjoy the right to participate in the decision-making processes that determine the allocation of the benefits (and costs) of public policies. Thus, social movements have accentuated a decline in the public's acquiescence and deference to élites and experts, and accelerated an increase in the public's interest in creating opportunities for direct participation and improving mechanisms for holding public officials accountable for policy decisions. Alan Cairns argues that the Canadian Charter of Rights and Freedoms has contributed to a sense on the part of many groups that participation should not be presented merely as opportunities, offered or withdrawn at the discretion of government officials, but should be enjoyed as quasi-rights.[13] Technology has given citizen groups access to technical information with which they can criticize and challenge governments; thus, these groups have provided valuable inputs to policy making—or alternatively have become vocal critics who can embarrass governments if ignored.

Second, an increasingly globalized economy has put political pressures on the State. In one respect, globalization has produced highly individualistic, more class-divided societies in which much of the upper stratum is less willing to sacrifice for the common good of society.[14] But globalization has also provided the terrain for the mobilization of social movements that are international in scope and for the development of a concept of global citizenship that presupposes universal rights and standards of justice. Consequently, we look to supranational institutions, as well as nation-states, to protect those rights. While the tolerance for, and practicality of, highly interventionist governments may have diminished, the role of the State in this environment remains important. It falls to states not only to protect individual rights, but to establish and promote a sense of political community (and individual responsibility to it) based on first principles such as democracy, freedom and justice. Thus to be seen to be legitimate, governments are under pressure to reform themselves to better embody and exemplify these first principles. Clearly, globalization is not just about markets, but about values as well.

The third source of pressures for democratization stems from the debate over the capacity of markets. While it is generally agreed that an essential aspect of democracy is choice, there is a sharp contrast between what neo-Conservative and social democratic governments believe are the best means for providing choice. From a neo-Conservative perspective, markets are the best vehicles for the expression of choice and individual freedom, and they are presumed not only to benefit, but to empower, individual citizens. Thus, the strategy of most neo-conservative governments has been to privatize policy to the market or impose market mechanisms on the delivery of policy. For example, neo-conservative governments issue vouchers to parents in order to promote choice in the selection of schools; and they use tax credits to allow parents to purchase the type of child-care services they desire in the market, rather than forcing them to rely on centrally allocated and government subsidized spaces in day-care centres. However, while markets work extremely well for many purposes, the creation of quasi-markets to deliver public policy often produces only an illusion of choice and frequently serves merely to accentuate existing inequities. For instance, if an adequate number of appropriate day-care spaces is not available, the possession of a voucher or extra money in the form of tax credits offers little real opportunity to exercise choice. Thus, the disillusionment with markets as vehicles of choice has led many people to look with renewed interest to democratic politics as the provider of choice.

Finally, to some degree, a push for greater responsiveness and accountability has emerged from within the public service. For example, the impetus for Public Service 2000 came from senior management, who saw a crisis in internal morale and a growing isolation of the federal government from Canadians. Although it is more characteristic of the "reinventing government" genre of reform with its emphasis on productivity and service, aspects of Public Service 2000—especially the interest in increased consultation—are also compatible with a democratizing impulse. The diversity and persistence of these pressures for change suggest that concern for enhancing democratic practices in Canada is not a fad that has appeared only fleetingly on the political agenda, but is instead a concern to which political leaders must direct serious attention if they are to maintain any degree of legitimacy and credibility with Canadians.

AN AGENDA FOR ENHANCING DEMOCRACY

Extending democratic governance in Canada will involve reforms at several levels, ranging from the basic institutions of parliamentary democracy to the micro level of workplace democracy within the public service. This chapter will explore briefly the potential for reform in four areas and provide an overview of the topics covered in the chapters that follow.

The Macro Institutional Level

Canadians' deep-seated and widespread discontent with contemporary practices of democracy may begin with anger at Prime Minister Mulroney and our current elected representatives, but it does not end there.[15] Rather, it extends to a disillusionment with our most fundamental democratic institutions and processes. This suggests that reforms aimed at enhancing democratic governance must start with the party and electoral systems, the Constitution and Parliament.

The representative and policy capacity of the party system in Canada has been in decline for several decades.[16] Parties are widely acknowledged to be largely exclusionary of women and minorities, inaccessible to many worthy potential candidates due to the costs of campaigns and, as brokers of interests which focus on leaders rather than issues, inept vehicles for the promotion of constructive policy debates.[17] Concern over the entire regime of regulation and financing of the electoral process was seriously provoked in the 1988 election because interest groups on both sides of the free trade issue spent money as never before. The 1993 election will be a critical campaign which may serve either to improve or further erode the credibility of the party system. Although it is early in the Tory leadership campaign as this publication goes to press, Kim Campbell, Jean Charest and the other candidates are promising a different kind of campaign and (wistfully) a different kind of government.[18]

• **Alexandra Dobrowolsky** and **Jane Jenson** examine the comprehensive and innovative package of recommendations presented in the 1992 report of the Royal Commission on Electoral Reform and Party Financing (RCERPF), which addressed the serious malaise of the Canadian party system. Because governments as well as parties spend money on elections, this issue has implications for government spending as well as for democracy. Dobrowolsky and Jenson offer explanations as to why neither the parties nor the social movements that share a democratizing agenda accepted the Commission's medicine. The problem with the RCERPF's approach, they argue, is that it treated interest groups as one of the causes, rather than as a consequence of, the party disease. When Parliament actually came to draft new legislation on electoral reform in February 1993, it disregarded the far-reaching reforms recommended by the Commission in favour of short-term political advantage and produced minimal changes to existing rules. This short-sighted response to the challenge offered up by the Commission, these authors conclude, is likely to produce more problems than it solves.

The 1991-92 round of constitutional negotiations leading to the Charlottetown Accord and the October 1992 referendum not only indicated that the *process* of constitutional renewal must be highly participatory and acceptable to Canadians, but it raised new questions about the *substance* and function of the Constitution in our society. A fundamental lesson that we learned from that round is that constitutions are one important means through which societies represent themselves to themselves. Constitutions are not just about "high politics"; they affect the stuff of everyday lives, such as jobs, education, taxes, health care and so on.[19]

• **Miriam Smith** addresses a new issue in Canadian constitutional politics, the recognition of economic and social rights. The debate over constitutionalizing these rights which took place in the 1991-92 Canada round raises fundamental questions about the very nature of the Constitution: Which purposes and whose interests should it serve? To what extent should policy choices (such as guarantees of free markets and rights to medicare) be enshrined? Would the constitutionalization of certain macro policy frameworks enhance democracy by providing minimal guarantees to all Canadians or diminish it by limiting the choices of future duly elected governments? While framed here in constitutional terms, the trade-offs involved in public spending on economic versus social policies are at the very heart of the debate over the future of the welfare state. Although interest in constitutional negotiations may have faded temporarily from the political agenda, Smith points out that debates about whether democratic governance would be well served by entrenching certain policy options in the Constitution are central ones that will resurface in the next round.

Although the limited space in this edition precludes an examination of parliamentary reform, the legitimacy of this institution is also under scrutiny due to its lack of representation of women and minority populations, its partisan bickering and its incapacity for policy review. Over the past decade several significant changes to Parliament have taken place. Beginning in the mid-1980s, the committee structure was expanded to promote more vigorous debate on proposed legislation and to assume a greater role in overseeing departmental policy and spending, as well as a stronger role in calling departmental officials—not just

Ministers—to account for the activities of government.[20] In addition, television has made the debates of the House of Commons readily accessible to the Canadian public. In March 1993, legislation on conflict of interest for members of Parliament and senators was finally tabled after being first promised by Prime Minister Mulroney in 1987.[21] If passed, and if compliance follows, the new rules should help to promote the perceived integrity of individual politicians. However, many keen observers of Parliament recommend a more major overhaul by further extending the influence of backbench MPs on the Government's agenda, creating a more collegial committee system to reduce excessive partisanship, allowing free votes on more bills (so that MPs can better represent their constituents rather than blindly holding fast to the party line under imposed discipline) and reforming the Senate.[22]

Naturally, substituting a more open and collegial model with more independently minded members on either side of the House of Commons *and* a more competitive and accessible party system will not be a task that the existing party and parliamentary élites are likely to take up with wild enthusiasm. However, MPs themselves may be more eager proponents because they share some of the public's discontent. As one member of Parliament was recently quoted: "[In my previous career] I had been successful, I was known in the community. But with the bestowal of public office, you instantly become a sleazebag."[23]

Forging New Relations with Citizens

Of course, the interest in citizen participation is not new, as such demands were voiced loudly during the late 1960s and through the 1970s. However, democratization of governance in the 1990s does not entail simply providing more opportunities for consulting citizens, but necessitates a re-evaluation of some fundamental premises. One basic issue focuses on the value of interest groups to society and the State, and a second centres on the distinction between citizens and consumers.

Many politicians, journalists and scholars view interest groups and social movements as part of the problem of governing and assert that groups overload governments, which leads to a situation of ungovernability. For instance, Barbara McDougall, in her capacity as Minister of Employment and Immigration, is typical of many Conservatives when she states,

> The problem, as I see it, is the fact that so many single or limited interest groups have established their presence on the national political scene that it is virtually impossible for any government to undertake a comprehensive policy platform and survive a subsequent election.[24]

A sea change in democratic governance will require that the positive contributions of groups be acknowledged. Not only do citizen groups connect individuals to issues and each other, they serve as vehicles for direct participation, alternative sources of policy expertise, effective mechanisms for communication of information and vocal watchdogs over governments.[25] In this light, social movements and interest groups can be seen as opportunities for extending policy discourse and promoting popular sovereignty. They are potentially part of the solution of enhancing democratic governance, not the problem.

However, a recognition of the positive role of groups must also acknowledge the fundamental inequality of society. The difficulty with superimposing democracy—which implies some measure of equality—on an unequal society is that some people count for more than others. From this perspective, a necessary function of the State is to compensate for the inherent inequities by including representatives of the less privileged groups in political institutions and consultations, and by providing assistance to these groups (perhaps in the form of public funding) so that they, too, can have a voice.[26] This is not to suggest that every group that asks the Government for money should receive it, nor does it imply that the existing funding programs of the Secretary of State and other departments are working perfectly well.[27] Rather, my point is that for a government to use citizen groups and social movements as the scapegoats for the difficulties inherent in governing, or to cut their funding for ideological reasons while at the same time asking these groups to be "partners" and service-providers, and to consult extensively on policy, is counter-productive. Of course, the more difficult challenge is to devise equitable arrangements for assistance.

Although neo-Conservative governments have given considerable attention to becoming more service-oriented and client-centred, as the rhetoric of Public Service 2000 suggests, they tend to define individuals as customers or clients, not citizens. The difference between the two notions is that a *citizen* is both an individual and a member of a collectivity; he or she self-identifies as part of that collectivity and, thus, cannot be completely separated from it. In contrast, a *consumer* is a "bundle of preferences waiting to be satisfied. Consumers are to be researched so that the service or product can be designed so as to best meet their wants—or so that new appetites can be stimulated and supplied."[28] The effect of this reasoning is that consumers are conceived to be atomized, private and self-interested units, rather than members of a political community who may be concerned not merely about the quality of service, but about the very nature of the goods and services being provided. Thus, reforming democratic governance cannot rely on the private sector metaphor of providing service to consumers, but must take up the political challenge of seeking participation by citizens.

Working from these fundamental premises, the task of creating a more participatory and democratic government might involve several interrelated steps: 1) expansion of mechanisms for citizen participation that provide realistic opportunities for large segments of society to participate;[29] 2) extension of a regime for regulating fairness in representation which both regulates the privileged and assists the disadvantaged; 3) provision of open access to information;[30] and 4) development of the capacity for self-management of policies and programs by groups and communities.[31]

In this volume, two chapters address the issue of government-citizen relations.

- In considering the question of fairness of representation, **Paul Pross** and **Iain Stewart** argue that the Conservative government has been contradictory in how it regulates different sets of interests. On the one hand, the Tories have been relatively lenient in the regulation of lobbying activity by clients (usually business interests who can claim "government relations" as a tax write-off) of professional lobbying firms. The review of the Lobbyists Registration Act by Pross and Stewart suggests a number of desirable reforms ranging from greater compliance mechanisms to more extensive reporting requirements by both third-party lobbyists and public servants. On the other hand, public interest groups which apply for a charitable status under the Income Tax Act have been quite tightly controlled due to the inflexibility of the definition of a charity under the Act. Pross and Stewart suggest that the designation of charitable status be expanded with a special category that would recognize the positive contributions to society made by public interest advocacy groups. This would make the regulation of these interests more visible and less discretionary.

- **Leslie Pal** and **Leslie Seidle** trace the unprecedented consultation exercise that was part of the Canada round of constitutional renewal beginning with the Bélanger-Campeau and Spicer Commissions in 1990 to the referendums of October 1992. They document for the first time the extent, specific form and cost of participation of each phase of the process and offer extensive analysis of the referendum campaigns in both Quebec and the rest of Canada. Pal and Seidle argue that the substance of the Charlottetown Accord was wedded to the process and that it failed to be ratified because of the peculiar nature of constitutional politics in Canada, not because the process was undemocratic. They point to a paradox of participation that affects all policy areas, not just constitutional politics: while wide participation holds the promise of greater legitimacy and support for a policy, an expanded number of players and agendas also exacerbates conflict. Rather than fulfilling the promise of participation, Pal and Seidle conclude that the "Charlottetown Accord succumbed to its paradox."

Changing the Public Service

The third element of a democratizing agenda involves changes within the State, because the politics of democracy are played out within the public service as well as between government and society. As noted, democratic governance requires both extending opportunities for participation *and* enhancing the capacity for strategic choice and legitimate action. While the concepts of democracy and governance are linked, and are essential to each other, the priorities of each occasionally collide.

There are at least four potential reforms that must be addressed within the public service. The first relates to the structural question of whether the representation of interests should occur *within* the State through a large number of specialized ministers and departments (for example, ministers responsible for women, youth or small business) or whether strategic trade-offs among related sets of interests could be better provided, without sacrificing representation, by a leaner cabinet and "super" ministries.[32] The second element is a process of "de-bureaucratization," or reducing the hierarchy and stripping away the layers of management, and thus, presumably, making the public service more flexible and responsive. However, public institutions are not infinitely elastic. This notion of responsiveness and accountability of public servants directly to the public runs smack into the traditional conventions of ministerial responsibility. The dilemmas posed by the incompatibility of these differing notions of accountability have yet to be fully addressed. Third, employment equity is associated with democratic governance because an institution whose workplace is not representative of the workforce cannot itself be seen to be legitimate.[33] Finally, workplace democracy involves adherence to traditional collective bargaining practices between labour and management.

Some of the managerial reforms introduced as part of Public Service 2000, although undertaken primarily with the intention of improving efficiency and serving clients, also deal with these aspects.[34] Streamlining of the public service began in 1992 through changes to the job classification system, which reduced the layers of management. The Public Service Reform Act (C-26), enacted in the fall of 1992, introduced amendments to the Public Service Employment Act and the Public Service Staff Relations Act that are designed to give greater authority to deputy heads to transfer and deploy employees at their current level throughout their departments, to provide greater clout to employment equity by making deputies publicly accountable for equity targets and to allow greater flexibility in the collective bargaining process.[35] Yet many critics fear that these changes will not expand, but may actually limit, the scope of bargaining and threaten the application of the merit principle. While the importance of some of the issues of workplace democracy and equity has been recognized, these reforms have run headlong into the financial restraint agenda so that positive change has been significantly slowed or, in the case of collective bargaining, usurped completely.

Although it is beyond the scope of this single volume to address all of the issues related to preparing the administration for more democratic governance, one chapter considers the key trade-offs between efficiency and democracy that are involved in institutional change and the managerial reforms.

- Four efficiency-democracy bargains which are central to the task of reinventing government organization are explored by **Bruce Doern**. These bargains are 1) choices between the size of government and the composition of services that will be demanded in the 1990s; 2) choices between the number of ministerial departments and the nature of representation; 3) issues related to the separation of policy functions from delivery mechanisms; and 4) choices on how to enhance citizen respect for, and confidence in, the public service. Doern concludes that "the number of cabinet portfolios should be pruned quite severely to help ministers focus on the large framework-oriented issues." Based on a comparison with the Next Steps program and the Citizen's Charter in the U.K., he also suggests that Canada's experimentation with special operating agencies should be vastly expanded and that, while the use of output "standards may help improve service delivery, there are areas where increased public investment is crucial to the provision of services."

Relationships with Other Governments

In spite of a decade of constitutional negotiations, Canadians are still trying to redefine relations among spheres of government. However, the intergovernmental relations of the 1990s must go well beyond clarifying the division of powers between federal and provincial governments. Two new relations need to be carved out. One debate focuses on the relations with the emerging governments of Aboriginal peoples; the other is a decentralization to, and disentanglement of, policy with local governments.

It will be a fundamental test of the first principles of democracy to recognize the legitimacy of Aboriginal peoples as distinct political communities, on the terms on which Aboriginal peoples wish to be recognized, and to negotiate just and enduring self-government arrangements.

- **Paul Chartrand** examines the issue of legitimacy in Canada's response to the claims by Aboriginal peoples for self-government. The establishment of a legitimate constitutional order, legitimate institutions and self-government arrangements depends not only on Canadian standards of legitimacy, but on those of Aboriginal peoples themselves. Chartrand argues that Canada has had difficulty in offering a principled response to the challenge by Aboriginal peoples. Two erroneous assumptions that fail to confront, and may even divert attention from, the issue of legitimacy have tended to dominate. One false premise is that Aboriginal peoples are a "racial minority" and the second is a liberal assumption of "equal treatment" for all who live in Canada. Both these assumptions make it very difficult to recognize Aboriginal peoples as distinct political communities with unique status. Moreover, the balance of power between Canada and Aboriginal peoples is by no means an equal one. "Canada has the upper hand in negotiations for Aboriginal self-government. It has the power to influence not only the identity of the claimants but also the very nature and scope of eventual self-government arrangements."

The debates over decentralization in the 1990s are not tied to a narrow vision of constitutional politics, but stem from a fundamental rethinking of political institutions and the concept of sovereignty. Confronted by an environment of internationalization of capital, global economies and global communication networks, the centrality of the concept of place has been supplanted and the primacy of the nation-state has been eroded. Globalization has at least two important implications for democratic governance. First, there is a growing consensus that choice on as many matters as possible should reside with local communities.[36] Thus, governments are moving away from the principles of national standards, universality and "one size fits all" policy and are seeking policy solutions that are community-based and community-delivered. This approach is exemplified by the community-centred shift in health care that is being promoted by both the federal and many provincial governments. Thus, the debate over decentralization of power cannot stop at provincial governments.[37]

The second reason for exploring the formal devolution of powers to local levels is that it is already happening on a *de facto* basis. In a globalized economy, the geographical locus of economic competition and development will no longer be the nation-state, but metropolitan areas.[38] The implication for Canada is this: federal and provincial governments should not only reassess the question of devolution of powers to local governments, but should also play an important role in promoting economic development and assisting in the reconstruction of urban infrastructure (in the broadest sense) in order to make Canada's metropolitan areas competitive in a global environment.

• The issues surrounding devolution to local governments are explored by **Harvey Lithwick** and **Rebecca Coulthard**. They argue that urban Canadians, who constitute almost 77 percent of the population, have been largely disenfranchised and that the failure to complete the logical process of devolution of powers has been a serious barrier to effective democratization. This disenfranchisement has had consequences of national economic significance because "problem laden urban areas are becoming a drag on the national economy, rather than its engine." Lithwick and Coulthard recommend an innovative program for urban economic and infrastructure development which would be supported by federal and provincial governments, and would be based on the creation of a Metropolitan Development Corporation in each of Canada's largest urban areas. Such an initiative, they suggest, would have long-term economic, as well as political, benefits that would "give real substance to our pursuit of more satisfactory and sustained economic growth, with its attendant social and environmental benefits."

ELECTION ISSUES

In addition to laying out an agenda for enhancing democratic governance in Canada, this edition of *How Ottawa Spends* also contributes to the central debates about democracy by exploring the policy issues that are likely to be key ones in the 1993 federal election. Four issues are identified as critical: 1) the Tories' record on management of the economy; 2) the debate over the North American Free Trade Agreement (NAFTA); 3) the dissolution of the "Sacred Trust" of social policies; and 4) education policy which, although it is not a federal responsibility, is centrally linked

to the debate over economic competitiveness and has become the
basis of one of the major social movements of the 1990s.

* The chapter by **Bruce Wilkinson** points out that the Mulroney
  government's economic agenda, which has centred on improving
  competitiveness, has led to the serious neglect of the issue of the
  balance of payments and, in particular, the current account deficits.
  Based on a review of the balance of payments record since 1984,
  Wilkinson's analysis reveals the magnitude of the problem: Canada's
  international indebtedness is now about 50 percent of the gross
  national product (GNP), dramatically greater than the comparable
  figure in the United States of about 6.5 percent of the GNP. Without
  significant policy changes, it is likely that foreigners will no longer
  be willing to continue lending to Canada. The proposal made by
  Wilkinson to deal with this problem is that the value of the Canadian
  dollar be lowered to a level of US$0.70 or less. Although this would
  impose a period of painful adjustment on Canadians, this pain would
  be less severe than the consequences of a policy that continues to
  avoid the problem.

* Just as the Free Trade Agreement (FTA) was the key issue of the 1988
  election, the more expansive NAFTA between the U.S., Mexico and
  Canada is likely to be a central debate in the 1993 election. **Ian
  Robinson** argues that the NAFTA, in its current form, will encourage
  strategies of destructive corporate competition that are based on
  reducing the costs of wages and environmental protection. This
  competition is likely to exacerbate income inequalities and undercut
  labour rights in all three countries. Robinson asserts that the NAFTA
  should be either reopened and fundamentally altered, or rejected. In
  its place, he proposes a pro-democratic trade policy that includes a
  continental "social dimension" similar to the European Community
  (EC) model.

In addition to their economic agenda, the other important
stamp of neo-Conservative ideology that the Tories will be called
upon to defend in the election campaign is social policy. Although
it has not been their top priority as restraint and deficit reduction
have been, social policy underwent a significant transformation
under the Conservative government in terms of the first principles.
This can be seen, for example, in the abandonment of the

long-standing principle of universality in the Family Allowances program, and in the choice of delivery mechanisms as demonstrated by their preference for use of the tax system. Moreover, as north-south economic integration accelerates, it will be social policy that provides the east-west glue to hold Canada together as a political community.[39] Thus, the substance of social policy should be a critical debate for all elections in the foreseeable future.

We also examine social policy from the perspective of process because policy making in this area has become profoundly undemocratic. One of the primary reasons that the Tories were able to effect such extensive and fundamental changes to social programs is that, in many cases, they proceeded through the "politics of stealth." Ken Battle, who coined the term, defines the politics of stealth as a process that "relies heavily on technical amendments to taxes and transfers that are as difficult to explain as they are to understand and thus largely escape media scrutiny and public attention."[40] Given the intense public debate that is likely to centre on social policy, two chapters are devoted to these issues:

- **James Rice** and **Michael Prince** provide an overview of the record of the Mulroney government on social policy over its two terms in office. They demonstrate that the Tories' approach has been characterized by three general features: 1) a record of expenditure restraint and program restructuring; 2) the prevalence of the politics of stealth and dominance of the Department of Finance as the central federal social policy institution due to its control over tax policy and intergovernmental transfers; and 3) a shift in targets as transfers to other governments have decreased while transfers to persons have increased since 1984. Rice and Prince assert that the result of this approach has been a lowering of the social safety net and a weakening of the bonds of nationhood.

- The latest of the Conservative government's changes to family benefits—the Child Tax Benefit created in 1992—is the subject of the chapter by **Ken Battle**. He provides extensive new data which show that, by the year 2000, fewer and fewer families will be getting less and less benefits. His conclusion is that, under the Conservatives, social policy "shows a distinctive pattern of progressive changes being undermined by regressive changes, which refutes their claims that they have created a simpler, fairer and more effective system of child benefits. The new system remains complex, inequitable and inadequate. "

In the final chapter, we depart from the *How Ottawa Spends* tradition to explore a policy field—public education—that is not a direct spending area of the federal government. However, the debate over reform of our school systems has become a key one as it affects all Canadians, many of whom are mobilizing as a grass roots movement that some believe will become *the* social movement of the decade.[41] While the federal government has no direct spending or regulatory jurisdiction over public education, it has claimed it as an issue of national concern and a central component of its competitiveness agenda.

- The primary concern of the federal government in education policy is to ensure that our schools prepare students to become future workers. **Saul Schwartz** explores the implications of the "ABCs" of one set of school reforms, known as intensification, that is intended to do this. He criticizes these reforms, which attempt to make schools more accountable by implementing programs of national standard-ized testing—testing that emphasizes the "old" basic skills of literacy and numeracy—and which promote parental choice in the selection of schools. Although Schwartz concurs that educational reform is a worthy and necessary challenge, he warns that the adoption of a simplistic approach could have some very negative unintended side-effects.

SPENDING AND A DEMOCRATIC AGENDA

Budgets, as expressions of priorities and values, are important components of democratic governance in both their substance and process. In 1993, the Conservative government chose to deviate from the usual practice of presenting a budget in late February. Instead, it offered a "mini-budget"—a rather substantial one—in the form of the Economic and Fiscal Statement delivered on December 2, 1992 and postponed the main budget until April 26, 1993.[42] The reasons for this strategy were twofold. First, there was a considerable gap between the fiscal and economic trends that had been projected in the February 1992 budget and the reality of the actual figures by year's end.[43] Economic under-performance probably was due to several factors: 1) the impact of the GST has driven a considerable degree of economic activity "underground" (that is, work is paid for by cash or barter and never claimed as earned income) so that the Government loses twice on taxation revenues—on the consumption tax and on income tax; 2) the economy was still undergoing a fundamental restructuring in which many jobs, especially in less competitive manufacturing industries, were being lost permanently; and 3) the recovery that was beginning to be felt by late 1992 was driven by exports, rather than by consumer spending, which provides governments with less revenue through consumption taxes.[44] Given the still burgeoning debt, the federal government wanted to signal to foreign lenders that Canada was not neglecting the problem. The second reason for this timing was a political strategy of presenting the "bad news" early so that it would be associated more with Mulroney than with the new Conservative leader. By delaying the main budget until the spring of 1993, the Government could use the budget presentation as an opportunity to congratulate itself on its record and claim any "good news" in terms of economic recovery to be a result of its own policies.

December 1992: The Not-So-Mini-Budget

Given the expectations being created by the fever of "Clintonomics" in the United States following the November election, many analysts looked to Finance Minister Don Mazankowski's December mini-budget to offer some commitments for infrastructure investment that might help jump-start an economy still stalled by the recession. However, those who had hoped for spending on infrastructure (in its broadest sense) were only minimally satisfied as the Government showed a lack of imagination in the type of infrastructure in which it chose to invest. While the Statement did commit $2 billion over five years ($225 million in 1993-94) to infrastructure development, it directed this to traditional types of infrastructure such as interprovincial highways, bridges and airports. There was little additional investment in human capital, which virtually all of the scholars analyzing implications of globalization argue to be essential to successful competitiveness.

The only commitments to human capital in the December mini-budget were $250 million over five years ($30 million in 1993-94) to lever money from labour and business for a national training effort and $300 million in Development Uses funds under the Unemployment Insurance program for initiatives to improve services (e.g. counselling regarding job search, skills training and mobility assistance) to long-service workers who have lost their jobs.

The December budget tried to stimulate employment by providing some assistance to small business, which account for 80 percent of new employment. This included relief (delivered as tax credits) from increases in unemployment insurance premiums for additional jobs (to a maximum of $30,000 per enterprise); a one-year 10 percent investment tax credit for purchase of equipment in small resource-based manufacturing enterprises and construction firms; and a raised ceiling for loans to small firms. In addition, the Home Buyers' Plan, announced in the February 1992 budget, was extended until March 1994. This program allows up to a maximum of $20,000 to be withdrawn, without tax penalty, from an individual's RRSP for purchase of a home. Minor modifications were also made to streamline the Research and Development investment credit and tax write-offs for junior oil and gas companies. The intent of all these measures was to stimulate the creation of jobs.

Despite these modest spending initiatives, restraint remained the dominant message and priority of the Economic and Fiscal Statement, as it had been in the Expenditure Control Plan which was first introduced in 1990.[45] In the December 1992 budget, there were four primary targets of cut-backs totalling $8 billion: 1) departmental operating budgets; 2) most interest groups and non-governmental organizations; 3) public service employees; and 4) the unemployed. These cuts were extracted by

- reducing government departmental budgets by a further 3 percent in 1993-94 (on top of a 2 percent reduction announced in November 1992 and an existing freeze on hiring and discretionary spending);

- cutting grants and subsidies to interest groups by 20 percent over two years. A wide range of groups were affected including arts and cultural organizations; consumer and environmental groups;

international development organizations; national social service groups; official language and multicultural groups; and Aboriginal political organizations;[46]

- imposing a two-year wage freeze for public servants and employees of non-commercial Crown corporations, as well as for cabinet ministers, members of Parliament, senators and the judiciary. The Government predicts that this freeze on salaries will save $450 million in 1993-94 and $700 million in 1994-95.[47] Combined with the two-year wage freeze introduced in 1991, it means that the process of collective bargaining has been suspended for a total of four years; and

- placing limits on the average benefits received by the unemployed under Unemployment Insurance (UI) and disqualifying voluntary quitters and those fired with cause from receiving benefits at all.[48] In fact, the largest single saving in the mini-budget's restraint program comes from these controls on UI recipients, which are expected to save $850 million in 1993-94 and $1.6 billion in 1994-95.[49]

The issue of process as to how the December budget was presented is important in the context of a discussion on democratic governance. The fact that it was not called a budget at all, but an "Economic and Fiscal Statement," allowed the Government to forgo the usual media lock-up and consultative processes, however limited these consultations usually are.[50] Thus, the media and opposition parties were caught somewhat less prepared than usual to critique the Statement, and this allowed the Government to get its message out in advance of its critics.

How well does this budget support the agenda of enhancing democratic practices? The answer is, not well at all. It showed neither strong leadership and imagination, nor support for democratic practices. First, the Budget does nothing positive to enhance government-citizen relations. The deep cuts to funding public interest groups, which appear to be ideologically based rather than significant cost saving measures, do not promote a democratic agenda and they demonstrate that the Conservative government views groups as expendable, worthy of minimal—if any—support by the State. Moreover, the greatest cuts were made at the expense of the most disadvantaged segment of society—the unemployed. In addition, the process of budget presentation (which appears to have been designed so as to stifle public criticism) was itself less democratic than in previous Tory budgets.

Second, the Budget seriously damages democracy within the public service because it suspends the collective bargaining process for another two years, which may place the entire regime at risk of being replaced by another system that would give even greater powers to management. If the savings were only modest, why did the federal government risk further straining labour relations with these wage controls? While we can only speculate, it appears that the greatest value of the 1992 wage freezes was symbolic.[51] They allowed the federal government to set an example for the provinces, where the indirect public sector wage bills are large (due to the number of employees in education, health care and social services), so that the provinces would find it difficult to ignore the issue of wage controls in developing their own budgets. In late 1992, the Reform Party, with its bureaucracy-bashing rhetoric, was showing considerable strength in the polls (especially in the West) so a tough stance on the public service played to the right wing of Conservative support. Finally, the wage controls have symbolic value as a signal to bankers and other private sector corporations that the federal government is getting its house in order.

While this budget did not significantly damage relations among governments, neither did it improve them. The federal government did not impose further cuts in transfers to the provinces, as it had in the first two years of its Expenditure Control Plan. But there were minimal efforts to invest in human capital or in urban infrastructure which is argued in the chapter by Lithwick and Coulthard to be essential to promoting both democracy and competitiveness at the local level.

April 1993: A Non-Traditional Pre-Election Budget

There were two inherently incompatible objectives in the final budget of the Mulroney years which was delivered by Finance Minister Don Mazankowski on April 26, 1993. One goal was to send the message to the business community and financial markets that the Conservative government was continuing to take a tough stand on restraint and deficit reduction, while the other goal was to antagonize as few people as possible in the period leading up to the election. In his statements to the media in the week before the budget was presented, the Finance Minister had created expectations that drastic restraint measures were likely.[52]

No radical moves came. The Budget contained no new taxes, no tax increases, and no cuts in transfers to the provinces or to individuals through the social programs. Indeed, the April budget contained few serious cut-backs at all, except potentially to public service jobs. However, it would have been very difficult to make significant reductions without touching either the social programs (which in 1994 will constitute 38 percent of the total outlays of the federal government) or transfers to other levels of government (which will be 12 percent of the total).[53] Cuts to transfers to individuals or provinces would have produced many disgruntled Canadians and provincial politicians at the wrong time. In contrast to the early years of the Expenditure Control Plan, the federal government in this budget wanted to foster co-operation, not confrontation, with the provinces. Most, including the New Democratic Party (NDP) governments of British Columbia, Ontario and Saskatchewan, recently had moved (as the federal government wanted them to) in the direction of severe spending restraint. Cuts to transfer payments might have undermined these provincial efforts. A radical restraint budget would also have constrained severely the policy options of the Tory leadership candidates. However, there were costs to presenting only a caretaker budget. The business community soundly criticized the Government for not taking more radical measures to contain the debt, and the day after the Budget was delivered, one of the smaller bond rating services downgraded the rating on federal government bonds, although other services did not lower their rating.[54]

The rhetoric of the April budget does not match its specifics. Although Finance Minister Mazankowski stated that the Budget would produce $30 billion in spending cuts and other savings over the next five years, most of these reductions either had been announced previously or will come late in this period (and thus may not occur at all). The Budget includes only $1 billion in new reductions for the 1993-94 fiscal year, of which $625 million will result simply from delaying the payment of the GST credit to low-income Canadians from January to April, which moves it into the next fiscal year.[55] This measure is merely "smoke and mirrors" accounting that hurts the poorest Canadians. Other restraint measures include

- cuts to departmental operating budgets were extended for a saving of $300 million in each of the next two years. When combined with the wage freezes and cuts of the December mini-budget, the total savings will be $7.5 billion over the period 1993 to 1998.[56] The Government estimates that these cuts will mean the elimination of 16,500 public service jobs across the country and possibly could result in the loss of an additional 33,000 public and related private sector jobs over the next five years.[57] To make these cuts, the Government said that it will "update" the Workforce Adjustment Directive in the summer of 1993;[58]

- regional development funding was reduced by $90 million in 1993-94 and by $100 million per year thereafter. The Economic and Regional Development Agreements (ERDAs) in forestry and mining will not be renewed as these areas are recognized to be provincial jurisdiction. This move accomplishes the transfer of responsibility (without financial compensation) for forestry and mining that had been proposed as part of the Charlottetown Accord;

- freezes in real terms to defence spending beginning in 1994-95;

- cuts to funding for interest groups are deepened by 15 percent in 1995-96 and by 20 percent in the following years. However, the savings will not be put towards deficit reduction, but will be reallocated to western grain transportation, Atlantic transportation and industrial milk subsidies;

- beginning in 1994-95, annual growth in spending for international assistance and by the university research councils will be limited to 1.5 percent;

- in 1995-96, operating subsidies to both the Canadian Broadcasting Corporation (CBC) and VIA Rail will be reduced by $50 million and by $100 million per year thereafter;

In its analysis of the economic outlook for Canada over the next five years, the Budget presents a rosy picture of prosperity. The Budget predicts real growth in the GDP of 2.9 percent in 1993 and 4.6 percent in 1994, compared with a meagre 0.9 percent in 1992. At the same time, inflation and interest rates are projected to remain low. However, unemployment, which is barely mentioned in the April budget, will remain high—11 percent in 1993 and 10.7 percent in 1994. The response by most economic analysts to this growth scenario was that it is extremely optimistic and even "highly conjectural."[59]

To what extent is this budget compatible with a democratic agenda? In several ways it is similar to the December budget: the Tories continued their ideologically based attack on interest groups and, depending on whether the Workforce Adjustment Directive is renegotiated with the unions or unilaterally changed, there may be considerable implications for democracy within the public service. In general, however, this budget will have little real impact because political events of the Conservative leadership contest and the general election will overtake it.

In one important sense, however, the April budget serves the interests of democracy well. In contrast to political circumstances in December 1992, there was by April a less decisive mandate by the Mulroney government to make fundamental and long-lasting changes. While the Tory leadership candidates stated (or at least hinted) that the restraint measures of Mazankowski's budget do not go far enough, the leading contenders also have stated that they will involve the Canadian public in the discussions of how to extract the more basic changes to government programs that deeper cuts would require. The Liberals and NDP want to open the discussion even further. They argue that the Conservatives' approach to deficit reduction, which is based on restraint and cutting government spending, has failed miserably. In contrast to a narrow focus on spending controls, the opposition parties advocate an approach of increasing revenues through economic growth based on investment in human capital and job creation to deal with high levels of unemployment. These alternative visions are appropriately debated in the course of an election campaign.

CONCLUSION

Is Canada becoming more democratic? As the following chapters discuss, some positive steps towards realizing a democratic agenda have been made recently at the federal level. These include the extension of the range of participants and the experimentation in mechanisms for consultation that were part of the last round of constitutional negotiations. At the administrative level, moves have been made to "reinvent" the federal public service to make it less bureaucratic and more responsive. However, in the past year alone, some important opportunities have been missed, although they may not yet be lost completely. The opportunities missed include the chance to overhaul the political party and electoral systems; to strengthen the regulation of lobbyists; to maintain a strategic centre of policy research and advising; to construct a federal-urban linkage with investment in economic development and human infrastructure in our metropolitan areas; to push for a pro-democracy trade policy; and to replace the politics of stealth in social policy with open debates about fundamental principles over universality versus targeted benefits.

There are several reasons why the Conservative government's attempts at democratic reform have been sporadic and tentative. First, the Government has not yet constructed and articulated for itself an agenda for democratic change and, thus, has not identified the individual reforms that are essential to realizing this agenda. Therefore, the reforms that have been made appear as stray cats without any support from the rest of the group. But to be fair to the Conservatives, many of the challenges of democratization are both relatively new and complex. Given the demands of governing with a shrinking state in a shrinking economy and an overcrowded constitutional agenda, the Government's attention has been diverted to other issues in the past two years. However, the issues related to democracy cannot be avoided much longer. Second, given the ideological orientation of the Conservatives, their emphasis in reinventing government has concentrated on promoting efficiency and productivity, and has centred on using market—rather than democratic—mechanisms. Third, due to the size of the public debt, some very difficult choices involving restructuring of the welfare state have had to be made by this government. But outside of constitutional politics, the

Tories generally have been reluctant to open the debates and accord Canadians sufficient integrity to participate seriously as citizens (with community rather than self-interest in mind) in making these hard choices—even if we do not like having to make them in the first place. Finally, the types of reforms inherent in a democratic agenda necessitate confronting some powerful interests, including the party élites and professional lobbyists. Instead of taking on these interests, our elected leaders have tended to displace the realization of reform over the longer run with political advantage in the short term.

Enhancing democratic governance does not necessarily entail spending more money and cannot be addressed adequately with dollars alone. Rather, the fundamental issue is about changing practices. But process, spending and policy outcomes are interdependent. One implication of changing democratic practice is that the choice of policy instruments may also need to change. Some of these may include market-based instruments and targeted policies (such as earmarked taxes) or community-based programs that, rather than adhering to national standards, differ from one community to the next. The use of market mechanisms is not necessarily antithetical to enhanced democracy, but the logic of democratic practice must rely on a political process of choice rather than a market-based one. The central dilemma of extending democracy is the same one that has challenged Canadian governments for decades: How do we maintain a sense of political community as a country, with national level interests and shared values rather than becoming a multitude of disaggregated communities with parochial interests.

This kind of transformation of governance cannot be undertaken by the federal government acting alone or in isolation. Rather, the federal government will need to engage the active participation and co-operation of citizens, interest groups and social movements, and other governments. Change must take place at the micro level of enhancing democracy within the workplace as well as at the macro level of reforming basic institutions. The purpose of this volume is to spark some discussion and debate about the challenges and numerous different potential directions for enhancing democratic practice. Perhaps the federal election campaign of 1993 will be an opportunity to extend these debates even further.

NOTES

I am indebted to my colleagues at Carleton University—Frances Abele, Katherine Graham, Jane Jenson, Allan Maslove, Leslie Pal and Gene Swimmer—and to Benjamin Little at Queen's University. Their incisive comments helped to improve this chapter immeasurably. My thanks also to my colleague and husband, Brian Little, for his careful reading, constructive suggestions and loaned metaphors. Carolyn Chisholm and Gordon Quaiattini provided superb assistance with the research.

1   The term "reinventing" government originates from the book by David Osborne and Ted Gaebler, *Reinventing Government: How the Entrepreneurial Spirit Is Transforming the Public Sector* (Reading, Mass.: Addison-Wesley, 1992).

2   The New Public Management is not restricted, or even original, to Canada. Similar reforms are evident in the U.K. under a Conservative government and in Australia under a Labour government. On the managerial reforms in the U.K., see Christopher Hood, "A Public Management for All Seasons?" *Public Administration*, 69 (Spring 1991): pp. 3-19; John Stewart and Kieron Walsh, "Change in the Management of Public Services," *Public Administration*, 70 (Winter 1992): pp. 499-518. For a discussion of administrative reforms in Australia, see Anna Yeatman, *Bureaucrats, Technocrats and Femocrats: Essays on the Contemporary Australian State* (Sydney: Allen & Unwin, 1990).

3   Glen Allen, "Maclean's/Decima poll: A verdict on politics," *Maclean's*, January 6, 1992, pp. 58-60.

4   As quoted in Ross Howard, "PC donor plan just diversion, critics charge," *The Globe and Mail* [Toronto], March 29, 1993, p. A5.

5   I have chosen to use the term democratic "governance" rather than democratic "administration" as many scholars do, because the types of changes that we are addressing in this volume extend beyond the administration to the political and constitutional levels. For another recent collection of essays on this topic, see Gregory Albo, David Langille, and Leo Panitch, (eds.), *A*

Different Kind of State? Popular Power and Democratic Administration (Toronto: Oxford University Press, 1993).

6   Feminist scholars writing on citizenship have made extensive contributions to the discussion of the value of participation in changing citizens from passive subjects to active agents. See Anne Phillips, *Engendering Democracy* (London: Polity Press, 1991); and Iris Marion Young, *Justice and the Politics of Difference* (Princeton, N.J.: Princeton University Press, 1990). On the value of democracy for enhancing political community, see Benjamin R. Barber, *Strong Democracy: Participatory Politics for a New Age* (Berkeley: University of California Press, 1984).

7   For a critique of the liberal and communitarian perspectives on citizenship, see Will Kymlicka, *Liberalism, Community, and Culture* (Oxford: Clarendon Press, 1989); Chantal Mouffe, "Democratic Citizenship and the Political Community" in Mouffe, (ed.), *Dimensions of Radical Democracy: Pluralism, Citizenship, Community* (London: Verso, 1992), pp. 225-39; and Anne Phillips, *Engendering Democracy*, chap. 2.

8   Stewart Ranson and John Stewart, "Citizenship and Government: The Challenge for Management in the Public Domain," *Political Studies*, XXXVII (1989): p. 20.

9   For a discussion of community development "partnerships," see Susan D. Phillips, "How Ottawa Blends: Shifting Government Relationships with Interest Groups" in Frances Abele, (ed.), *How Ottawa Spends 1991-92: The Politics of Fragmentation* (Ottawa: Carleton University Press, 1991), pp. 208-09.

10   On the reaction of the development organizations to the proposed changes to CIDA, see Canadian Council for International Co-operation, "External's Takeover of CIDA" (Ottawa, February 16, 1993). The changes to the Canada Council and the SSHRC were announced as part of the February 1992 budget and put forth as legislation in Bill C-93. See House of Commons, *Minutes of Proceedings and Evidence of the Legislative Committee on Bill C-93*, Issue 3 (February 24, 1993), pp. 7-27. On the reaction of the academic community, see Tim Stutt, "Academics Confront MPs

on SSHRCC/Canada Council Merger," *Bulletin*, vol. 40, no. 4 (Ottawa: Canadian Association of University Teachers (CAUT), April 1993), p. 1.

11   For the metaphor of herding cats, I am indebted to Brian Little.

12   The notion of the democratization of everyday life is borrowed from Alberto Melucci, *Nomads of the Present: Social Movements and Individual Needs in Contemporary Society* (London: Hutchinson Radius, 1989). See also Jane Jenson, "Changing Discourse, Changing Agendas: Political Rights and Reproductive Policies in France" in Mary Fainsod Katzenstein and Carol McClurg Mueller, (eds.), *The Women's Movements of the United States and Western Europe* (Philadelphia: Temple University, 1987), pp. 64-88.

13   Alan C. Cairns, "Constitutional Minoritarianism in Canada" in Ronald L. Watts and Douglas M. Brown, (eds.), *Canada: The State of the Federation 1990* (Kingston: Institute of Intergovernmental Relations, Queen's University, 1990), pp. 71-96; and Alan C. Cairns, "The Past and Future of the Canadian Administrative State," *University of Toronto Law Journal*, 40 (1990): p. 339.

14   On the impact of globalization, see Paul Kennedy, *Preparing for the Twenty-first Century* (Toronto: Harper Collins, 1993), chap. 3; Kenichi Ohmae, *The Borderless World* (New York: Harper Business, 1990); and Robert B. Reich, *The Work of Nations* (New York: Vintage Books, 1992).

15   On the public's views about political leadership and institutions, see Canada, Citizens' Forum on Canada's Future (Spicer Commission), *Report to the People and Government of Canada* (Ottawa: Supply and Services Canada, 1991), pp. 96-109.

16   For an overview, see Alain-G. Gagnon and A. Brian Tanguay, "Introduction: Canadian Parties in Transition" in Gagnon and Tanguay, (eds.), *Canadian Parties in Transition* (Scarborough: Nelson, 1989), pp. 2-22. See also the chapter by Alexandra Dobrowolsky and Jane Jenson in this volume.

17   The Liberal leader, Jean Chrétien, further damaged the image of an open, fair and democratic party process when, in the fall of 1992, he began personally appointing the nominees in local ridings to ensure that strong candidates were chosen and the process was not hijacked by single issue "fanatics." Technically, it is not against the rules of the Liberal Party for the leader to appoint nominees, but the convention has been to allow local constituencies to select their candidates by more democratic means. "Liberal nominations: Chrétien subverts democracy," *The Ottawa Citizen*, April 3, 1993, p. A3.

18   Patrick Boyer, a long time, articulate advocate of parliamentary reform, has presented a comprehensive package of specific reforms including a stronger role for parliamentarians, better access to information and tighter regulation of lobbyists. As a contender for the Tory leadership, Boyer has offered an even more radical suggestion which is intended to strengthen the role of caucus: the requirement that cabinet ministers be appointed by their fellow caucus members, rather than by the Prime Minister. See Mark Kennedy, "Boyer wants ministers chosen by caucus MPs," *The Ottawa Citizen*, April 3, 1993, p. A3.

19   Jane Jenson, "Beyond Brokerage Politics: Toward the Democracy Round," and David P. Shugarman, "The Social Charter" in Duncan Cameron and Miriam Smith, (eds.), *Constitutional Politics* (Toronto: James Lorimer, 1992), pp. 204-14, 157-77.

20   Sharon L. Sutherland, "Responsible Government and Ministerial Responsibility: Every Reform Is Its Own Problem," *Canadian Journal of Political Science*, XXIV, 1 (March 1991): pp. 91-120.

21   "New conflict rules tabled," *The Ottawa Citizen*, March 12, 1993, p. A4.

22   Peter Dobell, "Restoring Parliament's credibility," *The Globe and Mail* [Toronto], November 17, 1992, p. A21.

23   Quoted in Graham Fraser, "Four years on Parliament Hill and how they grew," *The Globe and Mail* [Toronto], November 24, 1992, pp. A1, A2.

24   Barbara McDougall, "The Concept and Practice of Democracy in Canada," *Canadian Speeches/Issues* (February 1991): p. 22.

25   Joshua Cohen and Joel Rogers, "Secondary Associations and Democratic Governance," *Politics and Society*, 20, 4 (December 1992): p. 443. The RCERPF also portrayed interest groups as a primary reason for the difficulties faced by political parties but, in their chapter in this volume, Dobrowolsky and Jenson strongly criticize the Commission's analysis of cause and effect. They argue that the RCERPF expressed little appreciation for the alternatives offered by social movements for enhancing democracy.

26   See Duncan Cameron, "Beyond the Market and the State: How Can We Do Better" in Daniel Drache and Meric S. Gertler, (eds.), *The New Era of Global Competition: State Policy and Market Power* (Montreal and Kingston: McGill-Queen's University Press, 1991), p. 446; Jane Mansbridge, "A Deliberative Perspective on Neocorporatism," *Politics and Society*, 20, 4 (December 1992): pp. 493-505; and Young, *Politics of Difference*, chap. 6.

27   For a discussion of government funding to interest groups, see Susan Phillips, "How Ottawa Blends," pp. 196-205; and Leslie A. Pal, *Interests of State: The Politics of Language, Multiculturalism and Feminism in Canada* (Montreal and Kingston: McGill-Queen's University Press, 1993).

28   Christopher Pollitt, *Managerialism and the Public Services: The Anglo-American Experience* (Oxford: Basil Blackwell, 1990), p. 125. On the distinction between citizen and consumer, see also Denis St. Martin, "Toward the Redefinition of the State-Citizen Relationship: Reforming the Canadian Bureaucracy" (Paper presented at Democratic Politics: 50 Years of Political Science at Carleton University, Ottawa, November 1992); Camilla Stivers, "The Public Agency as Polis: Active Citizenship in the Administrative State," *Administration and Society*, 22, 1 (May 1990): pp. 86-105; and Yeatman, *Bureaucrats, Technocrats and Femocrats*, pp. 2-3.

29   Over the two terms of the Conservative government, experiments have been made with new and multiple modes of public consultation, including Environment Canada's ground-breaking work on developing "multi-stakeholder" consultations; the now very popular use of 1-800 numbers that allow citizens to register their concerns by telephone; electronic town hall meetings and, of course, public opinion polling. However, polling does not qualify as real participation because it provides no mechanism for feedback to the public and because, increasingly, it is being used by the Tories not merely to assess public opinion as input into policy, but to figure out how to sell or market policy back to the public. The Government's guidelines on consultation are provided in Privy Council Office, Communications and Consultation Secretariat, *Public Consultation: A Practical Approach* (Ottawa, March 1993).

30   Governments naturally tend to be secretive and must be prodded into providing the public with information paid for by their tax dollars. While Access to Information legislation was passed in 1987, serious concerns have been raised recently that the process for obtaining information under the Act is slow, confusing and costly. The statistics on the use of the Access to Information process for the 1991-92 fiscal year show that its use is in slight decline and that the process is slow. Although the Act is supposed to ensure information is delivered to applicants within 30 days, the statistics show that 18.7 percent of requests took between 31 and 60 days, while 20 percent took at least 61 days to complete. In fact, only about 31 percent of requests were fully met at all. "Use of Access to Information Act in decline," *The Ottawa Citizen*, April 5, 1993, p. A3.

31   However, self-managing "partnerships" should include real power-sharing, involving mechanisms of both democracy and accountability, and must not merely be arrangements in which government controls the partners or in which existing inequalities are cemented. See Gregory Albo, "Democratic Citizenship and the Future of Public Management," and David Langille, "Putting Democratic Administration on the Political Agenda" in Albo, Langille, and Panitch, *A Different Kind of State?*, pp. 30-31 and pp. 234-35, respectively. For a more positive perspective on

partnerships, see Kenneth Kernaghan, "Choose Your Partners—It's Innovation Time," *Public Sector Management*, 3, 2 (1992): p. 16.

32   This issue was put on the table by the Conservative government in late 1992 with the de Cotret report (as yet not made public), but given the short period before a federal election and the political danger of throwing a number of ministers out of work in that critical period, there has been no action on the de Cotret report. However, the question of the appropriate size of Cabinet has become an issue in the Conservative leadership race and will probably be an election issue as well.

33   In spite of the positive rhetoric over the past eight years, changes in employment equity have been slow: women still comprise only 16.1 percent of the management category, while the other designated categories of disabled persons, visible minorities and Aboriginal peoples are a mere fraction. Public Service Commission, *Annual Report, 1991* (Ottawa: Supply and Services Canada, 1992), p. 20.

34   For a list of the initiatives undertaken to improve productivity and restructure the administration, see Treasury Board of Canada, *Modernizing the Federal Government* (Ottawa, 1993); and Ian D. Clark, *Getting the Incentives Right: Toward a Productivity-oriented Management Framework for the Public Service* (Ottawa: Treasury Board of Canada Secretariat, 1993).

35   Gene Swimmer with Kjerstine Kinaschuk, "Staff Relations under the Conservative Government: The Singers Change but the Song Remains the Same" in Frances Abele, (ed.), *How Ottawa Spends 1992-93: The Politics of Competitiveness* (Ottawa: Carleton University Press, 1992), pp. 267-312.

36   The principle of "subsidiarity," originally derived from the European Community, is sometimes applied—loosely and perhaps even metaphorically—to describe this growing interest in decentralization in Canada. Here, subsidiarity has been interpreted to mean that "power should devolve on the lowest, most local level at which decisions can reasonably be made, with the

function of the larger unit being to support and assist the local body in carrying out its tasks." As quoted in Gilles Paquet, "The Future Scope of Government: The Strategic State" in Jean Chrétien, (ed.), *Finding Common Ground* (Hull: Voyageur Publishing, 1992), p. 90.

37   In his extensive analysis of alternative means to more democratic administration, Jerry Frug strongly advocates decentralization to local governments. However, he makes the important point that success of such efforts may depend on establishing institutions of co-ordination and co-operation between cities. Frug advocates the creation of regional agencies which would be empowered to deal with specific inter-local problems. See Jerry Frug, "Administrative Democracy," *University of Toronto Law Journal*, 40 (1990): pp. 576-77.

38   Thomas Courchene makes the case that "the economies of scale and scope associated with the concentration of the information and services infrastructure means that these international cities become not only growth poles but the essential connectors outward towards the Londons and Tokyos and inward to their regional hinterlands. Already, Barcelona, Toulouse and Montpelier are forging economic links that will take them out from under Madrid and Paris and into an EC framework. Transferred to Canada, what this means is that, for a distinct society to have meaning in an economic sense, it must evolve around an international city: without Montreal, there would be no Bloc Québécois!" Thomas Courchene, "Mon pays, c'est l'hiver: Reflections of a Market Populist," *Canadian Journal of Economics*, XXV, 4 (November 1992): pp. 762-63.

39   Courchene, "Mon pays, c'est l'hiver," pp. 767-72. He also argues that the present system of fiscal transfers will need to be reformulated to shift from an emphasis on the prosperity of place (provinces) to an emphasis on the prosperity of people.

40   Ken Battle (writing as Grattan Gray), "Social Policy by Stealth," *Policy Options*, 11, 2 (1990). See also the chapter in this volume by Ken Battle.

41   Since the chapter by Saul Schwartz was prepared for this volume, unofficial reports indicate that Ottawa's interest in public education is becoming even more serious and that a federal "learning strategy" will be announced in the next Speech from the Throne. This strategy would give Ottawa the lead in setting national goals in education and may involve the linkage of these goals to tax transfers to the provinces. However, it is not yet clear how the provincial governments will react to this unprecedented intrusion into their jurisdiction. See Jennifer Lewington, "Ottawa seeks role in guiding education," *The Globe and Mail* [Toronto], April 13, 1993, pp. A1, A5.

42   It was the Tories who regularized the timing of presentation of a budget in about late February. Under the Trudeau Liberals, budgets were presented at irregular intervals and at less predictable times of the year.

43   The February 1992 budget had predicted a net public debt of $447.3 billion for the 1992-93 fiscal year and $469.8 billion for 1993-94. The Economic and Fiscal Statement 10 months later had revised those figures to a debt of $457.2 billion in 1992-93 and $489.7 billion in 1993-94 ($20 billion more than initially projected). See Department of Finance, *The Budget Papers* (Ottawa, February 25, 1992), p. 106; and *Economic and Fiscal Statement* (Delivered in the House of Commons by The Honourable Don Mazankowski, December 2, 1992), p. 18.

44   I am indebted to Allan Maslove for this analysis. Not surprisingly, Ontario has experienced the same forecasting problem in its budgets for similar reasons.

45   For an analysis of the 1991 and 1992 budgets, see Frances Abele, "The Politics of Fragmentation" in Abele, *How Ottawa Spends 1991-92*, pp. 14-23; and Abele, "The Politics of Competitiveness" in Abele, *How Ottawa Spends 1992-93*, pp. 11-16.

46   Cuts to interest groups are evident in the grants and contributions provided by individual departments; see Department of Finance, *Estimates: Part II of The Main Estimates, 1993-94* (Ottawa, 1993).

47　　These figures include defence personnel. In his assessment of the
existing wage control measures, Gene Swimmer notes that personnel costs constitute a relatively modest portion—12 percent—
of the total federal budget. "The point is simple: public sector
wages did not cause the deficit, and the restraint of wages would
not solve the deficit problem." Swimmer with Kinaschuk, "Staff
Relations under the Conservative Government," p. 285.

48　　The disqualification of voluntary quitters immediately raised the
concern that women who had been victims of sexual harassment
or who could not find adequate child-care arrangements would be
unfairly penalized. Before passing the enabling legislation, the
federal government attempted to delineate a list of legitimate
reasons for quitting a job. See "40 'just' reasons for quitting a
job," *The Ottawa Citizen*, February 20, 1993, p. D8; and Jeffrey
Simpson, "The unemployment insurance debate: Colourful, loud
and irrelevant," *The Globe and Mail* [Toronto], February 16,
1993, p. A16.

49　　*Economic and Fiscal Statement*, December 2, 1992, p. 15.

50　　Over the years, the Department of Finance has attempted to
provide somewhat more extensive consultations leading up to the
Budget, but it is still essentially a secretive process. However,
some of the provinces—notably Ontario—have been much more
innovative in public consultations surrounding the Budget. In
Ontario, the Treasurer usually brings together a number of groups
with different perspectives on an issue for discussions and often
includes other cabinet ministers in addition to the Treasurer. In the
last few years, the Treasurer has gone so far as to circulate a pre-
budget document that gives some hint as to the directions in which
the Government is thinking of moving and, thus, to facilitate more
relevant and detailed discussions on real options.

51　　My thanks to Gene Swimmer for suggesting this line of argument.
As Swimmer observes, the use of special legislation by the federal
government to send employees back to work after the 1991 public
service strike and to impose wage controls is antithetical to
democracy, particularly because it is possible that a 0 percent
wage increase could have been negotiated. See Swimmer with

Kinaschuk, "Staff Relations under the Conservative Government," pp. 287-94.

52   Alan Freeman, "Cuts to dominate federal budget," *The Globe and Mail* [Toronto], April 26, 1993, p. A1.

53   See the chart "Projected Federal Expenditures by Sector-1994" in the *Fiscal Facts and Trends* which appear as an appendix of this volume.

54   The Finance Minister immediately launched a savage counter-attack saying that the Canadian Bond Rating Service has used incorrect figures in its assessment. Bruce Little, "Firm lowers bond rating," *The Globe and Mail* [Toronto], April 28, 1993, pp. A1-2.

55   Canada, Department of Finance, *The Budget 1993* (Ottawa: April 26, 1993), p. 60.

56   The federal government used the April budget as an opportunity to congratulate itself on its record since 1984 and, in particular, for cutting the annual growth rate of federal program spending (all spending except service on the debt). However, one reason that the increase in program spending was small in 1993-94 (0.9 percent over 1992-93) is that the $2.2 billion Family Allowance program has been replaced with the Child Benefit program which is paid through the tax system rather than as a program expenditure.

57   "Federal budget may cost 50,000 jobs," *The Globe and Mail* [Toronto], April 27, 1993, p. B1.

58   The Workforce Adjustment Directive is an agreement (implemented after the 1991 strike) between the public service unions and the federal government. It provides substantial security to permanent employees whose positions have been declared surplus or have been contracted out. The opportunity to make job cuts at the department level, rather than across the board, will be extended under the practice of "operating budgets" which were introduced in the public service as of April 1, 1993. Operating

budgets have eliminated central agency controls over person-years and have granted to departments the authority to reallocate operating resources (including people, operations and maintenance costs, and minor capital) in order to achieve more cost-effective program delivery. While this is a worthwhile endeavour to improve the efficiency and flexibility of the public service, it may have long-term, but initially quite invisible, effects on the character of the public service. The concern is that operating budgets, combined with the new method of appointment and deployment to level, may make it easier for department managers to replace individuals who have retired or resigned with more junior people or to make term appointments. And, in spite of the provisions of the Workforce Adjustment Directive, the federal government still retains considerable flexibility to contract out, and may acquire even more if this Directive is set aside by the government. The longer-term implications of replacing experienced public servants with term or casual personnel or with "consultocrats" (consultants on contract) is that valuable institutional memory and expertise may be lost permanently. Combined with the loss of research and advising capacity that was a result of the elimination of the Economic Council of Canada and Science Council of Canada in 1992, and the reductions in funding and potentialy diminished relations with university-based researchers created by the merger of the Canada Council and SSHRC , there may be a serious diminution in the strategic capacity of governance.

59   Bruce Little, "Ottawa banks on '80s-style boom," *The Globe and Mail* [Toronto], April 27, 1993, pp. A1-2.

CHAPTER 2

Reforming the Parties: Prescriptions for Democracy

Alexandra Dobrowolsky
Jane Jenson

Résumé : La Commission royale sur la réforme électorale et le financement des partis (CRREFP) s'était donnée pour mission de soulager les maux de la démocratie canadienne au regard des partis fédéraux. Malgré les prescriptions nobles et logiques qui lui avaient été imparties, les plus innovatrices des recommandations formulées par la Commission au sujet de la réforme des partis et du financement des élections semblent aujourd'hui avoir été mises de côté. La CRREFP avait proposé d'accorder aux partis un pouvoir accru en matière d'orientations politiques et de représentation, d'ouvrir l'accès au financement d'élection et de contrôler les dépenses des indépendants. Dans ce chapitre, il est question des raisons qui ont poussé à la fois la circonscription naturelle—les partis—et la circonscription éventuelle composée de ceux qui s'inquiètent de l'état de la démocratie à rejeter les solutions avancées par la CRREFP. La Commission invitait les partis à amorcer une réforme interne et à agir dans leur intérêt personnel à long terme et dans celui de la démocratie. La circonscription traditionnelle, d'abord au sein du Comité parlementaire spécial sur la réforme électorale puis à la Chambre des communes, a envisagé les recommandations de la Commission dans un contexte à très court terme. Pour sa part, l'autre circonscription a été déçue du fait que la Commission n'avait pas exprimé l'intérêt qu'avait pour elle le bien-être démocratique. Il ne s'est donc pas encore formé d'alliance de parties en quête de la démocratie.

Abstract: The Royal Commission on Electoral Reform and Party Financing (RCERPF) set out to remedy the ills of Canadian democracy at the federal party level. Despite its ambitious and coherent prescriptions, the Commission's most innovative recommendations for reforming parties and election financing now seem to have been shelved. The RCERPF proposed strengthening the policy and representative capacity of the parties, making access to election financing more open, and controlling independent expenditures. This chapter examines why both its natural constituency—parties—and a potential constituency of those also concerned about the health of democracy have refused the RCERPF's medicine. The RCERPF's recommendations called for the parties to reform themselves and to act in their own and democracy's long-term interest. The traditional constituency, first in the parliamentary Special Committee on Electoral Reform and then in the House of Commons, treated the recommendations in terms of quite short-term calculations. The alternative constituency, in turn, was put off by the Commission's failure to acknowledge its stake in democratic well-being. Therefore, no alliance of democracy-seekers has yet been made.

Early Thursday morning, February 13, 1992, as the first westbound flights transported much of the Ottawa Press Gallery to Vancouver for the fifth weekend of constitutional conferences, Pierre Lortie and his four fellow Commissioners presented their final report to the remaining media. The Royal Commission on Electoral Reform and Party Financing (RCERPF), after just over two years of consultation, research and deliberation at a cost of less than $20 million, had produced an ambitious and lengthy set of proposals for updating the law regulating elections and parties, and their financing. The Commissioners' goal was to initiate reforms that would enhance the promise of the Canadian Charter of Rights and Freedoms that Canada is a "free and democratic society." As a result, their recommendations were not narrowly designed simply to address the details of regulation and financing. The proposals constituted a crusade against the widespread malaise concerning the well-being of democracy and democratic political institutions in Canada.

The new practices and processes of constitutional reform—including wider public consultation in forums like the Spicer Commission, the five weekend conferences for "ordinary Canadians," and Aboriginal circles—were direct responses to accusations that the Meech Lake Accord was anti-democratic because it resulted from closed-door negotiations by 11 white men in suits. The RCERPF was created in November 1989 because of similar dissatisfaction with the "free trade election" of 1988. The parallel campaigns waged in that election by groups like the Business Council on National Issues and the Pro-Canada Network had taken advantage of constitutional ambiguity about legislation restricting campaign spending to candidates and registered political parties. The Chief Electoral Officer chose not to challenge such "independent spending" because the relevant section of the Canada Elections Act, which predated the Charter, had been found to be unconstitutional by the Court of Queen's Bench of Alberta in a 1984 case involving the National Citizens' Coalition.[1] Such unlimited independent expenditures during election campaigns threatened the existing regime of financing and regulation organized around the principle of spending limits. As it developed new rules for the conduct of elections, the RCERPF would have to balance Charter rights and social movements' and interest groups' aspirations for influence in elections against the principle of the regulatory regime. Hence not only the rules, but the very definition of Canadian democracy was at stake.

Just as those involved in constitutional politics explicitly recognized the democratic stakes, so too did the RCERPF. Indeed, "democracy" was the first word spoken by Pierre Lortie as he opened the public hearings in March 1990:

> Democracy is our way of political life. The goal we have set for ourselves is an ambitious one. We intend to develop a blueprint for an electoral law that will effectively meet the needs of Canadians well into the next century, reinforce their confidence in our democratic process and their members of Parliament and reflect our values and democratic institutions.[2]

Yet the creative and comprehensive suggestions made in the final report, *Reforming Electoral Democracy*, have not attracted the attention that might have been expected in this era of rethinking fundamentals.[3]

One explanation, of course, is the timing. Perhaps there was simply no more space on the political agenda, given the fever pitch of constitutional negotiations, for yet another debate about first principles. We will argue here, however, that while the timing of the report's release, in the midst of the constitutional conferences, was unfortunate, the silences surrounding the prescriptions of the RCERPF have deeper sources. Put simply, the Commission was too radical in its suggestions for some—the political establishment in particular—and too traditional for others, especially those currently most involved in demanding the democratization of politics in the broadest sense.

On the one hand, *Reforming Electoral Democracy* challenged parties and politicians to rise above their immediate self-interest and invest in their future. It called for them to reform themselves and create more equitable and legitimate democratic institutions. Implementing the Commission's vision of the responsibilities of political parties required a fundamental shift in the self-definition and actions of parties and politicians. Not only would those already on the inside be forced to be more welcoming to new parties and efforts to mobilize minority opinions, but parties and parliamentarians would have to abandon many of their old ways. For example, the Commission's report called on parties to mount meaningful political debates in order to elevate political discourse, give their activists a larger role to play, and fight fair elections with limited expenditures. This different conceptualization of parties was too strong a medicine for many political insiders to take. So too was the Commission's insistence that the financial regime be used to increase access and demonstrate openness to competitors to the existing three parties, as well as to groups whose record of participation in the mainstream parties has not been commensurate with their presence in the population. In exchange for such self-reform, the RCERPF promised a reduction in the malaise now facing both politicians and the traditional institutions of representation.

In the interest of long-term well-being, the RCERPF called upon the regulators to improve the regime which regulates them. It is the parties in Parliament who must pass new legislation implementing this vision of what democratic institutions should be. The Commission tried to engage their sense of fair play, or equity. Thus far, the parliamentary parties have not risen to the challenge.

On the other hand, for those working outside of the traditionally defined institutional realm, the RCERPF's recommendations seemed irrelevant, even threatening. The Commission consistently treated the activities of "interest groups" in electoral and non-electoral politics as one of the *causes* of the parties' difficulties, rather than as a *consequence* of the mistrust many Canadians feel for the brokerage parties. Therefore, while reluctantly acknowledging that non-party groups may now provide representation, *Reforming Electoral Democracy* devoted a good deal of energy to exhorting the parties to change themselves in order to displace the alternative.

In doing so, the Commission expressed little appreciation of the availability of multiple strategies for enhancing democracy. In particular, it was remarkably silent about the recent upsurge of social movement politics. This type of politics encompasses not only the representation of "interests," but also the representation of diversified world views and the opening of alternative, non-traditional political spaces. Here the extension of legitimate political activity and debate is endorsed and promoted. Such politics, moreover, is founded on a discourse of democratization, which seeks to reduce inequalities of power and practices of exclusion. Several decades of social movement mobilization has created an awareness of multiple political struggles, beyond and around elections.

The unintended outcome of this silence about the work of social movements is that the Commission lost an opportunity for appealing to an important potential constituency. Outreach to such democracy-seekers might have generated allies who could pressure parties and politicians to implement the report's recommendations for more equity and access, and for reconstituted parties responsive to the claims for better representation. It might also have diffused the Commission's analysis beyond the walls of Parliament and the back rooms of parties. In contrast to the constitutional debates then, a propitious moment was not seized which could have prolonged and perpetuated the dialogue on improving Canada's democratic institutions.

The result of this uneasy mix of radicalism and traditionalism was that the RCERPF wrote a final report that pleased few in its natural constituency, not the parties because it called on them to reform, indeed transform, themselves. It also failed to attract a potential constituency from among those who have been so involved in promoting a new discourse of democracy—many social movements—because the report frequently labelled them "interest groups" and identified them as part of the problem.[4] The result has been a profound silence about the Commission's most innovative and important proposals for rethinking the rules of Canadian democracy.

The foregoing commentary is expanded upon in the next three parts of this chapter. First, we provide the context for the RCERPF by characterizing the current political parties in Canada. Second, we discuss, in some detail, the RCERPF's response to these parties' failings. In the third section, we describe how and analyze why many of the most progressive and innovative recommendations of *Reforming Electoral Democracy* have, to date, been shelved despite the real need for reform.

THE PARTY "DIS-EASE"

The Commission faced the unenviable task of prescribing for the democratic malady of the federal parties. The current condition can be traced to Canadian parties' long-standing and finely honed practices of brokerage. These parties, like all others, seek to build broad electoral coalitions in order to gain the support required to win elections. Over the years, however, the federal parties have continually interpreted the imperatives of "brokering interests" as confining parties and their leaders to positions that are both opportunistic and short-term.[5] Parties have become vehicles for leaders who serve as the political glue of the coalition, rather than for articulated political projects. These practices are not restricted to the party in power. The opposition, cognizant of the success of the leading party, most often scrambles for a position best characterized as "we'll do the same, but better." In these ways, electoral opportunism, centred on leaders, replaces public policy debate.

These brokerage tendencies have a lengthy, if not always venerable, tradition.[6] Almost 90 years ago, French scholar André Siegfried commented negatively on Canadian parties' tendency to shun debates of principle. He depicted the typical party as simply "a machine for winning elections," concerned exclusively with the conquest of political power.[7] Now, as in the past, parties have perfected this avoidance behaviour to the point where there is a serious neglect of long- or even medium-term policy thinking. This constricts the possibilities for wide-ranging debates and the space for pluralistic alternatives, both of which are desirable outcomes in the eyes of democracy-seeking groups.

Even more of a threat to democratic practices is the tendency of parties, once in office, to implement policies and even large-scale projects of reform which have not been systematically considered either by their own party organization or by the electorate. In short, the policy innovation that does occur is discussed and developed far from the public eye—in the bureaucracy, during federal-provincial negotiations, or by the select few researchers and writers of royal commissions. For instance, the Conservatives' conversion to free trade between the 1984 election (when Brian Mulroney rejected it) and 1988 (when the Tories planned to implement it without any electoral consultation) was only the latest in a long line of policy reversals or major initiatives taken without democratic consultation.

Other options for public scrutiny in a democracy have also become problematic. For instance, the Canadian media, trained on decades of brokerage politics, have tended to reinforce the leader/image focus and have relegated substantive discussions in favour of juicy sound-bites. New technologies, including not only the electronic media but also polling and political consulting, have accentuated the trend.[8]

The heart of the problem of brokerage politics is that the accommodation of interests that does occur takes exclusionary forms. Politics tends to be conducted in back rooms and on the basis of exchange relations of elite accommodation. Therefore, opportunities for political discourse are closed down rather than opened up. The "interference" of non-elites is discouraged in such a situation. Their presence risks complicating well-cultivated techniques for achieving elite consensus.

This latter point leads to perhaps the most damning criticism of the existing brokerage parties. Many assessments of Canada's parties stress their role in representing social cleavages and generating social stability.[9] Parties were meant to consolidate interests, then transform them into policy alternatives for transmission to government. In fact, they were to function as organizers, aggregators and harmonizers of interests which otherwise might be weakly integrated.[10]

It is, however, precisely the parties' failure to provide representation by incorporating the diversity of Canadian society, despite vocal demands from the many groups concerned, that strikes the observer of party politics at the federal level. The under-representation of women, Aboriginal peoples, visible minorities, and the oppressed and dispossessed leads one to question whether parties are performing their alleged function of social integration.[11] Calls for senate reform and representation in the House of Commons can be interpreted as a response to doubts that federal parties have the ability to accommodate even the country's regional interests, which was the main rationale for the brokerage system in the first place.

Given these limits, it is not surprising that some people and groups have sought alternative routes to representation. For example, drawing conclusions about the limits of party politics, interest groups and social movements have tended to focus their activism on a variety of institutional locales. Task forces and commissions, the public service, and various constitutional forums have become prime access points. [12]

Additionally, social movements have increased their prominence as representational forms, in and of themselves. [13] They have claimed victories of their own: the women's movement success in the 1981-82 constitutional round is a prime illustration. [14] Furthermore, following the mobilization around opposition to both free trade and constitutional reform, there has been a growing resort to coalitional politics. For example, the labour movement, Aboriginal organizations, women's groups and associations for disabled persons, among others, have made alliances around not only the immediate issues, but the broader goal of halting the Tories' neo-liberal agenda. [15] Through such initiatives, the coalitions are offering themselves as alternatives to the three major parties for organizing democratic debate and providing policy innovation. The effect, if not the intent, has been to reduce further the parties' representational capacity and legitimacy.

A summary diagnosis of the brokerage parties' "dis-ease" would read as follows: the refusal to provide adequate opportunities for political discourse and to engage in less exclusionary practices; the neglect of policy thinking; the absence of alternative national projects; and the failure in terms of formal, let alone substantive, representation of difference. Both the growth of alternative modes of representation and a resurgence of democratic discourse have counteracted these ailments. The Royal Commission on Electoral Reform and Party Financing shared much of this diagnosis and it set out a specialized course of treatment.

PRESCRIBING REFORM

The RCERPF deliberately chose to interpret its mandate very broadly and provide a response to the debates about democratic governance that had shaped so much of politics in the late 1980s and early 1990s. It also devoted a great deal of attention to the conditions under which Canadians vote in an effort to make the electoral system more "voter friendly" and therefore more democratic. Because our primary concern is the way the Commission interpreted its mandate to prescribe for parties and thereby also improve democracy, we do not consider the recommendations regarding voting regulations.

The RCERPF consulted widely. It held 42 days of hearings and received almost 900 briefs. It also organized a number of symposia and workshops, bringing together commissioners, researchers, party workers, MPs and election officials to consider much of the wide-ranging research programme. Lastly, the Commission established a consultative process for Aboriginal peoples.[16]

From the hearings and the data that it collected, the RCERPF concluded that serious problems existed for parties as representative institutions.[17] In the final report, the Commission stated:

> Canadians appear to distrust their political leaders, the political process and political institutions. Parties themselves may be contributing to the malaise of voters.... Whatever the cause, there is little doubt that Canadian political parties are held in low public esteem, and that their standing has declined steadily over the past decade. They are under attack from citizens for failing to achieve a variety of goals deemed important by significant groups within society.[18]

Given its analysis of the depth of the representational crisis, the Commission promised to do more than tinker with the law. It recommended an overhaul.

Reforming Electoral Democracy provided a detailed account of the ills of democracy at the federal party level. It identified practices of exclusion which had restricted access to positions of political power for significant segments of the Canadian population including women, Aboriginal peoples, ethno-cultural groups and "visible minorities."[19] It explicitly addressed the perception that elections were unfair and drew attention to the inequitable distribution of money and partial access to the media. It expressed concern that the political parties were neglecting their responsibilities for political education and policy development. What parties do best is conduct elections. For the RCERPF, this activity was a necessary, but insufficient, expression of their obligations to Canadian citizens.[20] Strong inducements were recommended to encourage parties to recapture the enthusiasm of Canadians for partisan activity and to increase the access of those heretofore under-represented. At the same time, the Commission called for greater fairness in the regime of election financing, ending the virtual exclusion of small and new parties from some forms of public funding. It proposed making the electoral process more welcoming to a variety of voices, thereby increasing rather than limiting competition.

This approach to electoral reform and party financing led the Commission to formulate six objectives around which it organized both its analysis and its recommendations. They were

- securing the democratic rights of voters;
- enhancing access to elected office;
- promoting the equality and efficacy of the vote;
- strengthening political parties as primary political organizations;
- promoting fairness in the electoral process; and
- enhancing public confidence in the integrity of this process.[21]

Versions of these objectives had emerged early in the RCERPF's process. Indeed, they provided the framework for the symposia and workshops that the Commission organized to reach out to a broader, specialized public and around which research results were incorporated.[22]

During its lifetime and throughout *Reforming Electoral Democracy*, the Commission demonstrated a real awareness that the representational capacity of the federal party system was in decline. Since the Charter came into effect, the courts have provided alternative routes to making claims. In addition, according to its analysis, the diversion of responsibility for decision making to the leader and Cabinet, and to executive federalism has been the culprit in diminishing the capacity of the party system. Most frequently mentioned by the RCERPF, however, was the increasing role of "interest groups" as alternatives to party politics for much of the population.[23] The final report suggests that problems with political parties have been "paralleled, if not caused, by the proliferation of special-interest groups" which attract activists away from parties, thereby posing a challenge to them.[24] For the Commission, parties are the primary political organizations because interest groups are incapable of either recruiting and selecting candidates, and thus organizing the institutions of parliamentary government, or "formulating policy that accommodates and reconciles competing regional and socio-economic interests."[25] Given this view of parties and their weaknesses, parts of *Reforming Electoral Democracy* read as a clarion call to the parties to get their act together or to risk being displaced by these other forms of political action.

As a start, *Reforming Electoral Democracy* set out recommendations for filling the representational deficits in the existing party system and, in particular, responding to the legitimate claims of women and Aboriginal persons for a place in the House of Commons. While quotas for female MPs were ruled out, there was a clear injunction to the parties to be more integrative.[26] The Commission had identified women as the most under-represented of the social categories it considered; enhancing access required action. As the Commission's report bluntly stated, "this virtual exclusion, particularly of women, from the corridors of political power is no longer acceptable."[27]

Recommendations proceeded on two fronts. Because it is well recognized that women, as a group, face financial barriers in seeking nominations and contesting elections, the RCERPF proposed moving the regulatory reach of the electoral law back to cover the nomination process, by setting nomination spending limits. Second, it suggested that political contributions to nomination contests be eligible for tax credits. While women might expect to be the main beneficiaries of these changes, which were originally put forth by them to the RCERPF, other less wealthy Canadians would also benefit. The third recommendation with respect to finance was to include child-care expenses as an allowable tax deduction for candidates.[28]

Proposals to alter the behaviour of parties (and not just potential candidates) constituted a wider front of reform. One recommendation was that parties use formal search committees and processes "that demonstrably promote the identification and nomination of broadly representative candidates."[29] Research in other jurisdictions, as well as in Canada, identified these procedures as most likely to alter the profiles of candidate pools. A second recommendation was for a financial incentive to parties to increase the percentage of women in the House of Commons. If the next election still produced a House that was more than 80 percent male, then any party nominating and electing a parliamentary delegation that was more than 20 percent female would have its reimbursement increased by the percentage of women it had elected.[30] The details of this scheme are less important than its overall aim: to use public funds—thereby demonstrating public interest in the gender composition of the House of Commons—to induce parties to nominate *and elect* more female candidates.

A second major representational shortfall acknowledged by the RCERPF was for Aboriginal persons. The issue of Aboriginal seats arose as part of a discussion of electoral boundaries in which the goal was to balance the principle of one person, one vote with the recognition of communities of interest.[31] With rare exceptions, even the most careful attention to communities of interest would fail to produce constituencies in which Aboriginal persons would come close to forming a majority or even a plurality. Therefore, *Reforming Electoral Democracy* recommended altering the geographical base of constituencies by creating province-wide Aboriginal seats where numbers warrant them. In brief, in those provinces where the number of self-identified Aboriginal persons voluntarily registered on a separate voters' list was greater than the proportion of the provincial population in each constituency (the electoral quotient), then the Electoral Boundaries Commission would create one or more province-wide Aboriginal seats. This different treatment was explicitly presented as necessary in order to achieve equality; in other words, it was linked to a discourse of affirmative action.[32]

For the Commission, the elimination of these representational gaps was not sufficient to increase the representational capacity of the parties and stop the dispersion of activism and the enthusiasm for "interest groups." More was needed, and the RCERPF called for a combination of state actions—public funding and regulation—to foster the kind of parties and party behaviour it considered necessary to reduce the democratic deficit.

It developed a set of initiatives to encourage parties to become "thicker" organizations with responsibilities beyond elections and the walls of the House. Under current law much inter-election activity, including nominations, is relatively unregulated and beyond the reach of the State. In the interest of generating institutions likely to provide the representation the Commission thought Canadians deserve, it recommended changes that would fundamentally modify parties as they are and transform them into the organizations they are meant to be. Indeed, *Reforming Electoral Democracy* actually defined parties as organizations created with the purpose of

> nominating candidates for election to Parliament; mobilizing electoral support for their candidates; engaging their members in discussion of democratic governance; providing forums for the development of alternative policies and programs; preparing their elected members for their parliamentary responsibilities; and organizing the processes of representative and responsible government.[33]

This definition not only gave the parties a central role in political life, it was also a marked departure from earlier rationales for electoral reform and party financing which tended to focus on candidates.[34] If these more substantial institutions were actually to come into being in any real way, many of the practices of brokerage politics would have to be changed.

The Commission was determined to nudge these activist parties into existence via a number of measures. First, it recommended that parties formalize their existence by adopting democratic constitutions, which would be consistent with the spirit and intent of the Charter.[35] Conceivably, among other things, such constitutions could commit parties to affirmative action and the recognition of equality. Second, the Commission's report was an advocate for the party activists so often bypassed in sequestered decision making and policy formulation. It called for more vital internal structures, the implication being that these would "serve the objective of building a broader and more active membership and of mobilizing that membership behind goals deemed important by the national party."[36] A third type of change had implications for the revitalization of party activism, but it was also primarily an effort to improve thinking about medium- and long-term policy development. The Commission recommended using public funds to establish party foundations.[37] These new institutions, linked to each party, would become primary sites for discussing policy alternatives. They were intended to have a salutary effect on the consideration of basic political choices as well as to improve the capacity for long-term thinking. Fourth, the Commission recommended altering the distribution of public funds for electoral reimbursement to strengthen the parties by giving them a greater proportion of public funds and by tying those funds to success at vote-getting, rather than to the parties' ability to spend.[38] Finally, the RCERPF recommended a series of reforms that would extend the regulatory regime into the nomination and leadership selection processes by regulating certain practices, setting spending limits and extending public funding into those realms of activity.[39]

The basic logic in all of this was that, while parties are private institutions, they do have public responsibilities for securing and enhancing democratic practices. The State funds parties because they perform essential functions. It regulates them for the same reason. Just as the State now regulates many dimensions of economic or cultural life because of their social importance (from banks to television and radio), so too should it regulate the parties. Not only are parties the institutions through which governments are selected, they also provide the means by which society represents itself to itself.

In some ways, these specific regulations were recommended in order to save the parties from themselves, i.e. to push them into acting appropriately. For example, the Commission was struck by the extent to which the courts in the United States, in reaction to public distaste for corrupt and racist party behaviour, had set up an elaborate regulatory framework for the primaries that effectively left the party organizations with only a nominal role in the nomination process of candidates in legislative and presidential elections.[40] Therefore, the recommendations for regulating nominations and leadership contests made in *Reforming Electoral Democracy* were meant to pre-empt such a diversion of a party function as well as to enhance access. Only with such changes would the parties have the capacity to play their role as primary political organizations.

The final report also contained a series of recommendations that would enhance fairness and electoral competition. These recommendations linked the goal of increased access for new actors, and the ideas they bring with them, to the goal of strengthening parties as institutions of representation. The Commission recommended inter-election registration procedures, by petition, for new parties.[41] In addition, it proposed a fundamental shift in the provision of public funding. Existing legislation makes public funds (reimbursement of up to 50 percent of allowable election expenses) available only to candidates who receive 15 percent of the vote in their constituency. The RCERPF recommended dropping the threshold to 1 percent. With such a change, any candidate wishing to participate in an election—and offer a different flavour from the three standard varieties—could also benefit from the "50 cent dollars" now spent by Conservative, Liberal and New Democratic Party candidates.

Current formulas for public funding of parties and candidates reward spending, whereas the Commission recommended rewarding success. For instance, parties now receive public funds for campaign expenses only if they spend at least 10 percent of their allowable limit. This regime rewards "big spenders" because the limit is set very high and it is usually only the three main parties that can spend enough money to get to this threshold. Smaller parties are thereby doubly disadvantaged. Not only do they have less to begin with, but they also receive no reimbursements for any of their spending.

To eliminate this inequity between those on the inside and those trying to get in, the Commission recommended reimbursing candidates and parties receiving at least 1 percent of the vote according to a formula which would recognize their vote-getting capacity; in essence, "the more votes, the more money."[42] Important for small parties, however, was the corollary: "some votes, some money."

These changes to funding were geared towards enhancing fairness. Very high thresholds for reimbursement of candidates' and parties' election expenses discouraged competition. The three major parties in Parliament designed this electoral regime in the past and recognize that it continues to work to their benefit. The Commission was daring the insiders to think beyond immediate self-interest and to consider principles of fairness and the health of democracy.

Also central to the Commission's conceptualization of fairness was its recommendation for limiting "independent expenditures," sometimes called "third-party spending."[43] These terms refer to the money spent for advertising by anyone other than a party or candidate during an election campaign. The issue is an important one because the Canadian regulatory regime depends on limiting expenditures by parties and candidates during elections. If these limits can be circumvented by groups and individuals who are not officially parties or candidates, then the notion of regulating the latter's election expenses obviously makes little sense. Most informed observers agree that it is the very presence of limits on how much parties and candidates can spend fighting elections which has kept election expenses in Canada under control. Moreover, these limits contribute to more competitive federal elections. They have meant that Canadian candidates, unlike their American counterparts, are not backed by rich and powerful Political Action Committees (PACs) which provide them with an overwhelming advantage over less equipped contenders. Nor do MPs have the same benefits of incumbency that their colleagues enjoy in the U.S. and which makes turnover rates so low there.[44]

The issue of independent expenditures is a thorny one. Concerns of free speech are clearly involved. The basic question is: Why confine the right to spend money to registered parties and official candidates during a crucial moment of electoral democracy? The RCERPF manoeuvred delicately through this thicket. It recommended severe limits to independent expenditures. No more than $1,000 could be spent by a group or individual, and this could not be pooled to create a larger fund. At the same time, internal communication within organizations like companies, unions, interest groups or any other organizational entity was deemed perfectly acceptable.

In making these recommendations, the Commission refused to make a distinction between "direct" spending, in which a party or candidate is explicitly identified, and "issue" spending in which a position is promoted without specifically mentioning a party or candidate. The RCERPF recognized that, as the 1988 election made clear, there was little need for the pro-Free Trade Agreement (FTA) Business Council on National Issues to call for a Tory vote. The choice for free traders was obvious. The lines between different kinds of spending were easily blurred.

The Commission accepted that the $1,000 limit would constitute a restraint on independent actors, but argued that this was defensible in order to achieve the competing goal of fair elections and a measure of equality among contenders. It claimed the Supreme Court of Canada would see this as a "reasonable limit prescribed by law as can be demonstrably justified in a free and democratic society" and, therefore, in conformity with Section 1 of the 1982 Canadian Charter of Rights and Freedoms.

The whole package that the RCERPF put together was a coherent one, proceeding from first principles, then translated into realizable recommendations. The initial response to the report was either muted (on the part of the parties) or quite critical (on the part of several high-profile groups representing the Canadians who would be most affected by the recommended reforms). For instance, upon release of the report in February 1992—despite the RCERPF-sponsored consultation among Aboriginal groups the Chief of the Assembly of First Nations, Ovide Mercredi, immediately rejected the proposal for Aboriginal constituencies, saying "it would relegate natives to 'lobby group' status.... Because few seats would be available to them it is not anything like the equal voice Aboriginal people are entitled to have in Canada."[45] Similarly, Judy Rebick, President of the National Action Committee on the Status of Women (NAC) called the RCERPF report "woefully inadequate" and asserted, "more dramatic action is needed to improve Canada's shameful record of only 13 percent women in Parliament."[46]

What was the problem here? Why were the spokespersons for Aboriginal groups and women rejecting much of *Reforming Electoral Democracy*? More striking even than the coolness of this reception, however, was the fact that those who were positive tended to focus on the narrower, more "housekeeping" elements of the report. The larger vision for reforming electoral democracy which underpinned *Reforming Electoral Democracy* has attracted much less attention.

REACTIONS: WHY REFUSE THE MEDICINE?

In this concluding section, we will argue that the recommendations of the Commission were put on the shelf of the medicine cabinet because its approach was too innovative in the way it conceptualized parties and too traditional in its understanding of routes to democratic representation. The result is that the Commission, as yet, has no real constituency. It has been rebuffed by its natural constituency—the parties and politicians most concerned about the functioning of elections and party financing. It has been ignored by a potential constituency—the social movements and other groups concerned with extending democracy in Canadian politics.

We will examine these two constituencies separately in the remaining pages.

The Natural Constituency

Utilizing a discourse of "party primacy," the RCERPF introduced a notion that was not completely familiar to Canadian ears, especially those at the federal level.[47] This notion stressed the importance of parties as *institutions* of representation that have responsibilities beyond fighting elections and organizing the House of Commons. As the definition of parties proposed in *Reforming Electoral Democracy* makes clear, the Commission worked with an understanding of liberal democracy in which parties operate as central, organic institutions. This more "European" notion of parties as ongoing institutions of democratic representation with public responsibilities provided a justification for additional state support in inter-electoral periods, as well as the rationale for extending the regulatory regime.[48] The insistence on a party constitution, a code of ethics, more equitable nomination and leadership selection practices, and monitoring of access were, among other things, evidence that the Commission expected political parties to be more than they currently are. It called on them to set their aspirations higher.

If enacted, its recommendations had the potential to dislodge the federal parties from their brokerage traditions of electoralist "policy taking" (whether from other institutions or other parties) and leadership politics. The parties might begin to move towards a situation where more than election strategy motivated policy stances and where viable institutions representing alternative projects linked individuals and the State.[49]

Simply stated, *Reforming Electoral Democracy* challenged the Government, parties and politicians to reform themselves. It called on them to change the law in ways which would alter their self-understandings, their existing practices and, indeed, the very logic of their behaviour. In such a context, it is not surprising that they might resist thorough-going reform.[50] The Commission asked the parties to put first principles ahead of immediate self-interest. This proved to be too strong a medicine for brokerage parties accustomed to short-term thinking and calculations of immediate advantage.

There was an additional way in which the Commission's conceptualization of liberal democracy challenged contemporary political discourse. In an era of neo-liberalism, in which the best state is supposedly the least state and market relations model all other social relations, the Commission presented a somewhat collectivist view and refused to equate equality in politics with equality in the market.[51] Throughout *Reforming Electoral Democracy*, it is clear that "public" is both a central concept and a "good word"—whether speaking of public responsibilities or of the right of the public to regulate. Given that the representative of the "public" in this context is the State, responsibility for overseeing the public interest rests with the State; it does not devolve to the private sphere. By advocating the use of public funds and promoting state regulation to achieve democratic ends, the RCERPF went against the prevailing political grain.

In the beginning, the Tory government's response was a cautious one. The report would be studied carefully, but there might be an election in the meantime. Speaking to the media after the final report, including draft legislation, was presented in February 1992, House Leader Harvie Andre told reporters, "the bill is not going to be simply stamped Government Bill and introduced in the House. We did not say in advance that we will accept it 100 percent and implement it as soon as possible...."[52] In fact, Andre expressed many reservations about the recommendations, such as the constitutionality of limits on advertising by third parties. He also refused to commit the Government to acting on the proposals before the next election, noting the "timing challenge."[53] That likelihood was even more reduced when he announced that the final report would be referred to the parliamentary Special Committee on Electoral Reform.[54]

The Government's reactions were predictable. Given the composition of the existing Tory caucus and the party's current neo-liberal agenda, no report would be palatable which called for a more active role for government and a more comprehensive, participatory notion of parties where connections between society and State are forged, rather than severed, through elite practices. Progressive Conservatives, in general, assessed the RCERPF's potential damage to their party's electoral advantage. For example, the Conservative Party, currently the most successful fundraiser, has begun to back away from the very concept of spending limits in elections, the bedrock principle of electoral regulation in Canada.[55] Theoretically and practically then, the Commission's report ran counter to the Tories' agenda.

The opposition parties shared the Tories' wariness, although they prudently endorsed some proposals. Liberal MPs Ethel Blondin and Mary Clancy thought the recommendations moved in the right direction for both Aboriginal peoples and women. Blondin stated, "This is a step to start correcting that inequality [historically facing Aboriginal people with respect to the Commons]."[56] For women, Clancy suggested, the proposals constituted "a positive action because they put the onus on parties to recruit and encourage women to run." Similarly, New Democratic Party (NDP) Leader Audrey McLaughlin commented that the RCERPF proposals "will go a long way, if implemented, to encouragement [for women] to participate."[57] Overall, however, spokespersons for the Liberals and the NDP joined the Tories' call for "further study" and echoed the difficulties of moving ahead before the next election.[58] There was little, if any, recognition of the Commission's grander vision.[59]

Thus, all parties refrained from wholeheartedly supporting the RCERPF's proposals, and nothing has been heard from them about the internal, non-legislated changes that would make them both more accessible and less electoralist in their focus.[60]

The response of the Special Committee on Electoral Reform was both critical of the Commission and crucial to the electoral reform process. The Special Committee's deliberations not only indicated the nature of parties' reticence about the RCERPF's proposals, but played a key role in influencing the speed of electoral reform and the direction it would take. In fact, it is on the basis of the Special Committee's recommendations, *not* the RCERPF's proposals, that new legislation was introduced on February 22, 1993.

The Special Committee operated on the basis of the all-too-familiar principles of short-term interest and electoral advantage. It assured the prominence of the three main parties whose representatives were the only members. Second, the members of the Special Committee weighed the costs and benefits of proposed changes to their respective parties. As just one example, the Special Committee failed to follow the Commission's lead in opening up inter-election registration procedures to new parties.

Instead, they maintained the rules that benefited the three traditional parties. Furthermore, neither the Tory nor NDP members of the Special Committee demonstrated much enthusiasm for the proposed change to a vote-based regime for reimbursing election expenses; both, no doubt, were tabulating that the change would generate a small loss in public funds to their respective parties. Throughout, the Commission's principle of fairness was factored out in favour of cost-benefit calculations which deviated little from the standard party equation.

What also became apparent from the Special Committee and, indeed, more broadly was that the RCERPF's activist state ran smack against neo-liberal roadblocks. From inside the Special Committee, Howard Crosby, Tory MP for Halifax West, complained that he "... had hoped electoral reform would yield less rule and regulation rather than more rule and regulation, less bureaucracy rather than more bureaucracy." He saw the proposed regulation of the nomination process as too bureaucratic. Likewise in the press, *The Globe and Mail* editorialist sharply criticized the Commission's supposed call for more regulation, more state.[61] The Chairperson of the RCERPF, Pierre Lortie, however, would not change course. While citing areas in which regulation would be reduced (broadcasting and voter registration, for example) Lortie refused to back away from the general principle of using rules and regulation. He maintained, "To the extent there is public money involved, you cannot totally avoid that process."[62]

In December 1992, 10 months after it was created, the Special Committee released its interim report, presenting legislative changes that the Committee described as "administrative in nature." The changes concerned procedures for registering parties and enumerating voters that would make it easier to get on the electors' list and would make voting more accessible, especially for Canadians away from home on election day or living abroad. The Committee promised, in the second phase of its work (which it claimed would also be completed before the next election, but that looks more and more doubtful), to consider broadcasting, disclosure of information about public opinion polls, decriminalization of certain election offences and election campaign financing, as well as some recommendations dealing with access to candidacy for disabled persons and those caring for young children. Put off to a third phase as matters that "simply cannot take effect before the next election" were Aboriginal constituencies and measures to increase the number of female candidates.[63] While Aboriginal seats are complicated matters involving redistricting which, arguably, might be best left until the Royal Commission on Aboriginal Peoples (which is also dealing with representation and citizenship) has presented its report, it is not obvious why the phase two changes to election financing could not include the recommendations about public funding to parties which improve the rate at which they elect women.

What is clear about the work of the Special Committee is that it decided, from the beginning, to rework the draft legislation proposed by the RCERPF although the legislation was designed not only to be comprehensive, but also to integrate all the elements of reform to make a philosophically, as well as legislatively, consistent package.[64] Instead, the Committee immediately "un-linked" all the pieces again. It also treated the recommendations of the RCERPF as only one among several to be considered with private member's bills and updates of earlier legislation also on the table.

The Special Committee rejected the RCERPF's assessment that electoral laws were unacceptably complicated as well as outdated and that their reform required nothing short of full replacement. The Committee preferred a piecemeal—and slow—approach, despite warnings that the next election might very well bring important Charter challenges to the existing legislation and its restrictions.[65] The Committee took 31 in camera meetings to draft its own legislation dealing with the administrative matters for phase one of its work. Rather than pursue a more comprehensive, coherent and open approach to reform, the Special Committee opted to plod through the nitty-gritty.[66]

As a consequence, Harvie Andre's prediction has been borne out: the representatives of the parties in the House have absolutely no intention of "stamping" the recommendations of the RCERPF into law. Whether they will accept any of the more innovative ones remains to be seen.

The Potential Constituency

While it is true that the parties and politicians have been less than enthusiastic about making sweeping changes to electoral democracy, it is also true that they have not been pressured to do so. The other potential constituency of the RCERPF—those concerned with making Canadian politics more democratic in general—immediately dismissed or failed to see the significance of the recommendations of *Reforming Electoral Democracy*. This cold response is linked to the RCERPF's discourse, especially its single-minded theoretical assault on "single-issue interest groups." The Commission elevated parties to the status of primary institutions of representation, not simply because they are the sole institution to present candidates, but also because it considered only parties capable of "accommodating interests." In its analysis, the Commission went to some effort to de-legitimate any pretensions that other types of organizations, whether interest groups or social movements, might have of contributing to broad-based democratic representation.

While it is the case that only parties elect members to the House of Commons, the other tasks of democratic representation are currently performed by *both* parties and social movements. In fact, the latter have promoted more expansive notions of democracy which reach beyond traditionally defined political spaces. Many women's movements, for example, have called for the democratization of the family as well as workplaces, thereby breaking through conventional political confines. Aboriginal groups which seek self-government are also deploying a discourse of democratization. The centrality of this theme of democracy to social movement politics was not taken into account by the RCERPF.

By lacking an appreciation of these developments, in part because it failed to apprehend the character of such social movements, the Commission could not relate its concerns about electoral democracy to those of others working for greater democratic well-being. More specifically, in using a model of parties as the only institutions that can accommodate interests, the Commission shifted from an analysis of parties as primary political organizations (that is, first in an order that includes *others*) to one of virtual exclusivity. According to *Reforming Electoral Democracy*, "citizens may organize themselves for political purposes into organizations such as interest groups or pressure groups. But only political parties can reconcile and accommodate diverse and competing interests to reach agreement on public policy."[67]

The report continually contrasted parties to "interest groups," "single-issue groups" and "special interest groups." These designations were presumably meant to include what are better named social movements.[68] Unfortunately, these labels tend to drive large social movement organizations—like feminist, nationalist, Aboriginal, gay and environmental groups among others—to distraction, precisely because they strive to be more "accommodative" than "special" and to integrate multiple concerns rather than "single issues." Elaborating inclusive world views which demonstrate the interrelations between an array of issues, forging political connections, networking and accommodating other movements and groups are all part of social movement strategy. For example, the major organization of the women's movement, the National Action Committee on the Status of Women, was a leading opponent of the 1988 FTA because of its perceived adverse effects on the whole economy as well as on Canadian sovereignty, and it worked in coalition with a diversity of other groups. Similarly, ecological groups are now mobilizing a diversified opposition to the North American Free Trade Agreement (NAFTA) because of the perceived negative environmental effects of low wage production. For social movements, issues and political linkages intersect and overlap. Therefore, the much-abhorred "special interest" and "single-issue" designations could, in and of themselves, explain the lack of support for a set of recommendations that insists on defining social movements this way. The problem, however, is an even deeper one than that of naming.

The interpretation of history embedded in *Reforming Electoral Democracy* overlooks the fact that the old-fashioned, structural-functionalist understanding of a division of labour between "interest groups which articulate interests" and "parties which aggregate interests" has been called into question by the multiple strategies of new kinds of actors in the last three decades. Since at least the 1960s, "the idea of unconventional political participation as a legitimate resource of democratic citizenship has spread out into the wider political community."[69] As the campaign for, and result of, the October 26 constitutional referendum demonstrated, Canadians are willing to take their political cues from non-party groups, and such groups are willing to claim the right to intervene in large political issues and to have their voices heard. There is a large, viable constituency for political action that is not bounded by the traditional routes of liberal democracy. Indeed, any detailed examination of at least the last decade of social movement politics in Canada demonstrates that these movements have faced and responded to challenges to accommodate a variety of interests, as well as to work in coalition with other like-minded groups.

Given the Commission's version of the detrimental consequences of "interest groups," it should come as no shock that social movements were less than impressed with *Reforming Electoral Democracy*. Because they seek multiple representational forms in their struggles for democratization, a call to trust the parties as the single means to a democratic end was unappealing. As a result, the Commission's proposals were received, at best, with indifference or scepticism and, at worst, with dismay if not disapprobation. Few social movement organizations endorsed the set of recommendations which seemed to be based on an effort to render them redundant.

Yet it may be appropriate for social movements to reconsider their position, particularly as Parliament continues to review the Commission's report. Precisely because social movement organizations in Canada follow a variety of strategies in making claims—sometimes acting autonomously, sometimes in coalition, and sometimes by pressuring one or more parties—they have a stake in electoral democracy. They are, moreover, no fans of the old-style, brokerage system. Many of these groups would be willing to support the kind of "thicker" party institutions for which the RCERPF called. The concerns of many social movements have much in common with aspects of the Commission's agenda, such as reconstructing parties in ways that introduce spaces for political debate and democratic practices; changing the faces of politics; controlling the power of money; and fighting against the efforts to "marketize" politics.

At the very least, social movements may have to reassess the Commission's recommendation on "independent expenditures" and contrast it to that of the Special Committee on Electoral Reform. In a surprise and very last-minute move, the Special Committee's December 1992 report suggested controlling independent expenditures by setting a $1,000 limit on "direct" spending. With this proposal, the Special Committee rejected the Commission's contention that it is impossible to make a distinction between direct and issue advertising. It was the Committee's half-hearted response to the RCERPF's efforts at regulating spending limits, which then became part of the legislation introduced on February 22, 1993.

Enacting this compromise will set limits on free speech without plugging all sorts of easily imaginable loopholes. In other words, it causes more problems than it solves, thereby making restraint less "reasonable" in the eyes of the courts. If legislated, the fight over spending limits would revolve around a very minimalist reform. Furthermore, without the full weight behind it of the principled reasoning that the RCERPF marshalled— precisely in order to convince the courts of the necessity of such a Charter right restraint—the limit is being set up for defeat. The likely result of a successful court challenge will be no limits at all, allowing elections to be financial free-for-alls. In such circumstances, social movement organizations, even in coalition, are likely to be vastly outspent, just as the opponents of free trade were able to marshal only 25 cents for every dollar spent by its proponents in 1988.[70] This gives some indication of the dangers involved in not paying sufficient attention to these electoral democratic developments.

In sum, the problem with the Royal Commission on Electoral Reform and Party Financing is not that it focused on expanding one democratic space: the political parties and elections. That, indeed, was its innovation and strength. Moreover, its call for fairness and generosity, as well as attention to first principles in electoral politics—in other words, for parties to rise above short-term calculations—helps explain why the mainstream parties, especially the government party, are thus far so little concerned with implementing the recommendations. The problem is that, unfortunately, the Commission failed to acknowledge that there are now multiple and intersecting paths leading to a more free and democratic society, including elections. In so doing, it failed to connect with those social forces which are also promoting an expanded discourse and practices of democratic citizenship. Yet, if not only parties and elections but politics in general are to become more democratic in Canada, that connection will have to be made, and quickly.

NOTES

Despite having benefited immensely from comments on an earlier version from Peter Aucoin, Alain-G. Gagnon, Pierre Lortie, David Mac Donald, Jon Pammett, Susan Phillips, Denis St-Martin and F. Leslie Seidle, we remain responsible for the analysis of this paper.

1   *National Citizens' Coalition Inc. and Brown v. Canada (A.G.)* (1984), 5 W.W.R. 436.

2   Pierre Lortie, "Opening Remarks at the First Public Hearing of the Commission" (Ottawa, March 12, 1990), p. 1.

3   The RCERPF reported in four volumes. The first two presented the analysis and recommendations, the third was draft legislation for implementing the recommendations and the fourth was a summary of "what the Commission was told." The overall title of the final report is *Reforming Electoral Democracy*.

4   It is important to distinguish social movements and interest groups. While social movements may create social movement organizations that behave in many ways like interest groups, they derive their organizational strength and expectations about behaviour from social movement ideology. See, for example, Susan Phillips, "Meaning and Structure in Social Movements: Mapping the Network of National Canadian Women's Associations," *Canadian Journal of Political Science*, 24, 4 (December 1991). In recent decades, social movements have stressed radical pluralism, coalitional politics and reconfiguring political discourse. At the same time, particularly in Canada, social movements have not eschewed a partisan connection. Indeed, this is an aspect of their political action that makes new social movements in Canada somewhat different from those elsewhere. See, for example, Alexandra Dobrowolsky, "The Stakes of Struggle: Democracy, Constitutionalism and Collective Actors in Contemporary Canada" (Paper presented at the conference on Democratic Politics: Fifty Years of Political Science at Carleton University, Carleton University, Ottawa, November 13-14, 1992). To illustrate, various organizations of the women's movement maintain ties with political parties and a willingness to engage in partisan

debate, as need be. In the same way, even as the organizational arm of the labour movement, the Canadian Labour Congress, alters its strategic orientation by increasing its involvement in coalitional politics, it maintains its long-standing link with the NDP.

5   See Janine Brodie and Jane Jenson, "The Party System" in Michael S. Whittington and Glen Williams, (eds.), *Canadian Politics in the 1990s,* 3rd ed., (Scarborough: Nelson Canada, 1990), p. 251; Harold D. Clarke, Lawrence LeDuc, Jane Jenson, and Jon H. Pammett, *Absent Mandate: Interpreting Change in Canadian Elections* (Toronto: Gage, 1991), pp. 9-10; H.D. Forbes, "Absent Mandate '88? Parties and Voters in Canada" in Hugh G. Thorburn, (ed.), *Party Politics in Canada,* 6th ed. (Scarborough: Prentice-Hall, 1991), pp. 255-57.

6   Similar critical comments on brokerage politics and democracy have a long history. For example, in the early 1940s, F.H. Underhill rejected Pendleton Herring's celebration of brokerage parties in "The Canadian Party System in Transition," *Canadian Journal of Economics and Political Science,* vol. IX, pp. 300-13, (1943). Writing in the mid-1950s, Michael Oliver assessed the possibility of revitalizing "genuinely creative political thought and action" which had fallen on hard times as brokerage parties struggled to bridge the English-French cultural gap, in *The Passionate Debate: The Social and Political Ideas of Quebec Nationalism, 1920-1945* (Montreal: Véhicule, 1991), p. 224 and chap. 8 *passim.* In the late 1960s, Gad Horowitz provided a stinging critique of the myths and undemocratic nature of broker-age parties in " Toward the Democratic Class Struggle" in Trevor Lloyd and Jack McLeod, *Agenda 1970: Proposals for a Creative Politics* (Toronto: University of Toronto Press, 1968), especially pp. 249ff.

7   André Siegfried, *The Race Question in Canada* (Toronto: McClelland and Stewart, [1906], 1966), p. 113.

8   Alain-G. Gagnon and A. Brian Tanguay, "Introduction: Canadian Parties in Transition" in Gagnon and Tanguay, (eds.), *Canadian Parties in Transition,* (Scarborough, Ont.: Nelson Canada, 1989), pp. 7-8.

9   See Frederick Englemann and Mildred Schwartz, *Political Parties and Canadian Social Structure* (Scarborough: Prentice-Hall, 1967), pp. 19, 55; John Meisel, "Recent Changes in Canadian Parties" in Hugh Thorburn, (ed.), *Party Politics in Canada*, 2nd ed. (Toronto: Prentice-Hall, 1967), p. 34; Conrad Winn and John McMenemy, *Political Parties in Canada* (Toronto: McGraw-Hill, 1976), p. 1.

10   For example, Meisel, "Recent Changes," p. 34.

11   See Sylvia Bashevkin, "Political Parties and the Representation of Women" in Gagnon and Tanguay, *Canadian Parties*; Lise Gotell and Janine Brodie, "Women and Parties: More Than an Issue of Numbers" in Thorburn, *Party Politics*, 6th ed. Both discuss women's formal and substantive under-representation. On state institutions as racist, nativist and exclusionary, see Daiva K. Stasiulis and Yasmeen Abu Laban, "Ethnic Activism and the Politics of Limited Inclusion in Canada" in Alain-G. Gagnon and James P. Bickerton, (eds.), *Canadian Politics: An Introduction to the Discipline* (Peterborough: Broadview Press, 1990), p. 581. For a concise discussion of positions on electoral reform and Aboriginal peoples, see Robert A. Milen, "Aboriginal Constitutional and Electoral Reform" in Robert A. Milen, (ed.), *Aboriginal Peoples and Electoral Reform in Canada*, vol. 9 of the Research Studies of the RCERPF (Toronto: Dundurn Press, 1991), especially pp. 38ff. For a discussion of class and party, see Leo V. Panitch, "Elites, Classes and Power in Canada" in Whittington and Williams, (eds.), *Canadian Politics in the 1990s*, pp. 199ff.

12   See Peter Russell's account of the assortment of task forces, commissions and conferences established in the last round of constitutional negotiations. *Constitutional Odyssey: Can Canadians Be a Sovereign People?* (Toronto: University of Toronto Press, 1992), chap. 10.

13   On interest groups, see K. Z. Paltiel, "The Changing Environment and Role of Special Interest Groups," *Canadian Public Administration*, 25, 2 (1982): p. 206; F. Leslie Seidle, (ed.), *Interest Groups and Elections in Canada*, vol. 2 of the Research Studies

of the RCERPF (Toronto: Dundurn Press, 1991). On social movements, see W.K. Carroll, (ed.), *Organizing Dissent: Contemporary Social Movements in Theory and Practice* (Canada: Garamond Press, 1992).

14   This "success" may have been a fleeting one, but it nonetheless signalled a symbolic victory. See Gwen Brodsky and Shelagh Day, *Canadian Charter of Equality Rights for Women: One Step Forward or Two Steps Back?* (Ottawa: Canadian Advisory Council on the Status of Women, 1989). On more recent struggles, see Alexandra Dobrowolsky, "Women's Equality and the Constitutional Proposals" in Duncan Cameron and Miriam Smith, (eds.), *Constitutional Politics* (Toronto: James Lorimer, 1992).

15   On coalition politics, see Duncan Cameron, "Political Discourse in the Eighties" in Gagnon and Tanguay, *Canadian Parties*, pp. 64-82. See also the case study of the Action Canada Network by Peter Bleyer, "Coalitions of Social Movements as Agencies for Social Change: The Action Canada Network" in Carroll, *Organizing Dissent*. "Older" social movements like trade unions are engaging in outreach to the "newer" social movements. For an interesting example of these efforts at linkages, see Canadian Labour Congress, *A New Decade: Our Future*, document 14 (Ottawa, 1991). For an illustration of how the women's movement has worked in coalition with others to oppose the Tory government's economic policy, see Sylvia Bashevkin, "Free Trade and Canadian Feminism: The Case of the National Action Committee on the Status of Women," *Canadian Public Policy*, 15, 4 (1989).

16   For a summary, see *Reforming Electoral Democracy*, vol. 1, pp. 4-6. Vol. 4 provides detailed information, including summary transcripts of these consultations and symposia; the English versions of the 23 volumes of Research Studies have been published by Dundurn Press.

17   It is worth comparing Lortie's "Opening Remarks" in March 1990 with later speeches. Initially he described the task facing the Commission as more narrowly focused on the franchise and regulation of finances. The argument was essentially that the law

was outdated, in particular in light of recent court decisions and the Charter. The context in which the mandate was interpreted quickly came to have an influence, however, as the hearings and research went forward. By September 1990, it was clear the Commission had understood that the suggestions it was hearing from the interveners "… were remarkably attuned to the opinion of a large majority of Canadians who are simply not content with the status quo, notwithstanding the obvious merits of our system." Pierre Lortie, "The Challenge of Electoral Reform: Combining Innovation with Continuity" (Speech to the Council of Governmental Ethics Law (COGEL), Anchorage, Alaska, September 14, 1990), p. 3.

18   *Reforming Electoral Democracy*, vol. 1, p. 221. See also Tables 5.1, 5.2, 5.4, which present the opinion data in detail.

19   It is notable that nowhere in *Reforming Electoral Democracy* did the Commission raise the issue of access for *all* citizens. While the financial limits which women faced in comparison with men were discussed, the unstated assumption remained that these women were drawn from similar professional and other backgrounds to men. While Aboriginal persons were described as under-represented, the problem identified was that their votes were less "efficacious" because they were geographically dispersed. Systemic or other barriers to poor and working Canadians did not figure in the analysis of the Commission.

20   As *Reforming Electoral Democracy*, vol. 1 said, in a classic understatement about Canada's brokerage parties, "overall, Canadian political parties have a reputation for being weak other than in the performance of electoral functions," (p. 295). In news conferences presenting the final report, Pierre Lortie was even more outspoken about the limits of existing parties. For example, he was asked directly whether the Commission's analysis of the parties' electoralist preoccupations and failure to engage in long-term thinking and its proposal for party foundations were not a bit exaggerated. He answered directly: "Non. Le régime institutionel pousse à la pauvreté au plan de l'élaboration des politiques…. Soumettre ces questions à une foundation politique peut certainement susciter une réflexion, offrir une base intellectuelle

plus fortes aux politiques, et éviter, comme actuellement, que le débat ne se résume au plus petit dénominateur." ["No. The institutional system promotes poverty in terms of policy development.... Setting these issues on a political foundation can certainly stimulate reflection, set a more solid intellectual basis for policies and avoid, such as is currently the case, the debate coming down to the smallest common denominator."] *Le Soleil* [Quebec], February 16, 1992, p. A11.

21   The motivation for these goals and the broad philosophical rationale are set out in *Reforming Electoral Democracy*, vol. 1, pp. 1, 6-18.

22   Lortie's speech, "The Challenge of Electoral Reform" (September 14, 1990), unveiled a perspective which, with variations, informed many subsequent public presentations of the Chairperson and the Commission as a whole. Lortie identified five "desirable characteristics of electoral democracy": to secure and strengthen the democratic rights of citizens as electors; to encourage effective representation within parliamentary government; to strengthen the capacities of political parties as primary political organizations; to establish fairness among parties and candidates in electoral competition; and to enhance public confidence in the integrity of the electoral process and representative government. These elements were a reworked version of five which had earlier appeared in an internal discussion document, "Electoral Democracy in Canada: A Sober Assessment of the Record" (July 29, 1990). The major difference between the two lists was the identification of strengthening parties as a primary characteristic. The speech made explicit reference to the fact that parties were having difficulties not only producing "accommodation," but also fulfilling their responsibilities for "enhancing the deliberative content of public debate and contributing to the resolution of political conflict." Lortie, "The Challenge of Electoral Reform," pp. 14-15.

23   On the Charter, see *Reforming Electoral Democracy*, vol. 1, pp. 2-3. On the general analysis of the diversion of representational capacity, see pp. 220-28. The analysis of interest groups often appeared in Lortie's speeches. For example, he characterized

"single issue" groups as having "diverted the focus and energies of many political activists," while the "proliferation of special interest groups" has made "it increasingly difficult for legislative institutions to mediate between conflicting group interests and to resolve social and economic conflicts" in "The Challenge of Electoral Reform: Combining Innovation with Continuity" (Speech to a RCERPF Symposium on the Active Participation of Women in Politics, Montreal, November 1, 1990), p. 11.

24   *Reforming Electoral Democracy*, vol. 1, p. 13.

25   *Reforming Electoral Democracy*, vol. 1, p. 13.

26   The concern with under-representation of women soon emerged. As early as September 1990, Pierre Lortie announced that effective representation had been hindered by the existence of "barriers and discriminatory practices" which interfered with equal access to representation. "The Challenge of Electoral Reform" (September 1990), pp. 11-13. This linking of "representation" to gender equity appeared in the internal document, "Electoral Democracy in Canada," p. 11. In mid-fall 1990, the Symposium on the Active Participation of Women in Politics took place at the École Polytechnique of the Université de Montréal. According to Commissioner Lucie Pépin, the Commission decided to provoke a discussion because it had heard too little about the issues in the public hearings. Lucie Pépin, "Notes pour une allocution lors de l'ouverture du colloque sur la participation active des femmes à la politique" (Montreal, October 31, 1990), p. 1.

27   *Reforming Electoral Democracy*, vol. 1, pp. 7-8. For a detailed analysis, see chap. 3, especially pp. 105-13, 268-73, including Table 5.10 which shows that, of the four groups considered (women, Aboriginal persons, visible minorities and ethno-cultural groups), the representational deficit for women was the largest (p. 269).

28   For these three recommendations, see *Reforming Electoral Democracy*, vol. 1, pp. 117-20.

29 *Reforming Electoral Democracy*, vol. 1, p. 121.

30 For example, if a party's MPs were 30 percent female and 70 percent male, its actual public funding would be 130 percent of its entitlement (to a maximum of 150 percent). This equity measure was designed to be temporary, subject to review after three elections and in place only until the overall number of women in the House reached 40 percent. See *Reforming Electoral Democracy*, vol. 1, pp. 268-73.

31 *Reforming Electoral Democracy*, vol. 1, chap. 4.

32 *Reforming Electoral Democracy*, vol. 1, pp. 10-11, 169-92. See also vol. 2, chap. 5 for the details of implementing Aboriginal constituencies. The final report, in vols. 1 and 4, describes in detail the special consultative process and the Committee for Aboriginal Electoral Reform, chaired by Senator Len Marchand, on which the Commission relied in developing these recommendations.

33 *Reforming Electoral Democracy*, vol. 1, p. 246.

34 See Jane Jenson, "Innovation and Equity: The Impact of Public Funding" in F. Leslie Seidle, (ed.), *Comparative Issues in Party and Election Finance*, vol. 4 of the Research Studies of the RCERPF (Toronto: Dundurn Press, 1991), pp. 123-25 and *passim*.

35 *Reforming Electoral Democracy*, vol. 1, pp. 246-47. In a related recommendation, the Commission encouraged parties to develop codes of ethics, pp. 286-90.

36 *Reforming Electoral Democracy*, vol. 1, p. 238.

37 The need for such foundations is described in detail and the recommendations are developed in *Reforming Electoral Democracy*, vol. 1, pp. 290-302.

38 *Reforming Electoral Democracy*, vol. 1, p. 371, provides data on this redistribution.

39   Public funding of nominations is recommended in *Reforming Electoral Democracy*, vol. 1, chap. 2, while leadership contests are discussed in chap. 3, and spending limits for both in chap. 6, pp. 358ff.

40   *Reforming Electoral Democracy*, vol. 1, p. 260.

41   This change would also have the perhaps unintended effect of strengthening the message that parties are more than election-fighting machines.

42   *Reforming Electoral Democracy*, vol. 1, p. 370.

43   *Reforming Electoral Democracy*, vol. 1, pp. 350-56.

44   See Herbert E. Alexander, "The Regulation of Election Finance in the United States and Proposals for Reform" in F. Leslie Seidle, *Comparative Issues in Party Finance*, pp. 31-33.

45   Patrick Doyle, "Let natives elect own legislators commission says," *The Toronto Star*, February 14, 1992, p. A4.

46   News release of the National Action Committee on the Status of Women, February 14, 1992. Other women's groups were also concerned that the proposals were too limited. See "Electoral reform aimed at women," *Calgary Herald*, February 21, 1992, p. C12.

47   This way of conceptualizing parties was not totally foreign. It is already institutionalized to some extent in Quebec where, as early as 1965, recognized parties were reimbursed for the inter-election cost of maintaining permanent offices in Montreal and Quebec. Later reforms made bloc funding for general organizational costs available. Jenson, "Innovation and Equity," note 21, p. 168. *Reforming Electoral Democracy*, vol. 1, pp. 239-43, surveys the inter-election recognition of political parties, including provincial jurisdictions.

48   On the European comparisons, see *Reforming Electoral Democracy*, vol. 1, chap. 5, which makes frequent comparisons with continental European experiences. In addition, Pierre Lortie, in

his testimony to the Special Committee, insisted on the European comparison, although the MPs thought that only Anglo-American cases were really relevant. See *Minutes of Proceedings and Evidence of the Special Committee on Electoral Reform*, issue no. 1, pp. 50-51.

49   By democratizing the parties and ensuring that political elites use this reformed institution instead of resorting to elite accommodation, the RCERPF attempted to reconstruct the party as a bridge between civil society and the State. For the metaphor, see Claus Offe, "The Separation of Form and Content in Liberal Democratic Politics," *Studies in Political Economy*, 3 (1980): p. 9.

50   For a discussion of earlier experiences with reform and the role of self-interest in making changes, see K.Z. Paltiel, "The 1984 Federal Election and Developments in Canadian Party Finance," in Howard Penniman, (ed.), *Canada at the Polls 1984* (Durham, N.C.: Duke University Press, 1988), pp. 140-41.

51   The distinction between the rights and freedoms of the market-place and the electoral process, and the differing notion of equality in each is made in *Reforming Electoral Democracy*, vol. 1, p. 14. See also the discussion of the difference between substantive and formal democracy on pp. 324-25. Lortie made the same point in testimony to the Special Committee. See *Proceedings and Evidence*, issue no. 1, p. 23.

52   Harvie Andre as quoted in Geoffrey York and Ross Howard, "Royal inquiry urges reforms for elections," *The Globe and Mail*, [Toronto], February 14, 1992, pp. A1, A4.

53   See Andre as quoted in York and Howard, "Royal inquiry." Editorial writers who favoured the recommendations were quick to point out that Andre's reaction suggested plans to dismiss the RCERPF or limit its impact to housekeeping. See, for example, "Don't shelve report," *Calgary Herald*, February 15, 1992, p. A4; "Rules for an election," *Edmonton Journal*, February 15, 1992; "Election reforms are long overdue," *The Toronto Star*, February 20, 1992, p. A24, which accused Andre of "whining about a 'timing challenge'" rather than getting on with it.

54   The Committee was established on February 14, 1992 and chaired by Progressive Conservative Jim Hawkes. It issued its third report on December 11, 1992, which was the first actually to address electoral reform; the first two considered the June 1992 Referendum Act. MPs Patrick Boyer and Peter Milliken, both of whom have long-standing interests in electoral reform, were members of the Committee.

55   According to the *Winnipeg Free Press*, Harvie Andre told the parliamentary Special Committee that, because of the Charter, spending limits would be "impractical after the next election" and that "there's scant correlation between spending and victory." Frances Russell, "If money does not talk, why is it so loud at elections?" *Winnipeg Free Press*, June 3, 1992, p. A7. The same article reports that Senator Norman Atkins (organizer of the 1984 and 1988 campaigns for the PCs) and David Angus (Chairperson of the PC Canada Fund) both argued against spending restraints.

56   Ethel Blondin as quoted in Patrick Doyle, "Let natives elect own legislators," p.A4. Her enthusiasm is hardly surprising; she was a member of the Committee for Aboriginal Electoral Reform.

57   Mary Clancy and Audrey McLaughlin, as quoted in David Vienneau, "Incentives urged to boost women's chances of election," *The Toronto Star*, February 14, 1992, p. A4.

58   York and Howard, "Royal inquiry," p. A4.

59   After some time had expired, on International Women's Day 1993, both the Liberals and NDP announced that they would strive to nominate more women in the next election. The NDP reiterated its commitment to 50 percent female candidates and reminded everyone of the existence of the Agnes Macphail Fund which provided about $1,200 to each woman running for the NDP. The Liberals promised to nominate women in 25 percent of the constituencies and to give about $8,000 this time to each candidate from the fund named after Judy LaMarsh. Both these funds were used in the earlier elections and, yet, in 1988, only 19.2 percent of candidates were women and, after the election, only 13.5 percent of the seats in the House were held by women.

See Chantal Maille with Valentina Pollon, *Primed for Power: Women in Canadian Politics* (Ottawa: Canadian Advisory Council on the Status of Women, 1990), p. 6.

60   There has been some movement in the area of spending limits. However, recent recommendations reflect more of a reiteration of past practice than an innovation. The Conservatives have proceeded to set spending limits for the 1993 leadership campaign: each candidate may spend no more than $900,000; donations will be processed through party channels so that they can be tax-credited; and the names of donors will be disclosed. This plan mirrors the practice of the Liberal party in its 1990 campaign. It has generally been described as a move to overcome voters' cynicism, but the ambiguities and lack of mechanisms for enforcement make achieving that end difficult. See Hugh Winsor, "PM plans tight rules on spending," *The Globe and Mail* [Toronto], March 5, 1993.

61   See "... and party organization," *The Globe and Mail* [Toronto], February 15, 1992, p. D6. In a set of two editorials, the *Globe* accused the RCERPF of "paternalism," as well as attempting to regulate too much. It termed the lever of public funding which the State has to influence party behaviour a "Faustian bargain," in an analysis that was much more negative about things "public" overall.

62   For the Crosby-Lortie exchange, see *Proceedings and Evidence*, issue no. 1, pp. 38-39.

63   *Minutes of Proceedings and Evidence of the Special Committee on Electoral Reform*, Third Report, (December 11, 1992), pp. 3-7.

64   See Lortie's interview with *Le Soleil*, p. A11.

65   On the Special Committee's strategy for unlinking the issues, see all of its *Proceedings*. The decision was taken at the first Committee meeting. On the Charter warnings, including the fear that such changes would result in the parties losing the possibility of reforming themselves, see Lortie's testimony to the Special Committee, *Proceedings and Evidence*, issue no. 1, pp. 35, 40ff.

66   For example, immediately after the Chairperson of the RCERPF had presented a detailed and concise overview of the principles underpinning the report and the coherence of the major lines of reform, Jim Hawkes avoided the larger issues, preferring to initiate a discussion of the details of enumeration costs. See *Proceedings and Evidence*, issue no. 1, pp. 27ff. Moreover, after inviting the Commission to one hearing, the Committee subsequently requested testimony almost exclusively from Elections Canada, especially the Chief Electoral Officer.

67   See *Proceedings and Evidence*, issue no. 1, p. 12. *Reforming Electoral Democracy*, vol. 1, pp. 222-23, simply asserts that these "interest groups" are incapable of accommodating and balancing a variety of interests. The discussion of interest groups proceeds through a series of assertions with remarkably few references to empirical literature to support them.

68   See *Reforming Electoral Democracy*, vol. 1, p. 222, where the examples of "environmental causes" and the "rights of women" are provided as "particular political interests" pursued "through single-issue organizations with the sole purpose of promoting a specific cause."

69   Samuel H. Barnes and M. Kaase, (eds.), *Political Action: Mass Participation in Five Western Democracies* (London: Sage, 1979), as quoted in Claus Offe, "Challenging the Boundaries of Institutional Politics: Social Movements Since the 1960s" in Charles Maier, (ed.), *Changing Boundaries of the Political* (New York: Cambridge University Press, 1987), p. 77.

70   *Reforming Electoral Democracy*, vol. 1, pp. 337-38.

CHAPTER 3

Constitutionalizing Economic and Social Rights in the Charlottetown Round

Miriam Smith

Résumé : Ce chapitre est consacré à l'incorporation dans la constitution des questions des droits économiques et sociaux dans le cadre des négociations constitutionnelles de Charlottetown. Il y est question des propositions formulées par le gouvernement fédéral en 1991 en vue d'enchâsser l'union économique dans la Constitution ainsi que du projet de charte sociale avancé par le gouvernement de l'Ontario. Ce chapitre retrace ce que sont devenus ces projets dans le courant du processus constitutionnel de 1991-1992. L'union économique et la charte sociale étaient toutes deux reprises dans la version finale de l'accord élaborée conjointement par les premiers ministres et les dirigeants autochtones à Charlottetown en août 1992. En revanche, les deux projets avaient été fatalement affaiblis dans le courant des négociations constitutionnelles.

Abstract: This chapter examines the constitutionalization of economic and social rights issues in the Charlottetown round of constitutional negotiations. It discusses the 1991 federal proposals to entrench the economic union in the Constitution and the Ontario government's social charter proposal. The chapter traces the fate of these issues through the constitutional process of 1991-92. Both the economic union and the social charter were included in the final accord reached by first ministers and Aboriginal leaders at Charlottetown in August 1992. Both proposals had been fatally weakened, however, during the constitutional negotiating process.

Two new issues in Canadian constitutional politics emerged in the 1991-92 round of debate and negotiations that led to the Charlottetown Accord. This round was aimed at brokering interests and regions that had been excluded from the Meech Lake negotiations and opening up the constitutional process to everyone from "ordinary Canadians" to the Aboriginal organization representatives who won a seat at the negotiating table. Yet the "Canada round" also witnessed the emergence of two relatively new constitutional issues—economic and social rights.

While many constitutions include statements of economic and social rights in general, such concerns have been absent from the Canadian constitutional debate. Over the decades, the constitutional debate has centred on finding an amending formula, entrenching a charter of rights, revamping the division of powers between federal and provincial governments, balancing regional demands, accommodating Quebec's aspirations and, since 1978, entrenching Aboriginal rights.

Constitutionalizing social and economic rights raises important issues about democratic governance in Canada. To what extent should we move beyond the traditional definition of the constitution? The traditional view of constitutions is that they establish the rules by which political institutions operate and the general relationship between the governed and the governors. In principle at least, constitutions do not set out particular policy choices; rather, they establish general and enduring rules of the political game within which a broad range of policy choices is possible. Of course, general political rules may inhibit certain policy choices and facilitate others. Constitutionalizing economic and social rights, however, takes these issues out of the political arena and beyond the control of democratically elected governors. In effect, constitutionalization would freeze our current conception of the rights of individuals, the role of markets and the role of the state. By removing such issues from the purview of democratic governance, changes would be more difficult to effect in the future.[1]

In addition, constitutionalizing policy issues mobilizes new sets of interests in the Canadian constitutional debate and creates another set of conflicts that must be resolved in an already very complex and heavily burdened process. Business, labour and social movements are touched very directly by economic and social rights. Such participants were more active players in the 1991-92 debates, in part because of a more open process that permitted group and individual input at various points (the constitutional conferences, the Beaudoin-Dobbie Committee, etc.).[2] In addition, the ties between such interests and key government players—the Ontario New Democratic Party's (NDP) ties to labour and the popular sector, and the Tories' ties to business groups—helped bring these actors into the constitutional process.

Therefore, the Canada round involved the constitution-alization of issues which have traditionally, in Canada, been left to democratic political channels. In the process, new actors and new interests were activated in the constitutional negotiations.

In the following sections, I examine how this situation came about. I begin by considering definitions of economic and social rights. The second section discusses some of the factors that led to constitutional discussion of such rights. Subsequent sections examine events between the release of the federal and Ontario governments' 1991 constitutional proposals and the negotiation of the Charlottetown Accord. The final accord reached by the first ministers and Aboriginal leaders on August 28, 1992 contained a much weaker version of the economic union and the social charter than that originally proposed by the federal and Ontario governments in 1991.

THE CONSTITUTIONALIZATION OF POLICY ISSUES

What are economic and social rights? In the recent and ongoing constitutional debates, economic rights are defined most often in terms of Canada's economic union. The economic union refers to the free movement of goods, services, labour and capital within a given territory (sometimes referred to as the "four freedoms").[3] There are many types of barriers which prevent this free movement in Canada: interprovincial trade barriers; preferential provincial tax policies; and federal policies that impede freedom of movement, such as regional benefits under unemployment insurance. Historically, federal policies ranging from the National Policy to the National Energy Program have "distorted" free markets, encouraged some kinds of economic development at the expense of others and benefited some regions of Canada more than others.

The cost of interprovincial trade barriers has been variously estimated. Some estimates put the cost at less than 1 percent of incomes.[4] Other studies have concluded that federal policies distort interprovincial trade at least as much as do interprovincial barriers.[5] As Thomas Courchene argues, however, static estimates of the impact of barriers underestimate other kinds of costs associated with barriers such as the risk of economic balkanization, the political effort expended at shoring up or obtaining barriers, and the effect of barriers on firm size, all of which may entail costs to the competitiveness of Canadian business.[6] Furthermore, interprovincial barriers run the risk of contravening international trade agreements such as the General Agreement on Tariffs and Trade (GATT), the Canada-U.S. Free Trade Agreement (FTA), and the impending North American Free Trade Agreement (NAFTA).

Some have argued that federal and provincial governments need to move beyond securing the economic union to reap the benefits of positive economic integration within the Canadian economic space. This would entail a greater degree of harmonization of federal and provincial policies so that the effects of policy divergence could be avoided. As with the economic union, this is a goal that could be achieved through interprovincial negotiation as well as through constitutional entrenchment.

To understand the politics of the economic union, we must understand the concept of the market itself. The economic union describes a situation in which markets determine the allocation of labour, services, capital and goods, and in which optimal allocations under the operation of the market are not "distorted" by the policies of *any* level of government. It is important to note that terms such as "freedom" and "market distortion" are value-laden. The free market itself cannot operate without some level of state intervention (e.g. provision of infrastructure). Furthermore, markets may not provide for certain kinds of goods (e.g. environmental protection). Market externalities, in the language of economics, may require state intervention if they are to be corrected. Therefore, the extent to which completely free movement of goods, services, labour and capital is desirable within Canada is above all a political question.

Proposals to entrench an economic union in the Constitution may take several forms. There are two powers in the Constitution Act (1867) that concern the economic union. Section 121 eliminates tariffs between provinces. However, it applies only to the circulation of goods (not to services, capital or labour) and has not been used effectively in the courts. In addition, there is Section 91—the federal trade and commerce power. However, judicial interpretation of Section 91 has recognized the provincial power to make laws that may affect interprovincial trade.[7] Other constitutional provisions that touch on the economic union include

Section 6 of the Canadian Charter of Rights and Freedoms, which assures mobility rights for all Canadians, with certain specified exceptions (residency requirements for the receipt of social benefits within a province, for example).

Constitutionally, the economic union could be strengthened in several ways. First, it could be regulated in such a way that it forestalls intervention by both levels of government. This would be a transfer of power from governments to markets or, to look at it another way, from government to citizens. Alternatively, the economic union could be regulated in ways that impair the provinces' ability to erect barriers, without interfering with the federal government's ability to "distort" the market. And finally, the economic union could be entrenched in the Constitution in a form that actually permits certain types of barriers.[8] As we will see below, this was the import of the Pearson Accord of July 1992, the forerunner of the Charlottetown Accord. Moreover, "positive integration" or harmonization of federal and provincial policies (and of policies across provinces) would limit the policy-making scope of all levels of governments. Depending on the type of harmonization envisaged, certain kinds of choices would be removed beyond the scope of democratic decision making: governments of whatever party would be prevented from undertaking certain types of policies.[9]

In contrast to the economic union, the social charter is a relatively new idea in the Canadian context. Such a charter would protect social rights for individual citizens just as the Canadian Charter of Rights and Freedoms protects political and civil rights. Social rights may be broadly defined as ensuring economic welfare and security for the individual. Unlike political and civil rights, social rights protect the citizen not from the State, but from the effects of the market. A social right to medicare, for example, protects the individual from having to seek medical services in the market-place. Again, in contrast to political and civil rights, which provide protection from state action, social rights require positive action by the State to ensure that all citizens are prevented from falling below a certain minimum.

Both the economic union and the social charter, in the forms proposed by the federal and Ontario governments in 1991, would limit the scope of democratic governance in Canada. The economic union would prevent both provincial and federal governments from carrying out interventionist policies that would transgress the "four freedoms." Potentially, the social charter would mandate the provision of services and transfers to citizens. In the case of the economic union, constitutionalization would prevent state intervention; in the case of the social charter, state intervention would be facilitated. In either case, the choices of the party in power and the influence of citizens through the electoral process would be circumscribed.

THE EMERGENCE OF ECONOMIC AND SOCIAL RIGHTS

Over the course of the eighties, a number of factors propelled economic and social rights onto the constitutional agenda. The economic union first emerged as a constitutional issue during the 1980-82 constitutional negotiations.[10] The Liberal government had proposed to strengthen the federal powers in both Sections 121 and 91 of the British North America (BNA) Act[11] as well as to entrench mobility rights.[12] This proposal would have given the federal government more authority under both Sections 121 and 91, as well as securing mobility rights in ways that would have limited provincial powers rather than the authority of the federal government. The federal proposal encountered stiff opposition from the provinces during the constitutional negotiations of the period and, consequently, only a weakened version of mobility rights appeared in the final Constitution Act (1982) as Section 6 of the Canadian Charter of Rights and Freedoms.[13]

There are several interesting dimensions to the Liberal proposals. The Liberal government was aiming at measures which would be centralizing and which would facilitate rather than undermine state intervention. This view is strengthened when the proposals are read in conjunction with the Liberals' economic agenda of the period.[14] From the National Energy Policy to foreign investment, the Liberal government was more interventionist than its Tory successors, even if many of its interventions floundered in the face of U.S., regional and business opposition.

The Liberals' failure to entrench a centralizing and interventionist economic union in the 1982 constitution resulted in the displacement of the issue onto the Macdonald Commission (the Royal Commission on the Economic Union and Development

Prospects for Canada). Although the Commission recommended the strengthening and modernization of Section 121, it also recommended that non-constitutional means be found to fortify the economic union. In particular, the Commission suggested the development of a code of economic conduct that would be negotiated by the first ministers and enforced by a commission composed of independent experts. This commission would eventually replace the courts as the adjudicator of disputes.[15]

Meanwhile, intergovernmental negotiations on interprovincial trade barriers throughout the eighties failed to make progress. Despite repeated protestations from both provincial and federal governments on the desirability of eliminating barriers, the intergovernmental talks stalled because provinces have a vested interest in retaining certain types of barriers. However, as the eighties progressed, pressures from both the GATT and the FTA threatened to make Canadian markets more open to foreign goods than to goods from other provinces and to make some interprovincial trade barriers the subject of U.S. countervail. These pressures resulted in the establishment of an intergovernmental Committee of Ministers on Internal Trade in 1987. Following a GATT ruling that forced Canada to dismantle barriers against foreign beer, the Committee succeeded in removing interprovincial barriers on beer as well as on public sector procurement of most government purchases over $25,000.[16] However, Quebec did not sign these agreements because of the failure of the Meech Lake Accord.[17] Thus, as of 1991, many interprovincial barriers remained in place.

Another factor that led to the constitutionalization of the economic union issue was the fact that the federal government's allies in the business community strongly favoured the elimination of interprovincial trade barriers. For the business community, the establishment of a North American free trade zone and the accelerating forces of globalization made an efficiently functioning economic union essential. Therefore, business (in both Quebec and Anglophone Canada) was eager to use the Constitution as a lever to create more efficient, less wasteful government. It also wanted to create political obstacles to state interventions in markets.[18]

By 1991 then, the major business associations all favoured the strengthening of the economic union. Both the Business Council on National Issues and the Canadian Manufacturers'

Association published position papers on the issue throughout the constitutional debate.[19] The Canadian Federation of Independent Business reported that its members overwhelmingly supported the removal of interprovincial trade barriers.[20] Similarly, a poll released by Michael Wilson at the height of the Pearson Accord negotiations showed that 86 percent of the Canadian Chamber of Commerce membership favoured the elimination of barriers.[21]

In contrast to the notion of economic union, social rights have never figured prominently in Canadian constitution-making. While some of the provisions of the Canadian Charter of Rights and Freedoms have been interpreted as imposing obligations on government, the only clear statement of social rights in the Canadian constitution is Section 36 of the Constitution Act (1982). This clause commits governments to promoting equal opportunities for Canadians, promoting economic development and providing public services. It also commits governments to the principle of equalization payments to ensure that provincial governments have sufficient revenue to provide "reasonably comparable levels of public services at reasonably comparable levels of taxation."[22] Even in this case, however, there are no clearly stated citizenship rights, but rather obligations between levels of government (and, even there, governments are committed only to the "principle" of equalization). As such, this section reflects the regional social contract rather than a social contract between governments and individual citizens.

The social charter idea had its origins in the same forces of globalization that propelled the constitutional agenda of business. The proposal drew its inspiration in part from the experience of the European labour movement with the 1989 social charter which had been an attempt to provide a counterweight to the "marketizing" effects of European Community 1992. In the Canadian case, the social charter was seen as a means of countering the increased liberalization of trade that had begun with the FTA and threatened to accelerate under NAFTA.[23] In part then, the constitutionalization of economic and social rights was an effort by governments, business and other social forces to respond to the phenomenon of globalization.

THE 1991 CONSTITUTIONAL PROPOSALS

In 1991, two important proposals were made to entrench social and economic rights in the Canadian constitution. The first of these was the federal government's own constitutional proposals, *Shaping Canada's Future*, which were released in September 1991.[24] The second was the Ontario government's proposal for the social charter.

The 1991 federal proposals addressed both the economic union and the issue of policy harmonization between federal and provincial governments. Without a doubt, these proposals were the most sweeping ever made on economic rights in a constitutional negotiation. The federal government proposed to amend Section 121 to guarantee free movement of goods, services, labour and capital. A number of exceptions would be permitted: equalization; provincial laws aimed at reducing regional disparity within a province; and any federal or provincial law that was declared by Parliament to be in the national interest. In the latter case, such a measure would have to be supported by seven provinces with 50 percent of the population.[25] In order to circumvent non-tariff barriers (such as regulatory practices) that might not fall under the purview of Section 121, the federal government proposed the expansion of the trade and commerce clause (Section 91) to allow the federal government to legislate "in relation to any matter that it declares to be for the efficient functioning of the economic union."[26] This new power (Section 91A) would require provincial approval under the "seven and 50" formula. In addition, provinces could opt out of the measure for three years, although the question of the renewability of the opt-out was referred to the Special Joint Committee of the Senate and of the House of Commons on a Renewed Canada (Beaudoin-Dobbie Committee).[27]

The Government also proposed measures to harmonize policy between levels of government. This was in keeping with the view of the business community that duplication between levels of government, and contradictory federal and provincial policies (particularly fiscal policies) needed to be eliminated. The Government proposed to develop fiscal policy harmonization with the provinces and to legislate these guidelines under the power of Section 91A.[28]

Why did the federal government put these proposals on the negotiating table? One critical factor was the federal government's reading of the Quebec situation. The Government was well aware of the debate which had begun to occur in Quebec, both before the Bélanger-Campeau Commission and within the Quebec Liberal Party (QLP). The QLP's Allaire report, for example, recommended not only a massive transfer of powers from the federal to the provincial governments, but also the strengthening of the economic union along neo-liberal lines. The federal government hoped that the economic union proposals would find favour with the Quebec government, which it was eager to have back at the negotiating table. The strong neo-liberal streak in the QLP and, indeed, in the Quebec business community implied that federal proposals which would limit the scope of government intervention (at both levels) and encourage policy harmonization would sell well in Quebec.[29]

Second, the federal government viewed the economic union as a way to reassert its nationalizing role in the face of both regional balkanization and Quebec's demands for enhanced provincial powers. If the federal government was going to be forced to trade away some federal powers at the negotiating table, the economic union provided a counterbalancing nationalizing dimension to the constitutional proposals. This might prove popular with Canadians outside Quebec who were increasingly attracted to a nationalizing and equalizing vision of the Constitution. While the expanded Section 121 would be enforced by the courts against both levels of government, and the new Section 91A provided a forum for interprovincial and intergovernmental agreements, the "four freedoms" were a transfer of power to all Canadians *equally*. The beauty of this was that the economic union promised a way to *nationalize* without *centralizing*, that is, to nationalize, apparently without transferring power to the federal government. Thus, it would appeal to the new charter-oriented political culture of English Canada without alienating Quebec.[30]

Finally, when read in conjunction with the harmonization provisions in the 1991 proposals, it is clear that the Canada round provided an opportunity to entrench the Conservatives' policy preferences in the Canadian constitution. By casting the proposal for the economic union in a way that would limit the future capacity of both levels of government to intervene, the Conservative government would leave its imprint on the Canadian constitution just as surely as had the Trudeau Liberals with their Canadian Charter of Rights and Freedoms.[31]

In contrast to the federal government's neo-liberal constitutional proposal, the social charter proposed by Ontario's newly elected NDP government suggested the constitutional entrenchment of a social democratic vision of the role of the State in Canadian society. The proposal for the social charter was framed in terms of social citizenship rights and as an expression of values shared by all Canadians. The proposal did not specify what values would be included in a social charter; instead, it merely suggested that the charter list "values and principles which Canadians wish to affirm and which should guide governments in the realm of social policy."[32] Short of justiciability, the proposal recommended enforcement of the social charter through intergovernmental co-operation, a reformed senate or an independent commission that could act as watchdog.

The Ontario government defended the proposal on several grounds. The Government emphasized its concern that the federal government keep its financial commitments to the provinces.[33] In addition, Ontario argued that the entrenchment of a social charter made economic sense:

> Our basis for international competitiveness must be a high level of technology, human skills and innovation, rather than low wages and high levels of human and environmental exploitation. The social charter will ensure that the social policy infrastructure cannot be destroyed for reasons of short-sighted political expedience or misguided economic theory.[34]

There were several pressures close to home that compelled the Ontario government to consider a social charter. The NDP government had inherited a substantial budget deficit from the previous Liberal government. As costs increased and revenue declined, federal transfers to the provinces—for health care and post-secondary education through Established Programs Financing and for the Canada Assistance Plan—had been cut.[35] Ontario's fiscal base was deteriorating. A social charter was seen, in part, as a means to hold the federal government accountable for declines in transfers and to ensure that the federal government could no longer cut funds to the provinces unilaterally.

Moreover, the social charter proposal was seen as providing the Ontario government with its own constitutional issue. Of all the actors at the negotiating table, Ontario was the only one without its own set of constitutional demands. Mindful that the Peterson government had acted as constitutional broker during the Meech Lake round, only to be defeated in the next provincial election, the Ontario government searched for a constitutional issue that would allow it to define a specifically Ontario interest in the negotiations. At the same time, the Government wanted an issue that could be defended as good for Canada rather than as simply another balkanizing and divisive demand. The social charter provided such a possibility. Polls showed that it was popular throughout Canada; thus, it could be presented as a gain for both Ontario and Canada in the negotiations.[36]

Taken together, the federal and NDP proposals were the most comprehensive ever made to constitutionalize economic and social rights. Of course, they proposed quite different versions of what should be entrenched in the Constitution. The federal proposals emphasized a neo-liberal vision of the role of the State in the economy, while the NDP government proposed a social democratic vision. What they had in common, however, was a nationalizing bent that attempted to counter the centrifugal currents of regionalism and Quebec nationalism with a new set of economic and social rights that all Canadians would share.

REACTION TO THE SOCIAL CHARTER AND ECONOMIC UNION PROPOSALS

Following the release of the federal and Ontario proposals, Constitutional Affairs Minister Joe Clark set up a series of constitutional conferences as well as the Beaudoin-Dobbie Committee consultations. These processes allowed for input from interest groups and individual citizens, as well as from provincial governments.

Provincial reactions to the economic union proposals were largely negative. The idea of a new federal power (Section 91A) did not find favour with the Quebec government. In general, the Quebec position was that the economic union should not be constitutionalized. Quebec business, including federalist groups, did not support the economic proposals.[37] The broad power of the proposed amendment was seen in Quebec as centralizing, despite the fact that the power could only be exercised by the federal government under the seven and 50 rule.[38] In part, this perception was due to the fact that the proposed Section 91A was poorly framed. While the provinces would have had a key role in the application of Section 91A through the seven and 50 rule, its framing as a new federal power aroused suspicion in provincial circles and it was difficult to sell politically in Quebec. Other provinces were also unenthusiastic about the constitutionalization of the economic union. While provinces favoured in principle the removal of barriers, they were sceptical of a proposal that would put decision-making authority in the hands of judges and of the proposed Section 91A, which they feared could be used by the federal government against provincial powers.[39] Thus, the federal strategy of nationalizing without centralizing failed, at least with respect to Section 91A.[40]

At the constitutional conference on the economic union in Montreal, participants from both sides of the debate were reluctant to enshrine economic principles in the Constitution, and the consensus of the conference (as reported in the media) was to eliminate the economic union from the constitutional discussions. The social charter, in contrast, found favour with delegates, although business groups claimed that social charter supporters had hijacked the conference process. Among delegates, as among provincial governments, the federal proposals were seen as a power grab.[41]

The social charter proposals in the form suggested by the Ontario government, on the other hand, lacked allies among the key constitutional players. Even within the social democratic camp, there were divisions over the Ontario proposal. Labour was somewhat lukewarm to the proposal, while the popular sector supported it. Among provinces, support was weak.

Perhaps most important, the entrenchment of a social charter, particularly in a form that would be enforceable or binding on government (whether enforced by the courts or enforced in some other way), contradicted the federal agenda. The Tory social policy record had been one of cautious retrenchment with a focus on deficit reduction. The import of the economic union proposals had been to roll back the State, not to further implicate it in the arena of social policy. Constitutionalizing measures that would potentially mandate social expenditure clashed with federal goals. Furthermore, there was substantial opposition to a social charter within the business community. During this period, the Business Council on National Issues (BCNI) used various tactics to push its goals, particularly those related to the dismantling of interprovincial trade barriers. The BCNI's views were solicited by the federal government; the organization spearheaded an effort to use annual company meetings to mount a drive for the business version of national unity, and it advertised the potential costs of dismantling Canada to put pressure on the Government to reach an agreement.[42]

The Beaudoin-Dobbie Committee's report reflected these political pressures. The report proposed the replacement of Section 121 with a new section establishing Canada as an economic union in which arbitrary and discriminatory prohibitions on the "four freedoms" would not be permitted. However, the report also suggested that exemptions should be permitted. Rather than enforcement through the courts, a disputes settlement mechanism would be established to adjudicate disputes. In addition to the revamping of Section 121, the Committee proposed a second statement of principle on the economic union which would be included as a companion to the social charter.[43]

On the social charter, the Committee recommended a nonjusticiable social covenant be added to Section 36 which would commit governments to health care; adequate social services and benefits; education; the right of workers to organize and bargain collectively; and the integrity of the environment. The change in wording from charter to covenant suggested that, rather than enshrining the social rights of citizens in the Constitution, the Government was simply making a promise to citizens. As both the economic union and the social covenant were to be monitored by an independent commission—to be established by the first ministers at a later date—the enforceability of the covenant was left to a further round of negotiations.

Therefore, by the time the intergovernmental constitutional negotiations resumed, a consensus had developed that an enforceable social charter was off the table and that the federal economic union proposal would have to be watered down. Proposals to entrench the "four freedoms" were still up for negotiation, although questions remained about potential exemptions and about the enforceability of such measures.

THE PEARSON ACCORD

In the negotiations that led to the Pearson Accord (July 1992), the precursor of the Charlottetown Accord, an agreement was reached on the transfer of powers between levels of government. This agreement met some provincial demands for particular powers (Ontario, for example, was keen to have training in the provincial jurisdiction). The main intent of the agreement, however, was to secure Quebec's assent to the constitutional deal.[44]

This agreement on the division of powers left the federal government vulnerable to the charge that it had given in too much to provincial demands. Once again, the federal government attempted to use the economic union issue to recoup its own political and economic agenda at the negotiating table. Given that the Section 91A power was not saleable in Quebec and that the policy harmonization measures had met with opposition, the federal government concentrated on securing a strengthened Section 121 that could be presented as meeting the needs of all Canadians without centralizing power.[45]

The federal strategy, however, proved difficult to achieve. Most provinces favoured the elimination of barriers, but each province had specific exemptions that it wanted to defend. The final Pearson Accord took up the proposal of the Beaudoin-Dobbie Committee to replace Section 121 with a new provision "that prevents the erection of interprovincial trade barriers by law or practice that arbitrarily discriminate on the basis of province or territory of residence, origin or destination and unduly impede the efficient functioning of the Canadian economic union."[46] This provision included a long list of exemptions: the principles of equalization and regional development; regional equity within a province or territory; and a list of 11 laws or practices relating to public security, safety or health, environmental protection, consumer protection, social services, land ownership restrictions, monopolies, marketing and supply management, labour practices (including pay equity), minimum wage laws, "reasonable public sector investment practices"; and even subsidies or tax incentives to encourage investment.

The new section would be enforced by an independent agency, established by the first ministers and jointly appointed by the federal and provincial governments. It would be implemented through a four-stage process of mediation and conciliation; screening; final determination and judicial review. While the decisions of the agency would be binding, the clause would only be justiciable to the extent of questions of law or jurisdiction.[47]

As the Beaudoin-Dobbie report had recommended, the idea of a non-justiciable and unenforceable statement of commitment to the "social and economic union" was also included in the Accord. This statement (with a list of principles similar to that of the Beaudoin-Dobbie report) would be monitored (not enforced) by a mechanism to be determined at a later first ministers' meeting. Thus, the potentially nationalizing dimension of the social charter proposal was picked up in the negotiations, but the Ontario proposal no longer had teeth.[48]

The Pearson Accord, then, reflected the failure of both the federal and Ontario agendas for constitutionalizing economic and social rights. Provincial opposition to the entrenchment of the economic union resulted in a weak clause that potentially undermined the intent of the original federal proposals; in fact, the Pearson Accord afforded constitutional protection to interprovincial trade barriers rather than eliminating them. Interestingly, this outcome had been foreseen by the Macdonald Commission, which had warned against the constitutionalization of the economic union issue because "a constitutionalized code formulated today would probably include so many opting-out, non-obstant and exception clauses that it would perhaps only legitimize what it was designed to prevent."[49]

This feature of the Pearson Accord immediately generated strong criticism both from the Tories' business allies and from within the Government itself. The BCNI, the Canadian Manufacturers' Association and the C.D. Howe Institute all publicly condemned the Accord's economic provisions.[50] More important, the two most powerful economic ministers in the Mulroney government, Donals Mazankowski and Michael Wilson, criticized the Accord publicly as a constitutionalization of the provinces' right to erect trade barriers.[51]

THE CHARLOTTETOWN ACCORD

The Charlottetown Accord (August 28, 1992) marked the final retreat from the federal government's proposals for economic union. The idea of a revamped and enforceable Section 121 with a list of exceptions was dropped entirely. Instead, the Charlottetown Accord set out a non-justiciable, social and economic union for Canada, again drawing from the list of values and goals provided by the Beaudoin-Dobbie report.[52]

Once again, a monitoring mechanism would be established by a first ministers' conference to mediate disputes; however, there was nothing in the agreement that specified what this mechanism would be. In the legal text of the Charlottetown Accord, a clause was added specifying that the commitment to social and economic union did not alter or affect the authority or rights of the federal, provincial or territorial legislatures.[53] Thus, it is clear that the social and economic union would have had little effect on the authority of governments.

As in the Pearson Accord, Section 36 on equalization was strengthened in the Charlottetown Accord. Meaningful consultation with the provinces would have to be undertaken before changes to equalization could be made, and a new Section 36(3) was added to commit governments to the promotion of regional economic development.[54] However, these changes still fell short of Ontario's demand for the protection of federal transfers.

Thus, the federal government failed to gain either its proposed new Section 91A or even a revamped Section 121 in the final constitutional accord. What had appeared in the Pearson Accord as a new Section 121 was contained in a political agreement at Charlottetown.[55] The political agreement formed a basis on which (binding) intergovernmental agreements might be negotiated. The premiers and the federal government agreed not to erect new trade barriers and to dismantle existing ones by 1996. The political accord established the same criterion for interprovincial trade barriers as developed in the Pearson Accord: none of the governments shall erect interprovincial barriers by law or practice that arbitrarily discriminate on the basis of province or territory of residence, origin or destination or that impede the "efficient functioning of the Canadian economic union."[56] As always, exemptions were suggested: federal equalization and regional development; provincial regional development policies; laws that restrict acquisition of land by non-residents; fish and agricultural marketing and supply management.

Moreover, the principles of economic union could not be used to ban laws and practices that were not a "disguised restriction on trade" (that is, their primary aim was not to create a restriction on trade). These included health and safety; environmental, consumer and language protection; social services; monopolies; labour practices; and subsidies and tax incentives for the purpose of encouraging investment, and exploration, development and conservation of natural resources.[57]

The Charlottetown Accord marked the failure of the federal strategy of constitutionalizing economic rights. Despite the differences between the Tory proposals and the Liberal position of 10 years previously, both efforts failed in the face of provincial opposition. While the premiers paid lip-service to the notion of economic freedoms, in practice they were unwilling to surrender powers that could be used to develop the economies of their provinces and to protect the position of their own provincial states.

CONCLUSION

The constitutionalization of economic and social rights through the debate and negotiations of 1991-92 is a relatively new phenomenon in Canadian politics. It raises questions about the very nature of the Constitution, about which purposes and whose interests the Constitution is to serve, and about the extent to which particular policies should be enshrined in the Constitution.

Through each successive round of Canadian institution-making, more issues have been loaded onto the constitutional agenda.[58] At the time of the Fulton-Favreau formula in 1964, the task was the patriation of the Constitution with an amending formula. At that point, Quebec was the only province interested in more powers. In Victoria in 1971, the problem of accommodating Quebec nationalism within the Canadian federation had deepened in the wake of the Quiet Revolution. In addition, the Trudeau government introduced the notion of an entrenched bill of rights into the debate.

In the constitutional round of 1980-82, a whole set of new issues and interests were joined in the constitutional fray. In addition to patriating the Constitution, agreeing to an amending formula and meeting the aspirations of Quebec, there were remobilized regional demands (from the West and Atlantic Canada) and the entry of women, multicultural groups and Aboriginal peoples into the constitutional debate. However, the patriation of the Constitution with an amending formula in 1982 merely created a new constitutional "problem"—that of securing Quebec's assent to the Constitution. The Meech Lake process showed, however, that the constitutional issue could not be confined to the agenda of governments. Aboriginal and women's groups contested the Quebec definition of the constitutional "problem" and fought for standing in the debate. Western Canadians mobilized behind demands for a restructuring of national political institutions and would not accept that senate reform be deferred to a later constitutional round. The increasingly charter-oriented political culture of Anglophone Canada had difficulty accepting that individuals, groups or provinces should receive special treatment.

By 1991 then, various societal demands were being channelled into the constitutional debate. This is not to deny the legitimacy of these demands, but merely to say that in a society without a written constitution or a society in which constitutional reform was not an issue, such demands would have expressed themselves differently in the political system.

The 1991-92 round, like each constitutional round that preceded it, saw the constitutionalization of new issues—in this case social and economic issues. A number of factors led to this development. Both economic union and the social charter were reactions to the increased globalization of world markets and to the construction of regional trading blocs. The social charter provided a social democratic anchor for the popular sector and the NDP in the face of the declining economic sovereignty of states and the spectre of lowest common denominator social and economic policies. The economic union issue, in turn, provided business groups and the Conservative government with an opportunity to cement the internal free market, potentially in ways that would reduce the future scope for state intervention.

Both these issues allowed the Ontario and federal governments to assert a pan-Canadian nationalism against the forces of regionalism and Quebec nationalism. While there are critical differences between the two proposals—one is neo-liberal, the other social democratic—both were calculated to appeal to the political culture of the post-Charter era and to the enduring popularity of "national standards" and "shared values." This similarity between the two proposals permitted the fusion of the economic union and the social charter in the "social and economic union" of the Charlottetown Accord, in which the unenforceable commitment of governments to economic freedom with social rights was affirmed.

Furthermore, the constitutionalization of economic and social rights was a convenient way for governments (federal and provincial) to deal with public concerns about the recession and economic restructuring. The proposals allowed government to discuss Canada's economic and social problems in the popular language of rights at a time when the fiscal crisis for both levels of government was constraining economic and social policy choices. And each government used the Constitution to solve problems that it had failed to solve with other strategies: for the Conservatives, the elimination of interprovincial trade barriers; for the NDP, the erosion of federal transfers to the provinces.

Once governments had placed economic and social rights on the constitutional agenda, they became embroiled in the dynamics of constitutional conflict. Groups such as business and the popular sector, which had not been closely involved in previous constitutional rounds, mobilized themselves in the constitutional debate. This process was facilitated by the ties between these groups and the parties in power at both levels. Ultimately, however, it was the combined force of provincial opposition to the economic union in the form proposed by the federal government that led to the watering down of the original proposals. Despite the multiplication of interests and actors in the constitutional debate, the amending formula still constrains the process, dictating provincial consent for constitutional change. While federal opposition would have doomed Ontario's social charter in any case, economic union encountered so much opposition—first in Quebec and then in other provinces—that it was rendered toothless in the final accord. Thus, the outcome was a defeat for both the Ontario and federal proposals.

If past constitutional rounds hold any lessons for the future, however, economic and social rights will not disappear from the constitutional debate. Once on the table, it is difficult to get a constitutional issue off the table. Thus, economic and social rights can be expected to resurface again in the next constitutional round.

NOTES

I would like to thank Susan Phillips, Bruce Doern, François Rocher and Radha Jhappan for their very helpful comments on the first draft of this chapter.

1   On these points, see Lars Ogsberg and Shelley Phipps, "A Social Charter for Canada" in Havi Echenberg et al., *A Social Charter for Canada? Perspectives on the Constitutional Entrenchment of Social Rights* (Toronto: C.D. Howe Institute, 1992), pp. 1-34; William B.P. Robson, "Examining the Case for a Social Charter" in Echenberg et al., *A Social Charter for Canada*, pp. 87-110.

2   On the process of the consultation in the Canada round of 1991-92, see the chapter by Leslie Pal and F. Leslie Seidle in this volume.

3   See Ivan Bernier et al., "The Concept of Economic Union in International and Constitutional Law" in Mark Krasnick, (ed.), *Perspectives on the Canadian Economic Union* (Toronto and Ottawa: University of Toronto Press, and Supply and Services Canada, 1986), pp. 35-153.

4   Nola Silzer and Mark Krasnick, "The Free Flow of Goods in the Canadian Economic Union" in Krasnick, *Perspectives*, pp. 155-94; Kenneth Norrie, Richard Simeon, and Mark Krasnick, *Federalism and the Economic Union in Canada* (Toronto: University of Toronto Press, 1986).

5   John Whalley and Irene Trella, *Regional Aspects of Confederation* (Toronto: University of Toronto Press, 1985).

6   Thomas J. Courchene, *Economic Management and the Division of Powers* (Toronto and Ottawa: University of Toronto Press, and Supply and Services Canada, 1986), p. 214.

7   See the discussion in the Royal Commission on the Economic Union and Development Prospects for Canada (Macdonald Commission), *Report*, vol. III (Ottawa: Supply and Services Canada, 1985), pp. 114-18; Bernier et al., "The Concept of Economic Union," pp. 44-64.

8   On these options, see Courchene, *Economic Management*, pp. 210ff; J. Robert S. Prichard with Jamie Benedickson, "Securing the Canadian Economic Union: Federalism and Internal Barriers to Trade" in Michael J. Treblicock et al., (eds.), *Federalism and the Canadian Economic Union* (Toronto: Ontario Economic Council and University of Toronto Press, 1983), pp. 3-50.

9   See Robin Broadway, *The Constitutional Division of Powers: An Economic Perspective* (Ottawa: Economic Council of Canada, 1992).

10   The federal government had commissioned a study of the issue in the early seventies. See A.E. Safarian, *Canadian Federalism and Economic Integration* (Ottawa: Information Canada, 1974).

11   The BNA Act and Constitution Act (1867) are the same act; the BNA Act was renamed in the constitutional repatriation of 1982.

12   Canada, *Securing the Canadian Economic Union* (Ottawa: Supply and Services Canada, 1980).

13   Thomas J. Courchene, "The Political Economy of Canadian Constitution-making: The Canadian Economic-Union Issue," *Public Choice*, 44 (1984): pp. 201-49. On Section 6 of the Canadian Charter of Rights and Freedoms, see Sanda Rogers-Magnet and Joseph Eliot Magnet, "Mobility Rights: Personal Mobility and the Canadian Economic Union" in Krasnick, *Perspectives*, pp. 195-270.

14   Peter Leslie, *Federal State, National Economy* (Toronto: University of Toronto Press, 1987), pp. 3-25.

15   Royal Commission on Economic Union, *Report*, vol. III, pp. 135-40.

16   *The Financial Post*, November 23, 1991, p. 8; David M. Brown et al., *Free to Move: Strengthening the Canadian Economic Union* (Toronto: C.D. Howe Institute, 1992), especially pp. 13-14.

17   *Winnipeg Free Press*, May 1, 1992, p. B19.

18   Business Council on National Issues, *Canada's Constitutional Future: A Response by the BCNI to the Government of Canada Proposals, "Shaping Canada's Future Together,"* (Ottawa: January 1992); Quebec Liberal Party, *A Quebec Free to Choose* (Quebec City: January 1991). See also business briefs to the Special Joint Committee of the Senate and of the House of Commons on a Renewed Canada (Beaudoin-Dobbie Committee), *Minutes of Proceedings and Evidence*, vol. 38, pp. 27-31, vol. 57, pp. 27-35.

19   Canadian Manufacturers' Association, "Canada 1993" in *A Plan for the Creation of a Single Common Market in Canada* (April 1991).

20   *Winnipeg Free Press*, May 1, 1992, p. B19.

21   *Winnipeg Free Press*, May 2, 1992, p. B19.

22   Constitution Act 1982, s. 36 (1-2).

23   John Myles, "Constitutionalizing Social Rights" in Echenberg et al., *A Social Charter for Canada*, pp. 52-63.

24   Canada, *Shaping Canada's Future Together: Proposals* (Ottawa: Supply and Services Canada, 1991).

25   Canada, *Canadian Federalism and Economic Union: Partnership for Prosperity* (Ottawa: Supply and Services Canada, 1991), pp. 22-23.

26   Canada, *Canadian Federalism*, p. 24.

27   Canada, *Canadian Federalism*, p. 24.

28 Canada, *Canadian Federalism*, p. 34. On these proposals, see David Schneiderman, "The Market and the Constitution" in Duncan Cameron and Miriam Smith, (eds.), *Constitutional Politics* (Toronto: James Lorimer, 1992), pp. 59-69; Donald C. Lenihan, "Economic Union: Notes on the Federal Proposals," *Network Analysis*, 1 (December 1991); Robin W. Broadway and Douglas D. Purvis, *Economic Aspects of the Federal Government's Constitutional Proposals* (Kingston: John Deutsch Institute for the Study of Economic Policy, 1991).

29 See Note 15. On the neo-liberal strand in the Quebec business community, see Miriam Smith, "Quebec-Canada Association: Divergent Paths to a Common Economic Agenda" in Daniel Drache and Roberto Perin, (eds.), *Negotiating with a Sovereign Quebec* (Toronto: James Lorimer, 1992); Alain-G. Gagnon, "Everything Old is New Again: Canada, Quebec and Constitutional Impasse" in Frances Abele, (ed.), *How Ottawa Spends: The Politics of Fragmentation 1991-92* (Ottawa: Carleton University Press, 1991), pp. 63-105.

30 On the Charter orientation of English Canadian political culture, see Alan C. Cairns, *Charter versus Federalism* (Montreal and Kingston: McGill-Queen's University Press, 1992).

31 Schneiderman, "The Market and the Constitution," pp. 63-69; Andrew Jackson, "The Economic Union" in Cameron and Smith, *Constitutional Politics*, pp. 70-8; Michael Bradfield, "Failing to Meet Regional Needs" in Cameron and Smith, (eds.), *Constitutional Politics*, pp. 92-104.

32 Ontario, Ministry of Intergovernmental Affairs, *A Canadian Social Charter: Making Our Shared Values Stronger* (Toronto, September 1991), p. 14.

33 Ontario Ministry, *A Canadian Social Charter*.

34 Ontario Ministry, *A Canadian Social Charter*, p. 3.

35 Allan M. Maslove, "Reconstructing Fiscal Federalism" in Frances Abele, (ed.), *How Ottawa Spends 1992-93: The Politics of*

Competitiveness (Ottawa: Carleton University Press, 1992), pp. 57-77.

36   Will Kymlicka and Wayne J. Norman, *The Social Charter Debate: Should Social Justice Be Constitutionalized?* in *Network Analysis*, 2 (January 1992), cited at pp. 1-2.

37   *Le Devoir* [Montreal], January 18, 1992, pp. A1, A12.

38   *Le Devoir* [Montreal], October 1, 1991, p. A2; October 7, 1991, p. 12.

39   *The Gazette* [Montreal], February 2, 1992, p. A5; *The Toronto Star*, January 31, 1992, p. A21.

40   *The Gazette* [Montreal], July 7, 1992, p. B1.

41   *The Gazette* [Montreal], February 2, 1992, p. A4; February 3, 1992, pp. A1, A2.

42   *Winnipeg Free Press*, June 2, 1992, p. A3; Business Council on National Issues, *Canada's Economic Union: The Advantages, Questions and Answers, the Costs of Fragmentation* (Ottawa, April 1992); *The Globe and Mail*, April 28, 1992, pp. A1, A2.

43   Report of the Special Joint Committee of the Senate and House of Commons on a Renewed Canada (Beaudoin-Dobbie Committee) (February 28, 1992), pp. 86-90.

44   *The Financial Post*, June 15, 1992, p. 3.

45   *The Globe and Mail*, June 9, 1992, pp. A1, A2.

46   *Status Report: The Multilateral Meetings on the Constitution*, Rev. (Ottawa: July 10, 1992), p. 3.

47   *Status Report*, p. 4.

48   *Status Report*, p. 2.

49   Royal Commission on Economic Union, *Report*, vol. III, p. 137.

50   *The Gazette* [Montreal], July 10, 1992, p. B5; *The Toronto Star*, July 23, 1992, p. A12.

51   *The Globe and Mail*, July 15, 1992, p. A4; *The Toronto Star*, July 23, 1992, p. A12.

52   *Consensus Report on the Constitution*, Final Text (Charlottetown: August 28, 1992), p. 2.

53   *Draft Legal Text of Charlottetown Accord*, (October 9, 1992), p. 44.

54   *Consensus Report*, p. 3.

55   *Political Accords, The Multilateral Meetings on the Constitution*, (Charlottetown: August 28, 1992), p. 1.

56   *Political Accords*, p. 1.

57   *Political Accords*, p. 1.

58   For an excellent description of this process over the last 30 years, see Peter Russell, *Constitutional Odyssey: Can Canadians Become a Sovereign People?* (Toronto: University of Toronto Press, 1992).

CHAPTER 4

Lobbying, the Voluntary Sector and the Public Purse

A. Paul Pross
Iain S. Stewart

Résumé : Les lobbyistes et les groupes de défense de l'intérêt public expriment les intérêts des particuliers au gouvernement. Les lobbyistes professionnels jouent un rôle important en ce qu'ils font circuler l'information entre le gouvernement et le milieu des affaires. De même, les groupes de défense de l'intérêt public permettent à des personnes qui conçoivent de la même façon ce qui est dans l'intérêt du public de faire connaître leurs opinions aux responsables des politiques et au public. Le gouvernement du Canada contracte des dépenses fiscales dans le but de financer ces activités. Le recrutement de lobbyistes est donc considéré comme une dépense d'entreprise aux fins de l'impôt sur le revenu des sociétés et certains groupes de défense de l'intérêt public, selon la nature de leurs activités, peuvent s'enregistrer comme organismes de charité. Malgré que les fonctions des organismes de charité et des lobbyistes professionnels se ressemblent et qu'ils bénéficient tous deux de dépenses fiscales, le gouvernement impose nettement moins de règles et de règlements aux lobbyistes qu'il ne le fait aux organismes de charités enregistrés. Il est question, dans ce chapitre, des règlements qui visent les lobbyistes professionnels aux termes de la *Loi sur l'enregistrement des lobbyistes* et de ceux qui s'appliquent aux groupes de défense de l'intérêt public enregistrés comme organismes de charité en vertu de la *Loi de l'impôt sur le revenu*. L'auteur avance que la réglementation plus rigoureuse des lobbyistes et l'élaboration d'un régime de réglementation plus souple au regard des organismes de charité seraient dans l'intérêt du débat sur la politique d'intérêt public au Canada.

Abstract: Both lobbyists and interest groups communicate the interests of individuals to government. Professional lobbyists act as an important vehicle for the transfer of information between government and the business community. In a similar manner, interest groups allow individuals sharing a common conception of the public good to express their opinion to decision makers and the public. The Government of Canada incurs tax expenditures which have the effect of supporting these activities. Thus, the retention of lobbyists is considered a business expense for corporate income tax purposes, and certain sorts of interest groups may register as charities. Despite the similarities of their function and the tax expenditure they both receive, the burden of regulation that the Government imposes on professional lobbyists is far less constraining than the regulatory regime pertaining to registered charities. This chapter examines the regulation of professional lobbyists, through the Lobbyists Registration Act, and the regulation of public interest groups registered as charities under the Income Tax Act.It is suggested here that discussion surrounding public policy debate in Canada would benefit from a more complete regulation of professional lobbyists and the development of a more flexible system of regulation for charities.

It is ironic that public consultation and lobbying should be considered vital features of modern democracy. Surely any well regulated democracy will engage its citizens in policy making through the medium of election and the party apparatus that makes the electoral system work. The fact that most citizens apparently no longer see the political party as a primary vehicle for communicating with government has led governments to find alternative means of communication and citizens to use other ways of influencing the decision-making process. For governments, public consultation, which is usually initiated by one of the administrative agencies rather than by the political arm, has become a widely used means of assessing individual and group views on policy issues. For individuals, there are four alternatives to the party system itself: individual petitions to agencies; individual petitions to MPs; the hiring of a lobbyist; and, finally, participation in an interest group. This chapter is concerned with the latter two and, in particular, focuses on how the regulation of lobbying, and the terms of federal tax expenditures in support of charities, affects the way citizens communicate with government.

Lobbying is defined as the process through which individuals and groups express their interests and attempt to influence public policy decisions in their favour. It may be carried out by individuals seeking decisions that benefit them personally, or it may be undertaken by formally organized groups promoting their special interest or some goal that they believe to be for the general public benefit. Lobbying is a necessary part of our complex policy-making system. However, because it affects government decisions that change the lives of millions and often involve immense public expenditures, special care has to be taken to ensure that it is carried out with integrity.

Two aspects of lobbying have generated public debate in recent years. The first is the development of paid "third-party" lobbying, which has become a major vehicle for business communication with government. This development has aroused public concerns about preferential treatment for wealthy interests and the transparency of the policy process. The second aspect is the proliferation of interest groups anxious to promote a great variety of ideas about the public interest. Just as the paid lobbyist has become an important adjunct to business lobbying, so public interest groups offer individual members of the public an affordable means of exerting collective influence on policy makers. Some of these groups use extreme measures to express their concerns and, consequently, excite public demands for group regulation.

Both third-party and public interest group lobbying raise concerns about government spending. Lobbying not only tends to lead to increased public spending, it is often financed in part through tax expenditures. Thus, corporate income tax regimes allow businesses to treat lobbying expenses as part of the cost of doing business, and many public interest groups are able to finance some of their advocacy activities through donations that are tax deductible.[1]

Official reaction to these issues has been quite different. On the one hand, care has been taken to avoid unduly inhibiting third-party lobbying; on the other, a considerable degree of regulation is deemed appropriate to constrain the lobbying activities of organized citizens. In this discussion, we shall look first at the recent debate over the regulation of lobbyists, occasioned primarily by a statutorily required review of the 1987 Lobbyists Registration Act. We will then examine the ongoing debate over the implicit regulation of public interest groups through the tax system. The most recent phase of this was triggered, in 1990, by Revenue Canada's publication of *A Better Tax Administration for Charities*. The debate centres on those charities involved in public interest advocacy and has to do with the inflexibility of the common law definition of a charity. Or, to put it differently, it centres on the apparent inability of the federal government to recognize that public interest advocacy groups need a tax status similar to that enjoyed by traditional charities.

THE LOBBYISTS REGISTRATION ACT

The goal of shedding light on the activities of lobbyists—and, to some extent, regulating them—was originally the project of a succession of parliamentarians on both sides of the House of Commons who promoted regulation through 20 private member's bills between 1969 and 1985. In 1985, this issue was taken over by Brian Mulroney who seems to have intended it to be part of a package of ethics reforms.[2] On September 9, in an "Open Letter" to parliamentarians, Mulroney stated that he would introduce legislation to "monitor lobbying activity and to control the lobbying process by providing a reliable and accurate source of information on the activities of lobbyists." Paid lobbyists would be required to register and to identify their clients. This would "enable persons who are approached by lobbyists for Canadian corporations, associations and unions, and by agents on behalf of foreign governments and other foreign interests, to be clearly aware of who is behind the representations."[3] By December 1985, the Minister of Consumer and Corporate Affairs had submitted a discussion paper on the subject to the House of Commons Standing Committee on Elections, Privileges and Procedure (the Cooper Committee) which, after holding hearings, issued a report on January 27, 1987.[4]

The report stated that "disclosure of information in this area is vital if we are to have an informed public.... [A] register is a tool which can be used by the general public to evaluate the pressures which are brought to bear on government."[5] The report proposed a broad definition of lobbying and lobbyists, suggesting that registration include "indirect lobbying" and those who "initiate and those who are paid to organize mass mailings or advertising campaigns to disseminate material designed to influence government through public opinion."[6] It concluded that only limited disclosure should be required: "If the lobbyist or the lobbyist's employer is required to furnish copious amounts of information we could create a situation similar to that found in some states in the United States where disclosure has been unmanageable both for the lobbyist and the state."[7] In the same vein, it urged lobbyists to protect themselves against further state intrusion by establishing a strong program of professional self-regulation. That the Committee had doubts about the likelihood of this advice being followed was made clear by its concluding recommendations: contingency fees should be prohibited; the registrar of lobbyists should be empowered to investigate suspected violations of the Act; and penalties for non-compliance with the Act should be "severe enough to make compliance a desirable and necessary goal on the part of lobbyists."[8]

Not all of these recommendations found their way into Bill C-82, "An Act to Register Lobbyists," which was tabled in the House on June 30, 1987, by Harvie Andre, then Minister of Consumer and Corporate Affairs. The Bill did accept the view that Canadian lobbying legislation should be concerned with attempts to influence the bureaucracy, as well as the legislature—an important divergence from the approach used in the United States. It also adopted the Committee's conclusion that administrative simplicity dictated that lobbyists need file only limited information. Andre claimed that, in proposing a system in which *registration* (but not *regulation*) was the goal, the Government sought to create a process that neither discourages the general public nor generates an uncontrollable demand for information.[9] By defining a lobbyist as anyone who receives payment to represent a third party before government, the legislation excuses both volunteers and those representing their own interests from registering, and so ensures that the new procedure does not impede access to government on the part of the general public.

The Bill provided that "professional lobbyists" who represent "clients" before government would be treated differently from other paid lobbyists. Within 10 days of undertaking to represent an interest on any one of a series of widely defined issues, these "Tier I" lobbyists were to provide their own name, the name and address of their firm, the names of clients and the names of corporate owners or subsidiaries of the client. They also had to file two types of information about the lobbying activity undertaken on behalf of clients: its area of concern (broadly defined in 52 categories); and the class of undertaking (e.g. the development of a legislative proposal, the awarding of a contract or grant) that lobbying was intended to influence. Registration would be required each time a lobbyist assumed a new undertaking. On the other hand, "Tier II" lobbyists, employees either of interest groups or corporations who spend a "significant part" of their employment representing their employer to government, would have to register only their name, and the name and address of the corporation or organization employing them. Neither Tier I nor Tier II lobbyists would need to submit financial information. Penalties would involve fines of up to $25,000 for failing to comply with the Act and up to $100,000 for knowingly filing false or misleading returns under the Act. The legislation made no provision for monitoring or verifying the information provided by lobbyists.

In this manner, the Bill favoured "simplicity" over the public's need to know who is talking to government about what. This commitment to keeping administrative requirements "simple" was carried over to the implementation stage.[10] As the regulatory impact assessment stated, "to minimize the burden imposed by the system, special care was taken to ensure that the Registry requires, within the intent of the Act, the registration of only the most necessary information."[11]

Criticism of the Act

Criticism of the Act has been harsh and consistent from the time Harvie Andre introduced it as a bill. Members of Parliament who had previously championed registration argued from the outset that the legislation went too far in simplifying the information required of some lobbyists. Some of the most influential firms, such as those that purported only to advise clients on lobbying strategy and those that engaged in indirect lobbying, would not be covered. The information required of Tier I lobbyists was less than the MPs had expected, and Tier II lobbyists were not even required to report their lobbying activities. Interest groups would not have to file any information concerning their objectives and supporters. Although Tier I lobbyists were required to register the undertakings they had entered into, they did not have to spell out the real subject matter of meetings.[12]

Critics also attacked the administrative arrangements (particularly the decision to set up a registry without giving the Registrar power to review or verify the information provided by lobbyists) and considered inadequate the limited fines for failure to register or for provision of inaccurate information. Such failings were taken as evidence that, although lobbyists had not vigorously opposed the regulation at the earlier stages and had been unconvincing in their testimony before the Committee, they were more active and more persuasive at the legislative drafting stage. The Government's draft was a disappointment to those members of Parliament who had lobbied for the legislation, but their efforts to introduce amendments were unsuccessful.[13] However, critics of the legislation did have one consolation. In an unusual move, the Government incorporated into the new act a provision to review the legislation three years after it came into effect.

That review became due in September 1992. An internal study was commissioned in the spring of 1992 and, by the end of that year, the task of conducting the review had been assigned to the House of Commons Standing Committee on Consumer and Corporate Affairs and Government Operations (the Holtman Committee). Two of the members of the Holtman Committee—John Rodriguez and Don Boudria—had been active supporters of reform in the 1986-87 Standing Committee on Elections, Privileges and Procedure, which had considered the original bill. During the review, the reformist position was also represented by MPs Derek Lee, Dennis Mills and Patrick Boyer.

As the review began in February 1993, many earlier debates were revived. In appearing before the Committee, the Minister of Consumer and Corporate Affairs, Pierre Vincent, carried forward his predecessor's claim that the Government was satisfied with the Act and its implementation: "... the existing law is good. I'm not aware of complaints from the public or any public-interest groups."[14] He proposed changing the time limit on prosecutions of unregistered lobbyists from six months to one year and requiring Tier II lobbyists to report the subject matter of lobbying undertakings in the same manner as Tier I lobbyists. He rejected the idea of requiring fee disclosures.

The Minister's position was shared by many lobbyists who, with the exception of those who consider the Act an unforgivable intrusion into client relations and a denial of their right to make representations to government, have found that the Act "has little real effect on their business."[15] Some even give it credit for bringing

> some objective, indeed official, acknowledgement of lobbying as a credible and legitimate function in national public affairs. And many lobbyists say the data on lobbying, now available because

of the registration process, contribute to a better understanding on the part of both practitioners and clients of how the business of public policy advocacy is being conducted.[16]

Most of the lobbyists' criticisms of the legislation are technical, and their greatest concern appears to be that the legislative review will push the Government a step further toward regulating the industry instead of merely recording its membership.

Among the reformers, Patrick Boyer has been especially active—raising the issue in the House, appearing at conferences and taking advantage of media opportunities to put forward a position in the tradition of earlier "House of Commons men" such as Jim McGrath and the late Walter Baker. Like them, he puts the role of the legislature in Canadian democracy at the centre of his concern over the effects of lobbying. For Boyer, "the practices engaged in by those who insert themselves between the people and those in their government and extract a fee for doing so ... [are] fundamentally undermining representative democracy and eclipsing Parliament."[17]

Boyer's position reflects the general conclusion among reformist critics of the registration process that the Lobbyists Registration Act has not achieved even the modest objectives set for it by Harvie Andre. This conclusion is substantiated not only by the belief among lobbyists that their business has been unaffected by the Act, but by the Government's own data. Thus in 1989, when proclaiming the regulations under the Act, the Lobbyists Registration Branch estimated that 5,000 Tier I and 10,000 Tier II lobbyists would register annually.[18] In reality, registrations have been one fifth of that number.[19] Although the 1989 estimates were little more than an educated guess, the shortfall is seen in the industry as a sign that many lobbyists are not registering. Lawyers in particular are said to be avoiding registration, although business leaders are also thought to be remiss. As *The Lobby Digest* commented indignantly,

It's a mystery how some corporate CEOs can spend what seems like half their life on the phone to, or visiting with, public office holders and yet not have their names appear on the Tier II registry. Meanwhile the manager of the Chamber of Commerce in Split Lips, Alberta registers because she takes a government official out to lunch every once in a while to press for better training programs.[20]

To some extent, these problems may be due to the newness of the procedure. Many business people and lawyers were slow to become aware of the Act or to understand how it affected them.[21] However, it has also become apparent that some lobbyists have sought loopholes in the Act and that registration contributes little to the process of rooting out influence peddling.[22]

Possible Reforms of the Act

Difficulties with compliance can be attributed to several factors: public indifference, lack of awareness of regulations, ambiguities in the legislation, limited administrative capacity, absence of investigatory and enforcement powers and inadequate sanctions. One major technical difficulty is the fact that the Criminal Code's statute of limitations on summary offences limits the ability of the RCMP to obtain prosecutions under the Act. The extension of the time limit to one year, while still too short, should make the Act more enforceable.[23] In addition, case law will eventually address the ambiguities surrounding the Act's disclosure requirements.

A more important problem is the limited authority of the Registrar, who is not empowered to investigate a registration or a failure to register. Even the formal authority to draw an apparent infraction to the attention of the RCMP is not contained in the Act. The obvious solution to this problem is to confer investigatory and monitoring powers on the Registrar, as has recently been done in some American states. However, the location of the Lobbyists Registration Branch in a line department is probably an important factor militating against this. Given the tendency of lobbyists to be friends of the government in power, it is almost inevitable that an occasion will arise in which the Registrar's status as a public servant will expose him or her to pressure to overlook unacceptable lobbying behaviour. As long as the Registrar's role is primarily to record, that conflict is unlikely to occur. However, the authority, and corresponding obligation, to investigate is bound to increase the probability that it will. These considerations have prompted some American states to give independent status to their lobbyists registration offices.[24] A Canadian equivalent would be to make the Registrar an officer of Parliament with a role similar to that of the Auditor General.

The Registrar's inability to monitor lobbying activity has been compounded by the failure of the Act to draw public officeholders into the registration process. Lobbyists are required to register, but not to provide proof of registration. Officials are not obliged to ask for proof of registration, check lobbyists' names and activities against the registry, report contacts with lobbyists or even record them. It would be feasible to require that some or all of these steps be taken in order to enhance monitoring of lobbying activity and provide proof of that activity should prosecution be necessary. However, such suggestions are brushed aside by those resisting reform, as either inoperable or bound to create "a nightmare of paperwork."[25] Yet, most officials keep appointment books. It would take very little extra effort to include the subject matter of meetings with records of appointments or to retain those records for a statutory period in case they should be needed by investigators. Similarly, by issuing registration cards to lobbyists, an easy means of verification would be provided that could be supplemented by requests to the Registration Branch— which is equipped with a computerized and presumably accessible registry—for information concerning the subject matter of lobbying undertakings. Similar approaches have been adopted by some American states.

Disclosure is a more difficult matter. Advocates of regulation have long urged wide disclosure in order to foster "transparency" in government. They have not, however, been able to counter effectively the argument that extensive disclosure will complicate the registration process, perhaps to the point of paralysis, without necessarily facilitating public awareness of lobbying activity. American experience with the Federal Regulation of Lobbying Act was frequently cited as a case in point during the 1987 hearings.

Nevertheless, the present system demands too little information. Although John Chenier, co-publisher of *The Lobby Monitor*, may be overly harsh when he describes the output of the "'computer convenient' numbering system" as "garbage in, garbage out," there is no doubt that the subject categories it uses are too vague and lend themselves more to obscuring the objects of lobbying than to making the process transparent.[26] In fact, Chenier believes that some lobbyists deliberately exploit the system's weaknesses in order to mislead critics and rivals of their clients. An uncomplicated remedy for this problem would be to require lobbyists "to reveal what specific piece of legislation they are trying to influence or name the particular procurement in which they are involved."[27] Information of this sort need not be voluminous.

Given the shortcomings of the subject classification system, it is not clear what benefit the Minister of Corporate and Consumer Affairs expects from his proposal to extend the subject reporting system to Tier II lobbyists. It may be an attempt to respond to the view that too little information is demanded of Tier II lobbyists. If so, the critics have not been satisfied and they point, in particular, to a growing concern that some corporate interests are registering as coalition associations in order to avoid revealing their individual connection with a lobbying undertaking.[28]

The most contentious issue related to disclosure has to do with the fees that lobbyists charge. Most lobbyists have obdurately resisted any suggestion that fees should be declared while reformers have been equally vigorous in their demands that fees should be disclosed. Ron Atkey of Osler, Haskin and Harcourt believes fee disclosure would turn "transparency" into "voyeurism." Gary Ouellet of Government Consultants International presents a view common among lobbyists when he argues that disclosure would be "unacceptable" to professionals. Bill Neville of the Neville Group takes another common position when he suggests that the solution "lies with the market not with the government."[29] Although one leading lobbyist endorsed fee disclosure before the Holtman Committee, the reformers have been unable to win on this issue.[30] In part, this may be because they have focused on reporting *fees*, rather than on reporting *project* costs. The former is interesting from a journalistic point of view, but provides virtually no context for the public to judge the significance of lobbying activity. On the other hand, when we are told, for example, that Hill and Knowlton Canada planned to spend close to $1 million in its campaign against the Ontario NDP's revisions of labour legislation ("Project Economic Growth"), and that Susan A. Murray was managing the "More Jobs Coalition" and by March 1992 had raised $200,000, we have some sense of the resources that special interests are prepared to put into a campaign.[31]

contingency fees

The question of whether contingency fees—fees that depend on the success of a campaign—should be banned aroused much debate in 1986-87 as well as in the current review. The corrupting influence of contingency fees is widely recognized. As Don Boudria puts it, "They are the ideal system to encourage abuse and unethical behaviour."[32] Consequently, rumours of large contingency fees attract media attention and foster public cynicism. In these circumstances, lobbyists are reluctant to endorse contingency fees but, at the same time, maintain that it would be difficult to impose tight restrictions on them: "Banning contingency fees sounds good; we're just not sure how you'd do it in practical terms."[33] Such positions were received sceptically by committee members, who repeatedly pointed out that a ban on such fees has been observed by Canadian lawyers for many years.[34]

A number of other themes were touched on in the Holtman Committee hearings. The issue of indirect lobbying has arisen here as it has in the debate over the role of interest groups and advocacy advertising during election campaigns.[35] Curiously, while in the latter debate all political parties have agreed that advocacy advertising should be severely curtailed during elections, the Government rejected the 1987 recommendation of the Cooper Committee that lobbyists report indirect lobbying. The Government has adhered to that position, but several of the reformers have revived the 1987 proposal and have urged it on the Government.

John Rodriguez prompted a good deal of heated discussion in the Holtman Committee by maintaining that officials of political parties should be banned from lobbying. He argued, first, that a ban is needed to ensure that such service is not undertaken for the sole purpose of securing access to government decision makers and, second, that a person active in the senior ranks of a political party must be—and be seen to be—able to address the general public interest, not simply that of a special interest.[36] However, this position was not encouraged by other members of the Committee and was avoided by witnesses.

Finally, MPs reviewed critically the desultory attempts to develop an association capable of fostering a code of professional ethics. Despite some intimations in 1987 from members of the industry that they were interested in building such an association, efforts to date have been unsuccessful. In the spring of 1991, Richard Bertrand of Executive Consultants tried to organize an association, but without success. Participants in a meeting on the subject said that, although the expected review of the Lobbyists Registration Act was an incentive, other factors inhibited organization. In particular, they did not feel that the professional ethics issue was sufficient in itself to provide the glue needed to hold an organization together.[37] In the meantime, the British government has introduced lobbying reforms that include a code of conduct and a professional practices committee, and at least one American state (Florida) has introduced a code of conduct in its revamped regulations.[38]

The code of conduct issue is strongly representative of the overall debate over lobby regulation at the federal level. There is considerable evidence produced regularly in the courts of the need for closer control over lobbying. Ironically most lobbying, legitimate and illegitimate, is financed as a tax deductible business expense. A small group of MPs have championed reform, supported by a handful of journalists. Their efforts have brought meagre results: little more than a registry of the more professionally minded lobbyists. The public is largely indifferent and increasingly cynical, according to the polls, about the moral tone of politics, but apparently uninterested in supporting reform. The media regularly report the more spectacular scandals, but take little interest in the nuts and bolts of reform. Leading lobbyists, as we have seen, have done little to promote a professional ethic. The Government has given minimal support to reform, confining legislation to an unenforceable "business card bill" and meeting the obligation to review the legislation with minor amendments and the proposition that "the existing law is good."[39]

PUBLIC INTEREST GROUPS AND CHARITABLE STATUS

If the regulatory regime that applies to lobbying firms as they represent private interests is surprisingly light, government constraints on the behaviour of groups advocating particular conceptions of the public interest are, by contrast, extensive, the more so because they are not clearly demarcated.

Public interest groups are formal organizations whose members have joined together to promote altruistically a common perception of the public interest. These groups play an important part in public consultation because they articulate alternative positions on policy issues, aggregate support around those positions and provide a mechanism through which their supporters can communicate with those who think differently. While these activities do not always endear public interest groups to the dominant interests in a policy community, their function in promoting and extending public discussion is increasingly recognized. In fact, with the continuing inability of traditional political parties to organize meaningful policy discussions within their own ranks, the role of such groups becomes more valuable. For these reasons, which we explore more fully below, the assignment of charitable status to a public interest has considerable significance.

Public interest groups are subject to most of the regulations that apply to firms and to trade, business and professional associations.[40] However, the majority of public interest groups are also subject to a further degree of regulation that is all the more powerful because it is implicit and discretionary. This additional burden of regulation is a consequence of their limited financial resources, a factor that all too frequently makes them dependent on the public purse.

Canadian interest groups receive an unusually high degree of financial support from government. Generally, this support comes either in the form of direct payments or through tax expenditures.[41] We are interested here in the practice of allowing registered charities to issue donors with receipts that can be used to reduce the calculation of income tax payable. Our concern lies in the uncertainty with which Revenue Canada administers charitable status. We will argue that this ambiguity, because it has important implications for many public interest groups and, thus, for the general public's capacity to communicate with government, raises the political question of whether charitable status should be redefined.

As a tax expenditure, charitable donations amount to a significant sum. For 1989, for example, Revenue Canada reported that some five million Canadians claimed donations to charity on their income tax returns for a total of nearly $2.5 billion, while businesses reported donations of a further $400 million. "The total cost to the federal and provincial treasuries in terms of foregone revenue is estimated at more than $1 billion a year."[42]

Although some organizers of public interest groups claim that charitable status imposes constraints that are too extensive to warrant registration, most seem to disagree.[43] Between 1986 and 1992, the number of registered charities grew by 10,000, from 55,017 to 65,000.[44] As Allan Arlett, then President of the Canadian Centre for Philanthropy, once put it: "There's no question that tax breaks encourage giving. It's not the only reason people give, but it's certainly a factor, particularly for higher-income donors."[45]

Charitable status not only gives groups access to a significant source of revenue,[46] but also provides important financial advantages. Charities' revenues and capital are protected from most taxation. They are exempt from federal income tax and, where goods and services are acquired for the non-taxable activities of the group, they are exempt from the goods and services tax. Charities also benefit from exemption from a variety of other taxes, including municipal taxes, provincial sales taxes and excise tax. These advantages serve to help groups to conserve the funds they raise through charitable donations.

The Regulation of Charitable Status

Organizations acquire charitable status through application to Revenue Canada, which reviews their purposes and activities to determine whether they fall under one or more of four "heads" that characterize the "good works" which the Income Tax Act associates with charities. That is, they must be organized primarily 1) for the relief of poverty and sickness; 2) for religious pursuits; 3) for the advancement of education; or 4) for "purposes beneficial to the community."[47] If Revenue Canada approves the application, it assigns a registration number which is subsequently treated by the group as one of its most important assets and, moreover, one that may be easily lost.

The application process, then, is the principal point at which Revenue Canada determines whether or not the aims and activities of an organization are charitable. However, Revenue Canada, after a routine audit or after receipt of a complaint, may also decide that the organization should be deregistered. The grounds for deregistration may be a failure to comply with the technical requirements of the Income Tax Act[48] or engagement in political activities prohibited by the Act. From the point of view of these groups, it is unfortunate that the Income Tax Act is vague as to what constitutes a "charity," a "charitable activity" or a "charitable purpose." This ambiguity has forced the courts to turn to common law for clarification and, at the same time, has exposed public interest groups to considerable regulatory uncertainty.

The nub of the problem is that, while the public in general seems to have accepted the idea that charitable status should normally be awarded to groups whose primary goal is to promote a particular view of the public interest, the common law definition of a charity is not as flexible. In 1917, Lord Parker of Waddington observed that

> [a] trust for the attainment of political objects has been held to be invalid, not because it is illegal, for everyone is at liberty to advocate or promote by any lawful means a change in the law, but because the Court has no means of judging whether a proposed change in the law will or will not be for the public benefit, and therefore cannot say that a gift to secure the change is a charitable gift.[49]

Since then, while the courts have continued to maintain that charitable activity does not include activity directed at changing specific legislation or policy, they have left some room for charities to engage in political activities that promote their charitable objectives.[50]

To clarify which political activities were allowable for charities and which were not, the Income Tax Act was amended in 1985, so that

> where a corporation or trust devotes substantially all of its resources to charitable purposes and a) it devotes part of its resources to political activities, b) such political activities are ancillary and incidental to charitable purposes, and c) such political activities do not include the direct or indirect support of, or opposition to, any political party or candidate for public office, the corporation or trust shall be considered to be constituted and operated for charitable purposes to the extent of that part of its resources so devoted.[51]

This did not, however, end the confusion about the type and level of political activities which could be undertaken by charities. If charitable organizations which expended "substantially all" of their resources on their charitable works were allowed to pursue political activities "ancillary and incidental" to their charitable ends, greater clarification was required as to what constituted "substantially all" resources and "ancillary and incidental" political activities.

Consequently, the phrase "political activities ancillary and incidental to charitable purposes" was elaborated in a 1987 Revenue Canada Information Circular.[52] In it, the political activities of charities are divided into three categories: activities not subject to limitations; prohibited activities; and political activities which are ancillary and incidental to a charity's objectives. There are no limitations on the provision of information and non-partisan views to the media, politicians or the bureaucracy, as long as the resources committed by charities in support of these activities are reasonable and as long as they are intended to stimulate informed public discussion. In contrast, overtly partisan activities, such as endorsing or opposing politicians, parties or named candidates engaged in electoral politics, are prohibited. Political activities which are ancillary or incidental to the charity's charitable objectives consist of attempts to influence and mobilize public opinion or gain support for the charity's position on an issue, either through communications, such as letter writing and media campaigns, or through events such as lawful public protests.

In its 1987 Information Circular, Revenue Canada also interpreted the meaning of the phrase "'substantially all' of a charity's resources," describing this as

> an expenditure test requiring that approximately 90 per cent of a charity's financial, physical and human resources be devoted to its charitable programs and activities over a program cycle.[53]

In effect, this means that charities may spend annually no more than 10 percent of their total resources to support political activities.[54]

From this discussion, it can be seen that the definitions used by Revenue Canada and the courts to describe charities and their activities do not readily encompass groups whose principal purpose is to promote general debate on public policy issues. Instead, charities are limited to a marginal level of political activity in support of their primary charitable objectives.

Problems with the Regulation of Charitable Status

Prior to the 1985 amendment to the Income Tax Act, and the 1987 Information Circular, charitable status allowed charities virtually no political activity.[55] The increasing policy activity of many groups in the 1970s and the early 1980s revealed the widening gap between their permitted political role and their actual activities. Revenue Canada warned a number of organizations that they ran the risk of deregistration if they continued to take stands on public policy issues.[56] The resulting outcry led Revenue Canada to consult with a committee of representatives drawn primarily from the major traditional charities in formulating the present regulations.

It is clear however that, while these revisions addressed issues that concerned the traditional charities, they did not resolve the overall policy problem of the conflict between the advocacy activities of charities and the restrictive regulations.[57] Nor did they address the administrative problem of interpretation in which officials continue to make determinations about the status of groups in an environment of uncertainty. Indeed, in the eyes of some interest group representatives, the way in which the rules are being interpreted now is particularly restrictive for public interest groups. A 1990 focus group study commissioned by Revenue Canada reported that there is concern among those who "feel they are treading a fine but unclear line between compliance and non-compliance."[58]

The authors' conversations with representatives of charitable groups underline this uncertainty.[59] Particular efforts, group leaders feel, are made by the federal government to challenge organizations that engage in public debate as a regular part of their charitable activities. Revenue Canada focuses on statements of purpose and frequently asks groups to revise them, sometimes in ways that seem contradictory to group leaders. Thus, one group concluded that "you can be an advocacy group, but you must not be lobbyists. Therefore you have to be very careful how publications are phrased...." Another group representative reported that

> when we applied for charitable status, Revenue Canada asked for a definition of "advocacy" (as found in the organizations statement of purpose). We defined it as information dissemination— education information.... Lobbying definitely will get you a no no from Revenue Canada.

Adding to the sense of uncertainty is the fact that Revenue Canada's prohibition on lobbying does not seem to extend to registration under the Lobbyists Registration Act. Departmental officials maintain that registrations made in conformity with the Act will not jeopardize a group's charitable status.

Revenue Canada's situation is unenviable. The ambiguity of the legislation it is charged with administering is only the first of its problems. Much more important is the fact that the activities of some advocacy groups periodically generate such intense public reaction that MPs routinely question their charitable status. So, for example,

> **Ms. Dawn Black (New Westminster-Burnaby):** On Tuesday [Apr. 28, 1992] I questioned the Minister of National Revenue on the charitable tax status of an American organization called Human Life International. The minister indicated that he would conduct a review ...

> **Hon. Otto Jelinek (Minister of National Revenue):** ... concern has been raised from both sides of the issue that she refers to, and I emphasize both sides. As a result, in order to maintain the integrity of the charitable organizations as a whole, I have today instructed my officials to review and investigate the activities of all politically active charitable organizations.[60]

Thus, the controversies surrounding a few groups envelope the entire spectrum of charities, creating a political issue of charitable status itself. Reviews are conducted, groups are audited and some carry their concerns to the media and politicians so that a new round of controversy develops, this time one in which Revenue Canada is at the heart of the storm. The Department soon acquires the sort of reputation for stifling legitimate public debate that is exemplified in the comment of one group official to the authors:

> The [Association] had applied for charitable status when I took up [my] position. The application was in process. I didn't pursue it because I knew it would fail. If you don't strictly fit the criteria, you use political means. You can have charitable status and still lobby if you have the right political connections. We won't try again until there is a change of government.

This is an extreme position. The assessment of an experienced interest group administrator currently working for an organization deeply engaged in public policy advocacy is probably closer to that held by most group leaders:

> Revenue Canada generally functions as an administrative body. As long as a group is running smoothly and gets its reports in, Revenue Canada won't initiate enquiries—even if charities are increasingly finding themselves moving away from their charitable mission and embracing advocacy.... However, Revenue Canada is responsive to complaints and follows them up.

In other words, Revenue Canada is not abusing its authority and is not out to control advocacy, but advocacy groups can be undermined by rivals. Furthermore, although there is clear evidence that Revenue Canada audits advocacy groups more frequently than other charities,[61] there is also anecdotal evidence that suggests Revenue Canada interprets charitable status as broadly as it can.

The Continuing Debate

Given the uncertainty surrounding the political activities of charities and the frequency with which the status of specific charities is attacked, one would expect efforts to be made to disentangle advocacy groups from traditional charities and to establish a framework that would limit the discretion currently exercised by Revenue Canada. The fact that such efforts have been few and inconclusive reflects the difficulties involved in the task and the nervousness of existing charities that the exercise might lead to a wholesale revocation of the privileges advocacy groups currently enjoy.

Nevertheless, the issue has not been ignored entirely. Indeed, it may be finding its way onto the public agenda largely due to the fact that the number of charities has grown so rapidly in recent years that traditional charities are beginning to call for a more rigorous system. Thus, in a 1991 brief The Canadian Red Cross Society argued that,

> the perception that anyone can obtain charitable privileges negatively affects the public image of charities as a whole. The large number of new registrants suggests the application process is not overly difficult. In addition, the criteria for awarding charitable status need to be reviewed. The registration of too many new charities impedes fund raising efforts as more and more charities vie for a share of the donation dollars, results in duplication of efforts and costs, and adds to public cynicism.[62]

The central thrust of the argument is that it is counter-productive to encourage too many charities to chase a limited pool of donations, but there can be little doubt that, in its reference to public cynicism, the Red Cross is diplomatically expressing its concern that controversy over a few charities undermines public confidence in the rest.

To date, this discussion has taken place largely within the charities community, and it has been overshadowed by a debate— much more compelling from the community's point of view— about the entire tax regime that applies to charities. This debate began in March 1990 when Revenue Canada organized a consultation with the charitable organizations around its discussion paper, *A Better Tax Administration in Support of Charities*.[63] This consultation is still in progress.

Although initiated by Revenue Canada, the consultation was thought in the policy community to be inspired by the Department of Finance, which many believe is motivated by two considerations: on the one hand, a desire to expand its tax base by eliminating as many tax expenditures as possible; and, on the other, a need to respond to private sector complaints that tax status gives charities an unfair advantage in the market-place.[64] For the traditional charities, which are the most influential in the consultation process, this threat to their revenue generating activities is of greater importance than the issue of registration. Revenue Canada has also downplayed the registration question, describing it as a "policy issue" rather than an administrative one, which is therefore outside the mandate of the consultation exercise. Indeed, the head of the Registration Directorate "reassured participants that the provisions of the Income Tax Act which permit registered charities to conduct limited non-partisan political activities are not the subject of the ... review."[65] The discussion paper's limited treatment of "political activities" merely reiterates the view the Department put forward in its 1987 Information Circular and invites comment only on its proposals to "publish information in plain language on what political activities charities may undertake" and to "require charities to provide more detail in their annual returns about the political activities they do undertake."[66]

Thus, the bias of the discussion paper is against those groups primarily interested in promoting debate over public policy. Its promise of a clear exposition of the rules relating to political debate is ominous and its suggestion that groups will be required to report their policy interventions more fully renews fears of policing and confining public debate. This fear is reflected in comments by representatives of the Coalition of National Voluntary Organizations (NVO), who made it clear that they are "uncertain of the government's intent with regard to the political activities of charities" and "concerned that the legitimate educational role of charities could be undermined by a broader interpretation of political activities."[67] The NVO leaders spoke for many charities when they welcomed the prospect of "clear and objective information on the concepts, definitions, and legal limitations on the 'political activities' of charitable organizations," but went on to assert a conviction that

> both advocacy and non-partisan political activity by charities when congruent with their mission is legitimate. The public interest can be well served by the educational work of charities in their areas of expertise.[68]

Such comments make it clear that the awarding of charitable status is currently more than an administrative matter. So does the statement of Revenue Canada itself that "departmental decisions in this area will usually be controversial. The aim should be to apply the legal principles fairly and consistently in all cases."[69] Our traditions of democratic government suggest that it is both unfair to officials to saddle them with a burden of discretion of this magnitude and detrimental to an underlying spirit of public involvement in policy making. As one interest group official told us,

> The way that the rules are being interpreted now is particularly restrictive for public interest groups. Partisan restraint is okay, but the good that public interest groups could do is being lost to the country.

In other words, the level of discretion accorded officials by the current system limits the capacity of tax expenditures to encourage public debate. This may be what society wishes. The proliferation of advocacy groups in recent years suggests that it is not. If it is not, and if society wishes to support a pluralistic debate on public issues, something must be done to resolve the ambiguities in the present system.

Some years ago, Revenue Canada recognized a similar problem in the case of amateur athletic associations and took a policy decision to accord them a status similar to that of charities. As a result, amateur athletic associations do not have to pretend that they are something other than they are in order to receive charitable donations, and public servants are not saddled with a politically dangerous burden of discretion in determining their status. What is needed today is a major public discussion about the possibility of according a similar status to certain public interest groups. Such a debate could reaffirm the important and enduring role of these groups in the policy process. The creation of a special status for such groups would remove much of the uncertainty many of them now face and would permit them to make strategic decisions on lobbying in light of efficiency and effectiveness considerations, rather than with an eye on regulatory consequences. A public debate on the issue would allow taxpayers to address the entire question of regulation of public interest advocacy and the implications of such regulation on freedom of speech.

Such a discussion would have to deal with some important issues. Patrick Boyer has pointed out that it would be crucial to avoid creating a Canadian version of the notorious American Political Action Committees (PACs), for example.[70] Nevertheless, such a debate would bring an end to the fiction that the matter of charitable status can be treated as an administrative issue of interest mainly to the charities community and it would force Canadians to consider the proper role of public interest groups in our democracy.

CONCLUSION

Politicians and journalists frequently ask why it is that the public is cynical about public affairs. The discussion that we have presented suggests one answer.

On the one hand, we see government moving reluctantly to regulate an industry whose ill repute is derived, in part, from the fact that some of its members trade on their status as "friends" of the Government. On the other hand, we find a different sort of lobbying—one that is capable of tapping the views of many members of the public—constrained by a persistent adherence to an archaic legal definition.

Both types of lobbying are important and, in many respects, necessary if the views of members of the public are to be brought to the attention of government. Both are sustained to some degree through tax expenditures: one through ability of corporations to treat lobbying as a business expense; the other through the tax credit for charitable donations. Yet lobbyists resist reform, even though they have been shown to be the cause of much profligate public expenditure, while the proponents of the public interest must work constantly in the shadow of deregistration. Surely, a system that encourages special interest lobbying, even as it discourages vigorous and open public interest representation, is bound to breed cynicism.

NOTES

A portion of the research reported here was supported by Social Sciences and Humanities Research Council Grant No. 410-91-1748. The support of the Council is gratefully acknowledged as is the participation of several interest group representatives, whose identity will not be revealed, in the study of public interest groups, which was funded by the grant.

1   U.S. President Bill Clinton has argued that lobbying expenses which are fully deductible for income tax purposes are "just another tax expenditure." "Parliament Ready to Review Lobbying Laws," *The Lobby Digest and Public Affairs Monthly* (February 1992): pp. 4-5.

2   Mulroney's intentions in introducing the proposal are discussed in A. Paul Pross, "The Rise of the Lobbying Issue in Canada: 'The Business Card Bill'" in Grant Jordan, *The Commercial Lobbyists: Politics for Profit in Britain* (Aberdeen: Aberdeen University Press, 1991), pp. 76-95. See also David Dubinsky, "Who-Whom? The Registration of Lobbyists in Canada" in Magnus Gunther and Conrad Winn, (eds.), *House of Commons Reform* (Ottawa: Canadian Political Science Association, Parliamentary Internship Program, 1991), pp. 131-59; Andrew Stark, "'Political Discourse' Analysis and the Debate Over Canada's Lobbying Legislation," *Canadian Journal of Political Science*, XXV, 3 (1992), pp. 513-34.

3   Mulroney's statement, with other documents relating to the issue, is to be found in Consumer and Corporate Affairs Canada, *Lobbying and the Registration of Paid Lobbyists* (Ottawa: Supply and Services Canada, 1985), pp. 32-33.

4   House of Commons Standing Committee on Elections, Privileges and Procedure (Cooper Committee), *Minutes of Proceedings and Evidence* (including the First Report to the House), no. 2, 2/33, (1986-87).

5   Cooper Committee, *Proceedings and Evidence*, pp. 8-9.

6   Cooper Committee, *Proceedings and Evidence*, p. 14. "Indirect lobbying" is the term usually used to describe campaigns designed to excite public opinion to support or oppose public policy alternatives, rather than to influence governments directly as the primary target.

7   Cooper Committee, *Proceedings and Evidence*, pp. 14-15.

8   Cooper Committee, *Proceedings and Evidence*, pp. 7, 8. The Committee suggested that the programme be administered by the Assistant Deputy Registrar General, an official of the Department of Consumer and Corporate Affairs also responsible for administering the Conflict of Interest Guidelines.

9   Consumer and Corporate Affairs Canada (CCAC), *Notes for Remarks by the Honourable Harvie Andre, Minister of Consumer and Corporate Affairs Canada ... to the Press Conference on Lobbying Legislation* (Ottawa, June 30, 1987); House of Commons Standing Committee on Consumer and Corporate Affairs and Government Operations (Holtman Committee), *Minutes of Proceedings and Evidence*, no. 53 (February 9, 1993), pp. 18-33.

10   CCAC, *Lobbying Legislation*, p. 4. The injunction was repeated frequently in the Standing Committee hearings, in the Committee's report and in debate on the Bill.

11   *Canada Gazette*, Part I, June 10, 1989, p. 2798.

12   The subject areas are defined in terms such as "federal-provincial relations," "environment," "foreign affairs," "government procurement," etc. Undertakings are described in categories such as "the introduction, passage, defeat or amendment of any Bill or resolution before either House of Parliament; the making or amending of any regulation ...; the awarding of any contract" and arranging a meeting with a public officeholder. *Canada Gazette*, Part I, June 10, 1989, pp. 2802-04.

13   See House of Commons, *Minutes of Proceedings and Evidence of the Legislative Committee on Bill C-82: An Act respecting the registration of Lobbyists* (Ottawa, April 27, 1988); House of Commons, *Debates* (daily version), July 25, 1988, p. 17923.

14   Ross Howard, "No need to tighten reins on lobbyists, minister says," *The Globe and Mail* [Toronto], February 10, 1993, p. A11.

15   For example, Pierre Fortier's remarks to the conference on "NGO and Business Lobbying in the 90's" (September 11-12, 1992) focused on the argument that regulation is counter-productive. Carleton University, Centre for the Study of Business-Government-NGO Relations, September 11-12, 1992 (proceedings forthcoming)

16   "The Lobbyists Registration Act Two Years Later," *The Lobby Digest and Public Affairs Quarterly*, 1 (November 1991): pp. 4-5. In fact, registration can be a boon to lobbyists. A significant proportion of the growing demand for lobbying services has been supply driven: when a lobbying firm finds out that another one has registered a particular client, it starts calling all its competitors to drum up business. The issue of supply driven demand has been discussed extensively by Sean Moore, "Registration of Lobbyists," (Presentation to the Institute of Public Administration of Canada (Ottawa, January 27, 1993).

17   Boyer takes a unique "integrated approach" to reform that would combine rules relating to lobbying, access to information and conflict of interest laws. The reforms he proposes combine the views of many critics. Specifically, Boyer would like to see: 1) more vigorous compliance/enforcement powers, including random audits/spot checks on registration; 2) the requirement that public servants maintain a log of contacts with lobbyists; 3) disclosure of the ownership of lobbying firms; 4) more detailed disclosure of the objectives of lobbying activity; 5) the banning of contingency fees; and 6) the registration of indirect lobbying (direct mail; advocacy advertising; coalition building). House of Commons, *Debates* (daily edition), November 20, 1992, p. 14292. "Boyer Seeks Reform of Public Ethics Laws," *The Lobby Digest and Public Affairs Monthly* (October 1992): p. 8.

18   "Lobbyists registration regulations," *Canada Gazette*, Part I, June 10, 1989, p. 2797.

19   On March 31, 1990, 473 Tier I and 2,355 Tier II lobbyists were registered; on March 31, 1991, there were 658 and 2,182, and on March 31, 1992, 790 and 1,961. See Consumer and Corporate Affairs Canada, Lobbyists Registration Branch, *Lobbyists*

Registration Act—Annual Report (Ottawa: Supply and Services Canada) for the years 1989-90, 1990-91 and 1991-92.

20   "Someone Has to Pay: But the Question Remains, How Much?" *The Lobby Digest and Public Affairs Monthly* (January 1993): pp. 8-9, 12.

21   See, for example, "Ontario Bar Ponders LRA," *The Lobby Digest and Public Affairs Monthly* (April 1992): p. 8.

22   See "Statute of Limitations Restricts Enforcement of Lobbyists Act," *The Lobby Digest and Public Affairs Monthly* (April 1992): pp. 1-2; Ross Howard, "Law shines only a low-wattage light on lobbying process," *The Globe and Mail* [Toronto], January 22, 1992. The suggestion that the Act has been of little use in the investigation of influence peddling derives from examination of newspaper accounts of a number of recent scandals. The most frequent triggers for investigations appear to be civil suits lodged by disaffected parties to lobbying undertakings or tips from public servants.

23   There has yet to be a successful prosecution under the Act.

24   "Scope of Lobbying Registration and Regulation Expand in U.S. States," *The Lobby Digest and Public Affairs Monthly* (October 1991): pp. 6, 8.

25   See, for example, testimony of the Minister of Consumer and Corporate Affairs before the Holtman Committee, *Proceedings and Evidence*, p. 53:21.

26   "Some lobbyists still won't let the sun shine in," *The Hill Times* [Ottawa], October 15, 1992. See also Note 10 *supra*.

27   "Parliament Ready to Review Lobbying Laws," *The Lobby Digest and Public Affairs Monthly* (February 1993): pp. 4-5.

28   Howard, "No need to tighten reins." The coalition issue has also emerged in the United States. See "U.S. Bill Ready," *The Lobby Digest and Public Affairs Monthly* (February 1992): p. 8.

29   "The Lobbyists Registration Act," *The Lobby Digest and Public Affairs Monthly*, pp. 4-5.

30   David MacNaughton, President of Hill and Knowlton Canada, told the Holtman Committee that disclosure of fees would "help dispel negative impressions of business," *The Globe and Mail* [Toronto], February 24, 1993.

31   "Government-Industry Relations in Ontario—A Mean Scene," *The Lobby Digest and Public Affairs Monthly*, 29 (March 1992): pp. 4-5.

32   Ibid. See also "Contingency Fees," *The Lobby Digest and Public Affairs Monthly*, 1 (August 1991): pp. 4-5. See also Howard, "Law shines."

33   William J. Fox (Principal, Earnscliff Strategy Group), Holtman Committee, *Proceedings and Evidence*, pp. 54-58. See also the testimony of Torrance Wylie, Chairman, Government Policy Consultants Inc., p. 54:21.

34   Ironically, the announcement in the 1992 budget that a fee would be charged for registration has aroused those who feel that the move violates the commitment to open access to government that is enunciated in the preamble of the Act. *The Lobby Monitor*, 3, 15 (May 11, 1992): p. iii; "Someone Has to Pay," *The Lobby Digest and Public Affairs Monthly*, pp. 8-9, 12.

35   F. Leslie Seidle, (ed.), *Interest Groups and Elections in Canada*, vol. 2 of the Research Studies of the RCERPF (Toronto: Dundurn Press, 1991). On the debate over the participation of interest groups in the electoral process, see the chapter by Alexandra Dobrowolsky and Jane Jenson in this volume.

36   Holtman Committee, *Minutes and Evidence*, pp. 54:29, 54:37.

37   "An Idea Whose Time Has Yet to Come," *The Lobby Digest and Public Affairs Monthly*, 1 (July 1991): p. 4. Holtman Committee, *Minutes and Proceedings*, February 4, 1993, pp. 52:9, 52:10.

38 "Scope of Lobbying Registration," *The Lobby Digest and Public Affairs Monthly*, pp. 6, 8. "British Parliament to Consider Registry and Code of Conduct for Lobbyists," *The Lobby Digest and Public Affairs Monthly* (December 1991): p. 5.

39 Howard, "No need to tighten reins." At the time that this publication goes to press, it appears unlikely that the Holtman Committee, which reviewed the Lobbyists Registration Act, will produce a report in time for action by the House of Commons before Parliament is dissolved for the federal election. In April, the Holtman Committee had difficulty convening to consider preliminary drafts of its reports because not enough Conservative members turned up to establish a quorum. See "Chairman Felix vs. Gang of Four," *The Lobby Monitor*, 4, 11 (April 5, 1993): pp. 2-3.

40 At times, even the same regulations seem to be more intrusive when applied to public interest groups. For example, administrators of acts of incorporation provide associations with "guidelines" that intervene far more extensively in their internal operations than companies would tolerate. G. Godsoe (Personal Communication, November 1992).

41 Susan D. Phillips, "How Ottawa Blends: Shifting Government Relationships with Interest Groups" in Frances Abele, (ed.), *How Ottawa Spends 1991-92: The Politics of Fragmentation* (Ottawa: Carleton University Press, 1991), pp. 183-213; William T. Stanbury, *Business-Government Relations in Canada* (Toronto: Nelson, 1992), pp. 137-40. The issues associated with the direct support of interest groups are discussed in A. Paul Pross, *Group Politics and Public Policy* (Toronto: Oxford, 1992), pp. 205-11.

42 Revenue Canada, Taxation, *A Better Tax Administration in Support of Charities* (Discussion Paper, Ottawa, 1987), p. 7.

43 This is clearly evident in an ongoing survey being conducted by the authors. Of the 34 public interest groups examined to date, 31 reported holding charitable status. For the 24 of these which provided detailed information on their sources of income, charitable donations represented 24.8 percent of their revenue.

44   Andrew Weiner, "Dollars to donors: Revenue Canada helps those who help the charities," *The Financial Post Moneywise Magazine*, March 1987; "Recession Influences Corporate Philanthropy," *The Lobby Digest and Public Affairs Monthly* (December 1992), p. 1.

45   Weiner, "Dollars to donors," p. 25.

46   It may also help groups avoid the problem of "free riders." The charitable donation receipt acts as an incentive to donors to support charities where otherwise they might take a "free ride" on group services and activities.

47   For example, relief of poverty includes food banks, low-cost rental housing; advancement of education might mean promoting "serious research in a recognized field of knowledge"; "purposes beneficial to the community" include preventing child abuse, rehabilitation and social welfare of the family "but only to the extent of preventing or alleviating distress." See Revenue Canada, *Registering Your Charity* (Ottawa, 1985). The adoption of these common law "heads" lies in *Pemsel v. Special Commissioners of Income Tax*, 3 T.C. 53 [1891], A.C. 531 [1888], 2 All E.R. 296. The last "head" is normally interpreted narrowly.

48   That is, deregistration occurs if it is established that the charity 1) carries on an unrelated business or, in the case of a private foundation, if it carries on any business; 2) fails to satisfy its disbursement quota; 3) ceases to meet the statutory requirements for registration; or 4) fails to file its various information returns. See C.H. Medland, "Limitations on Charities Under the Income Tax Act" in Wolfe D. Goodman, (ed.), *Charities and the Tax Man and More* (Toronto: Canadian Bar Association—Ontario, Continuing Legal Education, October 16, 1990), p. 2.

49   *Bowman v. Secular Society Limited,* [1917] A.C. 406 (H.L.).

50   *McGovern and Others v. Attorney General and Another,* [1982] Law Reports, Chancery Division, pp. 321-54.

51   Section 149.1 (6.1) and Section (6.2) of the Income Tax Act repeats the formulation for charitable organizations, in the same terms.

52   Revenue Canada, *Registered Charities—Ancillary and Incidental Political Activities*, Information Circular IC 87-1 (Ottawa, February 25, 1987).

53   Revenue Canada, *Ancillary and Incidental*, Appendix A. The reference to "program cycle" introduces a further important limitation. As a program cycle is usually defined as one year (although provision is made for longer time spans), charities are restricted to a maximum of 10 percent of their total resources being used to support political activities annually. The Information Circular also stipulates that a charity must disburse at least 80 percent of its receipted donations from the previous fiscal year on its charitable activities. This is intended to keep fund-raising costs down to an acceptable proportion of the revenues raised. It also, however, serves to limit the funds available for political activity to under 20 percent of donations received. Should other non-charitable expenses be incurred in the same period, the available finances could be quite small.

54   It is interesting to note that, of the 31 charities participating in our study of public interest groups, the 20 providing information about their lobbying expenditures reported that they spent only 11.4 percent on lobbying. Several of the registered charities included in the study objected to our question on the grounds that it led them into an apparent contravention of Revenue Canada's interpretation of permissible activity. However, most did agree that they engaged in a range of activities associated with lobbying, e.g. presenting briefs to policy makers, meeting with officials, etc., in order to present a view of a public policy issue.

55   See Revenue Canada, *Registered Charities—Political Objects and Activities*, Information Circular IC 78-3 (Ottawa, February 27, 1978).

56   George Rohn, Director General of the Canadian Mental Health Association, was reported to know of 16 groups receiving warnings. Ian Morrison, Chairman of the Coalition of National

Voluntary Organizations, claimed that many of the 126 organizations in his group would not admit to being threatened because they "don't want to draw attention to themselves." He cited the experience of the Quebec Social Rehabilitation Association, a prisoner rehabilitation organization, which was denied charitable status because it had publicly argued against the building of more prisons. See *The Chronicle-Herald* [Halifax], April 4, 1984; Andrew Cohen, "Who makes the rules?" *Canadian Associations*, June 1984. See also *Maclean's*, May 23, 1983.

57   "Traditional" charities are defined as those for which "substantially all" of their resources could be seen to be devoted to traditional charitable purposes and for which political activities could not possibly be seen as partisan.

58   Charities Tax Measures Research, Phases 1 & 2, *Final Report* RCT/PSB-141-03393 (Prepared for Revenue Canada Taxation by Longwoods Research Group, Ottawa, July 1990).

59   The following comments from the authors' study of public interest groups give a clear indication of the problems facing advocacy groups with charitable status. Officials of eight "public education" groups (the category most likely to contain groups whose activities would expose them to charges that they were engaged primarily in public policy advocacy) told the authors that none was confident of their group's maintaining its charitable status. Of these eight, two had to reword their statement of purpose in order to accommodate Revenue Canada, four have been challenged by Revenue Canada (three of which were also audited), four believe it is more difficult today to obtain charitable status than it was before the 1985 changes, and one clearly believed that it would not meet present criteria for charitable status.

60   House of Commons, *Debates* (daily edition), April 30, 1992, p. 9925.

61   In 1990, the Auditor General of Canada noted that "over the past four years [1986-90] audit coverage has averaged about one-half of one percent of registered charities." In contrast, in the authors' study (focusing on public interest groups), 9.6 percent of the

sample had been audited.

62   The Canadian Red Cross Society, "Response to Revenue Canada's Discussion Paper: A Better Tax Administration in Support of Charities" (Ottawa, March 1991), p. 4.

63   Revenue Canada, *A Better Tax Administration in Support of Charities* (Ottawa, 1990).

64   Interview with J. Shand, President, Canadian Society of Association Executives, May 15, 1992. Traditionally, charities have been carefully regulated as to the extent to which they may compete with private enterprise. In recent years, the distinction between charitable and business activities has become less and less distinct, with commercial concerns launching enterprises—e.g. in the health-care field—that have been traditionally associated with the non-profit sector in Canada, and with charities deriving revenue from related businesses.

65   Revenue Canada, *Minutes of Charities Consultative Conference* (Ottawa, May 11, 1990), p. 16.

66   Revenue Canada, Taxation, *A Better Tax Administration in Support of Charities*, p. 18.

67   Coalition of National Voluntary Organizations, "Response to Revenue Canada's Discussion Paper, *A Better Tax Administration in Support of Charities*" (Ottawa, January 1991), pp. 6, 1. *The Lobby Digest and Public Affairs Monthly* (December 1990): p. 1, also reported concern among "some public interest groups and charities," worried that the review "is likely to put a damper on what many organizations say is a vital part of their work."

68   Coalition of National Voluntary Organizations, "Response," p. 6.

69   Revenue Canada, discussion paper, 1987 (Draft version circulated prior to consultation conference), p. 41.

70   "Boyer Seeks Reform of Public Ethics Laws," *The Lobby Digest and Public Affairs Monthly*, 35 (October 1992): p. 8.

CHAPTER 5

Constitutional Politics 1990-92: The Paradox of Participation

Leslie A. Pal
F. Leslie Seidle

Résumé : Malgré l'échec définitif de l'*Accord de Charlottetown* le 26 octobre 1992 à l'issue de référendums menés au Québec et dans le reste du Canada, le document n'en demeure pas moins le résultat d'une participation tangible et nombreuse au processus démocratique. Les Canadiens ont sans aucun doute réagi au consensus de l'élite qui sous-tendait l'Accord, mais dans ce chapitre, les auteurs avancent que le processus même a eu une incidence sur l'issue. Après l'échec de l'*Accord du lac Meech* en 1990, il est devenu manifeste que le processus de formulation constitutionnelle ne pouvait plus relever uniquement des premiers ministres. Il fallait trouver des façons de donner voix au chapitre aux particuliers et aux groupes d'intérêts divers. Ce chapitre retrace l'exercice de consultation inégalé échelonné de 1990 à 1992 et rend compte du tour de force de devoir concilier les éléments des diverses étapes du processus tout en venant à bout d'un programme en évolution rapide (et dont les éléments étaient souvent contradictoires). Le processus a abouti à une entente subordonnée à de nombreuses conditions et très ténue qui appelait la tenue d'un référendum. Malgré l'échec de l'*Accord*, celui-ci pourrait très bien devenir l'assise des négociations constitutionnelles à venir. Ayant déjà servi une fois, le référendum est appelé à être intégré au processus de réforme constitutionnelle du Canada. Cependant, d'un point de vue général, l'échec de l'*Accord de Charlottetown* laisse supposer que même une participation vaste et diverse n'aboutit pas à un consensus. En fait, elle risque plutôt de donner lieu à un mécontent renouvelé à l'égard de la démarche politique.

Abstract: Despite its ultimate defeat in the October 26, 1992 referendums in Quebec and the rest of Canada, the Charlottetown Accord was the product of real and substantial democratic participation. Canadians undoubtedly reacted against the élite consensus behind the Accord, but this chapter argues that the process itself contributed to the results. After the failure of the Meech Lake Accord in 1990, constitution-making could no longer be a first ministers' monopoly. Ways had to be found to include citizens and varied interests. The chapter traces the unprecedented consultative exercise from 1990 to 1992, and demonstrates the challenges this posed for reconciling the dynamics of the various phases and for managing a rapidly expanding (and often inconsistent) agenda. This process led to an agreement which was qualified and tenuous, and also created pressure for a referendum vote. While defeated, the Accord may well become the "floor" for a future round of constitutional negotiations. Having been used once, the referendum will become, in effect, a part of Canada's constitutional amending formulae. In broad policy terms, the failure of the Charlottetown Accord suggests that even extensive and varied participation does not yield consensus. Rather, it may generate fresh disaffection with the political process.

The rejection of the Charlottetown Accord on October 26, 1992 by six provinces, the Yukon and many Aboriginal peoples raises fundamental questions about Canadian democracy. How could a document that was the result of unprecedented public participation and consultation, and which had the unanimous support of federal, provincial and territorial governments, as well as Canada's four national Aboriginal associations, be rejected? The conventional immediate explanation was that the referendum results were a repudiation of élites and of a process which critics claimed political leaders had tried to manipulate from the beginning. We believe the explanation is not that simple.

Fundamentally, the Charlottetown Accord failed because of the peculiar nature of Canadian constitutional politics, not because the process was undemocratic. First, political leaders negotiated against a backdrop of turbulent and contradictory forces: 1) widespread mistrust of representative politics; 2) mutually incompatible governmental, regional and group agendas; and 3) deep suspicions about the protection and extension of citizens' rights. Neither the Accord they fashioned nor the referendum itself could reconcile these forces. Second, the democratization of the constitutional process was undertaken somewhat reluctantly by politicians, more as a result of lessons learned from the earlier, failed Meech Lake Accord exercise than out of genuine conviction. The referendum, in particular, was chosen more by default than by design, and strategists were not prepared for the new campaign dynamics. Third, while broad participation gave the process needed legitimacy, it also increased the number of players, types of issues and forms of consultation. This increased the odds that formal negotiations would yield numerous compromises, thus increasing the number of potentially dissatisfied constituencies.

This most recent constitutional round holds several sobering lessons for Canadian democracy. On matters of substance, the

Accord could well become the "floor" for any future constitutional negotiations. Commitments made at Charlottetown (for example, on Aboriginal self-government) will colour non-constitutional policy fields. On matters of process, the Canada round model of extensive consultation and a referendum are likely to become standards in any future constitutional process, and broader participation will also be demanded in non-constitutional arenas. Wider participation is often argued to hold the promise of greater consensus and legitimacy for resulting policies. The paradox of wider participation, however, is that multiplying players and agendas sometimes heightens conflict and induces paralysis. Rather than fulfilling the promise of participation, the Charlottetown Accord succumbed to its paradox, as might Canadian governance more generally unless we reflect on the lessons of 1992.

THE CONSTITUTIONAL ARENA

Constitutions contain more than the rules by which political institutions function. They also symbolize and express the core values of a political community. Constitutional reform, therefore, is always difficult because the practical and symbolic stakes are so high. The Liberal government of Pierre Trudeau nevertheless succeeded, in 1982, in patriating the Constitution and amending it to include the Canadian Charter of Rights and Freedoms. This success came with a high price: Quebec did not sign. René Lévesque was then Quebec's premier, and many argued that no constitutional deal would have satisfied his separatist government. Even so, both the process (patriation without Quebec's agreement) and the result (a charter that could potentially override Quebec's language laws) were broadly criticized in Quebec as a betrayal of federal promises, made after the defeat of the 1980 Quebec referendum, to renew Canadian federalism. So, while the Constitution applied legally to Quebec, it had not been willingly accepted by its government. This omission persuaded the Mulroney government to co-operate with the government of Robert Bourassa (elected in 1985) to bring Quebec formally into the constitutional fold. To universal surprise, all 11 governments agreed to the Meech Lake Accord in 1987. Over its three-year ratification period, however, it was relentlessly attacked as both giving too much to Quebec and undermining the achievements of 1982 (especially the Charter). It died on June 23, 1990.

On the twisting path that led to Charlottetown, political leaders were not free to take any direction they pleased. In large measure the strategies, the players, the issues and even the outcomes of the Charlottetown exercise were determined by the sour legacies of the Meech Lake Accord and, in Quebec, of the "humiliation" of the 1982 patriation. Principal among those legacies were the following.

- **Symbolic Imperatives.** For many Quebec nationalists, the 1982 constitution was a humiliation and betrayal.[1] What Quebecers wanted fundamentally was a sign of contrition from the rest of Canada, some figurative, familial embrace disguised in constitutional language. Constitutional discourse thus flowed along two channels—a legalistic/substantive one and an emotional/symbolic one. The first involved specific issues like spending power; the second, the language of honour, shame, enthusiasm, pride, humiliation and insult. When the Meech Lake Accord collapsed, it was inevitably interpreted as a "rejection" by the rest of Canada of Quebec's aspirations. However, the overt and clear symbolism of the constitutional negotiations as a form of embrace or compensation for Quebec only irritated others who felt they too deserved to be recognized, affirmed and respected.

- **Constitutional Players.** Alan Cairns suggests that the Charter, and the intensely political process that spawned it, shifted the Constitution's centre of gravity to a more populist base.[2] A wide array of organizations and interests, including women, Aboriginal peoples, ethno-cultural minorities, disabled people and official language groups, fought over the Charter's final wording. As a result, many of them claim the Charter as their own and jealously guard their constitutional gains. The Meech Lake Accord was attacked by virtually every major Charter group. Women's organizations (except in Quebec), ethno-cultural groups, Francophone and Anglophone minority communities, and Aboriginal associations were the most visible and vocal. They were joined by a loose coalition of social policy advocates (who feared that constraints on the federal spending power would prohibit coherent new national social programs) and Anglo-Canadian nationalists (who feared emasculation of national governmental powers).[3] After Meech Lake, it was clear the constitutional process could no longer be a matter only for governments.

- **Issue Loading.** As the number of players multiplied, so did the number of issues and, perhaps more importantly, the *types* of issues. Reconciling competing governmental agendas was difficult enough, as the 1982 experience had shown. With the Meech Lake Accord, however, a host of Charter groups and others demanded to be part of the process. Even if, in a literal sense, they could not be at the table, their concerns would have to be addressed in a new round. Indeed, the final agonies of Meech Lake reinforced the importance of excluded interests. The first ministers' agreement of June 9, 1990 (an effort to save the Meech Lake Accord) promised further constitutional discussions on gender equality rights, the role of the territories, official language minorities, Aboriginal rights, a statement of "constitutional recognitions" (Canada clause) and the Senate—an agenda clearly designed to appeal to the loose but large coalition of Meech Lake opponents.

- **Post-Meech Lake Strategies.** The confluence of symbols, players and issues constrained the strategic options open to Brian Mulroney, Robert Bourassa and the other premiers. First, after the collapse of the Meech Lake Accord—almost universally regarded in Quebec as an absolute minimum—it was impossible for Bourassa to engage openly in another round of negotiations. And yet, the Quebec premier was not warm to sovereignty, so his strategic challenge lay in keeping the door open to negotiations while remaining apart from any humiliating horse-trading.[4] Second, the federal government knew that, if it were to pursue negotiations, it would have to adopt a much more open and democratic process.[5] The issues would have to be discussed thoroughly and broadly *before* decisions were taken; there could be no "seamless webs" as in the Meech Lake process. At the same time, however, the amending formula and federalism meant that at some point there would have to be intergovernmental negotiations. Indeed, the core issues from the point of view of Ottawa and the provinces—quintessentially *governmental* issues—had not really changed. These would now have to be addressed simultaneously with a range of other issues and a larger cast of potential constitutional players.

THE "CANADA ROUND"

While it was evident when the Meech Lake round ended that constitutional politics would have to become more democratic, it was far from clear what this would entail. Canada had only limited experience with processes other than executive federalism (sometimes supplemented by committee hearings). Moreover, accepting the objective of democratization does not necessarily lead to agreement on the methods to achieve it; the degree to which a particular method is democratic is a matter of judgement.

Two indicators that are relevant in assessing the democratic nature of a political process are 1) Who participates? and 2) How do they participate? The range of potential participants in constitutional reform is wide: from a few elected representatives (for example, first ministers) to all eligible voters. As for *how* citizens participate, the possibilities extend from passive attention to reforms decided by political élites to approval of amendments in a binding referendum. This section reviews the process of constitutional politics in the post-Meech Lake period leading to the Charlottetown Accord, with particular reference to these two indicators. The process is divided into three phases: 1) the cathartic phase; 2) the consultation and agenda-setting phase; and 3) the negotiation phase. This section concludes with an account of how it was decided to take the unprecedented step of putting the Accord before the people in a referendum.

The Cathartic Phase

The phase that began in autumn 1990 was "cathartic" because, at the instigation of political leaders, it allowed citizens to "let off steam" and included efforts (notably in Quebec) to overcome the disappointments of the Meech Lake round. The processes sponsored by the federal and Quebec governments differed markedly; the Quebec process set a new agenda for constitutional renewal and, arguably, widened the gulf between Quebec and the rest of Canada.

The death of the Meech Lake Accord meant that what most Quebecers had seen as "minimal demands" had proved unacceptable to the rest of Canada. It was, therefore, time to consider other avenues and, in Bourassa's view, Quebec did not have to wait for the rest of Canada to establish a consensus before examining its own future.[6] The Quebec government moved quickly to provide a forum. On September 4, 1990, the National Assembly unanimously approved Bill 90, establishing the Commission on the Political and Constitutional Future of Quebec.

The Commission's composition was unprecedented: half of its 36 members were members of the National Assembly, three were members of Parliament from Quebec and 15 were chosen from a number of sectors of Quebec society. Business was strongly represented by Michel Bélanger and Jean Campeau, its co-chairpersons, and four other members. The other sectors represented were trade unions, co-operatives, education and culture. The Commission's consultation methods were more traditional. It relied mainly on televised public hearings (see Appendix 5.2), and it invited submissions from a total of 55 outside specialists.[7]

While most witnesses before the Commission called for major constitutional changes, no consensus emerged on Quebec's "future" (this was not surprising given the almost even split between federalists and sovereignists among the members). Instead, the Commission concluded that "two courses are open to Québec ... a new, ultimate attempt to redefine its status within the federal regime, and the attainment of sovereignty."[8] It recommended the following process, which the National Assembly approved through Bill 150 on June 20, 1991:[9]

- A referendum on sovereignty would be held between June 8 and 22 or October 12 and 26, 1992. If sovereignty were approved, Quebec would acquire "the status of a sovereign State" exactly a year after the referendum vote.
- In the meantime, the National Assembly would establish a "Committee to Examine Matters Relating to the Accession of Québec to Sovereignty" and another "Committee to Examine Any Offer of a New Constitutional Partnership."

While the Bélanger-Campeau Commission was at work, the Quebec Liberal Party re-examined its own constitutional position. On January 29, 1991, the report of a committee chaired by former party president Jean Allaire was released. It proposed a new "Canada-Quebec structure" involving "exclusive, discretionary and total authority in most areas of jurisdiction" (22 were identified).[10] The Liberal Party adopted the report in March. Thus, by mid-1991, initiatives within Quebec had set deadlines as well as a threshold for assessing an eventual constitutional "offer" (although a number of political leaders outside Quebec called the Allaire report unacceptable).

Around the time the Bélanger-Campeau Commission was preparing to begin public hearings, pressure for a consultative initiative grew at the federal level (some argued that it would be unacceptable simply to wait for the Bélanger-Campeau Commission to report). What emerged was what one commentator later described as "the most eccentric and populist royal commission in the country's history."[11] The initiative—both innovative and experimental—was the Citizens' Forum on Canada's Future, chaired by Keith Spicer (who, for the duration, vacated his post as Chairperson of the Canadian Radio-television and Telecommunications Commission).

While the word "constitution" was absent from the Spicer Commission's mandate, its work was obviously intended to allow Canadians to "let off steam" about broader issues that simmered below the surface during the Meech Lake round (and would affect future discussions). The Forum was to provide "an opportunity to discuss the values and characteristics fundamental to the well-being of Canada ... [including] both shared Canadian characteristics and interests, and the identity and concerns of specific regions and groups."[12] As for who would participate, Prime Minister Mulroney said that "every Canadian who wants to will be able to have a say";[13] Spicer said he wanted to hear from a million Canadians. Mulroney also indicated the Forum should "use modern Canadian communications technology, today's electronic railroads, to bring people together."[14] The Forum used several innovative means to consult Canadians:

- A toll-free "Idea Line" provided information about the Forum's consultation process and collected callers' views.
- Some 5,300 group discussions were held, many of them led by one of the moderators engaged by the Forum, and others by various organizations across the country. The focus was to be on the 14 discussion points the Forum developed and, subsequently, revised when it became clear they were too long, detailed and directive (an example of the Forum's experimental approach and an issue that

provoked controversy among forum members). Those participating in group discussions, and others who received the Forum's information kits, were encouraged to send in an "individual response form."
• Six "electronic town hall meetings" linked participants in as many as seven provinces and territories; most were broadcast on the Parliamentary Channel simultaneously in English and French.[15]

The Spicer Commission encountered criticism (for example, of its initial $27.4 million budget) and considerable scepticism.[16] Its report of June 27, 1991 presented "findings and suggestions" on issues such as official languages, Quebec's distinct society, senate reform and Aboriginal self-government. Spicer endorsed a constituent assembly and leaned towards a referendum on constitutional reform.[17] As a whole, however, this was far from a road-map for Canada's future. Bearing in mind the Forum's deadline and hopelessly broad agenda, it was not surprising that it failed to "go beyond ventilating opinions on the country's problems and search in depth for solutions."[18] The Spicer report's diagnosis of the country's ill humour—particularly the anger with political leadership—was jarring at the time, but in retrospect seems accurate. Whatever its ultimate value, the Spicer Commission was a central element in a cathartic phase that perhaps was necessary before the items on a new constitutional agenda could be identified.

The Consultation and Agenda-Setting Phase

While the Spicer and Bélanger-Campeau commissions engaged in consultation, this aspect of their work was rather open-ended because neither of the governments concerned had presented a particular constitutional proposal. For this reason, it is fair to say that the "consultation and agenda-setting phase" really began with the release of the federal government's proposals, *Shaping Canada's Future Together*, on September 24, 1991. There is no doubt this was the broadest set of proposals the Government of Canada had ever sponsored. In part, this was a response to the claims of exclusion that marred the Meech Lake round; it also reflected the strategic value of taking account of "concerns expressed by Canadians from all walks of life" in what was called "Canada's round."[19] The proposals were relatively detailed (in some cases, draft legal texts were included), but they were not cast in stone. Prime Minister Mulroney stated that "we seek improvements to our proposals and we expect changes."[20] In this context, broad participation was actively encouraged: "Every Canadian will have the right—and the responsibility—to participate."[21] The chief vehicle at the federal level was the Special Joint Committee on a Renewed Canada (initially chaired by Senator Claude Castonguay and Dorothy Dobbie, MP; Senator Gérald Beaudoin later replaced Senator Castonguay).

While the Joint Committee had a demanding mandate (it was to report by February 28, 1992), it was part of a much broader consultative process, one without parallel in Canadian history. The comprehensive data on the principal aspects of this process provided in Appendix 5.2 lead to a number of observations on the *scale* of the consultations. During 1991 and 1992, a consultative body of one form or another was established in every province and territory.[22]

Only one final report (in the Yukon) was issued prior to release of the federal proposals; the latter thus provided a principal focus for the consultations (as the reports often acknowledged). In two provinces there were successive exercises. The New Brunswick Commission on Canadian Federalism was appointed in September 1990 and reported in January 1992; subsequently, the Legislative Assembly appointed a Select Committee on the Constitution. In British Columbia, a Legislative Assembly committee had a brief life during the Vander Zalm Social Credit government; another was launched early in 1992 under the Harcourt NDP government.[23] The numbers of participants were impressive, both in their own right and compared with the Meech Lake round (see Appendix 5.1). In each of three cases (Ontario, Alberta and the second British Columbia committee), over 400 individuals appeared as witnesses. The data on participation reported in Appendix 5.2 call into question the perception that interest groups "dominated" the process. Excluding the Bélanger-Campeau Commission, only the federal committee heard more presentations from associations and interest groups (categorized as "groups" in Appendix 5.2) than from individuals (during the Meech Lake round, more groups than individuals testified before five of the seven committees).

Finally, the consultations were marked by considerable innovation. A full treatment is not possible here, but a few examples illustrate some of the new methods used:

- Four consultative bodies included non-elected citizens: the Nova Scotia constitutional committee had only non-elected members; the New Brunswick Commission included only two MLAs; and there was non-elected representation in Newfoundland and Manitoba.
- Participation beyond the hearings process was often encouraged. In Nova Scotia and Newfoundland, a toll-free telephone line allowed callers to register their views. In New Brunswick, focus groups and personal interviews supplemented the hearings, and a "citizens' assembly" was held with a total of 60 participants (including the Committee).
- In some cases, an "interactive" approach was used. A number of provincial committees published interim reports, thus prompting reaction and providing a focus for further consultations. The Nova Scotia committee published a discussion paper in newspapers, along with a questionnaire soliciting citizens' views.[24]

One of the most innovative consultative exercises during this period was separate from, but linked to, the Joint Committee. By early November 1991, following some experiments in consultation—including town hall meetings, which were abandoned after no witnesses came forward in St. Pierre Jolys, Manitoba—the Joint Committee was at an impasse.[25] According to Arthur Kroeger (a senior federal deputy minister who later headed the conference secretariat), the federal decision to organize a series of national conferences meant that, if the Committee remained deadlocked, the federal government would receive some assessment of public response to its proposals; if the Committee resumed its consultations (which it did, using the traditional hearings approach), the conferences could provide "further insights into public attitudes."[26]

Four of the six conferences held between January and March 1992 were sponsored by research institutes; the fifth was jointly sponsored by the federal government and the group of institutes; and the sixth, on "First Peoples and the Constitution," was organized by the federal government in collaboration with the national Aboriginal associations. This unprecedented "outside" sponsorship entailed risk for the federal government but was considered an important way to foster a perception of neutrality and credibility.[27] Another fundamental innovation was the composition of the conferences. Newspaper advertisements invited prospective participants to apply; following a screening process, the institutes invited a proportion of such participants, ranging from 8 to 23 percent of those attending.[28] Each conference included 64 ex officio participants (principally the Joint Committee and government representatives). Associations and interest groups also accounted for a significant proportion of participants.[29]

While the conferences had no decision-making mandate, they played an important role in at least two respects. First, there is little doubt that the plea for accommodation by many of the participants injected hope at a time when the way forward was far from clear (CBC Newsworld allowed as many as 1.3 million viewers to share the experience).[30] In addition, the conferences played a role in shaping the constitutional agenda. For example, the proposed House of the Federation was virtually buried at the Calgary conference; the proposed new federal power to manage the economic union (Section 91A) was trounced in Montreal; and, prompted by well-organized lobbying at the Montreal conference, the idea of a social charter (proposed by Premier Bob Rae) moved well up the agenda.[31] What David Milne has referred to as the "feisty independence of the conferences," combined with their credibility and visibility, probably gave them an influence greater than intended. Political leaders could hardly quarrel with the main conclusions; nor could the Beaudoin-Dobbie Committee. As a consultation exercise, the conferences drew out and crystallized public response that was nascent or unformed (at least on certain issues) and helped improve the public climate. On these counts, this ambitious experiment has to be declared a success.

The Negotiation Phase

Throughout the intensive period of consultations that continued into early 1992, the next step was never clear. While the requirements of the amending formula meant that eventually formal discussions with the provincial governments would have to take place, some federal statements implied Parliament might act alone after the Joint Committee reported[32]—possibly by approving and providing legitimacy to "offers" to Quebec. It was doubtful this plan could have succeeded. While the federal government might have claimed it was acting in the national interest, most, if not all, the premiers would have condemned such a unilateral move, which would have undermined the parliamentary initiative. Nevertheless, the gambit remained as a fall-back and suggestions that it might be used coloured other governments' strategic calculations.

The Beaudoin-Dobbie report called for intergovernmental discussion to begin "as soon as possible."[33] Several premiers agreed and Ontario Premier Rae was particularly adamant in condemning possible unilateral federal action.[34] When Joe Clark convened a meeting on March 12 to review the report, Ontario caught the federal delegation off guard with a detailed plan for a multilateral process, most of which was accepted.[35]

While multilateral meetings eventually spanned a period of more than five months, the most intensive phase was the round of meetings chaired by Clark (from March 12 to June 11, 1992). This phase, while rooted within the structures of executive federalism, departed from the traditional intergovernmental process. First, the number of delegations was increased. The federal and provincial governments (excluding Quebec during this phase) were joined by leaders of the two territorial governments and the four national Aboriginal associations (Assembly of First Nations, Native Council of Canada, Inuit Tapirisat of Canada and Métis National Council). Territorial and Aboriginal representatives had participated in the first ministers' conferences on Aboriginal constitutional matters from 1983 to 1987 but not at other previous intergovernmental constitutional meetings. A second departure was the extent of the support network. A co-ordinating committee comprising each delegation's most senior officials was established, along with four working groups for the following areas: people and communities (notably, the Canada clause and the amending formula); institutions; Aboriginal peoples' inherent and treaty rights; and roles and responsibilities (the distribution of powers, economic union and the social charter). The responsibility of chairing these bodies was shared. The co-ordinating committee and one working group each had a single federal chairperson; the other working groups were co-chaired.[36] While the number of officials allowed in the meeting room was restricted, those attending numbered in the hundreds: the average number of accredited delegates for the meetings Clark chaired was 289; at the Toronto meeting (May 25-30), 435 delegates were registered.[37] A further contrast with the past was the candour demonstrated in statements to the media. The March 12 agreement had indicated there should be "regular public reporting of progress." At the end of each day, and sometimes at other points, Clark and others provided a fairly full account of points of debate and decisions reached.

As for the agenda, the federal government had hoped to focus discussion on the Beaudoin-Dobbie report. However, the March 12 agreement made it clear that other reports would be "starting points for discussion." The broad area of responsibility assigned to each working group, the larger number of delegations and the norm of (generally) proceeding consensually led to an expanded agenda; this was particularly the case in the working group on "roles and responsibilities," where several provincial governments added items. While a broad agenda was strategically necessary, some have suggested that the longer agenda made the process more laborious and meant that a good deal of time and energy was spent debating issues lacking sufficient political support. Even so, the March-June process was significant because so much of what became the Charlottetown Accord was developed during that period.

In the absence of full agreement when the meetings chaired by Clark concluded, the spectre of unilateral federal action reappeared. Parliament was recalled for July 15 to "confirm an agreement or advance ... constitutional amendments."[38] Following a meeting with Mulroney on June 29, the premiers (except Bourassa) met twice and, on July 7, reached agreement on a Triple-E Senate. The reaction in Quebec was very hostile, but Premier Bourassa (reassured that the "substance" of the Meech Lake Accord was pinned down) agreed to join the multilateral process. He was present for the final four meetings chaired by Mulroney, which led to the August 28 Charlottetown Accord.

This period in Canada's search for a renewed constitution concluded with major decisions being taken in the same forum that had become so reviled after it produced the Meech Lake Accord. Gone were the numerous advisers and flow of paper so much a part of the Clark meetings; the approach was closer to the one

Mulroney used in 1987 and 1990. In the end, the country's senior political leaders alone struck the final compromises and hoped that Canadians, more than a little fatigued from the many twists and turns, would accept the outcome.

Settling on a Referendum Process

During the phases reviewed above, the possibility of a referendum on constitutional reform hovered in the shadows, but was never far from the minds of political leaders. Even so, debate was never really joined on the democratic value of this unprecedented step (there had been only two national referendums in Canada, one on prohibition in 1898, the other on conscription in 1942).[39] In the end, the 1992 referendums did not emerge by design; however, they carried democratization of the constitutional process further than generally expected.

In considering the option, political leaders faced the legal requirement for a referendum in Quebec. More generally, they were aware that popular support for referendums was considerable,[40] but were conscious of the political risks, particularly if the results reflected regional division.[41] While some political leaders were hesitant, others promoted the idea. Since its founding in 1987, the Reform Party led by Preston Manning had been a strong advocate of referendums on major public policy issues. The party gained influence in Alberta and British Columbia, both of which adopted legislation requiring a referendum before constitutional amendments were introduced for legislative approval.[42] In April 1991, federal Liberal leader Jean Chrétien suggested a constitutional referendum before finalizing amendments.[43]

The May 31, 1991 Speech from the Throne indicated the federal government would introduce "enabling legislation to provide for greater participation of Canadian men and women in constitutional change." By autumn 1991, it became clear that the federal government was considering a referendum as a way to overcome provincial opposition to a constitutional "offer" to Quebec (whether developed through intergovernmental agreement or approved only by Parliament). As Constitutional Affairs Minister Joe Clark put it, the purpose would be "to secure the agreement of the people of Canada, in effect to reach around those premiers who did not agree."[44] However, in the face of opposition from the Progressive Conservative caucus, Clark hesitated and subsequently suggested possibly relying on a series of provincially administered referendums.[45] The matter was put on hold until late March 1992 when Mulroney reportedly convinced the caucus that, because of the uncertainty that the multilateral process would lead to a firm offer to Quebec, a national referendum might have to break the impasse.[46]

When legislation (Bill C-81) was finally introduced, the sponsoring Minister, Harvie Andre, did not address the democratic principles at stake, such as how a referendum could enhance the legitimacy of eventual constitutional reform. He referred to the legislation as a "precautionary measure"; it was "a matter of management prudence" to have "this instrument at hand to use in dealing with any eventuality."[47] However, disagreement over certain aspects of the referendum framework strained the all-party consensus the Government had so assiduously cultivated during the Beaudoin-Dobbie process. Opposition MPs criticized the proposal because it neither limited the number of campaign committees nor applied spending limits (the committees were, however, required to register if they planned to spend over $5,000 and to report on their finances after the referendum). Some argued for following the principles of Quebec's 1978 Referendum Act: only two committees (one for each side of the question) are allowed, and each is subject to a spending limit.[48] In committee, government spokespersons contended that allowing only two committees would not likely withstand a Charter challenge. The Government agreed, however, to impose on each registered committee a spending limit based on the number of constituencies in which it intended to campaign. This did not satisfy the NDP critics, and all but five of the party's MPs voted against the Bill at third reading.[49]

The "instrument" was thus at hand when first ministers met in Charlottetown during the last week of August. They decided the proposed amendments should be put to a vote across Canada, with Quebec holding a separate referendum on the same question but on the basis of its legislation. In the near-euphoria of the moment, they apparently believed this would allow the formal ratification process to proceed expeditiously and avert the risks associated with possible changes of government (as occurred in the Meech Lake round). At the same time, this would get around the difficulty of holding referendums in some but not all provinces. Quebec's Bill 150 required a vote no later than October 26; British Columbia and Alberta had their referendum requirement; and Premier Clyde Wells had stated that Newfoundland would most probably hold a referendum on any proposed amendments.[50] As Mulroney explained later, the country's national leaders were no doubt aware that it would be impossible to explain convincingly why some, but not all, Canadians should have a direct say as to the country's constitutional future.[51] Democratic values may have been on their minds, but the referendum process that resulted from their decision can justifiably be characterized as democratization by default.

THE CHARLOTTETOWN ACCORD

The Charlottetown Accord was lengthy and complex, but had three noteworthy structural characteristics. First, by the standards of Meech Lake and federalist Francophone opinion, it contained remarkably few gains for Quebec. This is important because the process of constitutional renewal that started with the 1986 Edmonton declaration,[52] and proceeded to the failure of the Meech Lake Accord, was designed to bring Quebec back into the constitutional fold. Whereas the Meech Lake Accord consisted predominantly of Quebec agenda items (distinct society, immigration, Supreme Court, spending power and veto), these items became part of a much larger and more complex agenda reflected in the Charlottetown Accord. For example, the distinct society recognition, while stronger, was embedded in a much longer and more complex Canada clause. The proposed elected senate, revisions to the House of Commons, and the long and complicated section on Aboriginal self-government were moulded in response to Quebec's concerns, but eventually overshadowed the items that responded to Quebec's demands.

A second significant structural characteristic of the Accord was the bracketing or balancing of virtually every one of its provisions. If constitutional documents could be submitted to an X-ray, this one would reveal an intricate internal system of neutralizers or checks that reduced the impact and import of its central provisions. The distinct society subsection in the Canada clause and the Aboriginal self-government section illustrated this characteristic admirably, though it was also evident in the sections on the Senate and the House of Commons, the Supreme Court, and the social and economic union.[53]

The Canada clause would have been inserted as Section 2 of the Constitution Act, 1867, giving it pre-eminence in constitutional interpretation. The first section of the Canada clause listed a series of characteristics that *together* should guide the courts. Among these was the provision that "Quebec constitutes within Canada a distinct society, which includes a French-speaking majority, a unique culture and a civil law tradition." A separate section immediately after the list of Canada's "fundamental characteristics" stated that "the role of the legislature and Government of Quebec to preserve and promote the distinct society of Quebec is affirmed." Critics like Pierre Trudeau argued that the Quebec government could use this to limit English language rights otherwise guaranteed by the Charter. But the clause could be used quite differently, since it stated only that Quebec's distinctiveness "includes" a "French-*speaking*" majority. Presumably it includes other things, such as a multicultural and multiracial society. Moreover, the Canada clause also said that "Canadians and their governments are committed to the vitality and development of official language minority communities throughout Canada" and that "Canadians are committed to a respect for individual and collective human rights and freedoms of all people." While it is true that the special role for the Quebec government to defend its distinct society was included in a separate and therefore perhaps somewhat stronger subsection, these other provisions in the Canada clause might have weakened any appeals to the distinct society clause as a basis for the abrogation of Charter rights.

The Accord's provisions on First Peoples were even more baroque. The Constitution Act, 1982 would have been amended to recognize "that the Aboriginal peoples of Canada have the inherent right to self-government within Canada," and this right was to be interpreted in light of the recognition that Aboriginal governments are one of three orders of government in Canada. Aboriginal governments would exercise their powers "to safeguard and develop their languages, cultures, economies, identities, institutions and traditions and to develop, maintain and strengthen their relationship with their lands, waters and environment so as to determine and control their development as peoples according to their own values and priorities and ensure the integrity of their societies."

These provisions were hedged by a host of qualifiers. No new rights to land were created and no existing Aboriginal or treaty rights were to be derogated, except as specifically indicated in self-government agreements. Aboriginal governments would have formed a third order of government in Canada and, given the phrasing in the self-government clause, would have been empowered to pass their own laws. Federal and provincial laws could have been displaced by Aboriginal laws, as long as the latter were not inconsistent with the preservation of peace, order and good government in Canada. The Canadian Charter of Rights and Freedoms would have applied immediately to Aboriginal governments, but those governments would also have had access to the "notwithstanding" clause. A new constitutional provision would have authorized Aboriginal peoples to undertake "affirmative action measures that have as their object the amelioration of conditions of individuals or groups who are socially or economically disadvantaged or the protection and advancement of Aboriginal languages and cultures." This would have been hedged, however, in that such programs could not contravene the equality provisions in the Charter (sections 15, 25 and 28) or the Accord's guarantee that Aboriginal rights were to apply equally to male and female persons.

The Accord's third distinguishing characteristic was its tenuousness. Criticisms that the Accord would doom Canada to endless constitutional negotiations were correct. The original Charlottetown consensus was littered with asterisks indicating the "details" of a given provision would have to be decided in future intergovernmental meetings; most of these were simply rephrased in the legal text as "commitments to convene meetings." Some outstanding examples included the nature of the common market (the exemptions to the application of Section 121 of the Constitution Act, 1867, and the mandate, role and composition of the dispute resolution agency), the delegation of powers to the provinces and virtually all important clauses pertaining to Aboriginal peoples. The potential agenda for future negotiations stretched well beyond view.

These characteristics were the direct result of the nature of the constitutional bargaining process and the constraints and agendas that drove it. Quebec received little, in part because of its strategic decision not to participate formally in constitutional talks until August 4, 1992. At that point, the other players had been engaged in discussions for over a year.[54] While theirs was far from a united front, it was at least an intricate web of common understandings around key issues that made it difficult for Bourassa to find allies or trade-offs that would allow significant gains, for example, on the division of powers.[55]

The internal checks, brackets and neutralizers in the Accord stem directly from the issue-loading ordained by the post-Meech Lake process, including the need to provide some visible response to the consultative process, for example in a Canada clause; to respond to Western demands for a Triple-E Senate and Aboriginal peoples' demands for self-government; to respect the Charter and signal support for the dualist vision of the country; and to balance social policy advocates' interest in a social charter with business interest in the economic union.

The nature of the agenda facing politicians leading to the Charlottetown Accord also explains its tenuous nature. The attempt to constitutionalize policy objectives and political identities, undertaken in a context of fiercely competing localities and some measure of mistrust, could yield only generalities. Providing any *specific* gain for any one player was difficult without specific gains for others. A constitution without hierarchies or advantages to any side was only remotely possible within a duet of ambiguities and cross-checks. The nature of the Accord and much of its specific content was, thus, a direct consequence of changes in the post-Meech Lake norms of constitutional consultation and decision making.

THE REFERENDUMS

Unlike the Meech Lake Accord, which went from intergovernmental agreement directly to provincial and federal legislatures, the Charlottetown Accord was put to the people of Canada. Had the Accord passed, the amendments would still have required legislative approval, as stipulated by the Constitution. In Quebec, the referendum had been a tool to force the pace of constitutional negotiation and ultimately to decide on any "offers" from the rest of Canada. As explained above, from the federal government's perspective a referendum was desirable because 1) British Columbia, Alberta and Quebec were to have one anyway; and 2) it would, if successful, give the Accord the needed legitimacy to carry it through a potentially lengthy ratification process. One national vote, therefore, was actually composed of two separate referendums, following different rules and marked by different issues and strategies. Outside Quebec, a poorly organized but single Yes side was defeated by widely disparate critics who were united only in saying No to one or another aspect of the Accord. In Quebec, the protagonists were more clearly defined and united on both sides, and the issues hinged much more solidly on provincial political and economic autonomy.

The Campaign outside Quebec

The Yes campaign in English Canada looked unassailable at the outset. Not only had governments and Aboriginal groups agreed on the package, but the Yes side could draw on the money and organization of the three main political parties. Moreover, public approval ratings of the Accord at the end of August hovered around 60 percent. It soon became clear, however, that the Yes side faced substantial obstacles. First, the "élite" consensus turned from an asset to a millstone. Strategists had anticipated that Prime Minister Mulroney's unpopularity would hamper the Yes side[56] and tried to neutralize it by establishing a committee of "notables" or eminent Canadians to carry a non-partisan Yes message. However, the committee never achieved prominence, and the consensus therefore was framed as one among élites.

Second, the consensus and commitment to the Accord was weak. While the NDP and Liberals supported the Accord, they expressed reservations. Liberal leader Jean Chrétien criticized the economic union and Senate. NDP leader Audrey McLaughlin noted problems with women's rights, gender equity in the Senate and representation of disabled people and other minorities. Alberta Premier Don Getty announced that he would resign after the referendum and thereby weakened the Yes coalition in the West. In the middle of the campaign, Newfoundland Premier Clyde Wells sought specific wording on the Senate in the legal text (its powers would be "parallel" to the those of the House of Commons) before he would fully support the agreement and fight for it on the referendum trail.[57] Manitoba Premier Gary Filmon spent the first two weeks of the campaign in London and B.C. Premier Michael Harcourt, after an initial period of intense criticism in British Columbia, left for California.[58]

This uncomfortable marriage of politicians reflected the uncomfortable alliance of organizations blended into the Yes campaign's "Dream Team." In its desire to be separate from the three parties, the Yes side decided to build its organizational infrastructure from scratch, thus consuming at least two precious weeks. But this unified organization still consisted of representatives of three rival parties and so there were inevitable disagreements over strategy and polling.[59] It took almost two weeks to launch a print campaign, and the disarray was palpable enough that Torrance Wylie, a veteran Liberal and one of Ottawa's top lobbyists, was recruited at the beginning of October to head the three-party strategy committee. Moreover, senior strategists tried to run the referendum as an election, which it was not. Things were no better at the provincial level. The Ontario Yes committee only established local committees in the first week of October and, even then, in only 65 of 99 electoral districts. A spokesperson admitted that there had been problems in building a "coalition among parties and organizations that have not worked together before."[60] A unified Yes campaign confirmed the image of an élite cabal and yet produced a badly co-ordinated, rigidly monolithic and uninspired campaign.

Finally, in addition to unanticipated liabilities in leadership and organization, the Yes side had a difficult message to sell. At first, the fact that the Accord was a compromise seemed a virtue, but this very quickly turned into a flaw that bedeviled its defenders. Flushed with confidence immediately after Charlottetown, for example, Mulroney tried to identify opponents with the Bloc québécois and the Reform Party. "I know there will be fights. And I know there will be challenges. And I know that the enemies of Canada will not be happy and they're going to be out in full force. They will encounter me and my fellow first ministers at every step of the road, fighting them off and fighting for Canada."[61] The "enemies of Canada" line caused an outcry, and by early September, the Yes forces were conceding that opposition to the Accord could indeed be patriotic and reasonable.

The Accord itself was difficult to defend, as discussed above. It was complicated, tentative, ambiguous and entangled. Because the Accord was a compromise among fundamentally different agendas, defence of any one item would immediately arouse suspicions that others had been sacrificed. For example, every claim the Prime Minister made that Quebec's interests had been met convinced Westerners that Quebec had received too much. Given these impediments, Clyde Wells tried a new argument on October 7; rather than simply saying that the agreement was imperfect, he claimed it was the best basis for constitutional negotiations over the next 20 or 30 years, or longer to come up with something "perfect." As he said in British Columbia, "Even if you don't agree that it's perfect, consider whether it's the right thing to do under the circumstances for an interim period."[62] But this argument simply reinforced the No side's claims that the Accord guaranteed perpetual constitutional bickering.

Given the structural weaknesses in its positive arguments, the Yes side increasingly focused on the negative consequences of a No vote through the referendum; Yes campaign discourse began to stress that a No would be the beginning of the dismantling of Canada. On September 28 the Prime Minister publicly tore up a list of 31 Quebec gains to show how the province would suffer without the Accord, and the Canadian dollar plunged by 0.51 cents against the U.S. dollar.[63] By mid-October, the financial markets had calmed down, the Canadian dollar had firmed and interest rates had fallen. Worries about the consequences of a No subsided. Given that the immediate result of a No vote would be the status quo, the "collapse of Canada" argument was discounted.

The liabilities of the Yes campaign in English Canada contributed to, and were magnified by, the unanticipated advantages on the No side. A Yes referendum victory had to carry every province; a No victory needed only one provincial rejection. The Yes campaign had to unite around the substance of the Accord; the No side did not have to co-ordinate at all, and indeed this was one of its major strengths. Mutually incompatible political interests from every corner of the political spectrum could attack the Accord for their own reasons and still contribute to a chorus of No's. They included Trudeau nationalists, radical feminists, English-rights groups, treaty Indians, groups representing disabled people and native women, as well as the Reform Party, and Liberals in British

Columbia and Manitoba; the list of opponents was a kaleido-scope of negatives. Given the Accord's character as a web of compromises and trade-offs, virtually every provision had the potential to mobilize some dissatisfied constituency. The No forces outside Quebec nevertheless developed four broad themes early in the campaign.

- **An Undermined Charter/National Government.** The new Canada clause, it was argued, would establish a "hierarchy of rights," giving the Quebec government special powers to promote Quebec's "distinct society," but would threaten the rights of women (who were mentioned in the clause) and disabled people (who were not). The Coalition of Provincial Organizations of the Handicapped (COPOH) said the exclusion of disabled people from the Accord was a "slap in the face" because handicapped individuals would have fewer rights than women or racial minorities.[64] The National Action Committee on the Status of Women (NAC) opposed the deal as "bad for women," although it also attacked the exclusion of the disabled people, visible minorities, and gays and lesbians, along with the Accord's spending power provisions (the NAC said the latter would make it impossible to exert national leadership in new social programs).

- **An Unworkable Government.** It was claimed that the Accord's institutional provisions on the House of Commons and the Senate, along with the likelihood of more intergovernmental negotiations to resolve asterisked items, would create political sclerosis. Articulated most clearly by the Reform Party, this argument claimed that the Accord's version of the Triple-E Senate was anaemic as well as impractical. Moreover, it had been won with the compromise of assuring Quebec that its representation in the House of Commons would never fall below 25 percent. An October 9 a *Globe and Mail* poll on the Quebec guarantee found support levels in British Columbia, the Prairies, Ontario and Atlantic Canada of only 11, 10, 15 and 26 percent, respectively. In Quebec, the proposal was supported by 76 percent of respondents.[65]

- **Too Much for Quebec.** It was argued that the Accord conceded special claims and powers to Quebec. The same *Globe and Mail* poll cited above found that while Quebecers supported the distinct society provision by a margin of 85 percent, the majority of non-Quebecers rejected it. Among No voters outside Quebec, 87 percent felt the Accord would give too much to Quebec; even Yes supporters agreed by a margin of 61 percent.[66] A *Maclean's*/Decima poll conducted on referendum day found that, while there was little common ground among non-Quebecers who voted No, the proposition that "Quebec got too much" was their leading reason.[67] Pierre Trudeau's *Maclean's/ L'Actualité* essay in late September provided intellectual legitimacy for anti-Quebec sentiments by arguing that Quebec's constitutional strategy was to blackmail English Canada with a series of escalating and insatiable "traditional demands"; the only way to stop incipient separatism was to call its bluff and refuse to accede.

- **Aboriginal Government.** Ovide Mercredi, the Grand Chief of the Assembly of First Nations (AFN), believed the Accord's promises of Aboriginal self-government marked a huge step forward for Canada's Aboriginal peoples, but he soon faced opposition from treaty Indians and native women.[68] The 61 chiefs in Manitoba reversed their initial support by early October, claiming that existing treaty rights would be eroded under new agreements struck with Ottawa and the provinces. The Manitoba chiefs felt Quebec was getting too much. Phil Fontaine, Grand Chief of the Assembly of Manitoba Chiefs (and Mercredi's rival for Grand Chief of the AFN), noted: "When we were instrumental in stopping the Meech Lake accord, we thought that what was being given to Quebec made everyone else into second-class citizens. This latest deal confirms Quebec's desire for superiority." The chiefs were also worried about trying to deal simultaneously with Métis and Inuit: "How can Canada meet its obligations to those of us it has failed in the last 125 years when you include the Métis and Inuit in this package and give them the same status?" opined Fontaine.[69] In addition, the Native Women's Association of Canada (NWAC) launched a court challenge to both the process and content of the Accord, arguing that designated Aboriginal associations were "male-dominated" and that the limited participation of Aboriginal women violated Charter guarantees of gender equality. The Federal Court of Appeal did not grant the remedies NWAC sought (increased funding and participation in first ministers' meetings) but did declare that Aboriginal women's freedom of expression had been restricted.[70]

There was much more to the No arguments outside Quebec than these four themes—including objections that the Accord did not go *far enough* in recognizing Quebec's distinct society and that it gave *too much* power to the Charter and the courts.[71] Despite the fragmentation of its message, the No side managed to weave together a vibrant tapestry of regional resentments against Quebec, group rivalries over status and rights, and nationalist support for central institutions. Yet, despite a consultative process wider and lengthier than any previous one in Canadian history, the Accord was still criticized as the product of élites.

The Campaign in Quebec

While the debate in the rest of Canada at times appeared fragmented because of the number of spokespersons and their differing priorities, in Quebec the focus was predominantly on the interpretation given to the Accord by two people: Premier Robert Bourassa and Parti québécois leader Jacques Parizeau. Interventions from federal spokespersons (Prime Minister Mulroney made a number of visits to Quebec) were fairly peripheral to a contest which, in many respects, resembled a provincial election. The No campaign accommodated Bloc québécois leader Lucien Bouchard without compromising Parizeau's lead role; Liberal dissidents such as Jean Allaire and Mario Dumont, President of the party's youth wing, also settled among the No forces.[72]

A further contrast with events in the rest of Canada was that the Quebec campaigns were launched quickly. In part, this reflected the foregone conclusion that the two party leaders would head the Yes and No committees. Furthermore, it was also necessary to proceed quickly in the National Assembly. Although Bill 36 (adopted in June 1992) had compressed the referendum timetable, the question had to be tabled in the National Assembly by September 9 in order to hold a referendum on October 26. In addition, Bill 150 had to be amended to stipulate that the referendum would be on the Charlottetown agreement rather than sovereignty. The National Assembly was convened on September 3, following approval of the Accord by a special convention of the Liberal Party on August 29, and amendments (Bill 44) were adopted on September 8. The question, identical in wording to the one Parliament later approved, was tabled on September 9 and adopted on September 16.

The two leaders' speeches in the National Assembly included elements of what became central themes in the campaign. Bourassa admitted he had not achieved all his objectives but claimed that "unprecedented gains" were made. He equated a Yes vote with political stability (thus anticipating the Yes committee's eventual slogan, "the future begins with a 'Yes'"). He admitted this would not mean the end of negotiations; however, as he saw it, approval of the Accord would end "this climate of constitutional crisis." A No vote, he argued, would mean the status quo; a setback leading to uncertainty.[73] Parizeau's principal lines of attack were set early. On August 24, he publicly questioned the Premier's capacity as a negotiator, saying Quebec did not gain enough, and criticized the division of powers section of the Accord, claiming that it was incomplete and would lead to years of discussion.[74] In the National Assembly he raised the tone, suggesting the Accord would constitutionalize discussions and disagreements ("chicanes"). In his view, a No vote would not mean uncertainty; rather, uncertainty would result if the "proposals" were constitutionalized (later, the No committee's slogan was "at this price, the answer is 'No'").[75]

Further damage to the Yes side resulted from an incident involving two of Bourassa's advisers. On September 14 Diane Wilhelmy, Bourassa's Deputy Minister of Intergovernmental Affairs, obtained an injunction preventing radio station CJRP Radiomutuel in Quebec City from broadcasting the tape of a cellular telephone conversation she had had with André Tremblay, a constitutional adviser to the Premier. Two days later, *The Globe and Mail* published extracts of the conversation in its editions outside Quebec. The *Globe* article focused on the two advisers' severe disappointment that Quebec had settled for "so little," particularly on the division of powers; Wilhelmy was quoted as saying: "It's a national disgrace, we should have left.... What a humiliation to arrive at such a point."[76]

During the ensuing two weeks, what came to be referred to as "l'affaire Wilhelmy" illustrated the difficulty facing those seeking to suppress information (even if obtained through questionable means[77]) in an era of photocopiers, fax machines and the Canadian Charter of Rights and Freedoms. The *Globe* article, faxed from elsewhere in Canada, quickly circulated among interested Quebecers. Part of it was read into the record of the

National Assembly by Parti québécois member Richard Holden; press reports thus included certain damaging passages of the Wilhelmy-Tremblay conversation.

On September 30, Wilhelmy reached an agreement with media representatives opposed to the injunction. A transcript of most of the conversation was released, on the condition that the recording not be played on radio or television. Arguably, publication of the transcript[78] had little effect since its essence was already in the public domain. However, the text corroborated what the headlines had said two weeks earlier. The impression was confirmed by reports of Tremblay's overly candid remarks to a committee of the Quebec Chamber of Commerce about Bourassa being exhausted towards the end of the constitutional negotiations[79] and by the comments of Moe Sihota, British Columbia's Intergovernmental Affairs Minister, to the effect that Bourassa "hit a brick wall."[80] While Bourassa continued to refer to Quebec's gains, "l'affaire Wilhelmy" left the Yes side at a disadvantage in countering the No committee's claim that Quebec had gained no new ground.

Mishaps thus put the Yes campaign on the defensive well before the writ was issued on September 27. Poll results reinforced the impression of waging an uphill battle. Here again, there was a contrast with the rest of Canada. Based on a review of publicly reported weekly CROP polls, the Yes side in Quebec never had the lead, even in the early days after the agreement was reached. The CROP poll conducted between August 25 and 28 indicated 41 percent opposed and 37 percent in support.[81] In successive CROP polls, the gap widened; according to the poll conducted between October 19 and 22, support for No was 52 percent, with 31 percent for Yes.[82]

The Yes campaign had some reason to be heartened by the outcome of the televised leaders' debate. Leading commentators credited Bourassa with a strong performance and a willingness to defend specific provisions of the Accord. Parizeau was criticized for tending to remain at the level of generalities and for giving the impression of already having embraced victory.[83] The post-debate CROP poll found that 46 percent of respondents believed Bourassa had won the debate; only 15 percent felt Parizeau was the victor. However, this apparently had little effect on voting intentions:

according to CROP, only 2 percent of respondents changed their mind as a result of the debate.[84]

Publicly reported opinion polls proved to be a fairly accurate predictor of the vote in Quebec. On October 26, 56.7 percent of Quebec voters rejected the Accord, while 43.3 percent supported it. The margin of 13.4 percent for the No over the Yes side was lower than in British Columbia, Alberta and Manitoba (see Appendix 5.3). Thus Quebec did not stand alone, as some thought might be the case early in the campaign when the Yes side was in the lead in the rest of Canada.

The Referendums and Democratization

Like any democratic process, the October 26, 1992 referendum can be assessed according to various criteria. One basic measure, voter turnout (see Appendix 5.3), indicates that, nationally, participation was 1.4 percent higher than the average for the last three federal general elections.[85] In Quebec, turnout was considerably higher than elsewhere; 82.8 percent of eligible Quebecers voted, compared with an average of 72.1 percent in the rest of the country.[86]

While there is no way of determining how well Canadians understood the Accord and its implications before they voted, they had ample opportunity to become informed. The federal government distributed a copy of the Accord to each household across the country. This may help explain the results of an Environics poll conducted on November 13 in which 70 percent of respondents said they had read at least some of the Accord.[87] In Quebec, each household also received a booklet, *Québec Référendum 1992,* distributed by the Quebec Chief Electoral Officer, in which the Yes and No committees stated their position. The publication allowed each side to communicate with electors in an unmediated way and to address substantive issues more fully than was often the case in the leaders' public statements. In Quebec, the leaders' debate (the first since the 1962 provincial election) attracted a high level of interest; a Neilson survey estimated that 2.14 million Quebecers watched all or part of the debate.[88]

Direct and indirect public funding helped the various organizations publicize their positions. Under the Quebec Referendum Act, the Yes and No committees each received $2,340,068 from public funds.[89] The federal Referendum Act did not provide for any such direct public funding to referendum committees. However, many registered committees benefited from free time broadcasts, which the Act obliged 10 networks to carry (except on stations in Quebec). Because the various Yes and No committees represented diverse interests, the free time broadcasts allowed a range of views to be communicated to voters.[90]

In Quebec, there was some discussion as to whether the legal framework unduly restricted the circulation of information. Under the Referendum Act, only Yes and No national ("umbrella") committees are legally recognized and allowed to incur "regulated expenses," which are limited;[91] it is an offence for anyone else to do so unless authorized by the official agent of one of the committees, in which case the spending counts against the committee's limit. Consequently, there is little room for non-registered entities to engage in spending related to the referendum options. While such restrictions on "independent expenditures" were upheld in court as recently as July 1992,[92] the definition of "regulated expenses" and the exemptions leave some room for interpretation.

For example, after seeking the advice of Pierre-F. Côté, Quebec Chief Electoral Officer, the Royal Bank of Canada decided not to distribute within Quebec the study it had commissioned on the potential impact of Quebec sovereignty. According to a press report, Côté had concluded that the study (which did not examine the Accord) could be considered as advertising directly favouring the Yes side.[93] Quebecers nevertheless learned about the study's conclusions because the Referendum Act does not restrict the media from reporting the details of a document held back from circulation; in addition, as with the Wilhelmy-Tremblay transcript, copies were obtained from outside the province. Later in the campaign, Côté reportedly considered but decided not to disallow distribution of the text of Pierre Trudeau's address at "La Maison du Egg Roll."[94]

Incidents such as these underline the tension between allowing free circulation of information and the principle—also eminently democratic—of fostering equity or "fair play" through spending limits. The latter risk losing their effectiveness if there are no checks on independent expenditures that directly support or oppose one side or the other (or if, as was the case at the federal level, government advertising is unchecked). However, the credibility of the legal framework may also be compromised if more general publications or assessments are barred from circulation. A less restrictive interpretation of the Quebec Referendum Act would have been more in keeping with the objective of full and open debate.

Looking at the referendum campaigns more generally, it is fair to say that those who perhaps underestimated Canadians' political astuteness were disappointed. A significant segment of the population did not seem greatly influenced by arguments about dire consequences and efforts to attach a broader meaning to the vote. While scepticism towards political leaders was no doubt part of this, the opportunities to become informed, both during the referendum period and earlier, may well have helped Canadians focus on the particular decision they had been invited to take in this unprecedented democratic exercise.

THE CONSTITUTION AND
CANADIAN DEMOCRACY

How democratic was the process leading to Canada's 1992 referendums, and what will be the effects in the constitutional domain and on the development of public policy more generally? As we have argued, the democratic nature of a process can be assessed in terms of numbers of participants and their directness of participation. On this basis, there can be no doubt that the 1990-92 round was markedly more democratic. It engendered efforts—many of them innovative—to broaden participation in the constitutional process and deepen the meaning of democratic rights in Canada. The numbers taking part were unprecedented: from the 2,400 individuals who appeared before committees, task forces and commissions (excluding the Spicer Commission) between November 1990 and September 1992 to the nearly 13.9 million citizens who voted in the referendums. This level of participation entailed significant costs; a conservative estimate of the cost of *federally sponsored* constitutional activities during the last round, including administration of the referendum, would be $300 million (see Appendix 5.4).[95]

Critics will argue that sheer numbers are not enough and that most of the new forms of participation were actually hollow and largely ineffective in the face of attempts at agenda control by élites. We disagree. While the consultations and referendums were imperfect instruments of democratic decision making, they met reasonable standards of participation and balance. Despite its apparent financial and organizational advantages, the Yes side lost. Interest groups were visible and vocal participants throughout this period, but individual citizens played an unprecedented role in public hearings, the constitutional conferences and, of course, in the referendum vote. Information was widely and freely available, and apparently read by millions of Canadians. The issues were thoroughly, almost numbingly, debated for an intense period of several months. While many Canadians were doubtless tired of the Constitution by October 26, they did not lack opportunities to participate meaningfully.

Yet many were unhappy with both the Charlottetown process and the Accord it produced. Critics have asserted that a *truly* democratic process could not have yielded so flawed a document. Our argument throughout this chapter is that the substance of the Accord was wedded to the process. While the broadened participation was laudable, it created a paradox. Not only the number of participants but their type increased, from governments and political parties to Aboriginal leaders and Charter-based groups. The number of arenas (a royal commission, legislative committees, other consultations) in which debate took place also increased. Moreover, in some cases, notably at the conferences in early 1992, "participation" extended to affecting both the agenda and content of potential constitutional reform. One consequence of these developments was heightened expectations. Consequently, when certain issues were dropped or received little attention, the Charlottetown Accord was criticized as unfair to a number of societal groupings. More fundamentally, as the agenda items multiplied, the negotiating climate became more complex and the number of linkages and potential trade-offs rose. Bearing in mind the differing interests of the 17 delegations and the nature of such negotiations, it is not surprising that few found their opening position accepted. The result was an untidy and unsteady compromise. The agenda had been greatly broadened, but there was considerable dissatisfaction at how far initial demands had been "bid down." The paradox is that more were involved, and in more meaningful ways, but many were still disappointed.

Another difficulty—discernible only with hindsight—was the challenge of reconciling the political dynamics associated with different phases in the process. At the time the multilateral phase began, the climate in the country seemed more favourable than even a few months before. While many accepted that it was now governments' turn, nearly six months of difficult private negotiations broke the perceptual link between the consultative phase and the eventual amendment proposals; the Accord itself was the work of governments and Aboriginal leaders. Moreover, the transition between the multilateral and referendum phases was neither planned nor smooth. As we have suggested, it was largely by default that Canadians ended up with a constitutional referendum. Those around the multilateral table apparently had given little thought as to how they would "sell" the complex and qualified "product" that emerged from Charlottetown, and key political leaders and strategists appeared uncomfortable with a campaign dynamic unlike that of a general election. Many Canadians' heightened awareness prompted resistance to efforts at cloaking the Accord in generalities and dodging substantive issues, thereby creating an opening for anti-politician, anti-élite sentiment.

What will be the constitutional consequences? First, on substance, the Accord may well become the floor for a future round. It is difficult to see how any proposal that did not include a recognition of Quebec's distinct society, a Triple-E Senate, Aboriginal self-government, and possibly a Canada clause and a social and economic union section, could be credible. Second, on process, any future round will have to entail wide consultations before formal negotiations begin. In addition, governments would be hard pressed to seek formal ratification of a future broad constitutional agreement without holding a referendum. We see this as a positive development; democratic approval of such fundamental changes is entirely justifiable.

Canada may have *de facto* altered its amending procedure in a most fundamental way. It is possible that bilateral or even multilateral agreements on minor constitutional changes might be approved using more traditional procedures.[96] But any proposed "package" that reflects a number of interests will immediately stimulate demands for wider participation and invite the paradox we have described. The irony is that, while the 1990-92 process witnessed significant efforts at democratization, the new (but still unsettled) thresholds for public participation, coupled with already difficult amending formulae, may make major constitutional change nearly impossible in the future. While the Accord's defeat drove constitutional issues off the national agenda,[97] Quebec nationalism and pressure for Aboriginal self-government could revive the search for constitutional renewal. The hurdles are now higher, and there is a danger that an inflexible amending formula in the face of fundamental demands for change may undermine the Constitution's legitimacy.

What of the referendum's implications for Canadian policy making more generally? The Accord's defeat appeared to stiffen Ottawa's resolve to protect its own powers, given the vague unease of many Canadians at the Accord's weakening of the federal government. The referendum also exposed deep anger, part of it linked to the recession, part of it directed at incumbent politicians and traditional forms of representative politics. A wide gap emerged between popular expectations—enhanced by greater opportunities for participation—and the realities of decision making by elected representatives. In future, governments might be more cautious about consultation and seek to govern even more by opinion poll. The latter is already in vogue in Ottawa, but it does not represent an increase in democratic involvement. A better course would be to assess carefully the opportunities for meaningful consultation, along with the constraints, before launching a particular process of public policy development. Beyond this, the uniqueness of constitutional politics suggests care in applying lessons to policy making more generally. Even so, the commitment to a more democratic society evident throughout this latest round means we should not discount the experience gained from Canadians' recent participation in seeking to renew the arrangements that govern their life together.

Appendix 5.1

**Meech Lake Round: Consultations
by Federal and Provincial Committees**

Jurisdiction	Composition	Hearings Process			Witnesses			Report Date
		Dates	No. of Sessions	Centres Visited	Individuals	Groups[a]	Govt/Elec. Reps.[b]	
Quebec	18 MNAs	May 12-25, 1987	8	Quebec City	17	20	0	May 27, 1987
Canada (Tremblay-Speyer)	5 Senators 12 MPs	Aug. 4-Sept. 1, 1987	15	Ottawa	29	48	9	Sept. 21, 1987
Prince Edward Island	5 MLAs	Feb. 2, 1988	4	Charlotte-town	9	21	0	May 12, 1988
Ontario	11 MPPs	Feb. 2- May 4, 1988	26	2	68	78	6	June 27, 1988
New Brunswick	7 MLAs	Sept./Oct. 1988 Jan. 25-Feb. 16, 1989	11	2	46	64	0	Oct. 24, 1989

Appendix 5.1

**Meech Lake Round: Consultations
by Federal and Provincial Committees**

cont'd

Jurisdiction	Composition	Hearings Process				Witnesses			Report Date
		Dates	No. of Sessions	Centres Visited		Individuals	Groups[a]	Govt/Elec. Reps.[b]	
Manitoba	6 MLAs; chaired by academic (non-elect.)	Apr. 6-May 2, 1989	12	7		211	93	7	Oct. 21, 1989
Canada (Charest)	15 MPs	Apr. 4-May 4, 1990	20	6		88	63	11	May 17, 1990

Source: See Appendix 5.5

Notes: [a] Associations, organizations, interest groups, spokespersons for political parties not represented in Parliament or a legislative assembly, local government representatives. When more than one person testified together, this is counted as one appearance.

[b] Government representatives (including officials); members of Parliament or a legislative assembly.

Appendix 5.2

Canada Round: Consultations by Federal, Provincial and Territorial Committees and Commissions

Jurisdiction	Composition	Hearings Process			Witnesses			Report Date
		Dates	No. of Sessions	Centres Visited	Individuals	Groups[a]	Gov't/Elec. Reps.[b]	
Quebec (Bélanger-Campeau)	18 MNAs, 3 MPs 15 non-elect. members	Nov. 6, 1990 - Jan. 23, 1991	11	11	74	227	1	Mar. 27, 1991
Yukon	2 MLAs	Feb. 25-Apr. 2, 1991	18	15	173	7	13	May 21, 1991
Canada (Beaudoin-Edwards)	5 Senators 12 MPs	Feb. 19-Apr. 30, 1991	32	16	143	62	5	June 20, 1991
British Columbia 1	14 MLAs	July 22-Aug. 8, 1991	6	6	91	9	0	Aug. 15, 1991

Appendix 5.2

Canada Round: Consultations by Federal, Provincial and Territorial Committees and Commissions

cont'd

| Jurisdiction | Composition | Hearings Process | | | | Witnesses | | | Report Date |
		Dates	No. of Sessions	Centres Visited	Individuals	Groups[a]	Gov't/Elec. Reps.[b]	
Prince Edward Island	7 MLAs	May 16-Nov. 7, 1991	10	2	25	9	0	Sept. 30, 1991
Manitoba	6 MLAs; chaired by academic (non-elect.)	Jan. 31-Feb. 12, 1991	24	5	172	56	1	Oct. 28, 1991
Nova Scotia	12 non-elected members	Sept. 23-Oct. 17, 1991	12	12	216	3	0	Nov. 28, 1991
Saskatchewan	6 MLAs	Sept. 23-30, 1991 Jan. 22, 24, 1992	7	5	15	15		Feb. 1, 1992
Ontario	12 MPPs	Feb. 4-Nov. 27, 1991	40	20	409	275	3	Feb. 5, 1992

Appendix 5.2

**Canada Round: Consultations by Federal, Provincial and
Territorial Committees and Commissions**

cont'd

Jurisdiction	Composition	Hearings Process				Witnesses			Report Date
		Dates	No. of Sessions	Centres Visited	Individuals	Groups[a]	Gov't/Elec. Reps.[b]		
Canada (Beaudoin-Dobbie)	10 Senators 20 MPs	Sept. 25, 1991-Feb. 11, 1992	38	14	75	175	47		Mar. 1, 1992
Alberta	16 MLAs	May 24-Sept. 27, 1991	27	14	420	126	4		Mar. 10, 1992
New Brunswick (Select Committee)	9 MLAs	Feb. 19-Mar. 9, 1992	6	Fredericton	26	18	0		Mar. 27, 1992
British Columbia 2	15 MLAs	Mar. 9-23, 1992	16	16	422	17	0		Apr. 2, 1992
Quebec (Offers)	16 MNAs	Aug. 28, 1991-Sept. 10, 1992	27	Quebec City	36	12	0		No Report

Appendix 5.2

Canada Round: Consultations by Federal, Provincial and Territorial Committees and Commissions

cont'd

	Hearings Process				Witnesses			
Jurisdiction	Composition	Dates	No. of Sessions	Centres Visited	Individuals	Groups[a]	Gov't/Elec. Reps.[b]	Report Date
Quebec (Sovereignty)	16 MNAs	Aug. 28, 1991-Feb. 11, 1992	38	Quebec City	44	14	0	Sept. 16, 1992
Newfoundland	8 MHAs 6 non-elected members	Nov. 12-21, 1991	11	10	56	17	1	Oct. 8, 1992

Sources: See Appendix 5.5.

Notes: The Northwest Territories Special Committee on Constitutional Reform and the New Brunswick Commission on Canadian Federalism did not hold public hearings and therefore are not included.

[a] Associations, organizations, interest groups, spokespersons for political parties not represented in Parliament or a legislative assembly, local government representatives. When more than one person testified together, this is counted as one appearance.

[b] Government representatives (including officials); members of Parliament or a legislative assembly.

Appendix 5.3

Results of the 1992 Constitutional Referendums

Province/ Territory	Yes (percent)	No (percent)	Rejected (Spoiled) Ballots (percent)	Turnout (percent)
Newfoundland	63.2	36.8	0.5	53.3
Nova Scotia	48.8	51.2	0.4	67.8
New Brunswick	61.8	38.2	0.6	72.2
Prince Edward I.	73.9	26.1	0.4	70.5
Quebec	43.3	56.7	2.2	82.8
Ontario	50.1	49.9	0.6	71.9
Manitoba	38.4	61.6	0.4	70.6
Saskatchewan	44.7	55.3	0.3	68.6
Alberta	39.8	60.2	0.2	72.6
British Columbia	31.7	68.3	0.3	76.6
Yukon	43.7	56.3	0.5	70.0
Northwest Terr.	61.3	38.7	0.7	70.4
TOTAL	44.6	54.4	1.0	74.7

Source: Elections Canada; office of the Directeur général des élections du Québec.

Appendix 5.4

Canada Round: Cost of Major Constitutional Activities

Activity	Cost (millions of dollars)
Spicer Commission	22.12[a]
Beaudoin-Edwards Committee	4.0[b]
Beaudoin-Dobbie Committee	4.2[b]
Canadian Unity Initiative, 1991-92 fiscal year	15.96[c]
Constitutional reform conferences (Jan.-Mar. 1992)	8.92[d]
Multilateral meetings (Apr.-Aug. 1992): operating costs	3.9[e]
Participation of Aboriginal peoples in constitutional discussions (Apr.-Aug. 1992)	8.0[e]
Production, printing and distribution of federal proposals, Consensus Report, legal text and related materials (Apr.-Oct. 1992)	21.3[e]
Toll-free telephone lines, guide/information distribution and other communication costs (Apr.-Oct. 1992)	12.3[e]
Advertising: production and purchase of television, radio and print advertisements[g]	25.0[e]
Support services for Minister responsible for Constitutional Affairs (Apr.-Aug. 1992)	11.3[e]
Public opinion polling on constitutional issues (Jan. 1991-July 1992)	1.41[g]
Federal referendum: administration	103.9[h]
Quebec referendum: administration	46.0[i]

Notes: Except for the referendum held in Quebec, all activities referred to in this table were sponsored by the federal government or Parliament.

[a] *Supplementary Estimates (B), 1991-92*, p. 61; Privy Council Office, Department of Finance, *1992-93 Estimates*, Part III, p. 25.

[b] *The Ottawa Citizen*, October 31, 1992, p. A3. The Beaudoin-Dobbie Committee spent some $1.45 million on fees to consultants (*The Globe and Mail* [Toronto], October 2, 1992, p. A5).

[c] *Supplementary Estimates (B), 1991-92*, p. 61.

[d] Information provided by a former senior staff member of the Constitutional Conferences Secretariat.

[e] *Supplementary Estimates (A), 1992-93*, pp. 71, 72, 76, 78; Treasury Board Secretariat, "Constitutional Initiatives" (Ottawa, n.d.)

[f] Does not include federal government advertising during fiscal year 1992-93 on non-constitutional issues related to national unity, including an estimated $11.9 million on "Canada 125," $6 million on "Knowing Canada Better" and $1.7 million on Canada Day (*The Gazette* [Montreal], November 25, 1992, p. B1).

[g] *The Globe and Mail* [Toronto], October 3, 1992, pp. A1-A2.

[h] *Supplementary Estimates (C), 1992-93*, p. 70.

[i] Information provided by a Quebec government official.

Appendix 5.5

PRINTED SOURCES

Meech Lake Round

Brock, Kathy L. *A Mandate Fulfilled: Constitutional Reform and the Manitoba Task Force on Meech Lake.* A Project Sponsored by the University of Manitoba Outreach Fund. October 1990.

Canada, House of Commons. Special Committee to Study the Proposed Companion Resolution to the Meech Lake Accord. *Report.* May 1990.

Canada, Parliament. Special Joint Committee of the Senate and the House of Commons. *The 1987 Constitutional Accord.* September 1987.

Manitoba Task Force on Meech Lake. *Report on the 1987 Constitutional Accord.* October 1989.

New Brunswick, Legislative Assembly. Select Committee on the 1987 Constitutional Accord. *Final Report on the Constitution Amendment 1987.* October 1989.

Ontario, Legislative Assembly. Select Committee on Constitutional Reform. Agenda: December 8, 1987-June 15, 1988.

Ontario, Legislative Assembly. Select Committee on Constitutional Reform. *Report on the Constitution Amendment 1987.* June 1988.

Prince Edward Island, Legislative Assembly. Special Committee on the 1987 Constitutional Amendment. *Report.* 1988.

Quebec, National Assembly. Commission permanente des institutions. *Journal des débats.* May 12-25, 1987.

Canada Round

Alberta, Legislative Assembly. Select Special Committee on Constitutional Reform. *Alberta in a New Canada: Visions of Unity.* March 1992.

Alberta, Legislative Assembly. Select Special Committee on Constitutional Reform. *Transcript of Public Hearings*, Subcommittees A and B, Volume I (May 24-June 1, 1991) and Volume II (September 9-27, 1991).

British Columbia, Legislative Assembly. Select Standing Committee on Constitutional Matters and Intergovernmental Relations. *Preliminary Report: British Columbia and the Canadian Federation*. August 1991. [Identified as "British Columbia 1" in Appendix 5.2].

British Columbia, Legislative Assembly. Special Committee on Constitutional Matters. *Report: British Columbia and the Canadian Federation*. April 1992. [Identified as "British Columbia 2" in Appendix 5.2].

Canada, Parliament. Special Joint Committee of the Senate and the House of Commons on a Renewed Canada. *Report*. February 1992.

Canada, Parliament. Special Joint Committee of the Senate and the House of Commons on the Process for Amending the Constitution of Canada. *Report*. June 1991.

Government of Newfoundland and Labrador. The Newfoundland and Labrador Constitution Committee. *Final Report*. October 1992.

Government of Saskatchewan. Task Force on Saskatchewan's Future in Confederation. *Report*. February 1992.

Manitoba. Manitoba Constitutional Task Force. *Report*. October 1991.

New Brunswick. New Brunswick Commission on Canadian Federalism. *Report*. January 1992.

New Brunswick, Legislative Assembly. Select Committee on the Constitution. *Final Report*. Fredericton: March 1992.

Northwest Territories, Legislative Assembly. Special Committee on Constitutional Reform. *Interim Report on the Activities of the Special Committee*. Yellowknife: March 1992.

Northwest Territories, Legislative Assembly. Special Committee on Constitutional Reform. *Report on the Multilateral Meetings on the Constitution.* Yellowknife: June 1992.

Nova Scotia. *Hansard.* Nova Scotia Working Committee on the Constitution. September 23, 1991-October 17, 1991.

Nova Scotia. Nova Scotia Working Committee on the Constitution. *Canada: A Country for All.* November 1991.

Ontario, Legislative Assembly. Select Committee on Ontario in Confederation. *Interim Report.* March 1991.

Ontario, Legislative Assembly. Select Committee on Ontario in Confederation. *Final Report.* February 1992.

Prince Edward Island, Legislative Assembly. Special Committee of the Legislative Assembly of Prince Edward Island on the Constitution of Canada. *Report.* September 1991.

Quebec, National Assembly. Commission d'études des questions afférentes à l'accession du Québec à la souveraineté. *Projet de Rapport.* September 1992.

Quebec, National Assembly. Commission d'études des questions afférentes à l'accession du Québec à la souveraineté. *Journal des débats.* August 28, 1991-September 16, 1992.

Quebec, National Assembly. Commission d'études sur toute offre d'un nouveau partenariat de nature constitutionnelle. *Journal des débats.* August 28, 1991-September 10, 1992.

Quebec, National Assembly. Commission sur l'avenir politique et constitutionnel du Québec. *Report.* March 1991.

Yukon, Legislative Assembly. Select Committee on Constitutional Development. *Report on the Green Paper on Constitutional Development.* May 1991.

INTERVIEWS

Eisan, Darryl, Intergovernmental Affairs, Nova Scotia. November 6, 1992.

Green, Wayne, Assistant Secretary, Social Policy, Cabinet Secretariat, Government of Newfoundland and Labrador. November 1992.

Hollett, Edward G., Special Assistant to the Premier, Government of Newfoundland and Labrador. November 1992.

Léger, Marc, Intergovernmental Affairs, Government of New Brunswick. November 6, 1992.

MacKay, Charles H., Clerk Assistant and Clerk of Committees, Legislative Assembly, Prince Edward Island. Various dates in October and November 1992.

Tanguay, Marie, Secrétaire de la Commission des institutions, Secrétariat des commissions, National Assembly, Quebec. Various dates in October and November 1992.

NOTES

We are grateful to the following colleagues for their generous advice and careful criticisms: Bruce Doern, Alan Cairns, Tom Flanagan, Alain-G. Gagnon, David Mac Donald, Susan Phillips, André Raynauld, Ronald Watts, Robert Yalden and Robert Young. We wish to thank Siobhan Harty, Policy Analyst at the Institute for Research on Public Policy, for her excellent research assistance and, in particular, for collecting the data for Appendices 1 and 2. Much valuable information was provided by Elections Canada, the office of the Directeur général des élections du Québec and various officials of Parliament, provincial legislatures, territorial legislative assemblies, the federal and provincial governments, and political parties; we greatly appreciate the co-operation we received.

1   Pierre Fournier, *A Meech Lake Post-Mortem* (Montreal and Kingston: McGill-Queen's University Press, 1991), p. 8. Guy Laforest, *Trudeau et la fin d'un rêve canadien* (Sillery: Septentrion, 1992), esp. chap. 1.

2   See Alan C. Cairns in *Disruptions: Constitutional Struggles, From the Charter to Meech Lake*, Douglas E. Williams, (ed.), (Toronto: McClelland and Stewart, 1991), chap. 4; Alan C. Cairns, *Charter Versus Federalism: The Dilemmas of Constitutional Reform* (Montreal and Kingston: McGill-Queen's University Press, 1992).

3   For an articulate version of this view, coupled with proposals for reform, see Philip Resnick, *Toward a Canada-Quebec Union* (Montreal and Kingston: McGill-Queen's University Press, 1991).

4   Bourassa clearly used the sovereignty option as a negotiating ploy to placate his nationalist wing after the Meech Lake failure. In early August 1992, at a Liberal Party youth delegate conference, he continued to try to play the nationalist card (calling Quebec a nation, a state, a people and a distinct society), but made it clear that renewed federalism was his clear choice. "Bourassa sets 10-day deadline to reach deal," *The Ottawa Citizen*, August 17, 1992,   p. A1.

5   On June 23, 1990, Prime Minister Mulroney said: "In the coming months and years, we must find a way to reconcile the need for public participation and [an] open democratic process with the legal requirements now in the Constitution." (Notes for an Address to the Nation, p. 3).

6   In the National Assembly on September 4, 1990, Bourassa observed that it was difficult to see a consensus emerging in the rest of Canada on either the will to reform the Constitution or how to do so. See *Le Devoir* [Montreal], September 6, 1990, p. 6.

7   Quebec, Commission on the Political and Constitutional Future of Quebec, *Report* (March 1991), p. 5.

8   Ibid., p. 73.

9   See ss. 1-4 of Bill 150. The Parti québécois voted against Bill 150; the reason, according to Guy Laforest, was that the legislation left the Quebec government too many avenues to get around holding a referendum on sovereignty. (See "Robert Bourassa et la maîtrise

du temps" in Douglas Brown and Robert Young, (eds.), *Canada: The State of the Federation 1992* (Kingston: Queen's University Institute of Intergovernmental Relations, 1992), p. 58.

10   Quebec Liberal Party, Constitutional Committee, "A Québec Free to Choose" (Quebec, 1991), pp. 35-38.

11   Michael Valpy, "Echoes of the future," *The Globe and Mail* [Toronto], June 28, 1991, p. A1.

12   Canada, Citizens' Forum on Canada's Future, *Report to the People and Government of Canada* (Ottawa: Supply and Services Canada, 1991), p. 149.

13   House of Commons, *Debates*, November 1, 1990, p. 15009.

14   Ibid.

15   The information on consultation reported here is summarized from Wendy F. Porteous, "Citizens' Forum on Canada's Future: Report on the Consultative Process" (Ottawa: Canadian Centre for Management Development, 1992). Porteous was Associate Executive Director of the Forum. An estimated 315,690 participants were involved in discussion groups; over 75,000 telephone calls were received.

16   For example, see Susan D. Phillips, "How Ottawa Blends: Government Relationships with Interest Groups" in Frances Abele, (ed.), *How Ottawa Spends 1991-92: The Politics of Fragmentation* (Ottawa: Carleton University Press, 1991), pp. 192-93.

17   Citizens' Forum, *Report*, p. 5. The main report did not present a conclusion on these matters, noting that "we must as a group leave serious analysis ... to specialists with more expertise and time than we have" (p. 135). On constituent assemblies, see Patrick Fafard and Darrel R. Reid, *Constituent Assemblies: A Comparative Survey* (Kingston: Queen's University Institute of Intergovernmental Relations, 1991); and Patrick Monahan, Lynda Covello, and Jonathan Batty, *Constituent Assemblies: The Canadian*

Debate in Comparative and Historical Context (North York: York University Centre for Public Law and Public Policy, 1992).

18   Valpy, "Echoes of the future," p. A1.

19   Government of Canada, *Shaping Canada's Future Together* (Ottawa: Supply and Services Canada, 1991), pp. viii, 49.

20   House of Commons, *Debates*, September 24, 1991, p. 2586.

21   Government of Canada, *Shaping Canada's Future Together*, p. 50.

22   According to Ron Watts, "the Charlottetown Agreement was based on the most intensive, extensive, exhaustive, and exhausting round of public consultations and intergovernmental negotiations that has ever been conducted in any country"; see "Canada in Question, Again," *Queen's Quarterly*, 99, 4 (Winter 1992): p. 797. To avoid excessive use of endnotes, sources have not been given for all the observations which follow. Readers are referred to the list of sources in Appendix 5.5.

23   The Members' Committee on the Constitution (appointed January 9, 1992) became the Special Committee on Constitutional Matters on March 17, 1992.

24   According to Brian Crowley, who served as the Committee's Secretary, the discussion paper thus reached some 300,000 households; 2,500 questionnaires were returned (Presentation to Canadian Institute of Public Administration annual conference, Winnipeg, September 1, 1992).

25   Meetings could not proceed because the Opposition members refused to attend. A senior member of the Committee's staff provided the following observations (confidential interview). The idea of holding town hall meetings reflected the influence of the Spicer Commission's innovations in consultation. Town hall meetings on Prince Edward Island had worked well, but the organizational challenges were greater in larger provinces. Some of the Committee's difficulties can be attributed to its tight

timetable and constraints on resources. When the Committee set its budget, it was conscious of media criticism of the Spicer Commission's spending. A higher budget would have allowed advance work to be carried out (none was done for the Manitoba visit).

26   Arthur Kroeger, "The Constitutional Conferences of January-March 1992: A View from Within" (Speech to IPAC/University of Victoria Conference, April 23, 1992), p. 1.

27   Peter Harrison, "The Constitutional Conferences Secretariat: A Unique Response to a Public Management Challenge" (Ottawa: Canadian Centre for Management Development, 1992), p. 5.

28   David Milne, "Innovative Constitutional Processes: Renewal of Canada Conferences, January-March 1992" in Brown and Young, *Canada: The State of the Federation*, p. 32.

29   At the Calgary conference, "individuals recommended by organizations" accounted for 29 percent of participants. See Canada West Foundation, "Renewal of Canada—Institutional Reform" (Conference Report, Calgary, January 1992), p. 2. In Vancouver, 47 percent of participants were from "experts/interest groups." See Harrison, "The Constitutional Conferences Secretariat," Figure 7.

30   Milne, "Innovative Constitutional Processes," p. 39.

31   On the economic union and social charter proposals, see the chapter by Miriam Smith in this volume.

32   *Shaping Canada's Future Together* stated (p. 50): "Upon receiving [the Committee's] report, the Government will propose a plan for a renewed Canada, for Parliament's consideration."

33   Canada, Special Joint Committee of the Senate and of the House of Commons on a Renewed Canada, *Report* (Ottawa: Queen's Printer, 1992), p. 99. For a summary of the report, see Peter H. Russell, *Constitutional Odyssey* (Toronto: University of Toronto Press, 1992), pp. 180-88.

34   "Ontario demands role in constitutional talks," *The Globe and Mail* [Toronto], March 3, 1992, p. A6.

35   The agreement was reflected in "Recommended Proposal for a Constitutional Process," an attachment to the March 12, 1992 news release issued by the Minister responsible for Constitutional Affairs. On Ontario's role, see "Reform process spurred by Rae," *The Globe and Mail* [Toronto], March 14, 1992, p. A4.

36   This information and the following observations about the working groups benefit from confidential interviews with a number of senior federal and provincial advisors. The working group on Aboriginal peoples' inherent and treaty rights was jointly chaired by three people representing the federal government, a provincial government and the Aboriginal associations, respectively.

37   Information provided by the Canadian Intergovernmental Conference Secretariat. Senior federal and provincial advisors who participated in previous rounds agreed in interviews that the number attending was unprecedented (although they noted that the greater number of delegations was a factor).

38   Notes for a Statement by Prime Minister Brian Mulroney, June 24, 1992, p. 1.

39   On the 1898 and 1942 referendums, see Patrick Boyer, *Lawmaking by the People: Referendums and Plebiscites in Canada* (Toronto: Butterworths, 1982); David Mac Donald, "Referendums and Federal General Elections" in Michael Cassidy, (ed.), *Democratic Rights and Electoral Reform in Canada*, vol. 10 of the Research Studies of the Royal Commission on Electoral Reform and Party Financing (Toronto: Dundurn Press, 1991); J.L. Granatstein, "Lessons from the plebiscite of '42," *The Globe and Mail* [Toronto], April 25, 1992, p. D2. For a thoughtful discussion of the role of referendums in furthering democratic values, see Patrick Boyer, *The People's Mandate* (Toronto: Dundurn Press, 1992).

40   In an Angus Reid-Southam News survey conducted September 25-26, 1991, 51 percent of respondents agreed that a

constitutional reform package should be approved through a referendum. See *The Gazette* [Montreal], September 28, 1991, p. A7.

41   This was particularly a concern in Quebec, where some remembered the reaction in the rest of Canada when, in the 1942 referendum, an overwhelming majority of Quebec voters opposed releasing Prime Minister King from his commitment not to introduce conscription. See Gilles Lesage, "Le NON du Québec à la conscription de 1942," *Le Devoir* [Montreal], October 2, 1992, p. B1; Granatstein, "Lessons from the plebiscite of '42."

42   See Reform Party of Canada, *Constitution, Schedule A* (Statement of Principles), especially points numbered 12 and 14. British Columbia passed its Constitutional Amendment Approval Act (Bill 81) on March 19, 1991; Alberta adopted its Constitutional Referendum Act (Bill 1) on June 26, 1992.

43   Transcript of a Speech by Liberal leader Jean Chrétien (Montreal, April 21, 1991), p. 6.

44   Quoted in Graham Fraser, "More questions than answers," *The Globe and Mail* [Toronto], April 14, 1992, p. A2B.

45   See Michel Vastel, "Au Canada de se prononcer sur les offres du Québec," *Le Soleil* [Quebec], January 26, 1992, p. A2.

46   Graham Fraser, "Fumbling on both fronts," *The Globe and Mail* [Toronto], June 8, 1992, pp. A1-A2.

47   House of Commons, *Debates*, May 19, 1992, p. 10839.

48   Critics at the federal level were joined by Quebec's Minister responsible for electoral reform, Marc-Yvan Côté (see "Opposition urges spending limits on vote," *The Globe and Mail* [Toronto], May 20, 1992, p. A3) and Quebec's Chief Electoral Officer, Pierre-F. Côté (see "Jugement sévère de P.-F. Côté," *Le Soleil* [Quebec], June 12, 1992, pp. A1-A2). On the origins of the 1978 Quebec Referendum Act, see Vincent Lemieux, "The Referendum and Canadian Democracy" in Peter Aucoin, (ed.),

Institutional Reforms for Representative Government, vol. 38 of the Research Studies of the Royal Commission on the Economic Union and Development Prospects for Canada (Toronto: University of Toronto Press, 1985), pp. 131-34.

49   On the issue of "umbrella committees" and the Charter see the comments of Margaret Bloodworth, Assistant Secretary (Legislation and House Planning), Privy Council Office in Canada, *Minutes of Proceedings and Evidence of the Legislative Committee on Bill C-81*, May 26, 1992, p. 3:101; Patrice Garant, "Un référendum doit être aussi bien encadré qu'une élection," *La Presse* [Montreal], June 3, 1992, p. B3. As amended (the Senate adopted Bill C-81 on June 18, 1992), each committee was allowed to spend an aggregate of 56.4 cents per elector in the constituencies in which it indicated (at the time it registered) its intention to support or oppose the question.

50   Bill 36, adopted June 19, 1992, shortened the referendum period (including debate in the National Assembly) from a maximum of 84 days to a minimum of 47 days. This allowed additional time for the multilateral process, a point the sponsoring Minister, Marc-Yvan Côté, did not acknowledge. See National Assembly, *Journal des débats*, June 2, 1992, pp. 1493-96. On June 10, 1992, Newfoundland adopted legislation (Bill 1) to allow it to hold a province-wide referendum and, on June 13, 1992, Premier Clyde Wells said, "I wouldn't bring [the proposals] to the legislature for approval without the approval of a referendum in Newfoundland" (CBC "Saturday Report", June 13, 1992).

51   "Mulroney sees tide turning toward Yes victory," *The Globe and Mail* [Toronto], October 23, 1992, p. A8.

52   The 27th Annual Premiers' meeting in August 1986 supported the idea of a "Quebec round" to deal with the five new conditions on the table with the election of a provincial Liberal government in Quebec.

53   All references to the Accord are to the "Draft Legal Text" signed on October 9, 1992, which itself was based on the August 28, 1992 "Consensus Report on the Constitution."

54   The July 7, 1992 first ministers' meeting on the constitution almost collapsed from the frustration of trying to figure out what Quebec's views might be. It eventually succeeded when the premiers simply decided to bargain among themselves. "The phantom of July 7," *The Ottawa Citizen*, August 17, 1992.

55   "Fight ahead for Bourassa," *The Globe and Mail* [Toronto], August 24, 1992, p. A5.

56   "Walking on a slippery log," *The Globe and Mail* [Toronto], September 9, 1992, p. A6.

57   "Politics intrudes on job of writing legal text of deal," *The Globe and Mail* [Toronto], September 29, 1992, p. A4.

58   "Fiery rhetoric leaving public cold, both sides say," *The Globe and Mail* [Toronto], October 1, 1992, p. A4.

59   "Reality shakes Dream Team," *The Globe and Mail* [Toronto], October 13, 1992, pp. A1, A2.

60   "Yes side sliding in Ontario, poll finds," *The Globe and Mail* [Toronto], October 8, 1992, p. A3.

61   "PM gears up to fight for accord," *The Globe and Mail* [Toronto], August 24, 1992, pp. A1, A2.

62   "Wells defends accord in B.C.," *The Globe and Mail* [Toronto], October 9, 1992, p. A6.

63   "Mulroney gets tough," *The Globe and Mail* [Toronto], September 29, 1992, pp. A1, A2. Later, the Prime Minister claimed that his tearing of the agreement was not impromptu, but strategic. It was designed to bolster Bourassa after the Wilhelmy tapes incident. He "had to go in" to turn things around and bide time until the Quebec leaders' debate. " Mulroney sees tide turning," *The Globe and Mail* [Toronto], p. A8.

64   "Accord puts handicapped in jeopardy, coalition says," *The Globe and Mail* [Toronto] September 4, 1992, p. A4.

65   *The Globe and Mail* [Toronto], October 9, 1992, p. A6. The poll
      was conducted by Com-Quest Research Group via a telephone
      poll of 1,526 eligible voters between October 1 and October 5.

66   "Quebec, B.C. heading for No vote," *The Globe and Mail*
      [Toronto], October 9, 1992, pp. A1, A2.

67   *Maclean's*, November 2, 1992, p. 17. This was cited as the main
      reason by 27 percent of No voters, followed by 22 percent who
      said, "The agreement is a poor one."

68   The Reform Party was the only prominent non-Aboriginal group
      to attack the self-government proposals, on the grounds that they
      went too far and would be too expensive. "Reform attacks native
      self-rule," *The Globe and Mail* [Toronto], October 5, 1992,
      p. A1.

69   On the other hand, Yvon Dumont, leader of the Métis National
      Council (which stood to gain substantially through the Accord),
      campaigned for the agreement as a true nation-building exercise.
      "Chiefs in Manitoba poised to reject Charlottetown deal," *The
      Globe and Mail* [Toronto], October 7, 1992, p. A7.

70   *Native Women's Association of Canada, Gail Stacey-Moore and
      Sharon McIvor v. Her Majesty the Queen*, Federal Court of
      Appeal, August 20, 1992, p. 15. Joe Clark tried to accommodate
      NWAC by having changes included in the legal text of the
      Charlottetown Accord to protect gender equality under Aborigi-
      nal self-government. NWAC was not impressed: "We're not
      happy, and we're not going to be happy until we can go in there
      and make sure these changes aren't taking away something we
      fought for," said Sharon McIvor, executive member of the group.
      It would oppose anything produced by the current constitutional
      process. "Wells, Clark agree on text," *The Globe and Mail*
      [Toronto] October 6, 1992, p. A7. In fact, NWAC launched
      another case on September 15, asking for an injunction against the
      referendum on the grounds that native women's interests had not
      been represented in the negotiations leading to the Accord. The
      Federal Court of Appeal rejected NWAC's arguments in its
      decision of October 16, 1992.

71   Harry J. Glasbeek and Michael Mandel, "Why the left should vote No in the referendum," *The Globe and Mail* [Toronto], October 19, 1992, p. A21.

72   Mario Dumont, "Libéraux pour le NON," *Le Devoir* [Montreal], September 10, 1992. For Allaire's case against the accord, see: "NON aux offres, et voici pourquoi," *Le Devoir* [Montreal], August 28, 1992.

73   National Assembly, *Journal des débats*, September 9, 1992, pp. 3308-09, 3312.

74   Parizeau argued, as early as August 23, that Aboriginal people received more than Quebec from the Accord. See "Même les autochtones ont obtenu plus que le Québec, dit Parizeau," *Le Devoir*, August 24, 1992, pp. 1,4); he reiterated the claim a number of times during the October 12 leaders' debate. The annotated version of the Charlottetown accord distributed by the No campaign contended that, compared to the recognition accorded Aboriginal peoples, recognizing Quebec as a "distinct society" was "very little" (Comité du NON, "Rapport du consensus sur la Constitution," pp. 14-15). On Quebec's "historic demands" see: Alain-G. Gagnon, "Canada, Quebec and Constitutional Impasse" in Abele, (ed.), *How Ottawa Spends 1991-92*, esp. pp. 64-75.

75   National Assembly, *Journal des débats*, September 9, 1992, p. 3321.

76   "Aide says Bourassa 'caved in'," *The Globe and Mail* [Toronto], September 16, 1992, pp. A1, A2.

77   Tremblay was speaking on a cellular telephone to Wilhelmy at her home in Ste-Foy. While details were not confirmed publicly, it was widely known that a journalist had intercepted and recorded the conversation.

78   *Le Devoir* [Montreal], October 1, 1992, p. A-4.

79   "Bourassa trébuchait sur l'anglais," *Le Devoir* [Montreal], September 17, 1992, pp. A-1, A-4.

80   "Referendum heat rises in West," *The Globe and Mail* [Toronto], October 8, 1992, pp. A1, A2.

81   Louis Felardeau, "Les sondages ne permettent pas de faire des prédictions," *La Presse* [Montreal], September 16, 1992, p. B1.

82   The polls were reported in *La Presse* [Montreal] on September 16, 21 and 28, and October 5, 19 and 24, 1992.

83   See Lysiane Gagnon, "Mince victoire pour Bourassa," *La Presse* [Montreal], October 14, 1992, p. B3.

84   *La Presse* [Montreal], October 19, 1992, p. B1.

85   The average turnout for the 1980, 1984 and 1988 elections was 73.3 percent. See Canada, Royal Commission on Electoral Reform and Party Financing, *Final Report*, vol. 1 (Ottawa: Supply and Services Canada, 1991), p. 52.

86   Voter participation in Quebec for the 1992 referendum was somewhat lower than for the 1980 Quebec referendum on sovereignty-association, when turnout was 85.6 percent (data provided by the office of the Directeur général des élections du Québec).

87   As reported in "Public Opinion and the Charlottetown Accord" (Calgary: Canada West Foundation, January 1993), p. 12. A CROP poll carried out in Quebec the week before the vote reported that 16 percent of respondents said they had read the entire Accord, and 43 percent at least part of it ("La majorité des Québécois disent avoir lu l'entente," *La Presse* [Montreal], October 24, 1992, p. B8). In a poll conducted for the Ontario government on October 19 and 20, 72 percent of respondents said they were familiar or somewhat familiar with the Accord ("Ontario knew Accord in trouble, polls show," *The Globe and Mail* [Toronto], January 11, 1993, p. A4).

88   *La Presse* [Montreal], October 16, 1992, p. B1.

89   Fifty cents for each name on the voters' list at the time of enumeration and on the register of electors outside Quebec at the time the writ was issued.

90   According to Fred Fletcher of York University (interview, December 7, 1992), some of the smaller committees produced rather creative free time broadcasts, and the national Yes committee found it difficult to respond to the range of views from the various No committees. In applying for registration, committees could seek an allocation of free broadcasting time. In order to qualify for the time, a $500 deposit was required; the deposit was returned if a committee was allocated free broadcasting time and used all of it. See Elections Canada, "Free Broadcasting Time" (1992). The number of committees allocated time on the 10 networks varied (there were 241 registered committees in all). For example, 34 Yes committees and 22 No committees qualified for free time on the CBC English AM radio network; 17 Yes committees and 14 No committees were granted free time on the CBC English television network (information supplied by Elections Canada). For an extensive analysis of the activity of the referendum committees, see "The Referendum on the Charlottetown Accord: An Assessment" (Calgary: Canada West Foundation, January 1993).

91   The spending limit was $1.00 for each eligible voter, which amounted to $4,872,965 for each committee.

92   *Robert Libman et le Parti égalité v. le Procureur général du Québec* (Cour supérieure, District de Montréal, July 30, 1992), pp. 40 ff.

93   Columnist Marcel Adam was highly critical of Côté's decision and expressed surprise that the Royal Bank would so easily have accepted it ("D'autres effets pour le moins douteux de la loi réferéndaire," *La Presse* [Montreal], October 1, 1992, p. B2). See also Lysiane Gagnon, "Non au charriage!" *La Presse* [Montreal], October 1, 1992, p. B3.

94   The decision was based in part on the fact that the publisher had planned the book before the referendum writ was issued, thus falling under an exemption from the definition of "regulated expenses." See "Le dg des élections a failli bloquer la diffusion du livre de Trudeau," *La Presse* [Montreal], October 7, 1992, p. B1 and Referendum Act, s. 404 (2).

95   In addition, millions of dollars in time, travel and related costs were spent by federal government departments mobilized during this period. For example, the budget of the Federal-Provincial Relations Office (in effect, the department for the Minister responsible for Constitutional Affairs) increased from $5.16 million (actual) in 1989-90 to $18.30 million (estimated) for 1992-93 (Privy Council Office, *1991-92 Estimates*, Part III, p. 21; Privy Council Office, *1992-93 Estimates*, Part III, p. 22).

96   As with the amendment on official language communities in New Brunswick, adopted by the House of Commons on February 1, 1993.

97   Federal statements in late 1992 indicated non-constitutional avenues to achieve some of the objectives of the Charlottetown Accord were being explored. Joe Clark suggested informal discussions on Aboriginal self-government could begin in January 1993 and that there was still widespread consensus that it would be possible to negotiate an end to duplication in some jurisdictions ("Clark undecided about future but still pushing parts of accord," *The Gazette* [Montreal], December 7, 1992, p. A7). However, in response to a post-referendum request from Quebec to transfer all manpower and training responsibilities, including the administration of unemployment insurance, federal Employment and Immigration Minister Bernard Valcourt indicated this was out of the question ("Ottawa balks at passing power to Quebec," *The Gazette* [Montreal], November 11, 1992, p. B1).

CHAPTER 6

Efficiency-Democracy Bargains in the Reinvention of Federal Government Organization

G. Bruce Doern

Résumé : Dans ce chapitre, il est question de quatre propositions d'efficacité démocratique qui sont les piliers de la refonte pratique de la structure et de l'organisation du gouvernement : choix quant à la taille du gouvernement et à la composition des services nécessaires dans les années 1990; choix quant au nombre de ministères et à la nature de la représentation; choix quant à la division organisationnelle des fonctions et des activités de politique; et choix à faire pour augmenter le respect des citoyens pour les services publics ainsi que la confiance qu'ils ont en ces services. Le chapitre se penche sur les choix récents faits par l'administration Mulroney et les compare à des changements récents survenus au Royaume-Uni, sous forme du programme Next Steps et de la charte civique sur les normes de service. Si l'efficacité et la démocratie ne sont pas antithétiques, elles donnent cependant lieu à des choix de plus en plus difficiles dans la mesure où les structures et les politiques du gouvernement peuvent à la fois rehausser l'efficacité et l'entraver, et le font. De plus, la structure de l'État est invariablement tributaire de points de vue divergents et équivoques qui envisagent la représentation démocratique comme un moyen et une fin en soi.

Abstract: This chapter examines four efficiency-democracy bargains that are central to the practical task of reinventing government structure and organization: choices between the size of government and the composition of services needed in the 1990s; choices between the number of ministerial departments and the nature of representation; choices concerning the organizational separation of policy functions from operations; and choices on how to enhance citizen respect for, and confidence in, public services. Recent Mulroney-era developments in these realms of choice are examined, as well as recent comparative developments such as the United Kingdom's Next Steps program and Citizen's Charter on service standards. Efficiency and democracy are not antithetical, but they pose ever more difficult choices since government structures and policies can be—and are—both efficiency enhancing and retarding. And the structure of the State is invariably tied to competing and often unclear views of democratic representation as both a means and an end in itself.

After more than a decade of bureaucracy-bashing and criticism of the very competence of government, the 1990s appear to be yielding to a call for a reinvention of government.[1] The call for reinvention and renewal stems from three converging concerns: a continuing need for greater efficiency in government structures and processes given the agendas that face Western countries, especially that of fostering international economic competitiveness; intense dissatisfaction with, and alienation from, traditional democratic politics and accountability regimes; and a latent and belated fear that a decade of deregulation and privatization, however much it may have witnessed the shedding of some activities that governments should not have been carrying out, may also have seen the gutting of some of the State's most basic capacities. Such capacities include effective representation, the ability to redistribute income from the richer to the poorer parts of society, and the capacity to set proper framework laws for the functioning of a competitive economy.

This chapter examines four efficiency-democracy bargains that are central to the practical task of reinventing government structure and organization.[2] Democracy and efficiency are not necessarily antithetical concepts. Each is often essential to the other's existence. But to some extent, they do collide and hence require the striking of bargains between them by different elements of the political system.

More particularly, the four efficiency-democracy bargains to be explored are

- choices between the size of government and the composition of the services most likely to be in demand for the remainder of the 1990s;
- choices between the number of ministerial departments and the nature of representation and who is being represented;
- choices between the organizational separation of policy functions from operational delivery activities and traditional concepts of ministerial responsibility for both policy and administration; and
- choices on how to enhance citizen respect for, and confidence in, basic public services given that citizens care not only about the input processes of government but also about the nature of the services delivered.

The chapter reviews recent comparative experience and analysis, and highlights their links—strong or weak—with Mulroney-era approaches to the structure of Canadian government organization. It is organized in five parts. The first section highlights some key conceptual issues in the nature of efficiency-democracy bargains. The next four sections deal in turn with each of the efficiency-democracy choices listed above. These sections examine comparative analysis including recent studies by the Organization for Economic Co-operation and Development (OECD), British experience with initiatives such as the Next Steps program for creating independent operating agencies, the Citizen's Charter on service delivery begun by British Prime Minister John Major, and Australian cabinet reorganizations which severely reduced the number of ministerial portfolios. These sections also highlight, where appropriate, related Canadian developments in the Mulroney era. Conclusions follow on the broad implications of these choices for Canada.

EFFICIENCY-DEMOCRACY BARGAINS: SOME CONCEPTUAL ISSUES

Two conceptual issues underlie the meaning of, and pressures for, the striking of the four efficiency-democracy bargains to be examined in the sections to follow: the nature of efficiency and its links to international competitiveness and organizational restructuring; and the diverse views of what democracy is or ought to be. I also stress that, in this diverse context, government organization is primarily a set of relationships with citizens and groups rather than just a bureaucratic entity separate from them.

Efficiency, International Competitiveness and Restructuring

Efficiency is usually understood to be primarily *allocative* efficiency, that is, the allocation of national resources to their highest value added use so as to maximize the total wealth of Canadians.[3] Efficiency also includes *administrative* efficiency, namely the capacity of the Government to achieve its goals with the minimum input costs. This second notion of efficiency is also vital because it is mainly the internal management processes of the State—the internal rules, norms and processes to which ministers and officials must adhere—that constitute what economists will often call inefficiencies and others will call the essential requisites of accountable democratic government.[4]

International economic competitiveness is understood for the purposes of this chapter to be only a larger variant of efficiency, albeit a vital one. International competitiveness imposes the inherent need for all Canadian policy makers to develop a greater capacity to adjust rapidly to changes in the world economy.[5] The core political corollary to this international rider is that it places a premium on the capacity of Canada's political institutions to obtain a working democratic consensus around key economic and social policies in order to face these global challenges. In many of these challenges Canada has international influence, but in others Canadians are policy takers, not policy makers.[6]

Efficiency is also linked to the larger dynamics of the organization of market-based production in the closing years of the 20th century. Sometimes referred to as the "restructuring" debate, the larger discussion has focused on the question of whether "western capitalist economies are beginning to generate entirely new forms for the organization of production."[7] Linked to concepts such as "post-Fordism," flexible specialization and Japanese-style management, these changes in organization suggest a profound shift away from vertically integrated "Fordite," or mass production based, manufacturing built on long production runs and point to a system based on two dimensions.[8] The first dimension is the need for more flexible production and human resource strategies, and the second suggests much more decentralized methods of production in both organizational and spatial/ regional terms.

Much as earlier centralized industrial processes helped form large public bureaucracies, so, not surprisingly, are these restructuring dynamics beginning to affect the nature of current public administration.[9] These changes are especially relevant to the discussion below of the nature of departmentalization and the separation of the policy and delivery functions. As we will see, some refer to this already as the "new public management."[10]

Contending Views of Democracy

The second conceptual issue is simply that of underscoring that democracy itself evokes many meanings and modes of expression. Various democratic modes and views compete for attention and support among Canadians in the 1990s. As other chapters in this volume indicate, choices tend to cluster around preferences for either traditional democratic representation through Parliament, Cabinet, political parties and established interest groups; or direct citizen representation and participation, often aimed directly at the public service as well as at the traditional democratic institutions. Structures and institutions such as federalism, the Canadian Charter of Rights and Freedoms, and international agencies become vehicles that can be used to pursue both types of democracy.

Of particular interest to us in this chapter is the fact that there appears to be a shift among many groups and citizens from demanding a role not just in the making of policy but also in some aspects of program delivery. Citizens also have many more direct points of contact, both conflictual and co-operative, between themselves and public servants.[11] These links have been developing at both the senior policy levels and the many points of direct service delivery. Public servants too, after a decade of being bashed by neo-Conservative governments and despite fears of greater privatization, are actively seeking ways to improve their own sense of self-worth and to restore pride in service delivery.

The above two conceptual issues regarding the efficiency-democracy equation lead to a further point that is too often ignored; government organization must, in the final analysis, be viewed as functioning in an embedded relationship with society.[12] Government is not just ministers and departmental bureaucracies in the abstract. It is also an amalgam of statutes, programs and policy instruments (spending, regulation, taxation, symbols) that interact with citizens and interests in a wide variety of ways. It is a relationship, not just a bureaucratic "thing."

These conceptual issues related to efficiency and democracy can be seen more concretely through the detailed examination, below, of the four efficiency-democracy bargains.

SIZE VERSUS COMPOSITION OF GOVERNMENT SERVICES

The first efficiency-democracy bargain involves choices between the overall size of government and the composition of government services. On the one hand, there is ample evidence from the collapse of the Soviet and eastern European Communist countries that monolithic and dominant states that disavow markets certainly produce an inefficient and uncompetitive economy, not to mention an undemocratic political system. On the other hand, there are certainly examples in the post-war period as a whole of countries with quite large state sectors (usually measured by public spending as a percentage of gross national product (GNP)) which have achieved both productive efficiency and social progress (e.g. Sweden and Germany).

Thus, it is evident that the aggregate size of the State can affect productive efficiency if the State is too large, but the issue of how large is too large is a matter of judgement. Equally, the size of the State can influence democracy through its infringement on the freedoms of some and its provision of needed services for others. Space does not allow a presentation of the data on Canada's size of government indicators compared with those of other countries.[13] For our purposes, it is sufficient to state that Canada stands, depending on the indicator (spending, taxation, regulation), somewhere in the middle of the pack among OECD countries. Canada's basic macroeconomic policies and actions have also been generally going in the same restraint and deregulatory oriented direction as have those of most OECD countries.[14]

Efficiency oriented concerns and pressures are likely to mean that the overall size of the Canadian government will have to be kept under stringent aggregate controls in keeping with the stances of its major competitor countries and markets. But it is the choices related to the composition of government activity, perhaps even more than its absolute size, that involve the crucial and difficult efficiency-democracy issues. This can be seen in two key examples: 1) functional areas of likely increased demand in public services; and 2) infrastructure and investment spending.

Despite the previously mentioned restraint policies of the last decade, analysts tend to agree that the 1990s will and should impose new pressures for increased intervention in three areas:

concerns about declining quality in education and health-care services; demographic changes arising from an older population and hence changes to pensions and health care; and environmental policy at the global, national and local levels. The burden of these pressures is that they suggest that governments will have to achieve further budgetary reform through changes to actual delivery, rather than through a repetition of 1980s-style controls on aggregate budgetary targets only.

The efficiency-democracy links here are complex but real. First, an expansion of demand for these services is likely and they are seen by democratic interest groups and citizen constituencies as vital for their own sense of what a democratic society ought to be able to provide. Second, there is wide disagreement among such groups as to precisely what these renewed services ought to be and how they ought to be delivered. Education and health care evoke widely different views about program goals and priorities. Environmental policy increasingly must address questions such as how much of policy can be delivered through direct regulation as opposed to economic instruments such as taxation and tradable permits.[15] Third, the character of these services, as distinct from social services delivered through simpler transfer payments to individuals, is such that very serious issues emerge as to how to secure efficiency in delivery. These services have the potential not only to grow but to grow explosively and inefficiently. Thus, earlier aggregate-oriented spending control methods are unlikely to be sufficient.

This is why so-called quasi-market approaches to delivery have been suggested and partially implemented in health care and social services.[16] Quasi-markets or internal markets involve the creation of more systematic buy-sell relationships among producers and customers (or their surrogates). The "quasi" aspect arises from the fact that the market is not a full-fledged one but instead may focus on improving supply-side or demand-side efficiencies. The logic in areas such as health care is that universal health care, combined with an ageing population and technologically expensive new services and cures, is creating a crisis in the efficient allocation of resources. A rationalization of resources has to occur and it will either come in the form of longer waiting lists or through other more sensible and explicit market-based methods. These kinds of pressures will have a major impact on the federal government even though it is not directly a health-care service provider. The impacts will first be provincial in nature but will quickly begin to affect decisions on federal financing.

The British have instituted a system of quasi-markets in their National Health Service and it is being examined in Canada and other countries.[17] In the U.K., special trust hospitals have been established and given increased independence to price and market their services. Many doctors have been allocated funds enabling them to purchase services from hospitals. The U.K. changes are radical and are clearly intended to overturn almost 50 years of traditional bureaucratically and professionally allocated services.

Analyses to date suggest extreme caution in reaching any judgements about the role of quasi-markets. Because of desirable and strongly held public and social service norms, there is strong democratic resistance to turning social services into market institutions. Early studies also suggest that quasi-market regimes will have to be quite tightly regulated especially to ensure that key aspects of universality of service are preserved or guaranteed. Nonetheless, once quasi-markets have been started and organizations/doctors experience some institutional independence as resource allocators, a constituency will have been created to press for more of the same.

Next, consider the issue of infrastructure and capital spending. Studies show that most OECD governments cut back on capital spending in the 1980s.[18] The consensus is that this has harmed economic efficiency because the underlying economic infrastructure for roads, bridges and capital works has been allowed to atrophy. An expansion of government investment (a bigger state) is called for in the sense of financing this investment, though not necessarily in terms of its delivery.

Indeed, the infrastructure issue raises a larger question about how capital investment decisions are accounted for and made in Canadian and other Western budgetary systems. The nature of the public budgeting system is biased against longer term efficiency-enhancing investment decisions because the system of budgetary accounts is essentially operational in nature.[19] Real capital budgeting or the use of social investment criteria are not encouraged. Spending on capital infrastructure or education is treated the same as spending on paper-clips or army underwear.

In summary, the link between the size of government, and efficiency and democracy is a complex one. The thrust of reform is likely to mean that Canada will have to restrain the size of government in an overall sense and in micro-industrial sector intervention simply as a result of economies becoming more and more integrated and watchful of each other's practices. But within this overall restraining ethos there will be areas where an expanded role for government can contribute to efficiency and, at the same time, enhance democracy through an intelligent and timely response to issues of great concern to Canadians as a whole. This includes a larger role in infrastructure investment, overall education and health care provision, and in key framework law areas such as environmental protection, albeit with a much greater use of complementary economic instruments.

THE NUMBER OF DEPARTMENTS VERSUS THE NATURE OF REPRESENTATION

The second efficiency-democracy bargain centres on the choices between the number of departments or ministerial portfolios in the Cabinet and the nature of representation. In efficiency terms, as the recent de Cotret review of federal agencies has struggled with, the question is whether Canada has too many ministerial cooks stirring the economic brew.[20] In democratic terms, the issue is how can a regionally and ethnically diverse country secure adequate representation except through a large cabinet, where decisions are actually made.

In recent years, the federal cabinet has consisted of about 40 ministers, one of the largest among Western governments. Both the British cabinet and the American executive structure have about a dozen major ministers or their equivalents.[21] And although the U.K. and U.S. systems leave room for various junior ministers and executive personnel to function in a second tier level, they clearly have fewer major executive departments headed by ministers (or ministerial equivalents) than does Canada. So, too, do the Japanese and Swedish systems.[22]

The Australian experience is also relevant to Canada. In 1987, the Hawke Labour government reduced the number of departments in the federal government from 28 to 16, with senior portfolio ministers released from detailed administration so that they could concentrate on broader policy. Initial assessments are far from complete. Some argue that budgetary reviews are now forcing a wider trade-off of resources in the broader groupings of portfolios.[23] On the other hand, one cannot show a direct link between portfolio change alone and enhanced Australian competitiveness.

It would seem reasonable to argue that a Canadian cabinet of 20 departments could function properly. If so, several practical puzzles would arise. The first puzzle concerns the identification of the portfolios that ought to be in a revamped structure. This requires a more detailed review than is possible here, but the Australian case is again instructive. Its 16 portfolios include Prime Minister; Attorney-General; Industry, Technology and Commerce; Transport and Communications; Immigration; Foreign Affairs and Trade; Employment and Training; Defence; Primary Industries and Energy; Administrative Services; and Arts, Sport, Environment and Tourism. It is not hard to envisage where interest group and regional battles over portfolios could occur if this were translated to Canada (e.g. only one primary resource department would greatly antagonize various resource interests), but difficult choices are inherent in the nature of the project.

A second conundrum concerns what to do with about 20 ministers who would get the chop. One option would be to institute a true system of junior ministers of state who would report to the senior portfolio minister rather than to the Prime Minister. This would be closer to the way the U.K. cabinet system works. The additional junior ministers would still be, in principle, superior to the current system because the legal and political basis of cabinet departments would be a much smaller number of departments.

The third practical issue concerns the indirect rather than the direct causal link between the number or complexity of departmental structures and efficiency and competitiveness. There is certainly a partial link. Experienced former political advisers and bureaucrats, such as Tom Kent, have argued that the Canadian cabinet structure is too unwieldy with the result that key ministers have greater difficulty keeping their eyes and brains focused on the medium- and long-term strategic issues facing Canada.[24] Kent advocates a cabinet of vastly reduced numbers. Otherwise, ministers will be prone to dealing with a series of ad hoc micro and sectoral interventions when pressured by special interest groups.

Bureaucratic theory also suggests that losses of time, money and scarce political goodwill can occur if the internal cabinet process consists of endless transaction costs incurred in negotiating across departmental lines. The proposition here is simply that the more ministers there are with real allocative or legislative authority, the more specific sectoral interventions there will be.

A final argument favouring a streamlined, vastly smaller cabinet focuses on the imperatives of international competition itself, on the one hand, and domestic interest group pressure on the other. Richard Phidd and I have argued, in a recent review of Canada's policy system, that Canada can no longer afford such an unwieldy executive structure, especially in the face of an ever-expanding system of domestic special interest groups.[25] An ever-greater premium is now placed on the federal cabinet being on top, and hopefully even ahead, of the international forces affecting Canada. This increasingly means the need to focus on, and be good at, dealing with the large framework policies needed for a competitive economy. It means that ministerial time spent on countless sectoral interventions is more and more costly relative to the challenges that Canada faces and, of course, relative to its severe budgetary deficit.

Moreover, such micro and sectoral interventions play into the hands of a domestic interest group structure that is more and more specialized and is, therefore, less and less likely to take a broad national and global perspective. The incentives and structures of Cabinet should increasingly be set up to challenge such a mélange of interests rather than to reinforce it. A much smaller cabinet would help force trade-offs to occur lower in the structure of the bureaucracy, leaving the broader *framework* trade-offs for the higher 20 or so ministers.

The counter-argument to the above points is usually dual in nature. First, transaction costs for policy participants is just another name for the democratic right to pressure and take part in policy making; therefore, much of it should not be viewed as a cost. Second, these transaction costs (democratic benefits) would also occur if there were fewer departments since such transactions would just become, in a system with many fewer ministers, intra-departmental battles *among officials* rather than battles among ministers. Moreover, democracy will not be served if only the weaker but deserving groups are restricted to the bureaucratic level while other well-heeled groups find direct access to the smaller cabinet. Ministers, however, are probably more transaction cost prone than officials simply because they are elected and bring more active political interests with them that have to be satisfied with real money.

The final question is: Where does a smaller cabinet leave the vital issue of regional representation within Cabinet? The Cabinet, according to this argument, is not just an executive agency but also a representative one.[26] The federal cabinet is big and unwieldy because regions must not only be accommodated but be seen to be accommodated. There is no doubt that regional imperatives are vital in Canadian cabinet-making and in the policy process. The extra regional imperative for the Cabinet has also arisen because of the weaknesses or skewedness of parliamentary representation. For example, there have been significant periods in Canadian political history when the governing party had virtually no representation in Quebec or western Canada. And the current appointed senate has long been discredited as a viable regional forum.

However, the federal cabinet and departmental structure has become big and unwieldy not just because of regional pressures. Growth has also been due to the need to symbolize, organizationally, new or emerging constituencies such as women, multicultural interests or science. It has also grown from perceived needs by prime ministers to reward ambitious politicians with the status of ministerial rank. In the 1960s and 1970s, when portfolio growth per se was most evident, the new departments were deemed to be (both in their time and subsequently) vital new aspects of the agendas of the day (environment; consumer and corporate affairs; regional development). Indeed, in a review of the main 30 or so cabinet portfolios of the late 1970s, I concluded that about half existed to co-ordinate the other half along some policy dimension of demonstrated political value or concern.[27] This could be seen as political pluralism triumphant or as a serious case of organizational gridlock.

The 1960s and 1970s were also times when portfolio structure was premised on the assumption of a fairly plentiful, or at least pliable, public purse. And it was a time when international imperatives, though hardly insignificant, were not dominant. Accordingly, the burden of logic in the 1990s seems to support the notion that efficiency in the important sense of maximizing the adaptiveness of executive government can be enhanced if the cabinet portfolio structure is significantly streamlined to a far smaller number of core cabinet portfolios, e.g. a dozen to 20. A somewhat greater focus on framework policy could emerge with Cabinet spending fewer transaction resources while keeping its eye more firmly on the larger economic and social issues.

But there is a necessary corollary to this recommendation for potentially greater efficiency and competitiveness. If nominal representativeness is reduced at the cabinet level, then it must be partly reconstructed elsewhere such as through strengthening Parliament, through the greater public scrutiny of special interests, and through devices such as an elected senate to improve vastly regional representation in national institutions. Some of these reforms were present in the defeated Charlottetown Accord constitutional reform package.

POLICY VERSUS OPERATIONS AND MINISTERIAL RESPONSIBILITY

The third efficiency-democracy bargain concerns the efficiency-inducing potential that might be derived from a greater effort to separate the policy from the operational, or delivery, aspects of public services. In this regard, I focus particularly on the Next Steps agency program that has been under way in the United Kingdom since 1988. Over half of the executive aspects of British government have been devolved into operationally independent agencies functioning on a virtually contractual basis with the parent department headed by the minister.[28] The Mulroney government's experimentation with such agencies has been much more modest. Fourteen special operating agencies have been launched including the Passport Office, the Government Telecommunications Agency, Consulting and Audit Canada, and the Intellectual Property Directorate.

The broad thrust of these policy-operation structural changes, along with privatization and the previously mentioned use of quasi-market approaches, has been characterized increasingly as the "new public management."[29] To appreciate the nature of this reform thrust, one must compare it with what would be called the old (but still significantly present) public management. This could be considered to be public administration functioning on classic Weberian lines and seeking to promote good responsible administration. The notion of responsibility evoked a primary concern with the public service's capacity to serve the elected government of the day with sound policy advice and to ensure accountability.[30] The focus here was also on input controls rather than on an output-oriented approach. When linked to our earlier discussion of the restructuring debate, the Weberian or large hierarchical bureaucracies were—and are—the structural parallel to Fordite private production systems.

A vital manifestation of this traditional system, especially in the context of cabinet-parliamentary government, is in the basic democratic principle that ministers should be and are responsible for policy and that officials and bureaucracies exist to administer. While the normative principles are clear, the realities of power and bureaucracy led to a continuous debate about whether there could in fact be such a "policy-administration dichotomy." Thus, it is argued that policy and administration create a seamless web of activities and that ministers will be criticized not just for "high" policy but for specific administrative choices as well.

This brief background is necessary to show both the continuities and discontinuities between the old and the new public management. First there is agreement in principle between the old and the new that ministers ought to focus on, and be responsible for, policy and that officials should implement it efficiently. But there are differences inherent in the structural form of delivery and in what it means for the doctrine of ministerial responsibility.[31] In the new public management, large departmental entities should be chopped into a parent department and smaller operating units functioning with as close to a market-based financial information and pricing system as possible. In this sense it is, directionally at least, a form of organization analogous to the new flexible post-Fordite systems of private production.

In terms of efficiency and competitiveness, the thrust of the conceptual argument is quite clear. It is argued simply that these systems are bound to be efficiency-enhancing because better costing, pricing, and allocative rationality and competition are built in. Benefits are also claimed at the level of the working *esprit de corps* of organizations. Smaller organizations delivering services will produce a more dynamic and better motivated public service. This in turn will enhance democracy because there will be greater sensitivity to, and focus on, the delivery of services to citizens.

The counter-arguments to this thrust are quite straightforward. Efficiency gains may well occur but there will be democratic losses in policy effectiveness and accountability in several senses. First, the doctrine of ministerial responsibility will be harmed because the implication is that, to some extent, ministers will not be held accountable quite as much as before for individual errors of implementation. Second, in the social services, professional and humanitarian goals will be sacrificed at the altar of competitive market urges. Third, public service unions often see this reform thrust as antithetical to their members' interests since it threatens jobs, challenges system-wide methods of determining pay and conditions of work, and indeed challenges the very notion of a single public service.

The formation of arm's length special or Next Steps-style agencies in the U.K. is the most direct example in a parliamentary system of a system-wide effort to separate policy from operations. The Next Steps program, instituted in 1988 by the Thatcher government, sought to convert as many as possible of the Government's service delivery functions into clearly designated quasi-independent agencies headed by a chief executive officer (CEO).[32] The CEO operates on the basis of a personal contract between himself or herself and the minister of the parent department. The contract specifies a fixed term and allows for higher than normal remuneration, including large performance pay bonuses.

Framework documents between the agency and the parent department are negotiated as well as annual performance agreements. The framework documents specify items such as key financial and service targets; agency objectives; relationships with the parent department; areas of managerial freedom; and the basis of the performance data that will be used for accountability purposes. The essence of the Next Steps regime was to create and foster a managerial, more output- and service-oriented culture in an array of smaller operating agencies. It would also free the minister and the central department to focus on policy matters. By April 1992, 72 Next Steps agencies had been established, covering more than 50 percent of the British Civil Service. The initial target in 1988 was to achieve a 75 percent goal by 1998.

There is little doubt that the Next Steps regime has changed public service management significantly in the U.K. But, not surprisingly, there is a mixed verdict regarding efficiency and other political criteria used for assessing the results. Some audit and anecdotal evidence undoubtedly points to micro-efficiency gains in particular agencies. After beginning in an intense atmosphere of ideological conflict, the Next Steps program now enjoys considerable cross-party support as a reform that is here to stay. Evidence also exists to support the view that some agencies and their employees have enjoyed an improved sense of their own *esprit de corps* and morale.

But again, claims regarding overall efficiency gains must be guarded because the Next Steps agencies are not in truth fully independent agencies. For example, performance pay applies mainly to the top of the organization rather than through the ranks. Key items such as pay and personnel structures are still centrally determined. Moreover, as traditionalists had predicted, the parent department and its minister do not always want to let the agency CEOs manage. The problem for ministers is that, while it is true that they ought to be focusing on policy, the system of ministerial responsibility inherent in parliamentary government also holds them accountable for particular decisions made in their name. A vigilant opposition in the House of Commons and in outside interest groups is unlikely, on a consistent basis, to play the game of separating policy from administration. As a result, it is a brave minister indeed who will follow along with the implied Next Steps logic.

In general, reforms aimed at separating policy from administration have some potential for enhancing efficiency but that potential is not automatic and is unlikely to occur unless the reforms are systematically rather than just experimentally introduced. In Canada, limited reforms in this area have been attempted only on a small experimental basis, involving the previously noted 14 agencies and emerging as part of the Public Service 2000 (PS2000) initiative.[33] In this regard, the Canadian program begun by the Mulroney Conservatives is far too timid to have much effect.

ENHANCING RESPECT FOR, AND CONFIDENCE IN, PUBLIC SERVICES

The fourth efficiency-democracy bargain concerns measures whose overall purpose is to restore respect for, and confidence in, the delivery of public services. These measures must, at the same time, accommodate the democratic pressure for direct citizen involvement in service delivery standards. Examples here include aspects of the Canadian PS2000 exercise begun several years ago by the Mulroney government, but, even more centrally, initiatives such as the U.K. Citizen's Charter program. Before discussing these in more detail it is essential to step back to observe some of the consequences of excessive bureaucracy bashing.

Government bureaucracies in one sense are the easiest of political targets. From the mid-1970s on through the 1980s, political parties of all stripes got extensive political mileage out of bashing the waste in government, invoking "fat cat" notions of national or provincial capitals, and rhetorically stereotyping the image of overpaid and underworked bureaucrats or insensitive striking public service unions.[34] In certain aspects, this kind of criticism was deserved and flowed from some reasonably objective analyses. In other aspects, it was purely ideological, it was a disguise for a larger attack on social programs, and it led to self-fulfilling prophecies. Thus, the more one said that government was weak or incompetent, the more the proper role of government was weakened. The morale of public servants also plummeted under this climate of attack. There were few defenders of bureaucracy.[35]

Throughout this period the public support for public services, as expressed in public opinion polls, did not plummet as much as the pattern of ideological criticism would indicate.[36] Public opinion suggested that Canadians wanted most of the public services they were receiving. In any event, by the late 1980s and in the early 1990s, governments were beginning to have some second thoughts about the excesses of bashing the State. The fear was now expressed that the excesses were leading to a gutting or hollowing out of the State. A reformed state was needed but also one that was a competitive and compassionate state, capable of playing its vital proper role in enhancing economic competitiveness and social cohesion.

As indicated earlier, there was also an increased desire among both traditional and new public interest groups for a direct role, sometimes in actually delivering services on contract or in monitoring standards for service delivery.

One manifestation of the desire to improve public services in Canada was the launching of the PS2000 exercise. It arose out of pressure from the senior public service itself which was concerned about the low morale and loss of self-esteem by a once-proud civil service. PS2000 was endorsed by the Mulroney Conservative government and involved a widespread review of public service organization and personnel matters, including issues such as contracting out and special Next Steps-style agencies. Importantly, it also dealt with the issue of administrative service standards and service to the public.[37] But the Canadian effort in this regard was modest in comparison with the extent of political leadership evident in the British Citizen's Charter initiative.

The Citizen's Charter program is an array of actions on a government-wide level that, in part, is a continuation of the Thatcherite legacy of privatization and, in part, is a departure from Thatcherism in that it reaffirms the importance of public services to the average citizen. It seeks to empower citizens to obtain redress for bad service, but it also seeks to establish and publish high service standards so that citizens may know what to expect and what to do when service falls below the required quality.

Thus, in his introduction to the 1991 White Paper on the Citizen's Charter, Prime Minister John Major stressed that, ever since he had been a local councillor in Lambeth 20 years before, his ambitions had been to "make public services answer better to the wishes of their users, and to raise their quality."[38] He went on to argue that he saw the Charter as a logical and natural complement to the Thatcher era's privatization and contracting out policies. The Charter was "about giving more power to the citizen." It was decidedly not, in his view, "... a recipe for more state action."[39] But, at the same time, it was to release the "well-spring of talent, energy, care and commitment in our public service."[40]

While the Charter was linked to further privatization provisions and to empowering citizens, its core was the requirement that all agencies in the U.K. government (departments, nationalized industries and local government) publish, and be held accountable for, standards of service delivery. By mid-1992, 18 charters had been published. Since a main part of the charter program is to enhance quality and pride in the public service, the program also includes an award—the Chartermark—for excellence in the delivery of public service.

An example of an agency's charter is the Jobseeker's Charter published by the Employment Service.[41] It specifies, among other things, the time a job seeker should have to wait to be seen (within 10 minutes) and the time it should take to answer the phone (within 30 seconds). It also specifies what the job seeker can expect from the Employment Service. The Charter also sets out what the responsibility of the job seeker is to help get the proper service and, hence, highlights the issues and realities of the co-determination of services between agency and citizen. Other charters, such as those for education and the health service, will publish so-called "league tables" that supply citizens with information on how schools are performing relative to others or how waiting lists at hospitals compare.

There is little doubt that the impetus for the Charter resides with the personal leadership of Prime Minister John Major. He has given it his personal political imprimatur. My own study of the Charter's impact on three British agencies gives it a guarded but positive assessment.[42] The charter program has helped sharpen the agencies' sense of knowing what kind of business they are actually in and it has assisted in furthering the operative and output-oriented nature of the Next Steps program. Indeed, it is through the combination of the Next Steps initiative and the Citizen's Charter that a better balance of reforms seems to be occurring. The charter program has also brought out, in surprisingly forthright ways, the close links between citizen responsibilities and public service delivery and thus has highlighted the public-private interconnectedness of the service chain. My analysis also concludes that for some areas of service delivery, the Charter itself cannot be a substitute for increased public investment in these services.

The Mulroney government has launched an internal review process on service standards. Centred in the Treasury Board, it has begun to canvass the views of agencies as to how to set and improve standards. Early indications are that the Canadian initiative will not have the necessary political leadership from the Prime Minister, nor can it likely be sold as a charter of service rights. The Canadian Charter of Rights and Freedoms and the recent constitutional debate over the Social Charter have undoubtedly led to an overuse of charter-like clarion calls.

However, what is healthy about some of the thinking regarding PS2000, the Citizen's Charter and the popularization of the "reinventing government" thesis in the U.S. is that it recognizes the positive role of government and the need to reinforce the proper role of the State without sacrificing some of the efficiency learning curves of the 1980s. While the connections between this line of reform and the broader allocative efficiency and competitiveness are also indirect, I have no doubt that they are important and essential for both a competitive and a democratic society in the rest of the 1990s.

CONCLUSION

The overall conclusion that emerges from this survey of efficiency-democracy bargains is that the impact of government organization, broadly defined, on efficiency and competitiveness, *and* on democracy, is not a simple one. Certain aspects of government organization reduce and retard efficiency and democracy, and other aspects enhance both. Moreover, in each of the four bargains explored, the specific notions of efficiency and democracy inherently or potentially involved must be made explicit in any discussion. Thus, efficiency embraces allocative, administrative, competitive and restructuring aspects which are interwoven. Democracy involves diverse preferences not only for traditional versus direct democracy, but also for the extent of democracy in the operation and delivery of policy versus the formulation of policy. The choices are also governed by the reality that government organization is embedded in a relationship with society rather than an abstract entity separate from it.

With respect to the size of government, it is clear that Canadian governments will have to rigorously restrain government, but in ways that go beyond the use of previous aggregate expenditure controls. This is because, although some traditional restraint measures will have to be maintained, they will have to be applied in the 1990s in the face of renewed and valid demands for better public services in areas such as economic infrastructure, education, health care and the environment. Accordingly, efficiency and democratic imperatives will involve efforts to deal with the actual diverse delivery aspects of such public services. From this basic premise, other specific implications flow concerning cabinet organization, the separation of policy and implementation, and the generation of renewed respect for, and support of, public services.

With regard to the basic structure of cabinet portfolios, I conclude, on balance, that the number of cabinet portfolios should be pruned quite severely to help ministers focus on the large framework-oriented competitive and social issues rather than on ad hoc micro and sectoral interventions. Although no system of cabinet structure can or should be entirely devoted to efficiency concerns only, the Canadian system does seem to me to be extremely unwieldy in the face of the increasing need to focus on larger international imperatives and to forge a working democratic consensus around the positions Canada should adopt to enable it to be competitive and socially cohesive. The current 40 plus cabinet portfolio system seems at times to be designed to promote micro, sector-specific interventions rather than to dissuade them. It is a luxury Canadians can no longer afford, nor is it apparent that it promotes any clear sense of accountability in basic policy terms.

The balance of evidence also suggests that policy and delivery mechanisms can be separated to a far greater extent than has been the norm in the past. In this regard, the modest Canadian experimentation with special operating agencies should be vastly expanded on a scale similar to the U.K. Next Steps program. In addition, improved and openly derived standards of service delivery, as in the U.K. Citizen's Charter program, can enhance confidence in and respect for the vital role of the public service. Even while recognizing that there are always some valid constraints in the wholesale transplanting of other countries' political innovations into the Canadian setting, one cannot help but notice that the Canadian program could go much further than it has, not only to secure some efficiency gains, but also to improve some aspects of public service morale and citizen involvement in the setting of service standards.

While the above conclusions are directionally similar, the analysis suggests that they must also be qualified in several important respects. First, none of the itemized reform areas have a direct unambiguous causal line between them and the achievement of enhanced competitiveness. Each is bound up in necessary qualifications having to do with the complexity of the actual relationships between markets and the State, and with the underlying democratic rationale for government institutions. Thus, for example, however crucial the size of government is to future competitiveness, so also is the precise composition of government activity. Direct sector-specific subsidization and regulation should be reduced. At the same time, infrastructure investment and broad areas of framework-oriented social regulation and social service provision in education and health care should be extended but also complemented with some market-based instruments of delivery.

Similarly, in the area of ministerial portfolio structure, the conclusion that Canada's cabinet is too unwieldy for future strategic policy making has to be qualified by the notion that, if representative aspects of cabinet formation are reduced, representation is likely to have to be strengthened elsewhere, e.g. in an elected senate or strengthened House of Commons. The key in these latter non-cabinet focused reforms, however, should be to strengthen the representation of the general interests of Canadians rather than forming another arena for unbridled special interest politics.

The policy versus delivery split inherent in Next Steps-style reforms, on balance, makes overall sense partly in efficiency terms and partly in terms of enhancing the morale and sense of mission of public servants. But it cannot be elevated to a pure principle because the realities of ministerial responsibility, especially as played out in the gladiatorial politics of the House of Commons Question Period or the two-minute television news clip, do not and should not always allow for neat separations of policy from implementation.

Finally, the early experience with measures such as the U.K. Citizen's Charter suggests that however much standards may help improve service delivery, there are areas where increased public investment is crucial to the provision of services. And such services are, in turn, crucial to long-term competitiveness and democratic advance.

What the full experience of the last two decades perhaps shows most of all is the need to reduce ideological blinkers and to be much more selective about which functional and organizational aspects of government are efficiency and democracy enhancing—and which are reducing. A thinking view of the State is far more important to Canadians than an ideological one that simply bashes bureaucracy and government or attacks market-based approaches as a form of ritual sport. The role of government will not shrink in real terms, but its composition can and should change. Both efficiency and democratic considerations require it.

NOTES

1   This chapter develops further some ideas initially set out in a paper written for the Government of Canada's Prosperity Initiative. See G. Bruce Doern, "Government Organization, Efficiency and Competitiveness in the Canadian Democratic Setting" (Ottawa: Government of Canada Prosperity Secretariat, June 1992). The Secretariat's permission to utilize parts of the paper in this chapter is greatly appreciated. Special thanks are also owed to my colleagues, Susan Phillips and Leslie Pal, for extremely helpful comments on an earlier draft.

2   See David Osborne and Ted Gaebler, *Reinventing Government* (New York: Addison Wesley, 1992). The reinvention label has been popularized by the Osborne and Gaebler book, but the analysis for Canada must go well beyond this American treatise.

3   See James A. Brander, *Government Policy Towards Business* (Toronto: Butterworths, 1988).

4   See G. Bruce Doern, "Canadian Macro and Micro Accountability Regimes and Economic Efficiency" (Paper prepared for the Economic Council of Canada's Government and Competitiveness Reference, Ottawa, February 1992).

5   See Michael Porter, *The Competitive Advantage of Nations* (New York: Free Press, 1990).

6   See Tom Courchene, "Towards the Reintegration of Social and Economic Policy" in G. Bruce Doern and Bryne Purchase, (eds.), *Canada at Risk? Canadian Public Policy in the 1990s* (Toronto: C.D. Howe Institute, 1990), pp. 125-48; and Robert Young, "Effecting Change: Do We Have the Political System to Get Us Where We Want to Go?" in Doern and Purchase, *Canada at Risk?* pp. 59-80.

7   See Paul Hoggett, "A New Management in the Public Sector?" *Policy and Politics*, 19, 4 (October 1991): p. 243.

8   See Robert Reich, *The Work of Nations* (New York: Simon and Schuster, 1991).

9   See Peter Aucoin, "Administrative Reform in Public Management: Paradigms, Principles, Paradoxes and Pendulums," *Governance*, 3, 2 (1990): pp. 115-37.

10   See R. Rhodes, (ed.), "The New Public Management," *Public Administration*, 69, 1 (Spring 1991).

11   My thanks to Susan Phillips for suggesting these points more explicitly than had been apparent in an earlier draft.

12   See G. Bruce Doern and Richard Phidd, *Canadian Public Policy: Ideas, Structure, Process*, 2nd ed. (Toronto: Nelson, 1992).

13   For details, see Doern, "Government Organization, Efficiency and Competitiveness."

14   See Howard Oxley et al., "The Public Sector: Issues for the 1990s" in *OECD Working Papers*, no. 90 (Paris: Organization for Economic Co-operation and Development, 1990).

15   See G. Bruce Doern, (ed.), *Getting It Green: Case Studies in Canadian Environmental Regulation* (Toronto: C.D. Howe Institute, 1990), chap. 1.

16   See Julien LeGrand, " Quasi-Markets and Social Policy" in *Studies in Decentralization and Quasi-Markets* (Bristol: School of Advanced Urban Studies, University of Bristol, 1990).

17   See Bob Hudson, "Quasi-Markets in Health and Social Care in Britain: Can the Public Sector Respond?" *Policy and Politics*, 20, 2 (April 1992): pp. 131-42.

18   See D.A. Aschauer, "Is Public Expenditure Productive?" *Journal of Monetary Economics*, 23 (1989): pp. 177-200.

19   See Douglas Auld, *Budget Reform: Should There Be a Capital Budget for the Public Sector?* (Toronto: C.D. Howe Institute, 1985).

20   During 1992, Cabinet Minister Robert de Cotret reviewed issues related to departmental organization and efficiency, and reported to Prime Minister Brian Mulroney. At the time of writing, no results of this review had been announced.

21   See Guy Peters, *Public Bureaucracy: A Comparative Perspective* (University of Alabama Press, 1988); and Gordon F. Osbaldeston, *Organizing to Govern*, vols. I & II (Toronto: McGraw-Hill Ryerson, 1992).

22   See Daniel Okimoto, *Between MITI and the Market* (Stanford: Stanford University Press, 1989); Hugh Heclo and H. Madsen, *Policy and Politics in Sweden* (Philadelphia: Temple University Press, 1987).

23   See Stuart Hamilton, "The Restructuring of the Federal Public Service" (Unpublished Paper, Canberra, 1990).

24   See Tom Kent, *Getting Ready for 1999* (Halifax: Institute for Research on Public Policy, 1989).

25   See Doern and Phidd, *Canadian Public Policy*, chap. 17.

26   See Herman Bakvis, "Regional Ministers, National Policy and the Administrative State in Canada," *Canadian Journal of Political Science*, 21, 2 (1988): pp. 539-67.

27   See G. Bruce Doern, "Horizontal and Vertical Portfolios in Government" in G. Bruce Doern and Vince Wilson, (eds.), *Issues in Canadian Public Policy* (Toronto: Macmillan, 1974), pp. 310-36.

28   See Peter Kemp, "Next Steps for the British Public Service," *Governance*, 3, 2 (April 1990): pp. 186-96.

29   See Rhodes, "The New Public Management," p. 1.

30   See J.E. Hodgetts, *Public Management: Emblem of Reform for the Canadian Public Service* (Ottawa: Canadian Centre for Management Development, 1991).

31   See Sharon L. Sutherland, "Responsible Government and Ministerial Responsibility: Every Reform Is Its Own Problem," *Canadian Journal of Political Science*, 24, 1 (March 1991): pp. 91-120.

32   See A. Flyn, A. Gray, and W. Jenkins, "Taking the Next Steps: The Changing Management of Government," *Parliamentary Affairs*, 43, 2 (April 1990): pp. 159-78.

33   See Canada, *Public Service 2000* (Ottawa: Supply and Services Canada, 1990). See also Canada, *The Historical and International Background of Special Operating Agencies* (Ottawa: Consulting and Audit Canada, 1982); and *Optimum*, 22, 2 (1991), (theme issue on special operating agencies).

34   See David Zussman, "Managing the Federal Public Service as the Knot Tightens" in Katherine A. Graham, (ed.), *How Ottawa Spends 1990-91: Tracking the Second Agenda* (Ottawa: Carleton University Press, 1990), pp. 247-76.

35   See Charles Goodsell, *The Case for Bureaucracy*, 2nd ed. (Chatham: Chatham House, 1985).

36   See Richard Johnson, *Public Opinion and Public Policy in Canada* (Toronto: University of Toronto Press, 1986).

37   See Canada, "Moving Forward with Service Standards: A Discussion Paper" (Unpublished paper, Treasury Board of Canada Secretariat, Ottawa, 1991).

38   See *Citizen's Charter* (London: HMSO Cm. 1599, July 1990), p. 2.

39   Ibid., p. 2.

40   Ibid., p. 2.

41   For further analysis of the Charter, see G. Bruce Doern, "The U.K. Citizen's Charter: Origins and Implementation in Three Agencies," *Policy and Politics*, 21, 1 (January 1993): pp. 1-14.

42   Ibid., pp. 12-14.

CHAPTER 7

Aboriginal Self-Government: The Two Sides of Legitimacy

Paul L. A. H. Chartrand

Résumé : Il est question dans ce chapitre des principes fondamentaux qui doivent légitimiser et assurer la continuité de l'autonomie gouvernementale des Autochtones. L'auteur tente d'y démontrer que la réaction du Canada aux revendications d'autonomie gouvernementale des Autochtones se fonde sur deux hypothèses qui n'abordent pas la question de la légitimité et qui détournent peut-être même de la question. La première hypothèse fautive est que les Autochtones constituent une «minorité raciale» et la seconde, plutôt libérale, veut que tous les résidants du Canada bénéficient d'un «traitement égal». L'auteur envisage trois façons d'aborder les revendications en matière de représentation des Autochtones : 1) la restructuration de la politique constitutionnelle; 2) des modifications proposées aux institutions en place, avec l'exemple des recommandations visant la création de circonscriptions électorales autochtones; 3) le processus de négociation de l'autonomie gouvernementale à l'échelon administratif. La question de la légitimité se pose dans les trois cas et le Canada n'y a pas encore trouvé de réponse qui fasse l'affaire.

Abstract: This chapter examines the first principles upon which legitimate and enduring Aboriginal self-government must be built. It seeks to demonstrate that Canada's responses to claims by Aboriginal peoples for self-government have been built upon two assumptions that fail to confront, and may even divert attention from, the issue of legitimacy. The first erroneous assumption is that Aboriginal peoples are a "racial minority," and the second is a liberal assumption that there should be "equal treatment" for all who live in Canada. Three types of responses to demands for Aboriginal representation are explored: 1) the new forms of constitutional politics; 2) suggestions for modifications to existing institutions, using the example of recommendations for the establishment of Aboriginal Electoral Districts (AEDs); and 3) the process of negotiations over self-government at the administrative level. All three cases raise questions about legitimacy that Canada has yet to answer appropriately.

One of the central contemporary debates about democracy in Canada concerns the recognition of Aboriginal peoples as distinct political communities. Only when they gain such recognition will it be possible to establish Aboriginal self-government founded on democratic first principles. Only if such principles inform the substance and process of a move towards Aboriginal self-government will the outcome be legitimate. Therefore, at the heart of the debate is the very legitimacy of Canada's national institutions, political processes and representation.

This chapter argues that the legitimacy of Canada's power over Aboriginal peoples is a core issue in current democratic politics. The Aboriginal peoples in Canada have long been subjugated politically and their social and economic circumstances are a matter of national embarrassment.[1] At this time, in various ways, they are asking Canada to justify its exercise of power over them and to explain its claims to resources and land. The legitimacy of Canada is at stake because the State's authority is being questioned. Canada is a country that believes it prefers reasoned order to violence, particularly in making constitutional change, and therefore it must accept such questioning.

Yet, Canada has had difficulty in providing a principled response to the challenge provided by the claim of Aboriginal self-government. Most debates about self-government are based upon two assumptions that fail to confront, and may even divert attention from, the issue of legitimacy. The first is that Aboriginal peoples are a "racial minority." The second is the long-standing and deeply embedded commitment to liberal values of individual equality which generates the premise that there should be "equal treatment" for all Canadians. Both these assumptions make it very difficult to recognize Aboriginal peoples as distinct *political* communities with unique status.

This chapter seeks to demonstrate the extent to which these assumptions about Aboriginal peoples and Canadian citizenship have informed the responses to claims by Aboriginal peoples for self-government. It also argues that they are profoundly inappropriate assumptions if self-government is to be grounded in principles which will generate legitimacy for it, as well as for other national institutions.

Aboriginal claims to "self-government," in the sense of greater political autonomy for Aboriginal communities, have generated state responses of three types. One is the new forms of constitutional politics, marked by Aboriginal leaders' unprecedented participation in the 1991-92 discussions leading to the ill-fated Charlottetown Accord. A second response involves only suggestions for modification of existing institutions, represented by a recommendation to establish Aboriginal Electoral Districts. Finally, a third response has been at the administrative level, through which various federal departments continue to negotiate new arrangements and administer policies intended to devolve some administrative powers to Aboriginal communities.

All three cases raise questions about legitimacy. There are two sides to legitimacy. Any challenge to the legitimacy of Canada must itself be legitimate. An illegitimate process will not easily secure acceptable and enduring forms of self-government. To achieve such, Aboriginal peoples must freely express their acceptance of their own representation in the process of securing political autonomy through self-government. This means that the legitimacy of Aboriginal self-government is ultimately in the hands of Aboriginal peoples. Government policies which ignore this proposition will not work in the long term.

In assessing the political relationship between Canada and Aboriginal peoples who are caught as enclave populations within its political boundaries, Canada has the clear upper hand in access to power and resources.[2] The balance of power is by no means even. In this relationship, Canada has considerable power to influence the identity of the "other side" involved, as well as the process of negotiating Aboriginal self-government. Government spending can shape the eventual nature and scope of Aboriginal self-government. Moreover, Canada is able to grant legitimacy to the challengers.

Both sides of legitimacy are at issue in politics in Canada and their presence explains why the road to self-government has been, and is likely to continue to be, strewn with obstacles.

ERRONEOUS ASSUMPTIONS

In the 1982 amendments to the Constitution, Aboriginal peoples secured recognition as political communities with collective rights. This constitutional status could provide the principled foundation for a new equality—the equality of "peoples" equal in dignity and respect.[3] Indeed, in the constitutional conferences and negotiations since 1982, many Aboriginal representatives have insisted on Aboriginal peoples being included in the process of crafting a new, legitimate order to replace the existing and unacceptable constitutional order. Their vision of equality, and claim to recognition as political communities, is clear. Despite this oft-stated position, however, the principles which underpin the vision of these Aboriginal leaders are frequently not the ones which are most apparent in everyday political discourse.

Instead, two very common—and mistaken—assumptions about the status and rights of Aboriginal peoples dominate. A first, albeit often unstated, premise for the legitimacy of the exercise of power over Aboriginal peoples by Canada is that they belong to a disadvantaged "racial minority" whose plight deserves benevolence from the State. A second rationale for the exercise of power is that, because Aboriginal people live in Canada, they must be Canadians. As such, they may not be treated differently from other citizens.

This section of the chapter criticizes these two assumptions, suggesting they are inadequate to the task of providing a principled grounding for self-government. It also, in doing so, provides evidence of the extent to which they are deeply embedded in everyday politics and even in proposals for reform. Only their elimination will generate a legitimate relationship between Aboriginal peoples and Canada.

One of the greatest barriers standing in the way of creating new and legitimate institutions of self-government is the notion that Aboriginal people constitute a "disadvantaged racial minority." Despite years of mobilization against this idea by Aboriginal peoples, the argument is frequently made and it often serves as a rallying cry for politicians and others attempting to block real change. Almost daily, the newspapers deploy a discourse based on the "race" assumption;[4] rarely is there a decent rebuttal.

The "race" notion has a long historical pedigree. It was present at the very beginning of Canada's existence as a country. Aboriginal peoples were excluded from the negotiations leading up to Confederation and were not, therefore, present at the constitutional creation of Canada. At that time, they were treated as "subject races," a status which permitted them to be subdued politically, "protected" from participation in the white settlers' land and market economies, and acculturated forthwith.[5] As such, Aboriginal peoples were not considered to be, or treated as, a political community or peoples whose participation mattered in the creation of a new constitutional order. The legitimacy of the new country (according to those who were included) did not depend on gaining the consent of Aboriginal "citizens," who were excluded.

This exclusion, as well as the "race" assumption which supposedly justified it, is evident in the subsequent actions of the courts and Parliament. Particularly revealing is the interpretation the courts gave to Section 91(24) of the Constitution Act, 1867. This provision arrogated to the federal government the exclusive power to legislate in respect to "Indians, and Lands Reserved for the Indians."

Section 91(24) might have been interpreted as a mandate for the federal government to conduct political and economic relations with Aboriginal peoples. There had been significant experience with such possibilities for this relationship. First Nations had already entered into treaties as distinct political communities.[6] Similarly, the Métis in Manitoba had entered Confederation as a distinct political community, with a constitutionally entrenched guarantee of land.[7]

Nevertheless, history gave short shrift to this alternative, which would have implied recognition of Aboriginal political communities. Instead, the courts accepted that Section 91(24) allowed the federal government to administer the everyday lives of the Aboriginal people it decided to locate on separate land called "reserves" and to define them as "Indians" for the purposes of its legislated policies. "Indians" were then excluded from participation in the settlers' Parliament, despite the fact that it claimed the power to decide their destinies.

The logic of legitimacy in this history was as follows. Principles of legitimate government applied only to the settlers, who were included in making the Constitution. Being "subject races," and therefore excluded, it did not matter that Aboriginal people were governed by laws in respect of which they had no say. This "first principle" of legitimacy of constitutional arrangements could hold sway, however, only to the extent that Aboriginal peoples continued to be treated as racial minorities rather than as political communities with full collective rights.[8] Recognition of "peoples" requires new principles.

The second assumption is that Aboriginal people are citizens of Canada and must, therefore, be treated as such. The political boundaries of Canada are assumed to enclose a natural community within which all citizens are treated as fungible items. The conclusion is, then, that existing institutions may legitimately assert power over Aboriginal persons.

Many, and probably most, Canadians take it for granted that Canada's very existence as a country depends upon its laws covering everyone who happens to live within the territory; such is the standard understanding of "citizenship" in everyday discourse.[9] Therefore, the seemingly logical conclusion is to note that Aboriginal people live *in* Canada; therefore, they must be Canadians. An easy next step is to argue that, if they are "Canadians," they are to be treated as everyone else; that is, they have the same rights and duties as all other Canadians.

Such a series of seemingly "logical" and deductive steps leads, however, to unfortunate results. With such reasoning, it is easy for politicians to raise the cry of "rule of law" and "one law for everyone" in discussions of Aboriginal self-government. Moreover, popular and public discourse can range widely over convoluted terrain.[10] For example, the experience of African-Americans can be used to support arguments for "colour-blind" policies. South African apartheid can be used to demonstrate the evils of separate political systems. The actions of white supremacist groups can be cited to generate distaste for differentiation of any sort.[11]

At this point, the second assumption joins the first. Liberal belief in individual rights becomes a basis for dismissing Aboriginal self-government as little more than an inappropriate recognition of "racial" categories. Therefore, while these two assumptions can be distinguished, and do not necessarily always operate together in popular discourse, there is a strong tendency for the two to be mutually reinforcing—and to narrow the space for any meaningful consideration of the legitimate recognition of Aboriginal political communities as the principle upon which to found arrangements for self-government.

Both of these assumptions must be discarded then. Only when Aboriginal peoples are viewed, not as "races" within the boundaries of a legitimate state, but as distinct political communities with recognizable claims for collective rights, will there be a first and meaningful step towards responding to Aboriginal peoples' challenge to achieve self-government. It is, then, absolutely crucial that the grounds for rejecting such assumptions be clearly and elaborately developed. The next sections of the chapter attempt to do so, with respect to constitutional and other institutional politics.

CONSTITUTIONAL POLITICS: "PEOPLES," NOT "RACES"

By 1992, Canadian politicians and the public had more than a decade of experience dealing quite directly with the claim of Aboriginal peoples that they should have a say in the constitutional make-up of Canada.[12] By then, political expediency compelled that Aboriginal political leaders be invited to participate directly and in unprecedented ways in negotiations about constitutional reform. Over the last decade, these Aboriginal leaders made it very clear that they refused to accept the existing constitution because it failed to recognize Aboriginal peoples' proper place within this fundamental institution. Therefore, in negotiations, they continued to press for major changes to the Constitution Act, 1982.

The most proximate goal for Aboriginal leaders in any such negotiations is to proceed beyond the 1982 recognition of the constitutional status of Aboriginal "peoples" by specifying the precise nature of their relations with Canadian public institutions. Section 35, enacted in 1982, recognized and affirmed Aboriginal and treaty rights, but it did not define those rights, nor did it specify whether self-government was included. When the constitutional conferences which took place between 1983 and 1987—as specified in Section 37 of the Constitution Act, 1982—failed to reach agreement and collapsed, 1991-92 was taken as a time when it would be possible finally to settle these matters.

The assumptions that Aboriginal peoples should be viewed as "racial" minorities living within the boundaries of a legitimate state clash with the recognition in the Constitution Act, 1982 of Aboriginal peoples as distinct political communities with constitutional status. The special status of "Indians" that was established by Section 91(24) of the Constitution Act, 1867 never caused much of a public stir as long as they were considered a "racial group" in need of special protection and treatment by the State. If, however, public policy is to be based not only on expediency, but upon enduring principles and legitimacy, it must derive from the latter and thereby banish concerns about "special status for racial groups."[13]

Since 1982, Aboriginal peoples have had constitutional recognition as distinct political communities. As such, they are now challenging Canada to rationalize its exercise of power over them.[14] In doing so, they are also arguing that this status allows—indeed requires—them to participate in the design of those institutions which exercise political power in Canada.

Of course, the idea of according special status to large groups of people within Canada, including the establishment of distinct public institutions, makes many people nervous. The idea of legal status is neither common nor well understood in Western countries, where status rarely has been recognized. Indeed, a Supreme Court decision dealing with "Indians" noted that "the principle of equality before the law is generally hostile to the very nature of status...."[15] Such thinking presents difficulties for any group promoting special status, particularly now that the Canadian Charter of Rights and Freedoms is both entrenched and utilized to promote values which are antithetical to the idea of "status."

This said, however, in addition to the constitutional recognition of Aboriginal "peoples" provided in Section 35 of the Constitution Act, 1982, the common law of Canada in fact already contains much that *does* accord legal status to Aboriginal peoples. The common law has, from the beginning, contained the basis for recognizing Aboriginal peoples as distinct, independent, political communities. That status lies in the Canadian courts' reliance on an analysis long established in the law of the United States in respect to Indian nations in that country.[16] This approach recognizes the inherent residual sovereignty of Aboriginal political communities. The legal doctrine is based on the courts' perception of the nature of the political relationship between the early settlers and the Aboriginal nations. In recent cases dealing with Aboriginal rights, the Supreme Court of Canada has affirmed its reliance on the American analysis, referring to the "nations" recognized in early British policy and action.[17] A crucial point of such legal analysis is that Aboriginal peoples are not defined in terms of "race." Rather, they are recognized as political communities, having all rights of such, including the right to determine their own membership according to their own political standards.

In the same way, Section 35 illustrates the impossibility of ascribing a "racial" basis to the identity of Aboriginal peoples. For example, Section 35.1 commits the federal and provincial governments to the principle that, before any amendment is made to certain constitutional provisions, a constitutional conference will be convened to which representatives of the Aboriginal peoples of Canada will be invited to consider any proposed amendment.[18] If "race" in the biological sense were the determinant of the identities recognized in Section 35, then the courts, as the arbiters of the Constitution, would require a test of racial identity. The logic of clinging to a racial understanding of constitutional recognition might then conjure up images of disappointed rivals for places at the constitutional conferences mandated in Section 35.1 bringing laboratory technicians and scientists to court to support their claim of being an "Aboriginal person" with standing to challenge the representativity of others. The implausibility of this scenario illustrates the point that the identity of Aboriginal peoples is a *political* issue, no different from the identity of Manitobans or Canadians. Thus, Section 35.1 can be read as recognizing a third set of constitutional actors, just as Section 35 recognizes the existence of distinct political communities with certain rights. Arguably, then, this section should be read as providing equality to distinct political communities with the capacity to forge their destinies within the boundaries of a united federation.[19]

Based on this argument, it is apparent that future considerations of Aboriginal self-government must jettison the notion that it would constitute "special treatment" for racial minorities.[20] In seeking self-government, Aboriginal leaders seek the power necessary to maintain cultures. The cultures they have in mind are unique ways of organizing society and promoting human values; they have little to do with the maintenance of biological "cultures," the notion suggested by the idea of "race." The cultures to be protected by self-government are distinct, historical political communities. Defined as such, the relevant issue—and the only relevant issue—is the way in which the claims of autonomy made by these communities can be accommodated within the federal institutions which now exist. The challenge is to design new—and legitimate—institutions.

THE FIRST HALF OF LEGITIMACY: CANADIAN INSTITUTIONS

Recognizing that Aboriginal people form historically and cultur- ally distinct political communities of "peoples," not races, re- quires a major adjustment in explanations available to Canadians about their past and present exercise of political power over Aboriginal peoples. While in 1867 constitution-making could exclude "subject races" and build institutions upon racism, continued exclusion since the Constitution Act, 1982, and the political mobilization of Aboriginal peoples is a severe challenge to the legitimacy of national institutions. Nevertheless, if 1982 was intended to herald a new deal for Aboriginal peoples, the constitution which Canada applies to itself still excludes them, because they have not participated in legitimizing it.

A basic principle of constitutional legitimacy is free con- sent. In the Manitoba Language Reference the Supreme Court explained the function of a constitution in this way:

> The constitution of a country is a statement of the will of the people to be governed in accordance with certain principles held as fundamental and certain prescriptions restrictive of the powers of the legislature and the government. It is, as Section 52 of the Constitution Act, 1982 declares, the "supreme law" of the nation...."[21]

A constitution is *legally* legitimate, then, only if it "has been adopted or amended by some pre-existing body or process that was legally authorized to adopt or amend the constitution."[22] A *politically* legitimate constitution is one which is generally accept- able to the people it governs because it was adopted or altered by persons or agencies that they generally accept as having the political right to decide such matters.[23] Normally, legal and political legitimacy are found together in a working constitutional document. When there is one without the other, it is political legitimacy that decides in the long run whether a constitution survives.[24]

Both the legal and the political legitimacy of the Canadian constitution are challenged by Aboriginal peoples. The political illegitimacy of existing arrangements is evident daily as Aboriginal peoples refuse to accept Canada's claim to assert power over them, whether the issue is taxation, gaming laws or land use. At the same time, the long odyssey of constitutional negotiations—the demand to be included and express concerns about the terms of the Charlottetown Accord—provides further evidence that Aboriginal peoples are demanding participation in the design of new institutions, which only such participation can legitimate.

Two illustrative arguments relating to the legal legitimacy of the Constitution can be made here. For example, it can be argued that the Constitution must be legitimized by the full elaboration of the existing Aboriginal and treaty rights that were inserted in Section 35. Aboriginal peoples cannot be seen as having accepted the legitimacy of the Constitution until there is a full elaboration of the nature and scope of Aboriginal rights, including self-government. In other words, because the process for arriving at agreement about the definition of the nature and scope of Aboriginal rights set out in Section 37 of the Constitution Act, 1982 failed, there are no grounds for arguing that Aboriginal peoples have accepted the current constitution. The condition on which that legitimacy depends has not yet been met. If an unwritten postulate at the very foundation of any constitution is the opportunity for constitutionally recognized peoples to negotiate and formally signify their agreement, this basic postulate has not yet been satisfied in Canada.[25]

The situation of the Métis in Manitoba provides a second illustrative argument. No government has fulfilled its constitutional obligations under the Manitoba Act, 1870.[26] The Métis agreed to join Canada on the basis of a set of constitutionally specified promises. These have not been kept and there is then, arguably, a breach of the bargain on the Canadian side. This breach negates the basis of the original agreement, because the federal government failed to carry out positive constitutional obligations. These obligations were part of the compact under which the Métis agreed to join Canada and, regardless of any legal constitutional result, the political legitimacy of the original bargain is tainted.

Despite the existence of such challenges to the political and legal legitimacy of the Constitution, these need not be construed as a threat to the political integrity of Canada. There are, however, serious challenges to the legitimacy of *existing* institutions. Establishing a legitimate constitutional order depends not only on

Canadian standards of legitimacy, but on those of Aboriginal peoples themselves.

REPRESENTATION IN INSTITUTIONS WITHOUT ALTERING THE INSTITUTIONS

The proposal for the establishment of Aboriginal Electoral Districts (AEDs) provides a good example of the limits to a policy of reform that does not address the issue of legitimacy. During the life of the Royal Commission on Electoral Reform and Party Financing (RCERPF), a Committee for Aboriginal Electoral Reform was constituted. The Committee consisted of five current and former Aboriginal members of Parliament, and it conducted extensive consultations within Aboriginal communities.[27] A first round of consultations took place in January 1991. Later in the spring, after the Committee was formed and a proposal for the establishment of AEDs was developed, a second round of consultations was organized with provincial, regional and national organizations.[28]

The Committee recommended establishment of Aboriginal constituencies in those provinces where numbers warranted them. The recommendations did not involve any constitutional change nor any major alterations in national institutions. They would have used existing legislation, namely the Canada Elections Act and the Electoral Boundaries Readjustment Act, to create federal AEDs as an appendage to the existing, geographically based, constituencies which now organize the House of Commons.

The identified goal of the Committee's recommendation was to redress perceived structural inequalities in the electoral system in order to make the system more *effective* in representing the interests of Aboriginal people as voters.[29] As such, the constituencies would provide an alternative for any individual Aboriginal voter who chose to register in an AED rather than in the constituency where he or she lived. Moreover, the existence of such constituencies would virtually guarantee that the number of Aboriginal people in the House of Commons would increase; therefore, the particular concerns of Aboriginal voters could be more frequently expressed, because more Aboriginal MPs would be available to raise them.

However, while dealing with the effectiveness of both voters and representatives, the Committee never considered the issue of *legitimacy* in respect to the exercise of state power over Aboriginal peoples as such. It took the existing institutions as they were and sought modifications of them. Despite the Committee's broad consultations within the Aboriginal communities and the expression of concern by other Aboriginal leaders about the initiative, the Committee continued to argue a position very close to one derived from the two assumptions which characterize so much of the Canadian debate about Aboriginal self-government.

The reasoning of the Committee is founded on liberal values, such as the idea that numerical minorities ought to be represented in legislatures in proportion to their number as individuals. This is a simple example of the notion that "anyone living in Canada is a Canadian" and, therefore, must be treated as all others.[30] In light of the Committee's expressed objective of providing effective representation of individual Aboriginal voters as Canadian citizens, it is surprising to find in the Committee's report arguments which conflict with the usual liberal assumptions. For example the Committee quoted, without disapproval, the view expressed by some of the leaders consulted that Aboriginal MPs would act as "ambassadors of their nations."[31] The report never indicated, however, how this corporate form of representation could be accommodated within a liberal proposal for individual political representation.

There is also evidence of race-based thinking in the Committee's report, which understood Aboriginal identity to derive from "Aboriginal descent." Thus, the structural problem was the paucity of MPs of "Aboriginal descent."[32] The problem with such reasoning is that, having adopted a "race" assumption, the Committee could not provide a test for distinguishing the claims of Aboriginal peoples from those of ethnic minorities.[33] Seeing the "slippery slope" of demands by all groups for constituencies representing their particular "community of interest," the Committee resorted to a practical political response to stop the "floodgates." This was that the Canadian Ethnocultural Council had informed the Committee that it was seeking integration in existing parties, rather than special status by way of particular constituencies.[34] In failing to provide a principle which distinguished Aboriginal claims to representation from those of other "minorities," the Committee on Aboriginal Electoral Reform took no steps towards specifying a sound principle for establishing the identity of legitimate claimants.

At times, the report of the Committee for Aboriginal Electoral Reform did seem to acknowledge that the legitimacy of national institutions was at issue. For example, the Committee reported that its consultations found that some Aboriginal leaders were concerned that the creation of AEDs would be seized upon as a "solution to the political marginalization of First Nations. Others suggested that, although there was significant merit in the Committee's proposal, the timing of the proposal is not appropriate and that it should wait until further constitutional recognition of Aboriginal and treaty rights."[35] Such concerns are founded on the idea that, while it is desirable in the long run to provide a voice for Aboriginal peoples in national institutions, a necessary *first* step is legitimizing the constitutional order as a whole.

Despite hearing such well-founded objections, the Committee remained more committed to its agenda of providing effective representation than to questions of legitimacy. Nothing swayed the Committee from its original commitment to realizing individual equality within existing representative institutions. It advocated, therefore, the establishment of AEDs, in parallel with efforts to gain constitutional reform or alone, in case the latter remained unrealized.[36] In doing so, the Committee explicitly rejected the alternative strategy of legitimizing all national institutions *before* Aboriginal peoples sought new places within particular institutions, like the House of Commons.

THE OTHER SIDE OF LEGITIMACY: ABORIGINAL REPRESENTATION

A state confronted with a challenge to its right to assert its power—that is, to its own legitimacy—must direct its response to a particular claimant. Of course, sometimes it is not difficult to do so. When the challenge comes in the form of armed confrontation, anyone pointing a rifle in your direction is immediately identified as a member of the "other side." This must have been true, for example, in the armed conflict at Batoche in 1885 involving the Métis and British-Canadian troops.

Sometimes, however, it is more complicated. Consider, for example, Aboriginal peoples in Canada, formerly free and residing in ancient homelands, but now caught within political boundaries imposed by outsiders who wish to appropriate the land for their own purposes. Here the response by outsiders to challenges to their actions may involve the exercise of another kind of power. In a situation in which power relations are unequal, the State also has the power to "recognize." In brief, the State retains the power to grant representativity to certain groups and to deny it to others.

This argument can be elaborated by the following historical references. When British settlers in Canada wished to appropriate land, in accordance with the kinds of formalities which would satisfy the legal minds of the day, they had no difficulty in recognizing the corporate identity of a relevant Aboriginal group and in finding appropriate representatives of that group with whom to formalize, or seal, the appropriation by means of a treaty.[37] Now, however, the same country is very nervous about recognizing that challengers to its legitimacy have a corporate identity; there is a major effort to transform formerly corporate entities (tribes, nations, peoples) into individual citizens or into predictable interest groups owing allegiance to outsiders' institutions of power. In this example, we see both the importance of a strategy of recognition and the power of a state to create its "opponent" or its "partner" by granting recognition.

The Canadian state, then, has a major interest in the identity of the claimants who challenge its authority, and it can use its power to affect consequences in three realms. First, the State has the power to influence the identity of the other side in negotiating self-government by its ability to grant recognition to a challenger and to refuse to recognize others. In such choices, the federal spending power is significant because the Government funds the Aboriginal organizations with whom it negotiates self-government. With this money, it is in a sense creating its opponent.

The second aspect involves the State's power to influence the process of claims-making. The State has the power, by granting recognition and using its spending power for example, to shape the form of negotiations and even to impose processes derived from Canadian political culture rather than any founded in Aboriginal cultures of decision making.

Third, both the State's power of recognition and its power over process ultimately give it great influence over the nature and scope of any forms of Aboriginal political autonomy resulting from such negotiations. For example, if Canadian governments choose to define and negotiate self-government with national associations (as they did in the constitutional talks) the results may well be different than if negotiations are held with regional associations (such as were involved in the James Bay and northern Quebec agreements) or if they undertake negotiations on the basis of "bands" as defined in the Indian Act (as in the Sechelt case in British Columbia).

Similarly, wide differences are likely if the scope of self-government is considered. Are all governmental matters to be dealt with between Canadian governments and small village communities, thus thrusting upon them issues that are irrelevant to their local circumstances? Are only local governmental issues to be included in the package of local Aboriginal self-government and the relevant communities proclaimed as "sovereign nations"? The capacity of small village communities to conduct governmental activities is obviously more limited than that of larger regional or national communities.

A state which uses its powers to influence the identity of Aboriginal individuals and communities, the process of negotiations and, thereby, the scope and nature of self-government is liable to find the legitimacy of the representatives it recognizes facing challenges within the Aboriginal communities. The issue is a key one in negotiating lasting self-government agreements, because disclaimers to any accord can be mounted on the basis of a challenge to the representativity of the party doing the negotiating.

Historically, the State has always exercised its law-making powers to influence the identity of Aboriginal persons and communities.[38] For example, the Indian Act of 1876 defined who was and, more importantly, who was *not* an "Indian" for the purposes of the Act. Essentially, the Indian Act definitions have been based on the original groups called "bands" which the State recognized in the 1870s. Within each band, the State granted "status" through a relationship with a male head of family and his descendants.[39]

State practices of recognition are sometimes reflected in Aboriginal organizational forms. For example, one national organization—the Assembly of First Nations (AFN)—bases its membership on the Indian Act definition of "Indians," rather than upon other grounds for self-naming such as treaty signatories, nations or peoples as defined by the usual political, social and anthropological factors. Moreover, government amendments to the definitions in the Indian Act have created confusion and political realignment amidst the ranks of "Indians" and Métis alike.[40]

State power of recognition within Aboriginal communities is also exercised by way of programs and policies which the State organizes within, or even devolves to, Aboriginal communities. For example, Employment and Immigration Canada's "partnership" strategy on employment and training, called *Pathways to Success*, illustrates the problem of establishing legitimacy of representation within Aboriginal communities.[41] The Department set up local management boards, comprising Aboriginal representatives, to oversee the program, review applications for funding under the Canada Jobs Strategy and make recommendations for resource allocations. Given the board members' control over the distribution of resources, recognition by the federal government may mean the opportunity to secure for one's group access to the power to influence the distribution of significant amounts of money. In this way, being recognized as a representative by the State may also be a source of power for Aboriginal groups, which may act to attract such recognition. Access to this source of power will be a subject of contest.[42]

The State also influences the process of claims-making, which it has the power to organize according to the usual rules of its political culture. Dealing with Aboriginal leaders who can supposedly speak for, and ensure acceptability of, negotiated positions with their constituencies suits Canadian political culture and political ideals. "Canada" is usually represented by agents of the federal and provincial governments. Canadian agents then seek from the Aboriginal community counterparts whom they can treat as similarly "representative."

For example, in the 1991-92 constitutional negotiations, it served the purpose of the Canadian agents to deal with large, representative and national Aboriginal organizations. Therefore, the federal government designated and financed, to a sum of over $10 million, four national Aboriginal organization—the Assembly of First Nations (AFN), the Native Council of Canada (NCC), the Inuit Tapirisat of Canada (ITC) and the Métis National Council (MNC)—to be part of the negotiations which eventually led to the Charlottetown Accord.[43]

From the perspective of Aboriginal communities, however, the legitimacy and representativity of these organizations is less obvious. The AFN and the NCC, in particular, do not purport to represent one single people, but collections of diverse groups for whom the matter of political solidarity is always particularly problematic. It has often been said that Aboriginal groups generally favour public decision making by a consensual process involving all concerned. Yet the very nature of the constitutional reform process, which responds to the exigencies of the Canadian political culture and structure, requires participation by a small number of Aboriginal leaders.

When, in accordance with the prevailing political culture of Canada, the State calls on the leaders of such national organizations to participate in processes of negotiating self-government, that decision has consequences for the potential to develop Aboriginal political structures based upon Aboriginal values and cultures. National Aboriginal organizations are likely to experience internal conflicts over the issue of representation. Internal power struggles erode the capacity of an organization to pursue common goals in negotiations with Canada. It is easy for others within the Aboriginal community to deny the legitimacy of the national Aboriginal association acting as a representative in order to disclaim agreement to any accord that might be reached between Canadian governments and Aboriginal groups. This stance serves as a key with which any agreement can be reopened by anyone wishing to do so. For example, when the AFN agreed to the terms of the Charlottetown Accord, some members of First Nations were quick to announce that they did not accept the Accord, because they did not consider that the leaders of the AFN were appropriately representative.

A second illustration of the State's influence on claims-making comes through its use of spending power. The rules of the game, that is the process, are much affected by differences in the amount of money that the federal government spends in preparation for, and during the course of, self-government negotiations compared with the capacity of village "nations" to spend, even if they receive state assistance. When the capacity of small communities to conduct governmental activities is contrasted with that of larger regional or national communities, the constraints and vulnerability of Aboriginal communities in this process are obvious. For instance, in 1993-94, the Community Funding program of the Department of Indian and Northern Affairs has allocated $8.9 million, a reduction of about $3.6 million from the 1991-92 fiscal year, to assist communities in planning and preparing for self-government negotiations.[44] Given the substantial number of communities involved, this does not represent a large sum of money for any particular community.

The State's influence also extends into the very dynamics of local communities, affecting culture and relationships, and these have consequences for the sorts of claims made. For example, some argue that the dynamics of local community life cannot be understood by looking only at events in the community.[45] It is necessary to understand that leaders must, if they are to influence policy, leave the community and travel to the capital, developing personal contacts and lobbying. There are at least two consequences which follow from this constraint. The first is that the local leaders who remain in the community retain significant political power within it. This distinction between "national" and "local" leaders may also result in conflicts over who is "really" representative. A system of direct contact between individual representatives and government agents has further implications. One is that the ability to have some influence in this way may be restricted to only larger groups that can afford to send their representatives to Ottawa.

CONCLUSION

In 1982, the Canadian constitution made a turn in the road by recognizing the existence of Aboriginal "peoples," largely as a result of political participation by Aboriginal representatives in the process of reform. The implications of the recognition of Aboriginal peoples as distinct political communities with a constitutionally recognized right of autonomy have yet to be worked out. Such recognition will require a fundamental shift in current thinking about the identity of Aboriginal communities. It is quite remarkable that, since 1982, there has been wide apparent support for the idea of Aboriginal self-government, despite the fact that many also believe that Canada is making concessions to a "racial minority." Perhaps the true test of support is to come with the gaining of significant Aboriginal autonomy, in the sense that self-defined communities can exercise the power to control resources for the public benefit of their communities.

In Canada, reasoned debate and constitutional and legal reform are a significant part of the negotiations of claims among groups within the State, rather than the use of direct violence and power. If that is so, and as long as it remains so, it is better to have a rational explanation for policy than to concede an unprincipled response for perceived political reasons or even to achieve "fairness" in a general sense. Yet the recognition of Aboriginal self-government can be placed upon principles that conform to the basic principles of constitutional federalism.

A shift to thinking about Aboriginal "peoples" as distinct political communities whose free consent is required to legitimize the Canadian constitution accords with accepted notions of federalism and constitutional legitimacy. If the claims of Aboriginal peoples challenge the legitimacy of Canada, then the process by which the challenge is made by Aboriginal people must itself be legitimate; that is, the negotiation and establishment of Aboriginal self-government must be acceptable and workable within the Aboriginal communities. This is the other side of legitimacy.

Canada has the upper hand in negotiations for Aboriginal self-government. It has the power to influence not only the identity of the claimants, but also the very nature and scope of eventual self-government agreements. The use of federal spending is a significant source of such government power. Federal expenditures, and federal policies generally, must heed the concerns raised, not only by the challenge to the legitimacy of Canada, but by the challenges posed by the issue of legitimacy of Aboriginal representation. The identity of Aboriginal representatives must be legitimized by Aboriginal communities. The legitimization of the exercise of power by Canada over Aboriginal peoples is still outstanding, but self-government agreements that are not legitimate in Aboriginal communities will not work.

NOTES

For helpful comments on earlier drafts of this chapter I thank Kathy Brock, Jane Jenson and Susan Phillips.

1   Ronald Wardhaugh, *Language and Nationhood: The Canadian Experience* (Vancouver: New Star Books, 1983), chap. 10.

2   The term "enclave" refers to political and not necessarily geographical communities; in geographical terms, 75 percent of Aboriginal peoples in Canada do not live on "reserves," and during the 1980s the urban Aboriginal population doubled. Native Council of Canada, *Some Facts about Aboriginal Peoples* (Ottawa, 1992).

3   Note that some claimants have relied upon the international law notion of "peoples" but that it is not necessary to rely upon it for purposes of recognizing the existence of constitutionally relevant political communities within Canada. On the rights of "peoples" at international law, with particular reference to Aboriginal peoples, see James Crawford, (ed.), *The Rights of Peoples* (Oxford: Clarendon Press, 1988); and Barbara Hocking, *International Law and Aboriginal Human Rights* (Sydney: The Law Book Co., 1988).

4   For example, the writer found one on the day this paragraph was written, "Warning termed racist propaganda," *Weetamah*, January 19, 1993, p. 2.

5   John L. Tobias, "Protection, Civilization, Assimilation: An Outline History of Canada's Indian Policy," *Western Canadian Journal of Anthropology*, Special Issue, 13 (1976).

6   See, generally, Peter A. Cumming and Neil H. Mickenberg, *Native Rights in Canada*, 2nd ed. (Toronto: The Indian-Eskimo Association of Canada and General Publishing Co. Ltd., 1971), Part IV.

7   See, generally, Paul L.A.H. Chartrand, *Manitoba's Métis Settlement Scheme of 1870* (Saskatoon: University of Saskatchewan

Native Law Centre, 1991); and George F.G. Stanley, *The Birth of Western Canada* (Toronto: University of Toronto Press, 1936);

8   The recognition of Aboriginal peoples as constitutionally recognized political communities within Canada will require a fundamental shift in traditional judicial analysis related to section 91(24). In cases which explained the relationship between special status and the Canadian Bill of Rights' injunction against racial discrimination, the courts considered "Indians," as defined by federal legislation, to be a racial group. For example, see *R. v. Drybones*, [1970] S.C.R. 282; 8 C.N.L.C. 273; *A. G. Canada v. Canard*, [1976] 1 S.C.R. 170; [1975] 3 W.W.R. 1; 8 C.N.L.C. 120; *R. v. Hayden*, [1983] 6 W.W.R. 655; [1984] 1 C.N.L.R. 148 (Man. C.A.).

9   For an example of this point, which surfaces regularly in public discourse, see Arlene Billinkoff, "Gambling battle symbolizes native grievances," *Winnipeg Free Press*, January 16, 1993, p. A7.

10   There is a more reflective version of this approach which seems to involve a deep commitment to liberal values of individual equality and to the political integrity of Canada. In this version, however, the threat is to the very legitimacy of "Canada." See, for example, Bryan Schwartz, *First Principles, Second Thoughts: Aboriginal Peoples, Constitutional Reform and Canadian Statecraft* (Montreal: The Institute for Research on Public Policy, 1986).

11   Will Kymlicka discusses the great distinction between apartheid regimes, the situation of African-Americans and Aboriginal peoples in *Liberalism, Community and Culture* (Oxford: Clarendon Press, 1991).

12   See David C. Hawkes and Marina Devine, "Meech Lake and Elijah Harper: Native-State Relations in the 1990s," Frances Abele, (ed.), *How Ottawa Spends 1991-92: The Politics of Fragmentation* (Ottawa: Carleton University Press, 1991), pp. 33-62.

13   For a typical example of the mistaken arguments on race, see Gordon Gibson, "Let's not use racism to tackle native needs," *The Globe and Mail* [Toronto], June 1, 1992, p. A19.

14   Bruce Ackerman has developed a principle of rationality concerning the legitimacy of the exercise of power; see *Social Justice in the Liberal State* (New Haven and London: Yale University Press, 1980). For purposes of this chapter, the notion described in the text is assumed as a general proposition and does not seek to rely on any particular explanation of it.

15   *A.G. Canada v. Canard* (1975), 52 D.L.R. (3d) 548; [1976] 1 S.C.R. 170; 8 C.N.L.C. 120, at 147, per Beetz, J.

16   The legal status of American Indian tribes as distinct, independent, political communities is described in David H. Getches and Charles F. Wilkinson, *Federal Indian Law: Cases and Materials*, 2nd ed. (St. Paul, Minn.: West Publishing Company, 1986), p. 277. In comparison with the Canadian reference to Aboriginal peoples, American Aboriginal peoples generally identify themselves as Indian tribes or nations.

17   *A.G. Quebec v. Sioui*, [1990] 3 C.N.L.R. 127, at 146 (S.C.C.).

18   The text is reproduced and discussed in Peter Hogg, *Constitutional Law of Canada*, 3rd ed. (Toronto: Carswell, 1992), pp. 694-95.

19   In 1977, Peter Russell argued that the application of the liberal philosophy of ethnic partnership to the Dene Nation's claim to survival as a distinct people within the Canadian state would entail the completion of Confederation. See Peter H. Russell, "The Dene Nation and Confederation" in Mel Watkins, (ed.), *Dene Nation: The Colony Within* (Toronto: University of Toronto Press, 1977), pp. 163-73.

20   For good discussions about ideas of "race" and Aboriginal peoples, see Russel Lawrence Barsh and James Youngblood Henderson, *The Road: Indian Tribes and Political Liberty* (Berkeley: University of California Press, 1980), esp. chap. 21;

Will Kymlicka, "Liberalism and the Politicization of Ethnicity," *The Canadian Journal of Law and Jurisprudence*, 4, 2 (1991): pp. 239-56.

21   *Re Language Rights under Manitoba Act, 1870* (1985), 19 D.L.R. (4th) 1, at 19.

22   Barry L. Strayer, "The Patriation and Legitimacy of the Canadian Constitution" (Cronkite Memorial Lecture, University of Saskatchewan College of Law, October 1982).

23   Ibid.

24   Ibid.

25   The Supreme Court's approach to constitutional interpretation has been expressed as follows: "... in the process of constitutional adjudication, the Court may have regard to unwritten postulates which form the very foundation of the constitution of Canada," *Re Language Rights under Manitoba Act, 1870* (1985), 19 D.L.R. (4th) 1, at 25.

26   See generally Chartrand, *Métis Settlement Scheme*.

27   For the report of the Committee, see RCERPF, "The Path to Electoral Equality: The Report of the Committee for Aboriginal Electoral Reform" in *Reforming Electoral Democracy*, vol. 4, Part 3.

28   The description of these consultations, including the publicity efforts and provision of toll-free numbers, is provided in *Reforming Electoral Democracy*, vol. 4, pp. 239-40.

29   This focus on the individual voter is very clear in the final report of the RCERPF as well, which discussed Aboriginal Electoral Districts in the chapter entitled "Equality and Efficacy of the Vote." *Reforming Electoral Democracy*, vol. 1, chap. 4. For a discussion of how AEDs fit into the RCERPF's own logic, see the chapter by Alexandra Dobrowolsky and Jane Jenson in this volume.

30   Indeed, in support of this position, the Committee's report quoted John Stuart Mill, the quintessential liberal theorist. See *Reforming Electoral Democracy*, vol. 4, pp. 248-49.

31   Ibid., p. 255.

32   Ibid., p. 243.

33   The RCERPF addressed this concern in another way. It elaborated four reasons why Aboriginal constituencies would not constitute an opening for other groups to make similar claims. The basic argument was founded on the unique constitutional and legal status of Aboriginal peoples in Canada, a status not available to visible minorities and ethnic groups. See *Reforming Electoral Democracy*, vol. 1, p. 11.

34   *Reforming Electoral Democracy*, vol. 4, p. 249.

35   Ibid., pp. 251, 256, 271.

36   Ibid., p. 256.

37   See how Treaties 8 and 11, for example, were signed; Rene Fumoleau, *As Long as This Land Shall Last: A History of Treaty 8 and 11 1870-1939* (Toronto: McClelland and Stewart, n.d.).

38   See Joe Sawchuk, "The Métis, Non-Status Indians and the New Aboriginality: Government Influence on Native Political Alliances and Identity," *Canadian Ethnic Studies*, XVII, 2 (1985): pp. 135-46. For an analysis of Aboriginal definitions by Aboriginal peoples and by outsiders, see Douglas E. Sanders, "The Bill of Rights and Indian Status" (1972), 7 U.B.C.L. Rev. 81.

39   Jack Woodward, *Native Law* (Toronto: Carswell, 1990), chap. 1.

40   Sawchuk, "Métis, Non-Status Indians."

41   Employment and Immigration Canada, *Pathways to Success: Aboriginal Employment and Training Strategy: A Background Paper* (Ottawa: Supply and Services Canada, 1991).

42   See the excellent discussion in Sally Weaver, "Political Representivity and Indigenous Minorities in Canada and Australia" in Noel Dyck, *Indigenous Peoples and the Nation-State: 'Fourth World' Politics in Canada, Australia and Norway* (St. John's: Institute of Social and Economic Research, Memorial University of Newfoundland, 1985), pp. 113-50.

43   This amount was targeted specifically to participation in the constitutional negotiations and is not part of the normal transfers from the federal government to Aboriginal representative organizations. In fiscal year 1993-94, Aboriginal political representative organizations received $5.6 million in grants and contributions from the Indian and Inuit Affairs Program of Indian and Northern Affairs Canada and $5.8 million from the Secretary of State. Indian and Northern Affairs, *1993-94 Estimates Part III* (Ottawa: Supply and Services Canada, 1993), p. 2-91; and Secretary of State, *1993-94 Estimates Part III* (Ottawa: Supply and Services Canada, 1993), p. 60.

44   In 1991-92, the Community Funding program provided $12.5 million in grants and contributions to Aboriginal communities to assist them in preparing for self-government negotiations; in 1992-93 and 1993-94, the amount of the transfer was $8.9 million in each year. Indian and Northern Affairs, *1993-94 Estimates Part III*, p. 2-93.

45   In the context of the United States, Robert Bee has observed that the dynamics of reservation political life cannot be understood by looking only at events on the reservation, but that one must also look to the relationship with Washington. See Robert L. Bee, "The Washington Connection: American Indian Leaders and American Indian Policy. The Manipulation of Policy in Indian Affairs," *The Indian Historian*, 12, 1 (1979): pp. 3-12.

CHAPTER 8

Devolution and Development: The Urban Nexus

N. H a r v e y L i t h w i c k
R e b e c c a C o u l t h a r d

Résumé : L'un des grands dossiers inscrits au nouveau programme national est le renouveau économique, tant à cause de la piètre performance de l'économie canadienne qu'en raison du nouveau programme économique de l'administration de Bill Clinton. Le développement économique des régions métropolitaines du Canada pourrait devenir le moteur du renouveau. Pour cela, il faudra à la fois des investissements dans l'infrastructure de ces régions et la mise sur pied de projets dans les collectivités urbaines, projets susceptibles d'entraîner une transformation économique. Cette dernière mesure ne pourra se concrétiser sans céder aux autorités locales l'autorité et les ressources nécessaires. Laissées à l'écart du débat constitutionnel sur la réorganisation de la régie nationale, les grandes villes canadiennes demeurent dépendantes et émasculées sur le plan fiscal. Par conséquent, on a effectivement dérobé aux Canadiens la possibilité de satisfaire leurs besoins dans les villes. De pousser la démarche de la dévolution jusqu'à inclure les régions urbaines constitue donc une occasion de multiplier les processus démocratiques et de faire valoir une stratégie valable de renouveau économique. La stratégie mise de l'avant est susceptible de provoquer un développement économique réel dans les zones métropolitaines.

Abstract: One of the dominant issues on the new national agenda will be economic renewal, due both to the dismal performance of the Canadian economy and the new economic agenda of the Bill Clinton administration. Economic development of Canada's metropolitan areas could serve as the vital engine of revitalization. This will require both appropriate investment in their infrastructure and the unleashing of initiatives in urban communities that are conducive to economic transformation. Central to the latter effort is the need for the devolution of powers and resources to the local level of government. Left out of the constitutional discussions for reorganizing domestic governance, the largest cities of Canada remain dependent and fiscally emasculated. As a result, Canadians are effectively disenfranchised in terms of meeting their urban needs. Completing the logic of devolution to include urban areas therefore offers the opportunity both to augment democratic processes and to promote a credible strategy for economic renewal. A strategy for fostering authentic economic development in metropolitan areas is proposed.

INTRODUCTION

The overriding national issues of economic renewal and devolution are rarely considered to be aspects of a common problem. This chapter sets out to demonstrate how in fact they are fundamentally linked at a juncture rarely considered by those concerned with national policies: the urban. This perspective also offers the possibility of finding original solutions.

Over the past few decades, there has been a steady devolution of powers from the federal to provincial governments frequently in the name of democratization, that is, of having services provided by that level of government most responsive to the needs of individuals and communities. The third level of government—the urban—is arguably the most democratic, being the one closest to citizens and, in general, the most transparent and accessible.[1] Robert Dahl has claimed that "as the optimum unit for democracy in the 21st century, the city has a greater claim, I think, than any other alternative."[2] Yet, urban areas have been virtually left out of this process of negotiating greater devolution with its attendant possibility of more democratic governance in Canada.

Perhaps the most important domain in which there has been a clearly visible effort to devolve powers and responsibilities has been the "constitutional," by which we mean the formal, legal relationships between orders of government. The needs of individuals in a modern society and economy have centred increasingly on matters of health, education, security, housing and communal infrastructure (roads, environment, waste disposal, clean water). These are all areas where responsibility has traditionally been assigned to the provincial governments, in the name of their greater proximity to those served. Massive transfers of resources to the provinces from the federal treasury have taken place through equalization payments and Established Programs Financing. The latter have evolved from conditional to unconditional transfers, further augmenting provincial paramountcy. Not content with the implied, if not explicit, controls Ottawa has continued to exercise, the provinces have sought to formalize their new powers and autonomy in the ongoing debate over constitutional reform. In an elegant statement of the case, Jean-Michel

Cousineau et al. show that decentralization is attractive for the following reasons:

1) to encourage policy innovation by intergovernmental competition;
2) to allow a closer match between public policies and citizen preferences;
3) to lower citizens' costs of signalling preferences; and
4) to create more encompassing interest groups and reduce "rational ignorance."[3]

Every one of the arguments made for greater provincial autonomy in the name of democratization applies with even greater force to urban governments. Proximity to taxpayer-voters, greater responsiveness, greater diversity, and so forth would all logically appear to call for formal devolution of powers from the provinces to this lower tier. Yet, as we shall see, such has not been the case. Functions have been "downloaded," but without matching revenues.[4] Or, if revenues are provided, they are almost entirely conditional.

A further reason advanced for keeping urban areas out of the picture is to avoid even greater complexities in intergovernmental negotiations which are already difficult.[5] In the light of our numerous debacles in the realm of intergovernmental affairs, this view is less than convincing. Indeed, Richard Loreto and Trevor Price argue exactly the opposite, that "in the larger provinces, the task of provincial guidance is too complex and bureaucratic, and central congestion could be positively lessened by allowing more initiative to the third level—municipal government."[6]

Exclusion from the devolution process has had a direct impact on urban communities, reducing their capacity to deal effectively with their mounting problems. As a result, these engines of the national economy have become increasingly ineffective, which has contributed in no small way to Canada's stagnation. Over time, the demand for traditional local government services has accelerated as a result of the process of urban economic and demographic development. Not only must that development be accommodated in terms of costly physical and social infrastructure, but its consequences in the social and environmental fields have proven to be overwhelming. As a result, local governments argue that they are incapable of delivering what is required of them or are being forced to attempt to do so with inappropriate financial and programmatic mechanisms. This constriction has led to a steady decline in the quality of urban life, most particularly in the larger metropolitan areas.[7]

Hence, the first hypothesis we wish to consider is that the failure to complete the logical process of devolution has constituted a serious barrier to effective democratization. Provincial governments continue to dominate most aspects of the public life of urbanites, who, as a result, tend to have a very limited say over the delivery of public services in their communities, especially those services in the fields of health, education, housing, etc., which are of primary importance to them. Moreover, in other fields which are the traditional domain of local governments, fiscal impotence has restricted both the quantity and quality of services provided. In other words, urban Canadians, economically and socially critical to the nation, find themselves with rather primitive public institutional machinery with which to establish and meet the important needs of community and individuals. It is in this sense that the urban majority might be said to be largely disenfranchised.

The second and related hypothesis is that this disenfranchisement has had consequences of national economic significance. Problem-laden urban areas are becoming a drag on the national economy, rather than its engine. They are incapable of maintaining, let alone expanding, the local physical infrastructure essential to support new development. Nor can they provide the high quality social infrastructure in the fields of health, education and the environment so necessary to attract modern competitive industries.

Our approach will be to examine, using recently released 1991 census data, the various demographic and economic forces acting on urban areas in the recent past and the pressures they continue to exert in terms of specific problem areas. We next examine the availability of resources in order to determine the degree to which urban needs are likely to be met now and in the future. The consequences of the alleged shortfall in the capacity of urban governments to attend to the legitimate and urgent needs of their constituents, and hence the failure of this vital dimension of democracy, will be critically analyzed. We then reconsider the economic significance of cities and their declining capacity to foster development. In the final section, we explore how this process might be reversed and even offer some degree of optimism for re-enfranchising urbanites.

DEMOCRATIZATION FROM AN URBAN PERSPECTIVE

By 1991, almost 21 million, or 76.6 percent, of all Canadians lived in urban areas. Half of all Canadians lived in urban areas with over 100,000 inhabitants, and almost 12 million lived in large cities with over 500,000 inhabitants.[8] The Census Metropolitan Area of Toronto is larger, in terms of population, than eight of Canada's 10 provinces. It is 68 percent larger than the four Atlantic provinces combined. Indeed, the image of the national capital as a minor town must be confronted with the fact that Metropolitan Ottawa-Hull, which now includes 921,000 persons, is larger than each of the four Atlantic provinces and, by the turn of the century, may well surpass Manitoba and Saskatchewan in size.

While these statistics are very recent, the broad trend has been essentially uninterrupted since before Confederation. What is remarkable is that, whereas the social and economic consequences of Canada's urbanization have completely transformed the nation, the same basic political-constitutional arrangements which were erected 125 years ago continue to define the nature of urban governance.[9] As a result, devolution and other system changes have failed to address the needs of urbanites as expressed primarily, but not exclusively, through democratically elected local governments. This failure frustrates the worldwide trend whereby individuals are striving to gain greater control over the forces that shape their lives. Much of the emphasis has been on political forces, but there is an important interaction between social and economic forces, and political ones that cannot be ignored.

In the social domain, the past quarter-century witnessed the creation of a wide variety of public institutions designed to help individuals, primarily those who are economically, physically or otherwise disadvantaged. However admirable the concern and immediately effective the level of assistance in providing a social safety net, one consequence has been the increased dependency of these beneficiaries on the State. And that dependency has, of necessity, reduced their ability to control their own lives. Former intermediating institutions in which they were active and influential participants—the family, the tribe, the church, the neighbourhood, the community—have been transformed or rendered redundant by the growing web of publicly created social institutions, over which individuals have much less control.

In no small measure this sweeping aside of such institutions was due to the fact that the initiatives in fields as diverse as health, higher education and welfare reform came from the necessarily remote but fiscally well-endowed federal government. The provinces also claimed their constitutional right first to deliver and then to finance (especially via federal transfers, unconditional if possible) such programs. Few, if any, of the initiatives came from the bottom up—from individuals, community organizations or the local level of government.

The rush, in the name of social justice, to capture these growing constituencies, who would then become clients, blinded their often well-meaning proponents to the long-term consequences: the erosion of their clients' capacity to exercise and expand their democratic rights through the traditional mechanisms of empowerment. A trade-off was made that favoured social justice over individual control, and we continue to live with the after-effects of that choice.

In the economic domain, rapid growth and growing internationalization in the postwar era also contributed to a significant erosion of individual autonomy. Consumer choices and employment opportunities are increasingly dictated by forces beyond the local market-place, in which the individual at one time had an important say. Decisions by national governments and multinational organizations in the realm of international trading arrangements, foreign investment policies, regulation of competition and investment incentives have become perhaps the overriding determinants of individual economic welfare. In such a world, the scope for local governments to influence the economic well-being of their constituents has been restricted.

URBAN NEEDS AND RESOURCES

The urban case has been asserted frequently, but its proponents have been unable to effect any substantial change. One problem is that the information necessary to make a persuasive case is still not available, although more and more is accumulating. A second problem is that no one with the ability to change things is listening.[10] Finally, the urban focus is too general, encompassing a great variety of fundamentally different communities. Our emphasis will be on metropolitan areas, as they are clearly the major problem areas that can no longer be dismissed.

Urban Needs

The continued growth of Canada's urban areas, in particular its major metropolitan areas, reflects and feeds back into the overall economic and demographic development of the nation. At present, the prolonged recession is having devastating consequences for the eastern metropolitan areas in particular, which face very high rates of unemployment, a glut in the housing and office markets, high rates of bankruptcy, and very low levels of consumer and business confidence.

In addition to these cyclical problems, there are a number of longer-term trends that more fundamentally influence the process of democratization. Such trends feature in the first instance a significant spread of metropolitan areas outward, which has led to the creation of new urban units which then tend to be joined to the larger area under the umbrella of some form of regional government.[11] Unfortunately, little, if any, thought appears to have gone into ensuring that such units are integrated into the larger metropolitan framework in a way that would complement the urban economy. In virtually all cases, including recent attempts in Ontario to reform regional governments, the search is for institutional accommodation (accountability, responsibility). However, reform has largely ignored solutions that would enhance functional effectiveness (e.g. social and economic development) in ways that would meet the unique needs of different communities. As a result, on the economic side at least, the synergy that would otherwise be expected from this urban growth and spread is often lost. What we observe instead is often mindless competition among local authorities in the same metropolitan area.[12]

Meanwhile, there has been a significant rise in urban poverty levels in general and for the growing number of female-headed, single-parent families in particular.[13] The escalation of urban poverty predates the current recession. Table 8.1 shows that, over the past quarter-century, there has been a nationwide decline in the incidence of poverty (of modest proportions for individuals but very significant for families). But the metropolitan dimension is quite different. The proportion of the poor residing in cities of over 500,000 rose from 22 percent in 1965 to 56 percent in 1990. Virtually all the offsetting decline was in small urban and rural areas where the proportion fell from 57 to 21 percent. What we have witnessed, therefore, is the "metropolitanization of poverty," a phenomenon that at one time was thought to be a unique American pathology.

Nor is this growing metropolitan poverty confined to the traditional groups of the uneducated and recent immigrants. The incidence of poverty among the university educated in these large centres has almost doubled since 1965. And, while the incidence of poverty among the aged has fallen, that among younger individuals, especially families with female heads, has increased sharply.[14]

Perhaps the most severe consequence has been the rapid growth of child poverty in urban areas. The failure of public policy, designed by higher levels of government, to protect this fragile group highlights both the problem and consequences of urban disenfranchisement.[15] This dramatic deterioration in the condition of inhabitants of the largest cities in Canada has been not only a tragic waste of our human resources, it has created an unprecedented need for social support and employment programs.[16]

In other domains as well, the growth of urban areas has created a variety of problems and needs. While subject to reporting biases, criminal data reveal higher and growing rates of crime, particularly violent crime, in the larger urban areas and especially in the core municipalities of metropolitan areas.[17]

With respect to the environment, the indicators are less definitive, but point to similar important problems and needs. One study of urban air quality reveals that for five key indicators, Montreal performed badly in all; Toronto, Calgary and Vancouver did so in four; and indeed only Ottawa, Winnipeg and Regina had a single problem area.[18] For water quality, one third of all households in urban areas of over 100,000 used water filters,

Table 8.1

**Structure and Incidence of Low Incomes
in Urban Canada, 1965 and 1990**

Population of Localities	Percentage of all Low Income		Percentage of Low Income among Pop. in Category	
	1965	1990	1965	1990
Cities over 500,000				
Individuals	10	33	29	37
Families	12	24	12	15
Total	22	56		
Cities between 100,000-499,999				
Individuals	6	8	36	34
Families	8	5	12	10
Total	14	14		
Cities between 30,000-99,999				
Individuals	2	5	38	37
Families	4	4	16	12
Total	6	9		
Small urban (under 30,000) and rural				
Individuals	14	10	56	30u
				23r
Families	43	11	34	10u
				9r
Total	57	21		
All localities				
Individuals	32	56	39	34
Families	68	44	34	12
Total	100	100		

Sources: N.H. Lithwick, *Urban Canada: Research Monograph Number 1, Urban Poverty*, (Ottawa: Canada Mortgage and Housing Corporation, 1971), Summary Tables 65-1; 65-2; Statistics Canada, *1991 Survey of Consumer Finances,* Ottawa, 1990. (Unpublished data).

Note: u = urban; r = rural.

purifiers, or bottled water compared with under 25 percent in small urban and rural areas.[19]

However partial, these data reveal a distressing conjunction of problems and an increase in their intensity over the past decades, particularly in the largest metropolitan areas. These findings are of concern, not just for the cities themselves, but for the entire country, precisely because the health of these centres is vital to the economic, social and cultural well-being of the nation as a whole.

Urban Resources

The ability of urban areas to meet their growing needs depends ultimately on the availability of fiscal resources. Traditionally, those revenues have come primarily from property taxes, transfers from higher levels of government and borrowing. More recently, municipalities have tried to increase their revenues by resorting to user fees.

The various sources of local government financing for selected years are presented in Table 8.2. The most dramatic change has been the reduced reliance on own-revenue sources over the past four decades. From a level of over 75 percent in the early 1950s, the proportion is now about half. It is clear that the decline in own-source revenues was the result of a steady fall-off of real property tax revenues. To compensate, there were very significant increases in provincial grants, primarily conditional ones. But these proved to be fiscal traps.

In 1990, the growing deficit in the federal government's budget led the Government to cap its Established Programs Financing for health and post-secondary education, and the Canada Assistance Plan. More recently, there have been cut-backs in Unemployment Insurance (UI) funding. This has forced many recipients onto social assistance which in some provinces is cost-shared with municipalities. The squeeze on the provinces as a result of both these reduced federal transfers and their own self-induced fiscal woes, led them in turn to squeeze social assistance (for example, in British Columbia, Alberta and Ontario) and to download functions to local governments. The provinces offered conditional grants to municipalities at the outset to sweeten the pill, then capped those grants without a matching reduction of mandated service levels when the crunch came.[20] Clearly, their

Table 8.2

**Local Government Revenues
by Source, 1953-88**

Source of Revenue	1953	1975	1988
		(percentages)	
Own source revenues:			
Real property taxes	63.6	39.6	37.5
Sales of goods and services	-	7.0	10.3
Other own source revenues	12.9	2.0	5.2
Subtotal	76.5	48.6	53.0
Transfers:			
Unconditional	2.9	7.9	5.5
Conditional	20.3	43.5	41.6
Subtotal	23.2	51.4	47.0
Total	100.0	100.0	100.0

Source: Harry M. Kitchen, *Property Taxation in Canada*, Canadian Tax Paper no. 92, (Toronto: Canadian Tax Foundation, 1992), Table 1.2.

fiscal dependency places cities in hazardous fiscal straits when funding gets restrained.[21]

Consider the downloading of social services. We have seen that these needs are clearly occasioned by rapid urbanization and economic stagnation, and that they are most severe in metropolitan areas. Such services cannot be funded efficiently from local revenues because of the potential mobility of recipients. Nevertheless, transfers in this area have recently been capped, leaving municipalities with an increasingly unsupportable welfare burden.[22] In the area of crime, service levels are again being squeezed. In Ottawa, for example, the total number of police personnel was the same in 1991 as in 1986, although the population of the city had increased by 25,000.[23] And so it goes on. That urban areas now face virtually insurmountable fiscal pressures should hardly be surprising.

Since 1975, the extension of user fees and other new revenue sources has offered some relief. However, the scale of that relief should not be overemphasized. The politically "safe" sources of user fees have now been tapped. Additional sources such as marginal cost pricing of public transit and parking, waste removal, police and fire services, and specialized education programs will be much more difficult to introduce.[24] It is also unlikely that proposals to share in provincial user fees, such as the lucrative tax on gasoline, will be kindly received by the hard-pressed provinces.

Urban Efforts

It might be argued that the reason the problems are growing is that urban areas are not making sufficient efforts to deal with them, either by raising additional revenues or by delivering better policies. The slower growth of local expenditures than would appear to be warranted by the growth in needs might be interpreted that way. For example, whereas federal expenditures in nominal dollars grew at an average annual rate of 10.6 percent from 1965-66 to 1991-92 and provincial expenditures grew by 12 percent annually, local government expenditures grew by 10 percent per year, although the local level represents the fastest growing segment of society.[25] In real terms, these growth rates were 3.4, 4.8 and 2.8 percent, respectively.[26] Furthermore, between 1961 and 1981, local government expenditures as a percentage of gross domestic product rose from 7.5 to 10.1 percent. However, in less than a decade of general fiscal retrenchment, between 1981 and 1988, that share declined to 8.8 percent.[27] Given the huge absolute and relative growth of urban areas, and the compounding of their problems, the overall growth of expenditure is much less than would appear to have been warranted. One reason may be that provinces assumed responsibility for a large number of formerly municipal functions such as health, social welfare and education expenditures, ensuring delivery by municipalities through conditional transfer financing. By 1980, provincial grants as a percentage of local gross expenditures in these three areas were 74.5, 52.2 and 65.8 percent, respectively.[28]

Most observers conclude that, despite these transfers, expenditures have been severely limited by the overall lack of revenues. Transfers have not grown as quickly as needs, and municipalities are restricted by the provinces, both in terms of what things they can tax and how much they can borrow. In other words, the level of expenditure is said to be determined more by revenue limits than by the unwillingness of local governments to fulfil their responsibilities. In general, this argument is persuasive, with one caveat—the reluctance of local governments to raise local property tax revenues. The property tax is not ideal from the politician's perspective, in that the base—the assessed value of real property—is rather slow growing, so that additional revenues must come from tax rate increases. And annual rate increases are very visible and highly unpopular. It is further alleged that the property tax is an unfair (regressive) one, but recent research has cast some doubt on that view.[29]

Under these circumstances, the argument that local governments are making their best efforts can be questioned. Certainly there would appear to be substantial room for increasing that tax if one considers the average burden on taxpayers. Harry Kitchen estimates that between 1971 and 1988, the share of personal income going to pay the property tax fell from 5.9 to 4.7 percent.[30] The problem is that other federal (the GST) and provincial taxes have increased the total tax burden on citizens, so that the hostility of local taxpayers to any increase in the property tax is in large measure a reaction to the cumulative burden of taxation.

As a result, a satisfactory appraisal of urban needs and the corresponding required effort is virtually impossible. The size of the deficit cannot be used to measure the gap because there are stringent limits imposed by the provinces on borrowing by municipalities. One solution is to focus on specific problem areas, but that would require very detailed micro studies. Table 8.3 provides a rather revealing score-card on the efforts of the various levels of government in one important, but not necessarily representative, area: environmental expenditures.

Table 8.3

**Expenditures on the Environment
by Level of Government, 1984-90**

Level of Government	1984-85	1990-91
Federal government		
As % of all environmental expenditures	11.1	8.5
As % of federal gov't. expenditures	0.4	0.4
Provincial governments		
As % of all environment expenditures	26.7	22.0
As % of prov. gov't. expenditures	1.2	1.2
Local governments		
As % of all environmental expenditures	62.2	69.5
As % of local gov't. expenditures	7.1	9.6

Source: Statistics Canada, *Human Activity and the Environment*, Cat. no. 11-509E, (Ottawa, September 1991), Table 3.2.

It is clear from this table that the federal and provincial efforts are both very limited and, more troubling, are actually declining as a proportion of the total effort being made. Only local governments have increased their share of their own budgets for environmental programs, thereby increasing their share of total environmental expenditures at all levels. As a result, one can only assert with admittedly weak evidence that there are substantial unfilled urban needs which are not being met because of the limited resources available to municipalities.[31] At best, problems are being serviced, not solved.

URBAN RESPONSES
Fiscal Responses

The natural response to fiscal tightness would be to raise property taxes, but we have seen that there are serious political limitations on that course of action. A number of tax reforms have been proposed, especially moving to Market Value Assessment on property taxation, but these reforms will, at best, correct certain distortions rather than give the local tax base greater revenue elasticity.[32] Significantly for advocates of tax increases, these reforms are encountering enormous opposition by local rate-payers.

One might well ask: Why not resort to debt financing, at least to fund new infrastructure, given the very long service life of such capital? Unfortunately, many municipalities were badly burned by the surge in interest rates in the early 1980s, which continues to impose a high cost on servicing outstanding debt. In the name of fiscal prudence many, if not most, municipalities in Canada now fund such infrastructure out of reserve funds or current revenues. That "prudent" strategy imposes enormous burdens on present generations for the benefit of those in the future who will likely be wealthier. This policy, like that of resisting tax rate increases, while safe, confirms that local governments are not making the efforts within their reach to deal with many of the challenges they face today.[33]

One favourite new source of revenue has been the local development charge, which attempts to generate revenues to cover the cost of many municipal services occasioned by new developments. This would appear to be a golden opportunity, but research on this levy reveals very serious consequences. It penalizes new home buyers and gives unearned profits to existing home-owners, which is both inefficient and inequitable. It also increases the cost of servicing and, hence, of housing. Two informed scholars on local government finance have concluded that "... the more closely one looks at the development-charge approach to financing municipal infrastructure, the less attractive it becomes."[34]

Service Cut-backs

In the face of fiscal timidity by local governments and inadequate funding from the provinces in particular (but also the federal government in the case of infrastructure financing), local governments have had to restrict their service levels. Many local government expenditure areas have service levels mandated by the province, leaving only discretionary areas to take the brunt of these cuts: staff releases, garbage collection, snow removal, library services, recreational facilities, and so forth, together with the steady decline in the maintenance and repair of urban infra-structure (see below).

There is some room for cynicism regarding these actions. At the same time that these cut-backs have been occurring, many municipalities have spent tens of millions of dollars on new head offices, culture halls, sports palaces and related monuments to themselves. No doubt these were felt to be necessary investments, but were they really the highest priority items on the municipal agenda?

The Infrastructure Crisis

The single, most problematic response to the fiscal squeeze on urban areas has been the cut-back in spending on physical infrastructure.[35] The very nature of capital intensive services such as roads, sewers, water systems, and so forth, is such that it is possible to run down the capital by not maintaining or replacing it, and to avoid building new systems required by rapid urbaniz-ation by increasing queues and letting quality standards slide. These actions have no drastic immediate consequence, just gradual deterioration of both very valuable stock and service levels. The long-term impact on private capital formation, productivity and economic growth is devastating.[36] Such deterioration is precisely what the Canadian Federation of Municipalities (CFM) alleges has been happening to urban infrastructure. In a number of recent publications, the CFM has attempted to estimate the level of resources needed to restore the infrastructure to an acceptable level.[37] By now, the number is probably of the order of $20 billion. While there are serious problems with the estimation procedures, virtually all other evidence supports the claim that there has been a drastic shortfall; and the various provincial ministries of urban affairs have accepted the claim. However, the provinces have insisted on federal participation before committing themselves to assist in funding the effort to rebuild the infrastructure, an invitation the federal government has consistently declined, primarily on cost grounds. Nor is it only the physical infrastruc-ture that is being run down. It is generally conceded that education, despite soaring budgets, has deteriorated as have health, social and cultural services.

Promoting "Local Economic Development"

The virtually universal response to the problems of the cities has been to try to find new industries that might expand the tax base and generate jobs. Most of these policies originate with local governments, although a variety of federal and provincial regional development initiatives have similar orientations. The reality is that local governments are minor players in the formulation and implementation of policies that impact on urban economic development. Those policies originate with federal and provincial governments, and national or international firms for the most part. Municipalities essentially respond to opportunities with the very limited and crude tools (planning, servicing) that are available to them.

What local governments emphasize are business promotion and provision of sites and services. Studies of these policies reveal in many cases a rather myopic approach, which equates business assistance with economic development and fails to include costs as well as benefits in the calculus that underlies decisions to provide fiscal and other incentives.[38] As we shall argue later, an emphasis on economic development is not inappropriate—indeed it is crucial—but a much more profound understanding of what that means is required.

Recent Initiatives

There have been bottom-up attempts to redress the situation. The effort by the CFM to get funding for infrastructure is one such attempt. But its failure, after a decade of hard sell, serves to illustrate the point being made in this chapter. Mayors from large cities and metropolitan areas, representing many millions of urbanites and pursuing policies that most urbanites would support, have been turned down flatly by the federal government. Of course the federal government knows full well that these mayors have no ability to deliver their voters, which speaks volumes about the truly marginal status of urban governments.

Another attempt now fashionable goes by the name of "disentanglement." Indeed, a newsletter on the subject is now produced by the Government of Ontario in co-operation with the Association of Municipalities of Ontario. The objective of the program is sensible: to assign functions to the level of government most capable of providing them. Significantly, however, no devolution of resources is envisaged. Moreover, like the constitutional debates, this effort presumes a detached, theoretical approach to power-sharing. By its nature, the competition for power in today's context will, in all likelihood, lead to further erosion of local government powers, not their augmentation. Such would appear to be what is being promoted between the lines in the 1991 Report of the Advisory Committee to the (Ontario) Minister of Municipal Affairs on the Provincial-Municipal Financial Relationship.

Other efforts at reform from above appear to be no less disingenuous. The creation of regional governments has, in general, served not to enhance local autonomy, but to mute it. Few reforms of regional government have been approved that would lead to greater authentic local autonomy. Simply stated, regional governments have been an attempt to achieve administrative rather than policy objectives, thereby failing to create the sophisticated and locally appropriate machinery needed for managing complex, multi-jurisdictional and multi-level systems of metropolitan governance.[39]

To summarize, there has been an erosion in the quality of urban life, especially in metropolitan areas, both in human and physical terms. Such an erosion is bound to affect the overall economic efficiency of urban areas by raising the direct cost of business, by increasing the cost of living (which translates into lower productivity and higher labour costs), and by reducing the amenity value of such places in attracting new firms. Efforts have been made, primarily by local governments, to deal with urban decline, but the lack of fiscal resources limits severely what they can do on their own. And all too often their modest efforts are misdirected, making matters worse.

Indeed, the way in which the situation has evolved and the manner of the response reveal much about the structural situation in which urban governments find themselves, limited by constitutional assignment to a highly dependent status. The failure of the provinces to devolve funds and powers to local governments has eroded the latter's capacity to be responsive to the particular needs of their citizenry. The homogenization and distortion of education, health and social policies by remote provincial bureaucracies are testimony to the damage done to democratic governance which requires greater local control and empowerment than the provinces have allowed. The only attempt by the federal government to get involved in devolution, the experimentation with a Ministry of State for Urban Affairs in the 1970s, was aborted due mainly to provincial opposition.[40]

The secondary consequences of non-devolution are even more problematic. Local governments, dependent on provincial largesse, quickly develop a subservient posture. Initiative is restricted and priorities are set in line with provincial needs, not those of the citizens who elect local governments. Not surprisingly, local governments have difficulty attracting the best possible political leadership and, in consequence and regrettably, some of their best officials get discouraged. Urban management tends to become second-rate, and the problems to which we have alluded simply get worse.

A further consequence of local government impotence is the decline of public support for and trust in it.[41] The sense of community purpose has given way to the narrow and selfish pursuit of self-interest. The common urban disease, Not In My Back Yard (NIMBY), is a symptom of that loss of faith. Without public support, attempts by local government to assert greater autonomy, to act more entrepreneurially and to take risks, even where there is a price to be paid, are simply non-starters. The saving grace is an occasional mayor with the vision, guts and brains to understand the situation and to build whatever local base he or she can to achieve more than the minimum generally available.[42]

A POLICY ALTERNATIVE

At this moment, it is unlikely that major political-institutional changes will be introduced to deal with urban disenfranchisement. Higher levels of government are disinclined to yield power. They certainly will not yield resources. And local governments remain parochial and divided, unable to combine forces to achieve any substantive changes. As a result of so many dead ends, and so much resistance to change, urban analysts appear to have grown weary and few imaginative proposals for authentic urban reform in Canada have materialized in the recent past. Nor have local officials yet come to realize what the name of the game is, and they have yet to take steps to play in the big leagues. Nevertheless, the conjuncture of recent events makes it an opportune time to see if a new initiative, taking an indirect approach that is less politically ambitious but ultimately more viable, might be considered.

Building on Metropolitan Economic Potential

One of the most puzzling omissions from much of the discussion about urban reform has been the economic significance of cities.[43] It is true that much attention is being paid by cities themselves to their economic development, however myopic their approach might be. But their national economic significance has not been recognized and, as a result, cities have not been prominent as vehicles for a development strategy. Some facts should be considered. First, economic activity, and leading economic activity in particular, is disproportionately located in the largest metropolitan centres, and hence these centres constitute the primary engine of national economic development. As one of many possible examples, the Census Metropolitan Area of Toronto, with 13.6 percent of Canada's population in 1986, produced 21.8 percent of the nation's value added output in manufacturing and employed 22.8 percent of the nation's manufacturing employees.[44] Moreover, much of new industry in high-technology fields is necessarily located in large metropolitan areas, adjacent to major universities and research establishments. One would expect, given these facts, that, especially in times of economic slow-down, we would pursue economic development policies building on the innate advantages of this economic core. Yet, it remains fashionable to pursue so-called regional policies which transfer key firms and plants from the economic base of the largest cities to less well-off regions. Both the federal and provincial governments pursue this politically attractive approach. The problem is that the costs far exceed the benefits, not only at the obvious level of the city affected but nationally as well. The costs are high because, in withdrawing a segment (a plant, firm, or research centre) of a complex economic system with its many interdependencies or linkages, a vast range of external costs are imposed on the urban and, hence, national economy. Locating this segment in a fragile area that has few, if any, comparative advantages and few linkages (neither of which appear to have been studied in most cases where such relocations have occurred) provides very modest offsetting benefits. And in addition to this direct net loss, taxpayers must pay for the huge incentives needed to entice these transplants.

Second, there has not been enough recognition of the central role economic improvement plays in contributing to social development. Not only are there immediate impacts in terms of reducing unemployment and raising incomes, but the quality of that employment and its sustainability are also affected. And the implications of more and better jobs for individual, family and community well-being are crucial. Moreover, economic development provides the tax capacity with which to finance local government services that have become eroded. The tendency in past years to see the economic, social and environmental domains as essentially separate and, indeed, incompatible led to policies such as the anti-growth crusade which did much harm in all areas.

Third, changes in the global economy generally, and in North America in particular, mean that industry can no longer survive if it produces purely for local, or even national, markets. Competition will eliminate all but the most efficient. And while many of the determinants of firm efficiency are internal to the firm, there are also external factors that can have a major impact. Such factors include the efficiency of infrastructure, especially in the areas of serviced land, structures, transportation and communication; the availability of high quality labour and the capacity to retrain labour frequently; the presence of entrepreneurial management; the willingness of financial intermediaries to participate actively in promoting new economic activity; the availability of scientific research and development facilities; and, most important, supportive, non-invasive public policies that let business do what it can do best while protecting the public from harmful side-effects. Many of these factors are determined by the quality of the local urban environment. Yet over the past few decades, as we have seen, that environment has deteriorated. Taxes have had to rise to finance local government due to the fiscal squeeze from the top down; local government policies have handicapped business in scores of ways in the name of amorphous planning goals; education and training, now significantly underfunded by any reasonable measure, increasingly appear to be out of touch with the requirements of a modern economy; and so on.

Fourth, business success is ultimately the result of individual efforts. Government macro policies are necessary to provide a helpful context in terms of exchange and interest rates, fiscal regimes, and so forth. The record of government's direct efforts to stimulate business should caution us about the limits of its effectiveness. If it were not for the current deficit problem, national and provincial governments would no doubt continue to pursue the golden grail of "industrial strategies" to kick-start the economy, learning nothing from billions of dollars wasted on megaprojects, failed attempts to pick winners, and so forth.

Fifth, increasingly national economic success has been the outcome of an aggregation of local success stories. The older paradigm of the economy as an amalgam of national industries is giving way to the newer paradigm of the economy as the composite of its local economies, each of which, on the basis of its unique local advantages and opportunities, must struggle in an open competitive environment if it is to succeed.

Sixth, Canadians, along with citizens in other Western democracies, are clearly tired of political-ideological battles and are telling their politicians to get on with stimulating an economic recovery. The temptation for those politicians is to go for the quick fix, for big spending programs with too little thought given to long-term effects. For the same dollars, we have the rare opportunity to lay the foundations for a serious economic development strategy, which can begin to restore Canada's flagging capacity to compete in a new and tougher international economy.

These facts point to an urgent and unique focus for an urban policy to address these salient issues, which, in addition, provides the possibility for rejuvenating our major metropolitan areas by reducing their dependency and encouraging them to focus on their central economic role and responsibilities.

Some Institutional Requirements

What is required is an authentic economic development program that aims to create in urban areas the conditions that will contribute to their accelerated economic development. American ideas such as urban enterprise zones would appear to have little relevance to our situation. Indeed, since each of our metropolitan areas has distinctive comparative advantages, an urban economic development policy must, in the first instance, identify those advantages, then develop strategic plans to take advantage of them. Such an effort can only be initiated by local governments. In addition, it must involve fully the local business, labour and community leadership. And it must attempt to maximize the "appropriate" contribution of the provinces as well as the federal government.

More specifically, we would propose the launching of a Metropolitan Development Corporation (MDC) for each of the five or six largest metropolitan areas, to be expanded to others as soon as feasible. An initial agreement would have to be reached among the public as well as private partners regarding the scope and scale of their respective efforts. All would participate in setting broad policy guidelines for the MDCs, but they should be run as an autonomous body, without day-to-day intervention. A broadly representative governing board is required to ensure that each MDC behaves in a responsible and accountable fashion.[45]

The MDCs would be given the initial responsibility to design a strategic development plan for each community as indicated above, indicating precisely those areas where government inputs of resources, programs, and so forth, at all levels are required and where policies that are harmful to urban economic development should be terminated or amended. Government inputs should not be used to support individual businesses. That task is best left to business itself.

In addition, we would propose the creation of a National Metropolitan Economic Development Banking System to provide venture capital to urban businesses that meet the criteria specified in the strategic plan, but purely on a business basis. In other words, all proposals must meet the test of the market-place. Again, management of the Bank would be independent but subject to the broad policy guidelines of a governing board consisting of representatives of the Bank of Canada, interested commercial banks, national and local business leadership, and key government finance officials. Ideally, each metropolitan area would have its own Metropolitan Economic Development Bank as part of the national system so that policies could be better tailored to local requirements.

All levels of government would be expected to contribute to enhancing the framework necessary to encourage economic development. Infrastructure to make the city more efficient, and to link it more effectively—depending on trading patterns—to other cities and export markets would have to be put in place. Key support institutions, such as universities and research centres, would be assisted primarily in those areas that would enhance the economic base of the city. Programs that prepare students for the emerging job market and help direct research toward applications in the most important fields, would be given highest priority. Tax and transfer policies would be reviewed with a view to increasing incentives for entrepreneurial activity. Policies to lower housing costs, improve amenities and, hence, keep labour costs competitive would be explored.

A concerted effort in this direction would give an enormous boost to the metropolitan economies and, more importantly, to the national economy, spreading benefits throughout Canada. It would expand the local tax base thereby speeding up the process of acquiring greater fiscal autonomy for the cities. It would also provide the basis for a coherent, cost-effective program for national and provincial governments as they search for spending programs to cope with unemployment and recession. The alternatives now being considered, building roads or repairing infrastructure without sufficient regard to where they would have the greatest developmental impact, reflect the kind of thinking that created so much of our present economic flabbiness.

Some Cautions and Grounds for Optimism

One of the most difficult tasks will be to distinguish what we are proposing as a development effort from most of what takes place at present under the same name. In fact, most economic development corporations in urban areas have little understanding of, and interest in, economic development as we use the term. Rather, they are interested in business development through promotion of exports and encouragement of new plants. But these efforts fail to take a long-term view of development. There is no strategic plan to identify sustainable advantages and build them, particularly in the "softer" domains such as achieving educational excellence, making the environment of exemplary quality, and supporting non-governmental communal development. These business development efforts have, in fact, polarized communities by setting the business interests against the rest of the community. As a result, urban economic development has acquired a bad name and triggers substantial grass-roots hostility. Such hostility will, of course, negate any serious development initiative.

But there is no alternative to serious development and, as a result, these subtle distinctions must be understood and communicated. Fortunately, there have been several examples of both regional and urban development programs that serve as attractive models for the MDCs. In the regional field the experiences of DATAR in France, the Geelong program in Australia, and the Appalachia Regional Development Act in the United States demonstrate that mission-oriented development planning can be effective.[46] One of the most encouraging recent cases of urban development has been Hamburg, where civic authorities created a development agency with assistance not from government but from local firms and banks. The result was that the economy was rebuilt with long-term, viable jobs that reflect its new comparative advantages in finance and communications.[47]

The National Interest in Urban Development

The details of such an urban development program remain to be worked out, but it is our view that the case for such a program is a strong one. With national elections on the horizon, it is the kind of initiative that an imaginative political party could debate and modify as needed. A program of this sort could help build a majority national urban constituency, replace vacuous promises about spending with a viable program, and forge an original link between an urgent economic initiative and political democratic reform. If the federal government should seize the initiative, not by deciding what has to be done but simply by agreeing to participate responsibly in urban-based initiatives, the provinces would have to join in because their urban constituents would not stand for their opting out.

It is clear that in the United States and, therefore, in Canada, there will be heavy emphasis placed on infrastructure development as the way to revive stagnant economies.[48] In the U.S., the motivations behind this orientation are complex, and important among them is the need for a response to the Los Angeles riots, much like the urban programs of the 1970s were responses to the riots in Watts, Newark, Washington and Detroit. These responses and their Canadian imitations had little lasting impact because the overriding concern was short-term cooling of the situation. With something like the MDC model, Canada can create a vehicle for channelling, in an effective manner, those initiatives that will yield more than short-term pay-offs. Indeed, such initiatives can give real substance to our pursuit of more satisfactory and sustained economic growth, with its attendant social and environmental benefits.

Finally, how is this option supposed to enhance democracy? It is our view that, by seizing such an initiative, urban governments would be taking the first giant step toward greater autonomy. We accept that it is unlikely that such autonomy will be granted voluntarily by the provinces. But, if substantial economic progress can be triggered by the MDC concept, then individuals in cities, and the cities themselves, will begin to take charge, creating over time social and communal mechanisms more in tune with what citizens want. In other words, the reform will not come through direct political change. It might, if properly managed, ultimately come about indirectly, beginning with economic development.

NOTES

We are indebted to Katherine Graham, Allan Maslove and Susan Phillips for excellent critical comments on an early draft.

1   There are numerous exceptions, where business or social activist minorities have disproportionate influence over local government policies. But special interests are at least as influential at the more senior level, although less easily detected. It can be argued that it is precisely this transparency that gives local government a much worse reputation than is warranted.

2   Cited by Jacques L'heureux, "Municipalities and the Division of Powers" in Richard Simeon, *Intergovernmental Relations*, vol. 63 (Toronto: University of Toronto Press for the Royal Commission

on the Economic Union and Development Prospects for Canada, 1985), chap. 5, p. 204.

3   Jean-Michel Cousineau, Claude E. Forget, and John Richards, *Delivering the Goods: The Federal-Provincial Division of Spending Powers* (Toronto: C.D. Howe Institute, June 1992), pp. 37-39. "Rational ignorance" refers to the fact that many voters do not bother to vote because the cost of becoming informed on many, if not most, national issues is greater than the perceived benefits.

4   Paul Waldie, writing for *The Globe and Mail* [Toronto], January 13, 1993, p. A8, says: "It's called downloading, but for city officials across Canada, it's more like passing the buck without the bucks."

5   L'heureux, "Municipalities," p. 201.

6   Richard A. Loreto and Trevor Price, (eds.), *Urban Policy Issues: Canadian Perspectives* (Toronto: McClelland and Stewart, 1990), p. 242.

7   There is a large volume of literature bemoaning urban neglect and demanding a new deal for urban governments. See, for example, David M. Nowlan, "Towards Home Rule for Urban Policy," *Journal of Canadian Studies*, 13, 1 (Spring 1978): pp. 70-79; Richard A. Loreto and Trevor Price, (eds.), "Conclusion: Provinces and Local Autonomy" in *Urban Policy Issues: Canadian Perspectives* (Toronto: McClelland and Stewart, 1990); and John H. Taylor, "Urban Autonomy in Canada: Its Evolution and Decline" in Gilbert A. Stelter and Alan F. Artibise, (eds.), *Power and Place: Canadian Urban Development in the North American Context* (Vancouver: University of British Columbia Press, 1986), chap. 1. Most of these authors argue for a devolution of powers and matching funding. Harvey Lithwick proposed federal involvement in a national (multi-level) approach to urban policy making as a way to lever provinces into accepting an enhanced role for urban governments. N. Harvey Lithwick, "Urban Canada, Problems and Prospects," (Report prepared for the Minister Responsible for Housing, Canada Mortgage and Housing Corporation, Ottawa, 1970). The Ministry of State for Urban Affairs

was created in 1971 to implement that proposal.

8   Statistics Canada, *1991 Census of Canada: Urban Areas, Population and Dwelling Counts*, cat. no. 93-305 (Ottawa, 1992), Table 3.

9   The persistent, if anachronistic, image of urban Canada as an agglomeration of small, diverse and weak entities enables provinces and the federal government to continue to redefine essentially urban issues, requiring urban solutions, in the non-urban frameworks that constitute their own partitioning of policy issues.

10   It may also be that local government politicians who most frequently complain about their powerlessness are less than sincere. Certainly, the extent to which they have shown leadership in dealing innovatively with their problems has not been impressive. There have been some individual successes, but the most striking phenomenon is their inability to act collectively. Indeed, even when opportunities do arise, they tend to want to make separate deals for themselves wherever possible.

11   For example, between 1966 and 1991 the population of the central cities of Montreal, Toronto and Vancouver combined declined by 7 percent, while their fringes grew by a factor of 24 times. For all 25 Census Metropolitan Areas, the fringe population grew by 11.6 times. Institute of Urban Studies, *Sustainable Cities*, Institute of Urban Studies Newsletter Supplement (Winnipeg: University of Winnipeg, Autumn 1992).

12   The loss of the Space Agency by the Ottawa metropolitan region was in part due to the inability of the various municipalities to see their common economic interest. N. Harvey Lithwick, *Economic Development in Ottawa-Carleton*, Research Study no. 4 for the Ottawa-Carleton Regional Review (Ottawa: Centre for Policy and Program Assessment, School of Public Administration, Carleton University, August 5, 1988), pp. 66-67.

13   There has been a continual shift of employment from the manufacturing sector to the service sector and, at the same time, a rapid rise in female participation in the urban labour force. In the case

of Metropolitan Toronto, for example, in the 25 years from 1961 to 1986 the share of manufacturing in the labour force fell from 30 to just over 20 percent, whereas the share of non-governmental services increased from 21 to 31 percent. Statistics Canada, *Census Metropolitan Areas Dimensions*, 1986 Census, cat. no. 93-156 (Ottawa, 1989), Table 15. In the same quarter-century, women increased from 33 to 45 percent of Toronto's labour force.

14   Indeed, based on international comparisons, Canada's poverty rate for single-parent households (mostly female heads) with young children is just under that of the United States (45 vs. 53 percent), but extremely high compared with the percentages in the United Kingdom (18), the Netherlands (8) and Sweden (6). Timothy M. Smeeding and Lee Rainwater, "Cross-National Trends in Income Poverty and Dependency: The Evidence for Young Adults in the Eighties" (Paper prepared for the JCPS Conference, Washington, D.C., September 20-21, 1991). The rates are for 1986 or 1987 and use as the definition of low income the proportion below the median income. See Statistics Canada, *Income Distribution by Size in Canada*, cat. no. 13-207 (Ottawa, December 1991), Appendix, Table 4.

15   The scope of this problem, and the harmful effects of public policy on these children, is described in Allan Moscovitch, "Slowing the Steamroller: The Federal Conservatives, the Social Sector and Child Benefit Reform" in Katherine A. Graham, (ed.), *How Ottawa Spends 1990-91: Tracking the Second Agenda* (Ottawa: Carleton University Press, 1990), p. 190.

16   One rough indicator of the scale of this social problem is the growth of food banks. Across Canada, this number rose from one in 1981 to 75 in 1984, 126 in 1988, and 292 in 1991. Jillian Oderkirk, "Food Banks," in Statistics Canada, *Canadian Social Trends* (Ottawa, Spring 1992), p. 7.

17   The national rate of violent crime reported in 1990 was 1.1 per 100 persons. In Montreal, Toronto and Ottawa, the rate was almost 20 percent higher. In Edmonton, the rate was 1.5, and in Vancouver, 1.6. These may be contrasted to the 1980 rates, where most of the metro areas had rates no higher than the national rate. Thus,

whereas the national rate increased by about 50 percent over the decade, the rates in the larger cities doubled. Canadian Centre for Justice Statistics, "Police Reported Crime Data in Canadian Municipalities, 1990" in *Uniform Crime Reporting Survey* (Ottawa, December 1991); and Statistics Canada, *Criminal and Traffic Enforcement Statistics*, cat. no. 85-205 (Ottawa, March 1982), Table 3.

18   Statistics Canada, *Human Activity and the Environment 1991*, cat. no. 11-059E, (Ottawa, September 1991), Table 4.1.1.2.

19   Statistics Canada, *Households and the Environment, 1991*, cat. no. 11-526, Occasional (Ottawa, 1991).

20   The most recent example is health care devolution in British Columbia. Responsibility to cut costs is being transferred to local authorities from the provincial government. Deborah Wilson, "B.C. to overhaul health-care system," *The Globe and Mail* [Toronto], February 3, 1993, p. A-1.

21   Paul Kantor explores this issue more broadly in "A Case for a National Urban Policy: The Governmentalization of Economic Dependency," *Urban Affairs Quarterly*, 26, 3 (March 1991): pp. 391-415. He concludes that "economic dependency of U.S. cities has increased as a result of federal urban-development and social welfare activities."

22   The Government of Ontario, however, has signalled its intention to assume full funding of welfare as part of its disentanglement negotiations. See below.

23   Canadian Centre for Justice Statistics, *Police Administration Statistics*, Annual Survey, selected years.

24   User fees do not address the equity issue. If the tax system were strongly progressive this would be of less concern, but such is clearly not the case.

25   Statistics Canada, *Public Finance Historical Data, 1965/66-1991/92*, cat. no. 68-512 (Ottawa, March 1992), Tables H1-H6.

26   We have used the implicit price deflator for government current expenditures. Statistics Canada, *National Income and Expenditure Accounts, Annual Estimates, 1926-86*, cat. no. 13-531 (Ottawa, June 1988); and Statistics Canada, *National Income and Expenditure Accounts*, cat. no. 13-001 (Ottawa, September 1992).

27   Harry M. Kitchen, *Property Taxation in Canada*, Canadian Tax Paper no. 92 (Toronto: Canadian Tax Foundation, 1992), Table 1.1.

28   Harry M. Kitchen and Melville L. McMillan, "Local Government and Canadian Federalism" in Simeon, *Intergovernmental Relations*, vol. 63, Appendix, Table 6-A1.

29   Kitchen, *Property Taxation*, chap. 3, gives a good review of the current literature on the question of the regressivity of the property tax. He finds that if it is not highly progressive, it is certainly not the regressive one so vilified by local government authorities. On the other hand, more recent evidence by the Property Tax Working Group for Ontario's Fair Tax Commission indicates that the tax is generally regressive, but with great individual variability in impact. *Highlights of Working Group Report*, (Toronto, 1992), pp. 7-11.

30   Kitchen, *Property Taxation*, Table 1.1.

31   See our discussion below on the infrastructure and fiscal crises.

32   Implementation of the economically rational Market Value Assessment system has encountered strenuous opposition in Ontario.

33   In a thoughtful essay, John H. Taylor attributes the essential risk averse behaviour of local leadership to the fear of reaction by taxpayers to significant alterations in the property tax burden. Taylor, "Urban Autonomy in Canada," chap. 11.

34   Enid Slack and Richard Bird, "Financing Urban Growth Through Development Charges," *Canadian Tax Journal*, 39, 5 (1991): p. 1304.

35   For a useful overview of the infrastructure crisis internationally, see OECD, *Urban Infrastructure: Finance and Management* (Paris, 1991).

36   David Alan Aschauer, "Infrastructure: America's Third Deficit," *Challenge*, March-April 1991, pp. 39-45.

37   Federation of Canadian Municipalities, *Municipal Infrastructure in Canada: Physical Condition and Funding Adequacy* (Ottawa, January 1985). See also reports from the various Canadian conferences on urban infrastructure. A summary of the situation, including the stances of the various governments, is contained in a paper by Canada Mortgage and Housing Corporation, "Urban Infrastructure in Canada" (Paper prepared for the Workshop on Infrastructure and Housing: Challenges and Opportunities, London, Ontario, June 18-19, 1992).

38   Lithwick, *Economic Development in Ottawa-Carleton*, especially chap. 4.

39   Roger B. Parks and Ronald J. Oakerson, "Metropolitan Organization and Governance: A Local Political Economy Approach," *Urban Affairs Quarterly*, 25, 1 (1989): pp. 18-29.

40   One balanced assessment of the Urban Affairs experiment is in Alan F.J. Artibise and Matthew J. Kiernan, *Canadian Regional Development: The Urban Dimension*, Local Development Paper no. 12 (Ottawa: Economic Council of Canada, December 1989), pp. 1-2.

41   At present, the level of public trust is higher in local government than in any other, but the trend is clearly downward.

42   The fact that local governments are circumscribed indeed limits their autonomy, but there remain significant domains where that autonomy can be expanded if local government wishes. "Whether they do is a question of local government initiative and responsibility," according to Harold Wolman and Michael Goldsmith, "Local Autonomy as a Meaningful Analytic Concept," *Urban Affairs Quarterly*, 26, 1 (September 1990): p. 25.

43   One exception has been the Organization for Economic Co-operation and Development (OECD). In an important report, *Revitalising Urban Economies* (Paris, 1987), a strong case is made for the social, as well as economic, benefits to be derived from urban economic development. Similarly, Christopher Brooks argues in "Rethinking the City," *OECD Observer* (October/ November 1992): p. 4, that "in spite of the importance of the city as a motor of economic growth, no co-ordinated approach exists in the OECD countries to deal with the impact of rapid change."

44   Statistics Canada, *Manufacturing Industries of Canada: Sub Provincial Areas, 1986*, cat. no. 31-209 (Ottawa, October 1990). Population data from the 1991 Census of Canada, *National Overview*, cat. no. 93-301 (Ottawa, 1992). Data on productivity and income differentials further support this argument about the vital economic core residing in the large metropolitan areas and their immediate peripheries.

45   There is mounting evidence that public-private partnerships can be extremely effective where carefully designed. Moreover, these partnerships need not be based solely on serving the needs of the business community. See, for example, OECD, *Environmental Policies for Cities in the 1990s* (Paris, 1990). One example given in the study is False Creek, Vancouver.

46   A good overview of both successful and (mostly) unsuccessful regional development programs is provided in Niles Hansen, Benjamin Higgins, and Donald Savoie, *Regional Policy in a Changing World* (New York: Plenum, 1990).

47   Theresa Waldorf and Carol Hall, "Old Hamburg Blooms Anew," *Newsweek*, International Edition, January 11, 1993, pp. 34-35.

48   President Clinton made infrastructure investment one of the key elements in his "Economic Blueprint," *New York Times*, June 2, 1992, p. A14. However, very few specifics have been provided, and the emphasis appears to be mainly Keynesian, where the amount to be spent is given greater significance than where. See also *Congressional Quarterly*, 50, 26 (June 27, 1992): p. 1901.

CHAPTER 9

Canada's Balance of Payments and International Indebtedness

Bruce W. Wilkinson

Résumé : Le Canada encaisse depuis quelque temps des déficits considérables de sa balance des paiements. Il en résulte que les dettes extérieures du Canada se chiffrent aujourd'hui à environ 50 p. 100 du produit national brut (PNB). La position concurrentielle du Canada à l'échelle mondiale, d'après ses produits d'exportation à base de ressources et les autres produits et services qu'il vend, est aujourd'hui beaucoup moins favorable qu'elle ne l'a été dans le courant des dernières décennies. Par conséquent, il existe un risque véritable que la situation empire et que le Canada soit confronté à une réticence croissante des autres pays de continuer à lui prêter des sommes énormes, comme ils l'ont fait dernièrement. Advenant cette éventualité, plusieurs modifications de structure s'imposeraient. Dans ce chapitre, l'auteur avance qu'il faudrait rabaisser la valeur du dollar canadien à environ 0,70 dollar US et que, à condition qu'il se produise au Canada les changements institutionnels et d'attitude nécessaires, il serait alors possible d'éviter de nouvelles poussées inflationnistes et de rétablir l'équilibre de la balance des paiements.

Abstract: Canada has recently been experiencing sizeable deficits in the current account of its balance of payments. As a result, its net international indebtedness is now about 50 percent of its gross national product (GNP). The international competitive position which the nation faces regarding its traditional resource-based export products, as well as other products and services, is much less favourable than it was in decades past. Consequently, there is a real possibility that the situation could become worse and that the country could experience a growing reluctance on the part of the international community to continue the massive lending that has been occurring of late. Severe structural adjustments would have to be undertaken if that were to occur. This chapter, therefore, argues that the appropriate response is to lower the Canadian dollar to about US$0.70 and that, providing appropriate institutional and attitudinal changes occur in Canada, new inflationary trends could be avoided and the balance of payments situation improved.

Since the Conservative government came to power in the fall of 1984, one important area of policy has been neglected—the balance of payments and the associated balance of international indebtedness. These have been treated, by and large, as unimportant residuals. The Government's repeatedly proclaimed emphasis in its management of the economy has been on achieving competitiveness in a global economy and upon certain policies which it has hoped would bring about this competitiveness, including

- trade liberalization to open up the Canadian economy to increased international competition and to stimulate greater efficiency;
- deregulation, privatization and fiscal deficit reduction to reduce the role of government in the economy and to give business a freer hand to operate as it sees fit; and
- in the last four years, the lowering of inflation in the hope of facilitating new investment.

The most recent emphasis has been upon improving the quality of education to provide more effective and adaptable employees for the business community.[1] But throughout the years, what has been happening to the balance of payments—in particular the current account of the balance of payments—has warranted hardly a word in government policy pronouncements. Nor has Canada's increasing net balance of international indebtedness received any attention although, as we shall see, both of these balances are, for Canada, much more adverse than their counterparts in the U.S. where they have received, and continue to receive, substantial consideration.

This chapter will highlight and discuss this important lacuna in the Government's policy agenda. The main theme is that the Government's ideology and policies, as they have been defined and followed to date, will not deal effectively with Canada's balance of payments deficits and increasing international indebtedness position. It argues that, without significant policy changes, Canada could eventually find that foreigners are unwilling to continue lending to it. At that time, some very dramatic and painful adjustments would have to occur in the Canadian economy.

The next two sections discuss the balance of payments and the balance of international indebtedness, and explain the nature of the growing problem they represent. Subsequently, an outline of the Conservative government's approach to the balance of payments will be provided. Finally, the need for additional depreciation or devaluation of the Canadian dollar is presented. The chapter argues, therefore, that a further significant decline in the international value of the Canadian dollar to US$0.70 or less is necessary for Canada to be able to compete more effectively in the world economy and to bring its expanding international indebtedness position under control. In addition, a number of supporting measures are discussed which will be needed if the lowered value of the Canadian dollar is to be effective in improving the Canadian competitive situation and in reducing the nation's net international indebtedness.

THE BALANCE OF PAYMENTS: THE RECORD

The balance of payments is a quarterly and annual record of all the economic transactions by the residents of Canada (governments, businesses and individuals) with the residents of the rest of the world. It consists of two main sections. The first is *the current account*, which records several things:

- all merchandise and services export and import transactions by Canadian residents with non-residents;
- interest and dividend receipts on capital owned or invested abroad and similar types of payments by Canadian residents to capital holders abroad; and
- transfers of funds in and out of the country as a result of inheritances and migration, as well as some other personal and governmental payments.

The second section is *the capital account*, which shows all net borrowings and lendings by Canadian residents, as well as inflows and outflows of direct investment which involves ownership and control of capital assets (such as factories, mines, retail stores, etc.). The main components of these two accounts since 1984, when the Conservative government assumed power, are summarized in Appendix 9.1.

Several trends are evident from the table. First, the surplus on merchandise export trade (that is, the excess of exports over imports) has been declining fairly steadily since 1984. The

293

improvement which appears to have occurred in 1990 was due not to a surge of exports, as it may seem, but primarily to changes in the way export statistics were recorded, so that more complete coverage and costing of exports occurred.[2] The gain in net exports for 1992 occurred because there was an earlier, and stronger, economic recovery in the U.S. than in Canada. If a full-fledged Canadian recovery occurs, we can expect the export surplus to diminish again. Second, the deficit on services trade (that is, the excess of imports over exports) has been growing quite steadily as well. Until 1989 this deficit was always less than the surplus on merchandise trade. In that year, it exceeded the merchandise surplus and has continued to do so since. An expanding proportion of this deficit—60 percent in recent years—has been due to travel and tourism. There are more Canadians going abroad and spending larger sums abroad than there are foreigners coming to, and spending in, Canada. Third, Canada's net interest payments abroad have expanded steadily as the nation's net international indebtedness has risen.[3] The consequence of these various changes is that the overall annual current account deficit has been increasing fairly regularly, equalling about $29 billion in each of 1991 and 1992.

These current account deficits are one measure of the extent to which Canada as a nation is borrowing from, or going more and more into debt to, foreigners. They must be distinguished from the deficits which get so much publicity in Canada, namely the annual deficits of the federal government (and, of course, the provincial governments). A portion of these latter government deficits entails borrowing from foreigners and, to that extent, overlaps with the current account deficits. But the current account deficits represent the net borrowing abroad by *all* residents of Canada, not just by governments.

The capital account entries in the balance of payments show the breakdown between direct investment and borrowing or lending via bonds and other money market instruments. If the statistics were complete, the balances on the capital account each year should equal those in the current account. Thus, for 1991, where the current account shows a deficit of $29.2 billion, the capital account should show net borrowing by Canadians of that same amount.

The excess of capital account borrowing of $5.8 billion greater than the current account deficit is labelled the "statistical discrepancy." It implies that either there were other imports into Canada that were not reported or that some capital outflows from Canada went unreported. Probably a bit of both occurred.

To put the current account deficits into context, it is worth relating them to the GNP. This is done in Appendix 9.2. Since 1984, when the current account had a modest surplus, the deficits have been an expanding share of the GNP. For 1991, the deficit was well over 4 percent of the GNP (see columns (1) and (2)).

At this point a deficiency in the Canadian method of balance of payments accounting must be highlighted. Generally, foreign-owned firms in a nation do not send home to their parent firms all profits in the form of dividends. Instead, they keep a portion of these profits as retained earnings and use them to finance new investment in the country in which they are located. The result of such transactions is that the foreign firm ends up owning more assets in its host country. In effect, the host country's international indebtedness increases.

To represent these transactions properly in the balance of payments, the retained earnings—the undistributed profits of foreign-owned firms in Canada which are being reinvested here—should be shown as an addition to investment income payments abroad. An offsetting entry should be made in the capital account showing increased foreign direct investment in Canada. Similarly, the profits which Canadian subsidiaries in foreign lands are keeping there and reinvesting should be reported as investment income receipts for Canada. An offsetting entry should be made in the capital account as an expansion of Canadian direct investment abroad. This is the method that the International Monetary Fund has recommended for years in its *Balance of Payments Manual*.[4] It is also the way that the U.S. and a number of other major nations have been presenting their balance of payments for years.

When adjustments of this type are made for Canada, the net effect, for most years, is to increase the size of the annual current account deficit, both absolutely and as a proportion of the GNP. The results are shown in Columns (3) and (4) of Appendix 9.2.

Another adjustment might also be made to the data. It was noted above that a statistical discrepancy has normally existed between recorded current account and capital account items. If this discrepancy were entirely due to unreported imports by Canada, the absolute size of the Canadian deficit would be increased in some years and reduced in other years. These results are shown in columns (5) and (6) of Appendix 9.2. The "true" figures are probably somewhere between these numbers and those shown in columns (3) and (4), as not all the discrepancy is likely to be attributable to the under-reporting of imports.

A final adjustment, which would consistently make Canada's current account deficit much larger than any numbers in Appendix 9.2 suggest, would be for *all* purchases and sales of goods and services to be reported according to the *national* ownership of the corporations involved. For example, sales of a foreign-owned company in Canada *to Canadians* (less purchases by that company from Canadian firms in Canada) would be considered as additional Canadian imports. Comparable adjustments would have to be made to the export side for Canadian firms producing abroad.[5] Detailed numbers are not available to make this type of estimate for Canada. But it is clear that, because foreign direct investment in Canada is $28 billion greater ($98 billion, if we allow for inflation) than Canadian direct investment abroad, Canada would have substantially larger net imports if this adjustment were made. For example, when this approach was used for the U.S., which (in contrast to Canada) has more direct investment abroad than foreign firms have in the U.S., the huge recorded U.S. trade deficit in 1987 (column (7) of Appendix 9.2) became a surplus of US$57 billion![6]

DOES THE BALANCE OF PAYMENTS DEFICIT MATTER?

The obvious question arises: Does the deficit matter? The short answer is, "Yes, a great deal." Consider why this is so. If a nation continues year after year to import more than it exports, it will have to borrow to make up the difference. This annual borrowing expands its indebtedness—which means that the costs of servicing the debt, such as interest payments, will be enlarged each year.[7] Consequently, the amount borrowed annually will have to increase to cover not only the continuing trade deficit, but also the growing service costs. This, in turn, raises the service charges again, which necessitates greater borrowing the next period, and so on.

Eventually, foreign lenders may begin to doubt the capacity of the nation to continue servicing its debt and to repay it. If that occurs and lending to Canada ceases, the nation would face the need to reduce sharply its net consumption and investment, in order to

- eliminate the annual external trade deficit on the sum of merchandise and services; and
- free sufficient additional goods and services for export to provide the foreign currencies to pay the service charges on the debt.

At the 1991-92 level of current account deficit, these adjustments would mean an initial annual reduction in the goods and services available to Canadians of $29 billion.

But this is not the end of the story. Foreign creditors, in addition to cutting off all new lending, are likely to begin withdrawing the funds they lent previously (e.g. by selling off government or other Canadian bonds so as to move their assets out of Canadian dollars). This would put tremendous downward pressure on the international value of the Canadian dollar, far more than that required to bring about the trade adjustment indicated above. It is likely that Canadians, too, would rush to move their liquid assets abroad. The attempted flow of capital out of Canada could be enormous—as occurred with Mexico in 1982. The Bank of Canada, in an attempt to stem the outflow and restore confidence in the dollar, would likely raise interest rates much beyond the levels seen in the fall of 1992, when doubts about the Canadian economy arose internationally.

No one can accurately predict what the outcomes might be. Certainly, the high interest rates would choke off investment spending and, therefore, reduce income, employment and government tax revenues, as well as worsen the already serious federal and provincial governments' fiscal positions. And the dollar could easily end up far lower than it otherwise would have been, with inflationary pressures much greater as well. It is certainly conceivable that the International Monetary Fund, supported by the main creditor nations, would step in and impose stringent austerity measures on the Canadian government as it has done on other major debtor nations. In summary, the shock to the Canadian economy would be very substantial indeed and much economic hardship would occur.

CANADA'S BALANCE OF INTERNATIONAL INDEBTEDNESS

A look at Canada's actual net indebtedness position and changes therein since the Conservatives took power in 1984 will help to clarify the situation. The numbers are summarized in Appendix 9.3. They show the net total of all the claims by the residents of the nation (governments, businesses and individuals) against all foreigners, less the claims by non-residents against those within the country. By the end of 1991, the Canadian net indebtedness had reached 41.8 percent of the GNP. For 1992, preliminary estimates suggest that the figure will be about 45 percent of the GNP.

These numbers actually understate the extent of the indebtedness, however. If past direct investment flows are measured in *current dollars* rather than past book values, Canada's net indebtedness is further increased. This is because much of the foreign direct investment in Canada occurred many years ago, whereas much of the Canadian direct investment abroad has occurred in the last decade or so. Thus, when price indexes for capital assets are employed, Canada's net international indebtedness for 1991 rises from about $270 billion, as reported by Statistics Canada, to about $325 billion, i.e. from about 41 percent of the GNP to 50 percent of the GNP![8,9] With this type of adjustment, the 1992 figure will approach 55 percent of the GNP! Clearly this type of situation is unsustainable.[10]

Some might argue that the very fact foreign lenders are currently willing to lend the funds Canada needs to cover its trade deficit and meet the service costs on existing debt must mean that there is no problem and that we should not be concerned about it. But this view does not consider the longer run adverse implications of a continuation of the current situation.

The history of the federal fiscal deficit has something else to tell us in this context. For many years, economists argued that such deficits were not a problem. Then, having ignored them for a long time, they suddenly recognized that there was a major, almost unmanageable, difficulty. Let us hope that we do not keep ignoring the balance of payments situation in the same way until it becomes unmanageable.

Borrowing for Consumption

A final point needs to be made with regard to the significance of continued, massive external borrowing and the accumulation of international debt. It has to do with the purposes for which the indebtedness has been incurred. The traditional economic view has been that when a nation borrowed abroad, it was not a matter of concern providing the funds were used for productive investment domestically. It was assumed that such investment would lead to additional domestic output and would, therefore, generate the funds to pay the service costs and, eventually, to repay the debt. This investment may also lead directly or indirectly to new exports or reduced imports.

This view, however, is questionable where the foreign borrowing was by governments, for even if the funds were used for fixed capital formation (schools, hospitals, office buildings, etc.), such capital would not necessarily lead to the production of exportable or import-replacing goods and services and, hence, a stream of revenues from which the debt could readily be serviced and eventually repaid. By the end of 1991, foreign holdings of Canadian bonds amounted to $202 billion—a sum which equalled 75 percent of all net Canadian indebtedness, including foreign direct investment.[11] About three quarters of these bonds have been issued by governments in Canada, chiefly the federal and provincial governments (see Appendix 9.4), so that the question immediately arises as to whether the borrowed funds were used to enhance the productive capacity of the economy. Suppose we take the view that *all* funds borrowed by governments that went into capital formation were used productively and will eventually enable debt-servicing to occur. What do we find? For the years since 1984, the federal government has employed little more than 1.5 percent of its total expenditures (on a national accounts basis) for capital formation (down from about 3.5 percent in the early 1960s). The provincial governments were only slightly better with 3.7 percent of their expenditures for capital formation (down from 14.5 percent in the early 1960s).[12]

Overall the message is clear. The high level of foreign borrowing by government has been overwhelmingly for current consumption purposes, rather than to expand the capital facilities of the nation. Even if one assumed that the portion of all government outlays going for education and training (about 16 percent) was basically an investment to enhance skill and productivity levels, the vast majority of government spending (and borrowing) has still been for consumption of one form or another, rather than for investment. And we have the additional concern today that even the portion spent on education is not being used as productively as it might be, given that nearly 30 percent of youths drop out of school before completing Grade 12 and that as many as 30 percent of high school graduates are not sufficiently literate to handle normal written instructions.[13]

The key question that arises is, Will the Canadian current account deficits and growing net international indebtedness reverse themselves automatically as time passes? The position taken in this chapter is that they are not likely to do so unless a further depreciation of the dollar takes place (beyond what has occurred since the summer of 1992) and a number of other policy changes are instituted. To highlight the need for change, the federal government's present approach will first be outlined, and a number of difficulties with it will be noted.

Before doing this, however, it is worth noting briefly, for comparison purposes, the American response to their current account deficits. They seem to have understood better than Canadians the arithmetic of accumulating indebtedness and compound interest. By 1984-85, when their current account deficit first exceeded US$100 billion and was about 2.8 percent of their GNP (see Appendix 9.2, columns (7) and (8)), great concern was registered by government officials, the news media and many economists about whether this situation could be sustained. For 1985-86, the U.S. net indebtedness was only 2.7 percent of U.S. GNP, yet substantial protectionist sentiment arose in Congress. As a consequence, U.S. officials met with the other members of the G-5 nations (France, Germany, Japan and the United Kingdom) and, on September 22 of that year, announced that they would intervene to reduce the international value of the dollar. The very next day the dollar dropped significantly and continued its decline (with some fluctuations) until, by the end of 1987, it was down 40 to 45 percent compared with its peak at the beginning of 1985. It rose again somewhat after that, but by mid-1992 it was lower by another 50 percent from its 1987 value.[14] The results of the depreciation were not immediate, but after about a two-year lag (the normal lag for exchange rates to produce their effect) the current account did improve and, by the end of 1991, the U.S. annual deficit was negligible compared with the U.S. GNP (see Appendix 9.2, columns (7) and (8)).[15]

THE CANADIAN FEDERAL GOVERNMENT'S POSITION

The federal position has involved a range of policies, the foremost ones being the negotiation of the Free Trade Agreement (FTA) with the U.S., thereby (supposedly) providing "secure access to the large U.S. market,"[16] and, more recently, the North American Free Trade Agreement (NAFTA). In addition, the Government has replaced the manufacturers' sales tax with the goods and services tax (GST) (which does not apply on export sales), and pursued the joint policies of deregulation and privatization. These, along with the reduction of inflation, are expected to improve Canadian competitiveness, stimulate exports and domestic investment, and generally lead to prosperity for the nation.

The growing deficits on the current account and the large increases in Canada's net international indebtedness have been given very little attention. Apparently, this is so for two reasons. On the one hand, the Government hopes that the above policies will, as they encourage international competitiveness and an improved export performance, produce a reduction in the growth of net foreign indebtedness and an increased capacity to service the foreign debt.[17] On the other hand, the Government—including the Bank of Canada—very much subscribes to the "new classical" view that sees the external deficit as primarily a consequence of domestic spending in excess of savings, particularly in the government sector. The idea in its simplest form is that as the Government spends more than its tax revenues, it borrows. This borrowing raises interest rates and thereby attracts capital inflows from abroad. These inflows push up the international value of the Canadian dollar, making Canadian production less competitive internationally and generating net imports. The "solution" is to reduce government expenditures. From this perspective, the exchange rate, or international value of the Canadian dollar, is seen primarily as a transmission mechanism, or residual, that merely reflects economic forces operating within the economy, rather than as a possible instrument which can have a determining effect upon exports and imports.[18]

The Bank of Canada (which is an agent of, and responsible to, the Minister of Finance) has focused its energies almost singularly on bringing down inflation. Growing current account deficits, which have consistently exceeded 3.6 percent of the GNP since 1989, have not been a concern of the Bank. Its policy over the last number of years has entailed hiking short-term interest rates in Canada to unprecedented levels above comparable U.S. rates—5.5 percent above the U.S. rate in the second quarter of 1990, for example—and keeping them high, even though the economy was deep in recession. The Bank has been concerned that a decline in the Canadian dollar (it was equal to about 85 cents at the time) would thwart its anti-inflationary goal.[19] The fact that its policies had ground the economy to a halt, raised unemployment and generated growing balance of payments current account deficits was not deemed to be of significance.[20] Instead, the Bank was able to express satisfaction about the high degree of confidence that foreigners had regarding the Canadian economy as they bought up Canadian debt,[21] even though it meant that the dollar was pushed to a peak of US$0.89 in the fall of 1991—a level that had not been attained for about 13 years—and Canadian products were, accordingly, less competitive in world markets. It should be noted at this juncture, too, that the drop in the Canadian dollar to about US$0.78 by the end of 1992, with most of this decline occurring in the last half of the year, was not because of bank policies but rather in spite of them. The Bank, in fact, worked to prevent the decline from being even greater.

THE CASE FOR A LOWER INTERNATIONAL VALUE FOR THE DOLLAR

The argument proceeds in three stages. First, there will be a critique of the Government's existing policies, and the reasons why they are not likely, in themselves, to rectify the balance of payments deficits will be given. Second, the less favourable international trading environment for Canadian products will be discussed so as to highlight the need for a lower value for the dollar. Finally, the extent of the required reduction in value will be considered, along with the importance of several supporting policies.

A Critique of Existing Government Policies

The view that the balance of payments current account deficit can be successfully disregarded because as the government deficit is reduced the external deficit will be eliminated, or at least brought under control, does not stand up for at least three reasons. First, this "twin deficits hypothesis"—as it has been labelled—is not empirically supportable. The Bank of Canada's own recent research[22] shows that rather than the relationship between these two deficits being positive, a *negative* and statistically significant relationship has existed! Where the fiscal deficit has declined, the external deficit has grown and vice versa. Therefore, curtailing the fiscal deficit is not necessarily going to remove the external imbalance, particularly given the high level of international net indebtedness which must be serviced. Second, the growing external deficits cannot be rationalized simply by arguing that there was an insufficient level of private domestic savings. As Richard Harris has shown, the appreciation of the Canadian dollar during the late 1980s (and the concomitant current account deficits) went beyond what could be explained by any private domestic spending boom.[23] Third, and perhaps most important, delaying any other remedial action regarding the external deficit in the hope that rectifying the fiscal deficit will do the trick ignores another reality.

A policy of attempting to lower government outlays (and/or raise tax revenues), while seemingly very commendable, implies more lay-offs, more unemployment, lower personal income tax receipts, higher unemployment insurance payments, higher welfare payments when unemployment benefits cease and reductions in consumption by those who are unemployed, and by those who still have jobs but fear being laid off. With lower expenditures from both the government and household sectors, little motive will exist for new investment either. The net result of this entire process could, therefore, be a *worsening* of the government deficit, not an improvement, and higher unemployment levels. Conceivably, the external trade deficit could diminish somewhat through these negative income effects, but the cost to the economy and, more particularly, to individuals would be high.

The other major component of the Government's policy needs to be questioned as well. This is the belief that controlling inflation, accompanied by the other measures mentioned above will in themselves be sufficient to bring about the desired new investment and increases in net exports.[24] First, it is not likely that a major relative improvement in Canadian manufacturing competitiveness will come about just through keeping the Canadian inflation rate *below* that in the U.S. for an extended period of time. Historically, Canada's performance on inflation has *not* been superior to that of the U.S. From 1960 to the end of 1991, for example, Canadian prices (as measured by the consumer price index) have grown at about 5.5 percent annually, whereas the comparable U.S. inflation rate has been just 5.0 percent.[25] Second, if relative productivity gain is the expected source of enhanced competitiveness then, even if it is possible to achieve such gains, it could be many years before the nation's international competitive situation is improved enough by this means alone to bring about the desired results. This may be longer than Canada can afford to wait. Some simple calculations will make this clear.

Consider the manufacturing sector. From 1985 to 1991, unit labour costs in Canadian manufacturing, measured in U.S. dollars, increased nearly 46 percent compared with those in the U.S.[26] (Recall that the United States accounts for about 70-75 percent of Canadian trade.) About 29 percent of this was due to slower labour productivity growth in Canada, and 21 percent was because hourly wage-salary increases in Canada had been greater. The remaining 50 percent was due to the appreciation of the Canadian dollar over this period.[27] Assuming the Canadian dollar had remained at US$0.85 and that Canada had been successful at keeping its inflation rate and growth rate of wages and salaries at the same level as that of the U.S., which they were in 1984-85 when Canada's current account was in approximate balance, Canada's productivity growth would have had to exceed consistently that of the U.S. for many years. To illustrate, if the U.S. had *no* growth in productivity in manufacturing, Canada's productivity growth would have had to be at a steady 2 percent per year *for*

19 years in order for its unit costs to be in line with where they were in 1986, relative to the U.S. Alternatively, if future U.S. productivity growth in manufacturing averaged 2 percent a year (a more likely scenario than zero productivity growth), Canada would have to have steady productivity expansion of 4 percent a year for 20 years to achieve the level it was at *vis-à-vis* the U.S. in 1986.

Moreover, the assumption of sustained, much faster productivity growth in Canada than in the U.S. is unrealistic. Over the past 30 years—1960-90—Canadian annual productivity expansion in manufacturing has been, on average, equal to that of the U.S. (about 2.9 percent) *not* consistently greater than the U.S. as the above calculations require.[28] Because the productivity performance of Canadian manufacturing has been, on average, about one half that of the U.S. over the past 12 years or so, it may be reasonable to expect improvements in excess of those in the U.S. for a period of time. But it is hardly reasonable to think that these improvements would be sustained for 20 years.

It is true that, over the past year, productivity gains have been occurring in industry—rather an unusual phenomenon during a severe recession because productivity normally does not improve during a recession. But these gains have come about primarily because firms have been quite ruthless in laying off staff and thereby increasing output per worker; the productivity gains have not occurred primarily as a result of new investment. It may be that productivity improvements from lay-offs are close to being exhausted. Or if they are not, all they may produce is more unemployment rather than great increases in output and, therefore, net exports.

Furthermore, to have large productivity gains over an extended period of time requires continuous increases in new investment embodying the latest technology.[29] For such investment to occur, there must be growing markets for the resulting output. In Canada, with all levels of government trying to lower their expenditures and reduce staff, and with private industry doing the same, the *domestic* incentive for new investment will remain subdued. Clearly, therefore, for years to come the main motive for most new investment will have to be to serve foreign markets. But if the Canadian dollar is maintained at too high a level, even this investment will not take place and the hope that

Canada will correct its current account imbalance becomes slim indeed.

The case for a depreciation of the dollar is made stronger when one considers the structural changes which have been occurring in the world and the domestic trading environment.

The Altered Global Trading Environment

Resource-Based Product. Canada has traditionally relied upon its resources for improvements in its trade account and, indeed, for its prosperity. Even today, resource-based products, either in raw or processed forms, account for about 50 percent of Canadian exports. However, Canada's international position with regard to such products is not nearly as favourable as it once was. For one thing a worldwide, long run decline in relative commodity prices has occurred over the last two decades.[30] For resource-producing nations like Canada, this trend reduces export revenues compared with import revenues. Consider also the changed circumstances for a number of the major individual resource products.

Regarding *agriculture*, even a resolution of the U.S.-European Community (through the General Agreement on Tariffs and Trade (GATT) dispute on subsidies) is not likely to mean major improvements in grain and oil-seed prices for years to come. And in future, as eastern European agriculture is modernized, we are likely to see a reduction in Western exports to that region; we may even see exports from there supplanting Western products elsewhere in the world. The Canadian poultry, dairy and horticultural segments of the industry will, as the FTA, NAFTA and GATT proposals are instituted, experience expanded imports. In *fisheries*, exports will decline with the diminution of the cod stocks off the East Coast and salmon stocks off the West Coast.

Mineral exports will be lessened too, as proven recoverable reserves diminish,[31] alternative world sources of supply are exploited and exploration expenditures within Canada, relative to those abroad, are reduced.[32] Simultaneously, the continuing move towards downsizing, more efficient use of mineral resources and the development of new materials technology is causing the demand for many metals to continue to grow more slowly than world GDP. For the *forestry* sector, lumber sales are likely to continue to be strong, providing resources are managed properly in Canada. But the development of alternative country sources of good quality pulp and paper supply (e.g. Brazil), and the U.S. move towards requiring more and more recycling of paper (particularly newsprint), will reduce markets for these Canadian products.[33] As recycling becomes mandatory, the necessary plants will not be built in Canada; instead they will be built close to the sources of used newsprint and to markets for the recycled product, namely near U.S. cities.

In the *energy* sector, natural gas exports to the U.S. will continue to be large. The big unknowns are price and whether, in years to come, Mexican gas reserves will be developed for export to the U.S. As for petroleum, conventional Canadian reserves are diminishing steadily. Although the nation has huge reserves in the oil-sands, large new investments would be needed to tap these reserves and such investment is not currently taking place. The Hibernia development off the East Coast will eventually increase supplies, but even so, the overall Canadian trade balance in petroleum products may well continue to decline. As for the remaining energy products—coal, electricity and uranium—major net export gains are not likely. As the Japanese and Koreans develop coal resources in China and elsewhere in eastern Asian, and are able to play different suppliers off against one another, Canadian exports and export prices to these nations could well diminish. Environmental issues regarding nuclear power and hydroelectric developments will continue to slow any expansion of uranium and net electricity exports.

In short, structural changes in the world and in domestic economies have worked together to reduce the strong trading advantage Canada has had historically in resource-based products. To strengthen its position in the face of these changes and to stimulate new investment and net export growth, a lower value for the Canadian dollar makes good sense.

One reaches the same conclusion when examining the changed world situation for other products and services.

Low Labour Cost Manufacturing. With the expanded global orientation of corporations, both large and small, and the high mobility of capital internationally, products requiring relatively unskilled labour are increasingly being manufactured and/or assembled in nations where wages and worker benefits are minimal. As more and more trade barriers are removed, Canada will have difficulty preserving its existing industries for these types of products, let alone expanding them. Its trade balance in such goods could become worse. Only with significant new investment to enhance productivity will some of these sectors be preserved. Such investment is unlikely to occur unless the resulting production can be competitive. Once again, then, the need for a lower Canadian dollar becomes apparent.

High Technology Manufacturing. Depreciation of the dollar should assist the high technology sectors to some extent too. The research and development (R&D) performance of Canadian-owned firms is, on average, poor compared with that in other developed nations (there are some shining exceptions, of course), in spite of Canada's having some of the most generous R&D incentives in the world. The performance of foreign-owned firms in Canada in this regard is even worse.[34] These latter firms often do the majority of their R&D in their home countries, near their head offices. Consequently Canada tends to get mere assembly plants or, as they are frequently called, "screwdriver" plants, which involve little transmission of the most current technology to the nation. The plants located here are primarily to serve local markets. Also, under the FTA and (more recently) the incipient NAFTA, as tariff barriers come down, there is no longer the incentive for foreign firms to locate in Canada even to serve the domestic market, and Canada has little remaining policy freedom to encourage or persuade foreign—in particular U.S.—firms to establish in Canada. Maintaining a lower value for the Canadian dollar, while far from an assured way of altering the situation, at least moves in the direction of making the country a more attractive place to invest to serve the Canadian as well as other North American markets.

The Services Sector. As noted earlier in this chapter, this sector is already running a deficit of over $12 billion annually, of which 60 percent is due to travel and tourism alone. This travel and tourism deficit has been growing ever larger as Canadians increasingly explore their roots in foreign lands during the summer and seek warmer havens during the winter (and avoid the GST via cross-border shopping). The other major component of services is business services, where the deficit—$4 billion in 1991—also continues to expand. Some segments of the services sector are competing quite effectively in international markets, such as insurance and financial services, but these form a fairly small part of the total sector. With the high degree of foreign ownership of Canadian industry, one can expect that net payments for royalties, trademarks, management fees and computer services will continue to be large. And with the move to greater liberalization of services via the FTA and NAFTA, there may well be a tendency for U.S. firms to centralize more service functions in the head offices of the parent company, which would enlarge these payments even more. Here again, the argument can be made that a lower value for the Canadian dollar is important if these pressures towards an even greater service account deficit are to be countered.

The message from this review of the severe challenges facing Canada's external trade sector is that no cause for complacency exists. There is little evidence to suggest that, if we but "stay the course we are now on," the balance of payments current account deficits and the nation's net international indebtedness will be reduced, and the types of potential difficulties mentioned earlier in this chapter avoided.[35] Structural and other adjustments need to be made in Canada. The way to bring these about is through an "expenditure switching" policy involving changes in relative prices. A further depreciation of the currency is, therefore, the obvious policy choice. Consider this policy in more detail.

A Lower Dollar

The basic argument for a diminished international value for Canada's currency is clear enough. It will make both Canadian exportable products and products competing with imports more competitive. The profitability of locating in Canada to serve both Canadian and foreign markets will be enhanced. And, over time, we could expect to see improvements in Canada's merchandise and services trade balances and, therefore, reductions in the current account deficit.

A depreciation now is preferable to a do-nothing approach which, as suggested earlier in this chapter, could lead to

- a substantial international crisis of confidence in the Canadian economy's ability to repay its debts; and
- a much lower value for the dollar and far higher costs for Canadians than would otherwise have been necessary if remedial action had been taken sooner.

A depreciation now is also a far more preferable approach for reducing the external deficit (and government fiscal deficits) than is a policy of trying to do these things simply through cuts in government expenditure, which (as noted earlier) will reduce income and employment. In contrast, a depreciation will have the desirable effect of not only encouraging exports and discouraging imports, but of *raising* domestic income and employment and, thereby, increasing tax revenues and helping to reduce the government budget deficit. With 11 percent unemployment in the Canadian economy (much more if allowance is made for part-time workers and discouraged workers), there is considerable room for these types of favourable income effects.[36]

An obvious question is, How much of a depreciation is necessary if Canada is to eliminate its current account deficit and begin reducing its net international indebtedness? Various estimates have been made in recent years, but this is not the place to attempt an extensive assessment of these. Instead, the recent, authoritative work by Richard Harris will be drawn upon to provide an indication of an appropriate value for the dollar.[37]

Harris has calculated that, based upon the difference in unit labour costs in manufacturing between Canada and the U.S., the Canadian dollar would have to be down in the US$0.70 range for Canada's competitive position to be restored. An alternative computation he made, which was focused on determining what value of the Canadian dollar would eliminate Canada's current account deficit, arrived at a figure of about US$0.72, providing that Canadian and U.S. growth were about equal.[38]

However, these estimates should be adjusted downward. As the calculations were being undertaken, the 1989 deficit on the current account was thought to be only $16.7 billion, but it was actually $22.9 billion, 37 percent more.[39] For subsequent years, the deficit mushroomed further—to $29.2 billion in 1991. In addition, the worsening competition situation for Canadian resource exports has become more evident since these estimates were made. Thus, given these developments, the dollar would have to be significantly *below* US$0.70 in order to balance the Canadian current account. Moreover, if the question had been changed to ask how a current account *surplus* could be generated (not just the deficit eliminated), so that Canada's huge net international indebtedness could be eliminated eventually, then obviously the value of the dollar would have to be lowered even more.[40] At the very least, then, Canada should be looking at a value for its currency of no more than US$0.70 if it is going to be an attractive place for firms to locate and if the current account of the balance of payments is not to be a continuing, or even worsening, problem.

OTHER ISSUES

A number of issues come to mind when considering the possible implications of a depreciated dollar; they all have to do with whether it will have the desired effect. Although they are not all fully within our control, we may be able to do something about some of them.

The "Hysteresis" Issue

One matter of concern is the possibility of "hysteresis" in trade flows—whether an extended period with an inappropriately high external value for the currency may produce adverse effects of a long-term nature which continue to thwart adjustment in trade even when the currency value is lowered.[41] This difficulty could emanate from a variety of sources. Highly educated and experienced scientists, engineers and other professionals may have left Canada due to a lack of opportunity here during the recent years of an overvalued currency, and they may not be interested in returning once the currency is reduced again. Canadian firms would, therefore, be short of the requisite people. Also, other skilled and educated workers who may not have emigrated may find that, because of being unemployed for substantial periods due to the overvaluation, their training has become outdated, their human capital has deteriorated and they are no longer well equipped to serve firms adequately in competitive world markets. Again, both foreign and domestic firms which have moved out of

Canada may have become acclimatized to operating completely from a U.S. location and, therefore, may have little inclination to relocate in Canada, particularly if the majority of their sales are in the much larger U.S. market. This is especially true for U.S. and other foreign-owned firms now that the FTA is in effect. Because the Canadian tariff is largely removed on Canada-U.S. trade, the motivation they originally had for locating in Canada to get behind the Canadian tariff and serve the Canadian market is gone. In addition, they may feel that if the FTA should ever be cancelled by the U.S. or if American authorities should choose to alter their rules to increase protection of their own industry, they would be better off to be in the U.S.[42]

No simple answer exists for this problem. One possibility is that Canada should not just let the dollar depreciate to US$0.70 or so, but that it should be *pegged* to the U.S. dollar, with perhaps a 5 percent margin on either side, to convince the international business community that the lower value would not be just a short-term phenomenon. Such action may significantly improve the long-term attractiveness of locating in Canada.

Reliance on the U.S. Market

Canada's enormous reliance upon the U.S. as a market for 70 percent of our exports presents an even more important potential difficulty for a further depreciation of the Canadian currency. Canada already runs a large merchandise trade surplus with the U.S. It has been declining, on average, since 1985, but it is still about $15 billion annually. (Our merchandise trade deficit with other nations in aggregate is about $8 billion.) To have major gains in our trade balance would therefore require net gains on trade with not only Third World countries, but also the U.S. A bigger surplus for Canada means a larger deficit for the U.S. Their current account deficits and net international indebtedness, although far smaller than Canada's in relative terms, are always of great concern to them. They are not likely to view lightly Canada's adding significantly to this deficit.

Although no straightforward solution exists, a number of possibilities come to mind. First, it is necessary to educate the U.S. administration and Congress on the seriousness of the Canadian situation. Their attention needs to be drawn to the far larger relative size of Canadian current account deficits and Canadian international indebtedness, compared with their own. It needs to be pointed out to them, for example, that Canada's net international indebtedness is 45 to 55 percent of our GNP (depending upon whether historical book values or current values of direct investments are used), compared with the U.S. figure of about 6.5 percent. And it needs to be noted that if a major international crisis-of-confidence occurred regarding the Canadian economy and Canada had to adjust abruptly to this, the loss in U.S. exports to Canada would be much larger than would occur over time as a result of an exchange rate realignment.

Second, over the longer term, Canada needs to give more than occasional lip-service to the need for the nation to diversify its export markets. In the past Canadian economists, as well as many other people both within and outside the Government, have ridiculed suggestions of various "third options" for Canadian trade on the grounds that Canada's proximity to the U.S. makes it our natural market. But the time has come to treat such options seriously. Asia is often cited as the growing market of opportunity, and indeed it is, although it may be difficult to counter the well established Japanese linkages and the growing influence of other nations, such as Korea. Latin America is much closer, and with the NAFTA (and possible extensions of it in the future), there may be more immediate opportunities in this hemisphere than in Asia for trade diversification. No one should minimize the many difficulties in developing markets for Canadian products in these nations. But other countries, such as Japan and Korea, have greatly diversified their markets. In the present circumstances, there are good reasons for Canada to try to do the same.

Inflationary Pressures

The greatest fear that most people have whenever the possibility of a depreciation or devaluation of the dollar is mentioned is that of a new round of serious inflation. The first thing to be noted is this: a significant decline in the Canadian dollar did occur in the last half of 1992, from about US$0.84 to US$0.78.[43] Yet, there have not been major demands for higher wages. Undoubtedly, this is related to the high unemployment rate, the increased proportion of part-time jobs, the general recognition that the federal government and most provincial governments face severe budget problems and really cannot entertain wage-salary increases, and the repeated announcements of lay-offs, within both government and the private sector. And this is the case even though the implication of higher prices for tradable goods, both exportables and importables, is that the purchasing power of people's incomes is, and will continue to be, diminished as the exchange rate change works its way through the system.

If the seriousness of our current account and net international indebtedness situation is given more attention in this country, and people are alerted to the fact that the nation's global position regarding our traditional resource-based export products (as well as labour-intensive and high-tech products and services) is much less favourable than in past decades, then the likelihood of limiting wage demands is going to be much higher than it otherwise would be. This would be particularly likely if governments took the lead in not just freezing salaries at current levels, but actually reducing them in nominal terms for MPs, MLAs, civil servants at all three levels and government enterprise employees. This action would have three positive benefits:

- it would set an example for all other sectors of the economy;
- it would be a step towards bringing government salaries back into line with private sector incomes;[44] and
- it would be a way of reducing government deficits that would be preferable to lay-offs, which only increase unemployment benefits and welfare costs.

Perhaps the greatest danger of new inflationary pressures from a further decline in the dollar may emanate from the resource-based export industries. As they experience higher profits when their international competitiveness and sales revenues increase, employees may demand (and receive) higher wages and salaries. If this occurs, demonstration effects may spread to other sectors where workers, seeing the greater incomes in the export industries, would want higher incomes as well—even though their productivity and the profits of their employers may not fully warrant them. If wage and salary increases are granted in these other industries for the sake of labour peace, their product prices will have to rise to accommodate the higher labour costs. General inflation could erode the competitiveness advantage of the depreciated Canadian dollar. This is what happened in the early 1980s as the dollar declined.

The problem is to contain these pressures. It is time to learn from the experiences of nations that have been more successful at limiting than Canada has been.[45] It seems pretty defeatist to say, as many are inclined to do, that inflation control methods in Canada—other than through massive unemployment—do not and cannot work. There is much room in Canada for attitudinal changes so that longer-term societal interests are assigned more significance and short-term individual interests are downplayed. And new institutions might well be developed, possibly along the lines of national wage-salary agreements, as some other nations have done successfully. A detailed discussion of the possibilities available to us is outside the bounds of this chapter.[46] But to ignore these possibilities, given the serious nature of the international situation Canada faces, would seem to be irresponsible.

Appendix 9.1

The Canadian Balance of Payments: 1984-92
(billions of dollars)

	1984	1985	1986	1987	1988	1989	1990	1991	1992
CURRENT ACCOUNT									
Merchandise									
Exports	111.3	119.1	120.3	126.3	137.8	141.8	146.5	141.7	157.5
Imports	-91.5	-102.7	-110.4	-115.1	-128.9	-135.3	-136.6	-135.9	-148.1
Balance	19.8	16.4	9.9	11.2	8.9	6.4	9.9	5.8	9.4
Services									
Exports	14.7	15.9	17.8	19.1	21.5	22.1	23.0	23.3	24.7
Imports	-19.1	-20.7	-23.0	-25.4	-27.5	-30.3	-34.3	-35.6	-38.0
Balance	-4.4	-4.6	-5.2	-6.3	-6.0	-8.2	-11.3	-12.3	-13.3
Investment income									
Receipts	6.4	7.6	7.7	8.0	12.0	10.1	10.0	9.7	7.7
Payments	-19.8	-21.9	-24.1	-24.5	-30.7	-31.6	-34.0	-32.1	-32.6
Balance	-13.4	-14.3	-16.4	-16.5	-18.3	-21.5	-24.0	-22.4	-24.9
Net transfers[a]	-.2	-.3	.3	-.1	.3	.3	-.1	-.4	.2
Current account balance	1.7	-3.1	-11.4	-11.6	-15.5	-22.9	-25.7	-29.2	-28.6
CAPITAL ACCOUNT									
Capital overflows									
(Increased Cdn. claims on non-residents)									
Direct investment	-2.9	-3.9	-5.7	-9.4	-6.5	-5.5	-5.1	-4.4	-3.3
Other outflows	-7.7	1.2	-5.1	-6.1	-13.2	-5.8	-4.2	-3.6	2.0[b]
Total outflows	-10.6	-2.7	-10.8	-15.5	-19.7	-11.3	-9.3	-8.0	-1.3

Appendix 9.1

The Canadian Balance of Payments: 1984-92

(billions of dollars)

cont'd

	1984	1985	1986	1987	1988	1989	1990	1991	1992
Capital inflows (Increased foreign claims on Cdn. residents)									
Direct investment	1.7	-2.8	1.4	4.6	4.5	2.4	6.8	5.9	4.7
Other inflows	13.4	14.9	23.5	25.7	31.3	31.9	27.9	37.2	23.9
Total inflows	15.11	12.1	24.9	30.3	35.8	34.3	34.7	43.1	28.6
Capital account balance	4.5	9.4	14.1	14.8	16.1	23.0	25.4	35.1	27.3
Statistical discrepancy[c]	-6.2	-6.3	-2.7	-3.2	-0.6	-0.1	0.3	-5.8	1.3

Source: Statistics Canada, *Canada's Balance of International Payments* (Ottawa: Supply and Services Canada, various years).

Notes: Totals may not add due to rounding.

[a] These include migrants' funds, personal remittances and various government transfers.

[b] This item was positive in 1992 because the Bank of Canada spent about $7 billion of foreign exchange revenues defending the Canadian dollar from further depreciation.

[c] These numbers record the difference between recorded current account deficits and net capital account inflows which, if there were no undetected transactions, would equal one another.

Appendix 9.2

Various Measures of the Current Account Deficit in the Balance of Payments, 1984-91

Year	CANADA[a]				U.S.			
	Official Current Account Balance		Current Account Incl. Retained Earnings[b]		Current Account incl. Both Retained Earnings and the Statistical Discrepancy		Current Account incl. Retained Earnings	
	billions of dollars	% of GNP	billions of dollars	% of GNP	billions of dollars	% of GNP	billions of dollars	% of GNP
	(1)	(2)	(3)	(4)	(5)	(6)	(7)	(8)
1984	1.69	3.9	-.26	-.01	-6.44	-1.49	-107.4	-2.8
1985	-3.10	-.67	-4.73	-1.02	-11.03	-2.38	-117.7	-2.9
1986	-11.39	-2.33	-13.19	-2.70	-15.89	-3.25	-141.4	-3.3
1987	-11.60	-2.17	-12.98	-2.43	-16.13	-3.01	-154.0	-3.4
1988	-15.49	-2.64	-16.86	-2.87	-17.45	-2.97	-126.5	-2.6
1989	-22.89	-3.64	-24.19	-3.85	-24.22	-3.85	-110.0	-2.1
1990	-25.71	-3.99	-25.71	-3.99	-25.45	-3.95	-92.1	-1.7
1991	-29.25	-4.49	-29.25	-4.49	-35.05	-5.38	-8.6	-.2

Appendix 9.2

cont'd

Sources: Statistics Canada, *Canada's Balance of International Payments: First Quarter* (Ottawa, 1992), Table 1; Statistics Canada, *Canada's International Investment Position* (Ottawa, 1988), Table 17, and 1991, Table 12; U.S. Department of Commerce, *Survey of Current Business* (Washington, D.C.: various years).

Notes: [a] Although it is more popular today to use gross domestic product (GDP) than gross national product (GNP), the latter is used here for ready comparison with the U.S., which used only GNP until quite recently. GNP is a measure of the total value of goods and services earned by Canadian residents regardless of whether they are earned inside or outside the country. It excludes the payments to non-residents on capital they own in Canada. GDP measures the total value of goods and services produced in Canada whether owned by Canadians or non-residents. It excludes returns on Canadian investments abroad.

[b] These numbers on retained earnings are only estimates. Statistics Canada does not report retained earnings on Canadian direct investment abroad and, since 1987, has included retained earnings on foreign direct investment in Canada with other adjustment factors such as revaluations (e.g. when take-overs of foreign-owned firms by other foreign-owned firms occur) and reclassifications. Thus for the years 1984-86, the reported retained earnings on foreign direct investment in Canada were subtracted from estimates of retained earnings by Canadian firms abroad. These estimates assumed that such earnings were the same percentage of retained earnings in Canada as Canadian direct investment abroad was of foreign direct investment in Canada. For the years 1987-89, retained earnings in Canada were estimated at $4 billion per year, while for 1990 and 1991, they were conservatively placed at zero. The same procedure as for 1984-86 was used to estimate retained earnings on Canadian direct investment abroad and to arrive at net retained earnings figures.

Appendix 9.3

**Canada's Net International
Investment Position, 1984-91**

	1984	1985	1986	1987	1988	1989	1990	1991
Net indebtedness in billions of dollars	-151.1	-173.6	-191.4	-204.7	-213.0	-231.9	-252.2	-272.4
Net indebtedness as a percentage of GNP	35.0	37.4	39.1	38.3	36.3	36.9	39.2	41.8
Net indebtedness as a percentage of GDP	34.0	36.3	37.9	37.1	35.2	35.7	37.8	40.4

Sources: Department of Finance, *Economic Reference Tables: August 1992* (Ottawa: 1992), Tables 3, 74; and Bank of Canada, *Bank of Canada Review: October 1992* (Ottawa: 1992), Table H2.

Appendix 9.4

Foreign Holdings of Canadian Bonds

Issuer of Bonds	Non-Resident Bond Holdings 1991		Percentage of Gov't. Expenditures Going for Capital Formation: Annual Averages, 1984-91
	billions of dollars (1)	percentage of total (2)	(3)
Government (incl. enterprises[a])			
Federal	65	32	1.7
Provincial	84	42	3.7
Local	4	2	13.3
Other	48	24	-
Total	202	100	

Sources: Columns (1) and (2), Statistics Canada, *Canada's International Investment Position* (Ottawa, March 1992); Column (3) Department of Finance, *Economic Reference Tables: August 1992* (Ottawa: 1992), Tables 52, 56, 58.

Note: [a] For the federal government, $9 billion of the borrowing was by government enterprises. Provincial enterprises accounted for $32 billion.

NOTES

1   On the federal government's interest in education, see the chapter by Saul Schwartz in this volume.

2   Commencing in 1990, Canada and the U.S. started to rely on each other's import statistics to record trade flows between them. Nations are generally much more particular about recording all imports than recording all exports because of the possibility that tariffs or other import restrictions may apply. Thus, when Canada commenced using U.S. import figures to report its exports, the numbers shot up because of the more complete U.S. coverage. At the same time, Canada commenced recording the value of *all* merchandise exports *not* at their point of shipment, as had been the practice, but at the Canadian borders just as the merchandise left the country. Thus, export values were inflated by the cost of freight and shipping from the point of production to the port of exit from Canada. For example, see Statistics Canada, *Summary of Canadian International Trade: December 1990* (Ottawa: Supply and Services Canada, March 1991), p. v.

3   Unlike interest charges, *net* dividend payments abroad have actually been diminishing as Canadian direct investment abroad has expanded. In 1991, the net outflow of dividends was down to its lowest level ever—only $54 million.

4   International Monetary Fund, *Balance of Payments Manual*, 4th ed. (Washington, D.C., 1977), pp. 104-05.

5   For a detailed discussion of the methodology of this approach, see De Anne Julius, *Global Companies and Public Policy: The Growing Challenge of Foreign Direct Investment* (New York: Council of Foreign Relations Press, 1990); and Julius, *Foreign Direct Investment: The Neglected Twin of Trade* (Washington, D.C.: Group of Thirty, 1991).

6   See Julius, *Global Companies* and *Foreign Direct Investment*.

7   Remember that these charges are quite different from service charges on the better known *federal* budget deficit, some of which

go to foreigners but the majority of which go to Canadian residents. (Of the net federal debt of $388 billion at the end of 1991, only about $60 billion or 15 percent was held abroad.)

8   These estimates were made by inflating the value of Canadian direct investments abroad using the U.S. Implicit Price Deflator for non-residential investment. This deflator was employed as a proxy for all Canadian direct investment abroad because 60 percent of it is in the U.S. Foreign direct investment in Canada was inflated using the GDP Implicit Price Index for non-residential capital formation in Canada as reported by the Department of Finance, *Economic Reference Tables: 1992* [Ottawa: Supply and Services, Canada), Table 43. One further adjustment made, which is not mentioned in the text, is that Canada's gold reserves were inflated to market values as at August 1992. This adjustment increased Canadian international assets by $4 billion. The foreign direct investment adjustments raised the net value of Canadian indebtedness by $60 billion.

9   The U.S. uses a more sophisticated approach to calculate current costs or replacement costs of their assets and liabilities. It involves a perpetual inventory approach to compute current values of plant and equipment, general price indexes to value land and replacement cost estimates of inventories. Limitations of time and resources prevented this type of approach for calculating the Canadian current values. See U.S. Department of Commerce, *Survey of Current Business* (Washington, D.C.), May 1991, June 1991 and June 1992. The U.S. has also used a "market value" approach to estimating its net international investment position. Indexes of market prices of the stocks involved in foreign direct investment in the U.S. and U.S. direct investment abroad are used in this calculation.

10   Richard Harris has shown that the crucial relationship is between the real rate of interest which has to be paid on foreign debts and the growth rate of real GDP. Where the real rate of interest is higher than the real GDP growth rate, then over time the debt to GDP ratio increases. In turn, the size of the trade balance as a proportion of the GDP necessary to prevent the foreign debt to GDP ratio from expanding under these circumstances becomes

even greater. The need for a large merchandise trade surplus is even more acute when the service account portion of the total trade balance is, itself, in deficit—as is the Canadian one. Richard G. Harris, *Exchange Rates and International Competitiveness of the Canadian Economy* (Ottawa: Economic Council of Canada, 1992), pp. 28-29.

Consider these basic relationships for the Canadian economy at the moment. Real GDP in 1992 rose only about 0.7 percent. Average real interest rates for the year, as measured by the prime corporate rate on short-term paper or the chartered banks' prime rate, were in the range of about 5.5 to 6 percent. In addition, total merchandise and service trade was in deficit by about $6 billion. Clearly, if these relative magnitudes continue, the ratio of foreign indebtedness to GDP will mushroom and be unsustainable.

11   There were $7.6 billion of foreign bonds held by Canadians, so net foreign holdings would be only $193.9 billion.

12   Municipalities performed somewhat better on this measure, but their borrowings were comparatively small. Note that it is quite appropriate to consider not just federal borrowing but also the borrowing by the other levels of government in this context, even though our focus is on the performance of the federal government. This approach is appropriate because the macro-policies which the federal government has followed have a great deal of influence upon whether these other governments have to borrow and whether they will be motivated and/or required to borrow internationally, rather than domestically.

13   Michael Wilson, *The Budget* (Ottawa: Department of Finance, February 26, 1991), p. 139. An alternative view might be that it is acceptable for the Government to borrow abroad for consumption purposes if it frees funds for domestic businesses to spend more on investment. However, as will be noted in the section of this chapter on the Government's position, increased government borrowing abroad was not accompanied by increases in investment outlays.

14   Federal Reserve Board of Cleveland, *Economic Trends* (September 1992), p. 18.

15   The situation was more complicated than is suggested here. For a concise discussion of what went on, see Paul R. Krugman and Maurice Obstfeld, *International Economics: Theory and Policy*, 2nd ed. (New York: Harper Collins, 1991), pp. 573-76.

16   Michael Wilson, *The Budget* (Ottawa: Department of Finance, February 20, 1990), pp. 52-53.

17   Wilson, *The Budget* (February 26, 1991), pp. 51-53, 108-11, 123-26; and Don Mazankowski, *The Budget* (Ottawa: Department of Finance, February 25, 1992), pp. 45-46.

18   Richard Harris, in *Exchange Rates*, pp. 26-27, discusses this point. A third possible reason for the Government's neglect of Canada's large current account deficit and growing net international indebtedness is that officials were not fully informed as to the magnitude of the annual deficits. As indicated in the table below, revisions in the Statistics Canada data in the second quarter of 1991 showed the deficit for the years 1987 to 1990, inclusive, as anywhere from 25 to 38 percent greater than had been previously reported. This revision may account for the 1992 *Budget Papers* finally indicating that the deficit was "worrisomely large"—although it did not give rise to any expression of concern by the Governor of the Bank of Canada or any suggestion by him, or the Government, that something ought to be done about it. Rather, the Government continued to assert, as it had done in previous budgets, that the deficits would decline in subsequent years. The further statistical revisions for 1988 to 1990, which were made in the second quarter of 1992 (after the 1992 budget was presented), raised the deficits for those years by another 11 to 17 percent. However, even without all of these adjustments, the growth in the deficits was evident, so it is difficult to assign much weight to this possibility.

**Current Account Deficits,
1984-91**
(billions of dollars)

Statistics Canada Estimates

	1984	1985	1986	1987	1988	1989	1990	1991
As of spring 1991	2.7	-2.0	-10.2	-9.2	-10.2	-16.7	-16.0	
As of summer 1991	1.7	-3.1	-11.4	-11.6	-13.9	-20.7	-22.0	
As of summer 1992	1.7	-3.1	-11.4	-11.6	-15.5	-22.9	-25.7	-29.2

Source: Bank of Canada, *Bank of Canada Review* (Ottawa), various
issues.

19   John W. Crow, *Annual Report of the Governor to the Minister of
Finance and Statement of Accounts for the Year 1989* (Ottawa:
Bank of Canada, February 28, 1990).

20   A good discussion of the bias of the Bank of Canada and the federal
government in general towards controlling inflation, regardless
of the implications for unemployment rates, is provided in Robert
M. Campbell, "Jobs...Job..Jo..J... The Conservatives and the
Unemployed," and in Fanny S. Demers, "The Department of
Finance and the Bank of Canada: The Fiscal and Monetary Policy
Mix" in Frances Abele, (ed.), *How Ottawa Spends 1992-93: The
Politics of Competitiveness* (Ottawa: Carleton University Press,
1992), pp. 23-56 and pp. 79-124, respectively.

21   John W. Crow, *Annual Report of the Governor to the Minister of
Finance and Statement of Accounts for the Year 1991* (Ottawa:
Bank of Canada, February 28, 1992), p. 11.

22   Stephen S. Poloz, *Fiscal Policy and External Balance in the G-7
Countries* (Ottawa: Bank of Canada, 1992).

23   See Harris, *Exchange Rates*, pp. 26-32. Harris notes that real business investment grew very little as a proportion of the GDP between 1984 and 1989 and, for 1989 (as a percentage of the GDP), was still two full percentage points *lower* than the average for 1974 to 1982 (inclusive) of 14 percent. (For the years since 1989, such investment as a percentage of the GDP has been even less--only 10.5 percent of the GDP for the first three quarters of 1992.) He did recognize a surge in household spending (including residential construction) during the late 1980s, however, which resulted in a significant decline in the personal savings rate (from 12.5 percent of the GDP in 1982 to 7.25 percent of the GDP in 1989.) But, he concluded that even this could not fully account for the appreciation of the Canadian dollar. Since he concluded his study, the economy has been deep in recession. Expenditures on housing, now at 6.2 percent of the GDP, are again down to no more than they averaged over the years used as the basis for his comparison, 1974-82, and consumer expenditures are retrenched. The large external deficit can hardly be attributed to this source.

24   A major assumption underlying these other policies, which include trade liberalization, privatization and deregulation, is that if the Government simply gets out of the way and lets the market work, the Canadian economy will prosper. The naivety of this belief in the light of the way in which the governments of other industrial nations—such as Japan, Germany, France and the U.S.—are deeply involved in working with, and furthering the objectives of, their national corporations is considerable. For a discussion of this issue, see Bruce Wilkinson, "Trade Liberalization, the Market Ideology, and Morality: Have We a Sustainable System?" in Ricardo Grinspun and Max Cameron, (eds.), *The Political Economy of North American Free Trade* (Montreal: McGill-Queen's University Press, 1993).

25   Canada, Department of Finance, *Economic Reference Tables: August 1992*, Tables 44 and 90; and U.S. Department of Commerce, *Statistical Abstract of the United States* (Washington, D.C., 1991), Table 769.

26   U.S. Department of Labor, Bureau of Labor Statistics, *Monthly Labor Bulletin* (Washington, D.C., December 1991).

27   Economic Council of Canada, *Pulling Together: Productivity, Innovation, and Trade* (Ottawa, 1992), p. 29. The Council actually based allocations numbers on a 41 percent, rather than a 46 percent, differential but the proportions will still be broadly correct.

28   The productivity growth rates for sub-periods within the 1960-90 time span, according to the U.S. Department of Labor, *Monthly Labor Bulletin*, p. 29, are

	Canada	U.S.
1960-73	4.5	3.3
1973-79	2.1	1.4
1979-90	1.5	3.1

29   Pierre Mohnen's recent work, entitled *The Relationship Between R&D and Productivity Growth in Canada and Other Major Industrialized Countries* (Ottawa: Economic Council of Canada, 1992), indicates that productivity growth is even more dependent upon R&D than on physical capital per se—although, new investment is obviously also necessary for the R&D to produce the higher returns.

30   Economic Council of Canada, *Au Courant*, vol. 13, no. 1 (Ottawa, 1992), p. 8.

31   Mine suspensions and closures during 1992 in excess of mine openings and reopenings reduced capacity by 81,000 tonnes daily, continuing a trend that commenced in 1990. Canada, Energy, Mines and Resources, Mineral Policy Sector, *Mineral Industry Quarterly Report: September 1992* (Ottawa: Supply and Services Canada, 1992), p. 17.

32   A recent survey conducted by the Mining Association of Canada shows that mining companies expect to increase the proportion of their exploration budgets spent outside Canada from 19 percent in 1987 to 43 percent in 1997. "Canada losing exploration dollars: Mining firms increasingly working outside country," *The Globe and Mail* [Toronto], September 18, 1992. Energy, Mines and Resources has been saying for some years that unless a major

expansion of exploration activity for base metal deposits occurred in Canada, there would be sizeable reductions in the recoverable deposits of these metals by the mid-1990s. Government of Canada, Energy, Mines and Resources, Mineral Policy Sector, *Canadian Mines: Perspective from 1990: Production, Reserves, Development, Exploration* (Ottawa: Supply and Services Canada, 1992).

33   A major concern motivating increased recycling in the U.S. is the garbage disposal problem, as paper comprises over 50 percent of the nation's garbage. See William L. Rathje, "Once and future landfills," *National Geographic*, vol. 179, no. 5, May 1991, pp. 116-34.

34   For example, see Advisory Council on Adjustment, *Adjusting to Win: Report of the Advisory Council on Adjustment* (Ottawa: Supply and Services Canada, 1989), chap. 10. Also, see Michel Demers, "Responding to the Challenges of the Global Economy: The Competitiveness Agenda" in Abele, *How Ottawa Spends 1992-93*, pp. 163-70.

35   Some may be inclined to assume that the current problems are merely cyclical phenomena. Those who would support this stance may like to point out that in the early 1960s, Canada's net international indebtedness as a proportion of the GNP was as high as it is today (44 percent in 1961) and then progressively dropped until it reached a low of 23.5 percent of the GNP in 1974. Thus, they may ask, "Why should we be concerned now?" However, the circumstances of the 1960s were far different than those of today. Those were years of enormous expansion in the world and Canadian economies. Canadian real GNP rose about 5.2 percent per year during this period, and output per capita expanded by 3.3 percent annually. (During the 1970s, it grew even faster—by an average of 4 percent annually.) Canada's many natural resource sectors and primary manufacturing industries relying on domestic resources were booming and new exports such as potash, sulphur, natural gas and canola were coming into prominence. In the latter part of the 1960s, the U.S. war effort in Viet Nam helped fuel other manufacturing sectors in the Canadian economy as well. These conditions are in stark contrast to the ones today, which we

have outlined above. It would, therefore, be inappropriate to use the experience of another era such as the 1960s and early 1970s to justify a complacent attitude regarding the present situation.

36   On the unemployment question, see the chapter by James Rice and Michael Prince in this volume.

37   See Harris, *Exchange Rates*, chap. 2 and pp. 43-45.

38   Harris also made two other estimates of what the exchange rate should be, one using the old purchasing power parity theory and the other using a particular concept of the appropriate "real exchange rate." The purchasing power parity theory is woefully deficient for present purposes as it does not begin to account for comparative changes in productivity between countries, or changes in competitive circumstances as discussed above with regard to the resource, labour-intensive or the high-tech and service sectors. So it is not surprising that by this calculation a Canadian dollar equal to about US$0.86 is supposed to be appropriate. If we bear in mind the large deficit in the Canadian current account for the years 1990, 1991 and early 1992 when this level of exchange rate prevailed, we can readily see that this approach is not relevant for the present purposes.

The second approach, entailing an estimate of the appropriate real exchange rate, is more relevant than the purchasing power parity approach in that it takes into consideration productivity growth differentials between nations. It suggests an exchange value for the dollar of about US$0.77 to US$0.81 would be appropriate, which is the range which existed in the autumn of 1992. But, even it does not address *directly* the problem of the deterioration of the higher unit labour costs in Canada or the worsened competitive situation of the various Canadian commodity and service sectors. So it has not been assigned any weight in this discussion.

39   See note regarding the revisions in these estimates.

40   Allowing for differences in production growth and inflation in the U.S. and Canada over the last year or two would not alter this conclusion. For example, in 1991 the inflation rates measured by

the consumer price index were 5.6 percent in Canada and 4.2 percent in the U.S. See Canada, Department of Finance, *Economic Reference Tables*, p. 138. As for productivity growth for 1991, Canada achieved a 0.7 percent rate versus 0.3 percent for the U.S. (Harris, *Exchange Rates*).

41   Harris, *Exchange Rates*, pp. 36-38, 47-48.

42   Canada has the option to cancel it too, on six months' notice, but is much less likely to do so because 70-75 percent of its trade is with the U.S., whereas only 25 percent of U.S. trade is with Canada. The most recent and best known example of an American-biased interpretation of the trade rules is the U.S. allegation that the Honda plant in Canada did not meet North American content rules for auto parts. This was like a warning to other firms, "Locate your plant in the U.S. or be vulnerable to our changing the rules and jeopardizing your exports to us."

43   This was a consequence of several factors: 1) the disruptions in the European exchange markets in August, which subsequently spread to Canada; 2) the Government's own fear-mongering that the country was going to fall apart unless Canadians voted in favour of the Charlottetown Accord; and 3) the growing awareness of the international economy that the nation has been experiencing huge current account deficits in the balance of payments and has been doing very little to resolve this problem.

44   Federal government wages in 1990, for example, were about 30 percent above comparable civilian wages and roughly the same situation prevailed for the other two levels of government. See S. Damus, *Canada's Public Sector: A Graphic Overview* (Ottawa: Economic Council of Canada, 1992), pp. 9-10.

45   John Cornwall, *The Theory of Economic Breakdown: An Institutional-Analytical Approach* (Cambridge, Mass.: Basil Blackwell, 1990), has a good discussion of the policies of the other nations which have been successful, in contrast to those which have been unsuccessful, at restricting inflation.

46   See Cornwall, *Economic Breakdown*; Campbell, "Jobs...Job..." ; and Campbell, "Coping With Globalization Instead of Just Talking About It," *Policy Options*, 13, 10 (December 1992): pp. 13-18.

CHAPTER 10

The NAFTA, Democracy and Continental Economic Integration: Trade Policy as if Democracy Mattered

Ian Robinson

Résumé : Ce chapitre se penche sur l'incidence éventuelle de l'*Accord de libre-échange nord-américain* sur la qualité et la stabilité de la démocratie au Canada et aux États-Unis et sur l'avenir de la démocratie au Mexique. L'auteur y pose que la qualité et la stabilité de la démocratie dépend de la quasi-égalité universelle des revenus et de la protection des droits des travailleurs, entre autres. Or les progrès à ces égards ne sont possibles que dans la mesure où les stratégies concurrentielles des entreprises visent l'augmentation de la productivité, l'amélioration des compétences des travailleurs et la hausse des salaires, et non les coupures salariales et l'élimination des avantages sociaux. Dans le courant des dix dernières années, les gouvernements des trois pays signataires de l'Accord ont rejeté cet argument et encouragé la concurrence salariale par divers moyens, dont des accords de libre-échange et de déréglementation qui facilitent le mouvement des capitaux et intensifient la concurrence internationale. Il en a résulté une iniquité grandissante, la pauvreté et la violation des droits des travailleurs dans les trois pays, quoique la gravité de ces problèmes s'amoindrisse du sud au nord. L'*Accord de libre-échange nord-américain* limitera encore plus le pouvoir de réglementation des gouvernements sur les entreprises puisqu'il donne lieu à la création, ni plus ni moins, de nouveaux droits de propriété privée pour les entreprises et qu'il exacerbe la concurrence qui s'exerce entre les gouvernements pour attirer les investisseurs privés et les conserver. Selon toute vraisemblance, l'Accord ne fera qu'aggraver les tendances sociales apparues dans les années 1980, et donc miner la qualité de la démocratie et ce, dans les trois pays signataires. À la fin du chapitre, l'auteur envisage différentes façons par lesquelles la politique commerciale pourrait être employée pour alimenter, et non miner, une démocratie forte à la fois dans les trois pays signataires de l'Accord et à l'échelle mondiale, niveau où ces problèmes doivent en fin de compte être réglés.

Abstract: This chapter considers how the North American Free Trade Agreement (NAFTA) will affect the quality and stability of democracy in Canada and the United States, and the prospects for democracy in Mexico. It argues that the quality and stability of democracy depend upon low levels of income inequality and the protection of labour rights, among other things. Progress on these dimensions is possible only if corporate competitive strategies are based on increasing productivity, worker skills and wages, rather than cutting worker wages and benefits. In the last decade, governments in all three NAFTA countries have rejected this argument and encouraged wage-based competition in a variety of ways. These include deregulation and trade agreements which increased capital mobility and intensified international competition. The result has been growing inequality, poverty and labour rights violations in all three countries, decreasing in scale as one moves north. The NAFTA will further reduce the capacity of governments to regulate corporate behaviour, by creating what amounts to new corporate private property rights and increasing competition among governments to attract and retain private investment. It is likely, therefore, to intensify the social trends of the 1980s and, as a result, to reduce the quality of democracy in all three NAFTA countries. The chapter's final section considers a number of ways in which trade policy could be used to strengthen, rather than undermine, high quality democracy in the three NAFTA countries and at the global level, where these problems must ultimately be solved.

Prior to the Tokyo round of the General Agreement on Tariffs and Trade (GATT), trade agreements were primarily about reducing tariff barriers to the free movement of goods across national boundaries. Since then, however, the scope of trade agreements has been greatly expanded to include not only goods but services, not only trade but investment and intellectual property flows, and not only tariff but non-tariff barriers to these flows. The new international trade agreements also prohibit discrimination between national and foreign-owned corporations, and create new corporate private property rights, possessed by both national and foreign investors. The trade agreements of the last decade amount to full-fledged frameworks of economic integration. These frameworks will function as economic constitutions, setting the basic rules governing the private property rights that all governments must respect and the types of economic policies that all governments must eschew. The North American Free Trade Agreement (NAFTA) goes further in this direction than any other agreement signed by Canada to date.

When dealing with constitutional design, it is fitting to raise fundamental questions and to clarify basic ethical assumptions. This discussion focuses on one such question: What effects is the

NAFTA likely to have on the quality of democracy in Canada and the United States, and on the prospects for the emergence of a democratic regime in Mexico? The questions most frequently raised about the NAFTA are whether it will promote economic competitiveness and growth in the three countries, and what its cost to national sovereignty will be. But competitiveness and growth are not ends in themselves; they are desirable only insofar as they improve human welfare, particularly that of the poorest segments of society. Competitiveness can be achieved in different ways, and economic growth can take different forms. Some of them are incompatible with improving the welfare of the majority, much less the poorest members, of the national and international population. There are good reasons to believe, as I will indicate, that democratic rights and institutions are the best way to increase the likelihood that corporate competition and economic growth will enhance the welfare of the less well off half of the population, in Third World as in First World countries.

Like competitiveness, nation-state sovereignty is not an intrinsic good. Its moral force derives from its contribution to empowering the people who live in these territorial units to make important choices about their own destiny. If some national objectives, e.g. protecting Canadians and the global environment, require binding international commitments that reduce the sovereignty of the State (as do all such commitments), then nation-state sovereignty is properly subordinated to popular sovereignty. As long as nation-states are the highest level at which high quality democracy exists, the nation and its sovereignty will have special moral and political significance. But we must be clear about the source of this special status.

Under this view, competitiveness, economic growth and national sovereignty either presuppose or serve the more fundamental political good of democracy and its associated rights and duties. To the degree that the pursuit of these subsidiary objectives involves trade-offs with the quality or stability of democracy, it is self-defeating and should be abandoned. Put another way, the pursuit of these goals only makes moral sense to the degree that it does not reduce, or preclude other ways of increasing, the quality of democracy.

This chapter argues that the NAFTA—in its current form— is likely to encourage corporate competitive strategies based on reducing wage and environmental protection costs, and intergovernmental competition premised on cutting corporate taxes and regulations to attract and maintain private investment. Competition of this sort will exacerbate income inequalities and undercut labour movement rights and power in the three NAFTA countries, and will not attack the root causes of the slow economic growth of the 1980s.[1] Increased income inequality and diminished labour rights will reduce the quality of democracy in Canada and the United States, and the chances that stable, high quality democracy will emerge in Mexico. The NAFTA, in its current and any modified form that continues to encourage these kinds of destructive competition, must therefore be rejected.

Rejecting the NAFTA will not be enough, however. The economic pressures associated with global under-consumption and intensifying international competition are already propelling us towards a less just and a less prosperous world. The NAFTA, if passed, will only intensify these trends by broadening their scope and accelerating their pace. New instruments of national trade policy, and new international economic agreements and institutions, must be constructed if the trajectories of our global and continental economies are to be deflected onto a happier course. Trade policy is only one area in which new thinking and institution-building are necessary. New mandates and powers will have to be assigned to the World Bank and the International Monetary Fund (IMF) as well.

Elements of a more democratic trade policy already exist, albeit in an underdeveloped form. The Auto Pact requires car producers qualifying for its benefits to link the value of the automobiles they build in Canada to the value of the automobiles they sell here and their Canadian content. It is simple and fair, and it has promoted dramatic increases in productivity, particularly in Canada.[2] The "social dimension" of the European Community (EC) provides for minimum EC-level labour and environmental standards to prevent corporate competition based on "externalizing" social and ecological costs. It also includes "structural funds" that provide poorer countries (and the poorer regions of rich countries) with transfers to help them meet these minimum standards. The labour rights provisions of American trade laws— and their Canadian equivalents, if such are created—provide the leverage for inducing authoritarian regimes to accept and enforce international minimum standards. Parallel provisions could be introduced with respect to environmental standards.

This chapter is divided into four sections. The first explains why low levels of income inequality and the protection of labour rights are essential to stable, high quality democracy. The second section outlines some of the most important ways in which the NAFTA would increase the mobility of capital and restrict the regulatory powers of governments relative to the baseline established by the Canada-U.S. Free Trade Agreement (FTA) and the Tokyo GATT. The third section considers how these NAFTA-induced changes would likely affect levels of economic inequality and labour movement rights and power in Mexico, the United States and Canada. The last section develops in more detail the above suggestions concerning a pro-democratic trade policy for North America.

DOMESTIC CONDITIONS OF HIGH QUALITY, STABLE DEMOCRACY

In a democracy, all adults have the right to vote for their political leaders, speak their minds on political issues, form their own political associations and run for political office. These rights are well protected and regularly exercised. Satisfaction of these minimal requirements of democracy still permits great variation in the degree to which all citizens are equipped—through education, income and leisure—to participate effectively in democratic politics, should they wish to do so. The degree to which political power is concentrated in the hands of a relatively small élite, by virtue of their structural position in the economy or their political connections, also varies greatly.[3] Finally, there are considerable differences in the share of "public decisions"—i.e. those with substantial implications for large numbers of citizens—that are determined or overseen by democratic processes.[4] These variations affect the *quality* of democracy within nations meeting the minimal definitional threshold.

Two of the most important "structural" determinants[5] of democratic quality are the level of income inequality and the level of protection for worker rights. High levels of income (and wealth) inequality are much more difficult to justify than low levels, and political systems—democratic or otherwise—that permit high levels of income inequality are much more difficult to legitimate than those that do not, other things being equal. High levels of income inequality are particularly corrosive in a democracy, however, because the official ideology of such a regime is one of equal citizen rights and dignity, equal political participation and equal economic opportunity. Where the system and its outcomes have no legitimacy among large numbers of desperately poor people, high levels of social mobilization and radical critiques of the existing order are to be expected. In the face of such mobilization, political and economic élites who wish to defend their wealth and power may feel that they have no viable alternative to repression. Recent work by Edward Muller demonstrates a strong and consistent relationship between low levels of income inequality and democratic stability, and between high levels of inequality and instability.[6]

Strong, broadly based and democratic labour unions and the protection of labour rights are important for several reasons. Strong, democratic labour movements reduce inequalities both through collective bargaining and through support for political parties that push for redistributive social and economic policies.[7] Second, because unions and union-affiliated political parties play this critical redistributive function, they are usually the primary targets of political and economic élites seeking to defend the power arrangements that create and sustain many inequalities. Labour rights violation levels, therefore, serve as a rough barometer of the willingness and capacity of political and economic élites to suspend democratic rights in order to preserve their privileges. Democracy is unlikely to develop or survive for long in a climate of labour repression, because labour rights overlap, to a substantial degree, with human rights and democratic rights. If we wish to increase the quality of democracy, we should protect and promote the growth of independent, democratic unions and the other social and economic policies that reduce income inequalities.

Some would argue that rapid economic growth naturally leads to democracy and that strong labour unions and redistribution to reduce income inequalities will slow or stall such growth.[8] The first proposition is undercut by the compatibility of rapid economic growth with Nazism and Communism before the war, and such economic "miracles" as Brazil and South Korea since. A more accurate view is that industrialization "naturally" leads to strong labour movements that generally push for democracy and redistribution. If, however, political and economic élites respond to these demands with repression, democracy does not advance.[9] The second proposition is belied by the postwar experience of the most successful newly industrialized country of all—Japan— which had both democracy and free trade unions throughout the years of its extraordinary growth. It should also be recognized that *before* they began their rapid growth and despite the existence of authoritarian regimes, South Korea and Taiwan exhibited income distributions at least as egalitarian as those in the most industrialized countries, and they continue to exhibit such patterns today.[10] Thus, a relatively egalitarian distribution of income seems to help, rather than hinder, rapid economic growth in less developed, as well as in more developed, economies.

THE NAFTA'S IMPACT ON STATE REGULATORY CAPACITY

The NAFTA is an extension of the deregulatory approach to international trade and economic integration found in the Tokyo round of the GATT and in the FTA. As such, its principal focus is on constraining governments' capacity to regulate the behaviour of foreign and domestic importers, exporters and investors. These restrictions amount to new private property rights that go well beyond those recognized in Canadian and Mexican law, if not those of the United States. In effect, what the Conservative government could not accomplish directly in the 1991-92 round of constitutional negotiations—the inclusion of private property rights in an amended Canadian Charter of Rights and Freedoms— due to provincial government opposition, it may yet accomplish through the NAFTA. Expanded protections for investor property rights stand in stark contrast to the absence of measures to increase the protection of labour rights and the environment. The argument that such concerns have no place in a trade agreement (narrowly defined to mean the free movement of goods and services across borders) is transparently empty, since investor and intellectual property rights have no place in such an agreement either.

These new private property rights will reduce the capacity of governments to protect and promote the social prerequisites of high quality democracy and high productivity growth in three ways. First, they will impose new *legal* restrictions on governments' right to regulate corporate behaviour without incurring unsustainable compensation burdens. Second, they will improve the security of foreign investors in Mexico, increasing *market* pressures on Canadian and American governments to reduce regulatory standards (and taxes) in their intensifying competition for corporate capital investment. Finally, the NAFTA will increase the domestic *political* power of foreign corporations by creating a new commonality between their interests and those of domestic businesses. This will occur because any policy that challenges the prerogatives of foreign investors will have to be applied to domestic investors to ensure NAFTA-consistency under the National Treatment principle. As a result, foreign transnational corporations (TNCs) will be able to rely, to an unprecedented degree, upon the political power of domestic business to defend their interests.

The principal new legal restrictions on the right to regulate are found in the chapters of the Agreement that deal with "technical standards" such as labour and environmental regulations, and the chapters that grant NAFTA "investors" new protections against regulation by all levels of government in all three countries. The National Treatment principle governs all of these chapters.

Technical Standards

The NAFTA's restrictions in this area go beyond those found in the FTA in several respects. They apply to measures taken by provincial governments; these were explicitly excluded from the ambit of the FTA. They also impose a tough new test on government regulations that are deemed to be trade restrictive. Like the Tokyo GATT and the FTA, the NAFTA recognizes a special class of legitimate regulatory objectives—in this case, the "safety or the protection of human, animal or plant life or health, the environment, or consumers"—which may be valid even if they restrict trade.[11] If a measure is found to be trade restrictive, a government seeking to defend it must first demonstrate that the intent of the measure was to realize one of these "legitimate objectives." This is not always easy to do, particularly if the measure serves several purposes.

In the FTA and the Tokyo GATT, a trade restrictive government regulation was immune to challenge if the test of legitimate objectives could be met. But under the NAFTA, a government which successfully meets this test must still meet a second, demonstrating that its measure was the "least trade restrictive necessary" to achieve its legitimate objective. While we have no experience with how this second hurdle will work, it could be quite onerous. In principle, the test seems quite unbalanced. The least trade restrictive way to achieve the objective may be much more expensive, less effective, or have many undesirable side-effects. Why should all other policy objectives—even those acknowledged to be "legitimate"—be subordinated to the objective of freeing the movement of goods, services and investment across borders? Trade freedom is not even guaranteed to promote economic growth, much less economic development, and still less democracy.

Given the considerable hurdles that must be cleared in order to defend successfully a regulation or policy deemed to be "trade restrictive," the burden that a challenger must meet in order to show that a measure is "trade restrictive" becomes very important. In many cases, the most promising way to meet this burden is to show that a government measure violates the National Treatment principle. Under this principle, a measure is trade restrictive if it discriminates in favour of national producers or investors compared with non-national exporters or investors. The NAFTA applies this principle to trade in goods and services, *and* to investments by NAFTA investors, while the Tokyo GATT applies it to trade in goods alone.

Over the years, GATT panels have developed a broad interpretation of what counts as "discrimination": an interpretation called "equal competitive opportunity" (ECO).[12] On this reading, a measure can apply the same rule to nationals and non-nationals and still be discriminatory if it has the *effect* of placing foreign exporters at a competitive disadvantage. For example, Northern Telecom has recently developed a non-ozone-depleting (i.e. CFC-free) way of cleaning printed circuits and microchips. Were Canada to require that all producers of such materials in Canada and all exporters of such materials to Canada employ a CFC-free process, this would place Northern Telecom's foreign rivals at a competitive disadvantage in Canada until they licensed the clean technology from Northern Telecom or developed their own.[13] This would be enough to qualify such a regulation as discriminatory, hence trade restrictive, according to the ECO interpretation. Language reflecting this interpretation is explicitly included in the NAFTA's Financial Services chapter. The interpretation may also be "read into" other chapters by future NAFTA panels.

The NAFTA will bring such broadly defined concepts as "discrimination" to bear on a wide range of government—particularly provincial government—activities not covered under the Tokyo GATT or the FTA. This substantially increases legal uncertainty and, with it, the likelihood of challenges to government measures. Responding to such challenges will increase the costs of regulation. Ensuring that the necessary, least trade restrictive tests have been met, to improve the chances of withstanding a challenge, will also cost money. All this is likely to have a chilling effect on efforts to raise standards or introduce regulations in new areas.

Investor Rights[14]

The Investment chapter proscribes seven different kinds of "performance requirements." Some of these restrictions are carried over from the FTA, but the prohibitions on technology transfer and world or continental "product mandating" are new.[15] The need for such requirements may increase in the coming years, owing to the changing TNC strategies that reduce the autonomy of their branch plants.[16] All of these performance requirements represent efforts to "manage" trade, on the assumption that this can promote economic development, particularly when dealing with vertically integrated TNCs that are able to set the prices of the goods and services that they import and export, rather than taking these prices as given by competitive markets.[17]

The most important managed trade principle governing Canada-U.S. trade to date—the 1965 Auto Pact requirements that the qualifying auto companies must produce vehicles in Canada valued at a minimum of 75 percent of the value of their vehicle sales in Canada and that such Canadian built vehicles must have at least 60 percent Canadian value added—is not included in the list of prohibited performance requirements. It is nonetheless weakened because the NAFTA will (over 10 years) reduce to zero all tariffs on autos manufactured in North America, provided they meet its North American "rules of origin" (i.e. content requirements). A car with 60 percent Mexican and 10 percent American content would easily meet this requirement. In such a case, the Canadian government cannot use tariffs to enforce the Auto Pact principle should TNCs decide not to comply with it. The FTA did the same thing with respect to the United States, but Mexico probably represents the more serious threat if the Big Three auto makers opt for a cost-externalizing competitive strategy. The only remaining incentive to comply with the Auto Pact, independent of lower Canadian production costs, is therefore the right to import parts from non-FTA/NAFTA countries duty-free for compliant Auto Pact corporations.[18]

The Investment chapter also requires that North American investors receive "national treatment" or "most favoured nation" (MFN) treatment, whichever is better. Since any law that singles out foreign investors for different treatment is by definition discriminatory, this principle appears to rule out attaching any special conditions or performance requirements of any kind to foreign investors as foreigners.[19] As noted above, this creates a new commonality of interests among foreign and domestic investors.

The Monopolies and State Enterprises chapter[20] will impose new constraints on two more traditional government strategies for inducing the co-operation of private investors—the creation of a public corporation to compete with them, or the creation of private monopolies subject to various conditions. Article 1502 permits the creation of new public or private monopolies, but requires governments to endeavour to "minimize or eliminate any nullification or impairment of benefits" that investors reasonably expected to receive under the NAFTA. Further, all monopolies, old or new, must act "solely in accordance with commercial considerations" and may not use their monopoly power to engage in "anti-competitive practices," such as "the discriminatory provision of the monopoly good or service, cross-subsidization or predatory conduct."

NAFTA investor rights go beyond those created by the FTA in two other important respects. First, the number of investors eligible for such protections will greatly increase. Investors seeking the more limited protections of the FTA's Investment chapter had to own the majority of shares or otherwise control the investment to be eligible for these protections. The NAFTA definition of "investment" merely requires *some* American or Mexican ownership or control. This appears to grant almost any publicly held business operating in Canada protection under this chapter, since most of them will have at least some American (or Mexican) ownership.

Second, the new investor-state dispute process created in the NAFTA's Investment chapter will permit investors who believe that one of their new rights has been violated to go before an international tribunal with binding arbitration powers, or to go to the domestic courts.[21] The tribunal will operate under the procedural rules of the International Centre for the Settlement of Investment Disputes (ICSID). The choice of venue will be the investor's. In contrast, under the FTA and the GATT, private investors cannot launch a direct challenge to any government measure. Instead, they must persuade their national government to launch such a challenge. The NAFTA investor dispute process will make it faster and less expensive for eligible investors to enforce their new property rights. This will result in more challenges and, hence, higher regulatory costs, even if governments successfully fend off all such challenges. When the governments lose, they will have to change their behaviour or pay compensation.

To sum up, the NAFTA will go well beyond the FTA and the Tokyo GATT in the restrictions that it imposes on state regulatory capacity by imposing new legal restrictions on governments and by reducing their bargaining power *vis-à-vis* domestic and foreign corporations, which will find it more attractive to invest in Mexico than has been the case to date. It also builds political bridges between the interests of foreign and domestic investors, thereby increasing the political power of the former in each of the three political systems. This makes it less likely that states will pursue the kinds of policies and regulations necessary to protect and promote high quality democracy and rapid productivity growth. The precise scale of these changes—like those that result from other constitutional amendments—is controversial because it depends upon the interpretations given to such key terms as "discriminatory treatment," "nullification and impairment," and "anti-competitive" by future NAFTA panels, national courts and ICSID tribunals. But the main drift of these changes is clear.

THE NAFTA'S SOCIAL AND ECONOMIC IMPACT: POLARIZATION

What does the NAFTA-reinforced shift in the balance of economic, legal and political powers among private corporations, governments and unions imply for the structural variables that I have argued are critical to democratic quality and stability: the level of income inequality, and the recognition and protection of labour rights?

No one constructs general equilibrium—or disequilibrium—models to answer questions like this. Nor are efforts to model narrower questions such as the NAFTA's net impact on Mexican or American employment or wages very convincing. They rest on unpersuasive assumptions and oversimplifications, and variations in even one of these assumptions can generate radically different results.[22] The analysis in this section is built upon two assumptions that are more plausible than many found in the standard economic models. First, the growing income inequality and the erosion of labour rights that characterized the 1980s was, to a substantial degree, the product of the trade liberalization and other market deregulation initiatives of that decade. Second, since the NAFTA will extend the scope and depth of these initiatives, it is likely to intensify the social trends of the last decade. Consider each NAFTA country in turn.

Mexico

Mexican income inequality has increased without respite since the end of the Cardenas presidency in 1940. By 1958, the incomes of the richest 5 percent were 22 times those of the poorest 10 percent; by the late 1970s, that gap had more than doubled.[23] In 1977, over 57 percent of all Mexican income went to the top 20 percent of the population alone.[24] This is 10 percentage points above the level consistent with stable democracy and considerably higher than is typical for countries with Mexico's level of per capita gross national product (GNP).[25] Income inequality data for Mexico in the 1980s are not available, but inequality has likely grown because Mexican wages fell by between 50 and 60 percent in this period. The ratio of total wage income to GNP reflected this decline, falling from its 1976 peak of 40.3 percent to about 26.6 percent in 1987 and then 23 percent in 1992.[26]

It is commonly supposed that the Salinas reforms and the NAFTA will reduce Mexican poverty and income inequality by encouraging new foreign investment that will reduce unemployment and increase wages. I cannot agree with this optimistic picture. In my judgement, the NAFTA is likely to exacerbate Mexican income inequalities for four reasons. First, the economic growth promoted by the NAFTA in the next decade is unlikely to result in anything close to full employment, so that labour market forces cannot be relied upon to increase Mexican wages.[27] Second, the NAFTA will destroy some unions and pressure those that remain to lower their wage demands, so that unions can only raise the income of Mexico's workers through collective bargaining to a very limited degree. Third, while the productivity gains associated with new foreign investment make possible substantial increases in Mexican wages while maintaining high profits, it is unlikely that TNCs will raise wages in the absence of government, union or full employment market pressures. Fourth, in the absence of strong private sector redistributive mechanisms, the burden of reducing inequalities falls primarily upon the same Mexican state that has presided over the growing inequality of the last 50 years. Unless there is a dramatic improvement in the quality of Mexican democracy, there is little reason to believe that the Mexican state will seriously try, much less succeed in, reversing historical trends. Consider each point in more detail.

The NAFTA is unlikely to eliminate Mexican unemployment—or, perhaps more accurately, underemployment.[28] The employment created by new foreign investment in the Mexican manufacturing sector[29] is unlikely to be much greater than the new unemployment, created by the NAFTA, in Mexican agriculture[30] and "import substitution industrialization" (ISI) manufacturing[31] sectors. Even in the 1960s, when the Mexican GNP expanded at an average of 6.5 percent per year, only about 300,000 new "formal sector" jobs were created each year.[32] NAFTA-induced investment is likely to be at least as capital intensive as that of the 1960s. But in the 1980s, the Mexican workforce has been growing at the rate of about a million new workers per year, and this rate is unlikely to decline much without a substantial reduction in Mexican poverty levels.[33] So, even if the economic growth rates of the 1960s could be doubled, and the problem of displaced workers in the agricultural and ISI manufacturing sectors is ignored, Mexican employment growth would not keep pace with workforce growth, much less reduce the existing pool of unemployed and underemployed workers.

Mexican unions will be under severe pressure for three reasons. First, much of the ISI manufacturing sector, one of the two sectors in which Mexico's unions are strongest, is likely to be destroyed for the reasons noted above. ISI firms and unions will only survive by taking dramatic wage cuts and reorienting to production for TNCs, to the degree that TNCs will buy from them.[34] Second, Mexico is privatizing substantial elements of the state sector, the other sector in which Mexican unions are strong. It is estimated that 600 Mexican public enterprises have been privatized since 1982.[35] Finally, President Salinas has already taken steps to divide and weaken the major unions in sectors such as oil and education that otherwise would have been relatively unscathed by ISI restructuring and privatization.[36] Taken together, these measures dramatically weaken the existing Mexican labour movement and, given the Mexican labour market, this can only push Mexican wages down.

Productivity increases make it possible for TNC employers in Mexico to follow Henry Ford's policy of dramatically increasing employee wages, even in the absence of unions, but Ford of Mexico evinces little interest in following its founder's example on this score, and neither do other TNCs operating in Mexico. The wages paid by the *maquila* remain about half those in the ISI sector, despite the *maquila's* much higher productivity levels.[37] Nor is it likely that Henry Ford would have behaved any differently had he been in charge today. He raised his workers' wages in the United States because, as he put it, they (and other workers like them) had to be able to buy his cars or he could not sell enough of them to make his new mass production methods pay off.[38] But Ford of Mexico does not see its Mexican workers as the principal market for the cars that it assembles in Mexico—its market is the United States and Canada, plus the top 20 percent of the Mexican population that enjoys standards of living comparable to the élites of the other two countries.

The Mexican state, as long as it is dominated by the ruling Institutional Revolutionary Party (PRI), is unlikely to do through taxes and transfers what it is unwilling to do through support for labour rights and credit for upgrading the productivity of small holder agriculture. Unfortunately, the 1988 elections suggest that the PRI is willing to resort to fraud and violence to preserve its grip on power.[39] State labour repression—and state tolerance for employer repression—seems to be increasing in Mexico for two reasons.[40] First, while unions affiliated with the ruling PRI put up relatively little resistance to the structural adjustments associated with the debt crisis, their acquiescence is steadily eroding. Some unions long affiliated with the PRI supported the breakaway social democratic party, the Party of the Democratic Revolution (PRD), founded by Cuatemoc Cardenas to contest the 1988 elections. The unions that remained loyal to the PRI face dwindling state patronage and increasing pressure from rank and file union activists for a more independent, democratic form of unionism. Only repression or a change in economic course seems likely to prevent growing economic and political opposition from the Mexican labour movement.

The second reason that increased labour repression is likely is the Salinas regime's economic strategy: Mexico as the primary low wage "export platform" for the North American market.[41] From this perspective, it is critical to keep Mexican wages competitive with those of every other country which might aspire to this position. Even with high levels of unemployment, the kind of highly mobilized, democratic labour movement that will emerge in Mexico if labour repression is not increased is quite capable of producing wage and benefit gains that the regime will consider incompatible with the global market niche that it wants Mexico to occupy.[42]

To sum up, if the NAFTA and other forms of deregulation go forward, it is unlikely that current levels of Mexican income inequality and labour and political repression will be reduced, even if the impressive gross domestic product (GDP) growth rates of the 1960s are restored or surpassed. Indeed, poverty and polarization are likely to grow. In this context, the chances of a Mexican transition to stable democracy are remote, however good the intentions of those promoting the current reforms. The

NAFTA is, therefore, likely to propel Mexico farther down the road to Guatemala rather than lift it up towards California.

Canada and the United States

Canada and the United States look very similar when compared with Mexico. Both are very rich and are stable democracies which exhibit income inequality levels that look very low *vis-à-vis* Mexico, though rather high by Organization for Economic Co-operation and Development (OECD) standards. Both countries have recognized and protected the rights of independent, democratic unions since the end of World War II, albeit with considerable regional variation in the scope of those rights and the effectiveness of their protection. While the issue in Mexico is whether trends encouraged by the NAFTA will permit the emergence of democracy, the issue in Canada and the United States is whether quality of democracy will be reduced, and if so, by how much.

In spite of their basic similarities, Canada and the United States began to diverge on several interrelated dimensions with direct bearing on the quality of democracy in the 1970s and 1980s. Perhaps most important, while the economic and political power of labour movements in both countries began to wane in the 1970s with "stagflation," intensifying international competition and more conservative governments in both national capitals and many states and provinces, it declined much more precipitously in the United States. The greater speed of declining American labour movement power was partially caused by, and accurately reflected in, its accelerated decline in "union density"; between 1955 and 1975, the share of the non-agricultural workforce belonging to unions in the United States steadily fell at an average rate of 0.15 percent per annum. Between 1975 and 1989, it plummeted at a rate of 0.85 percent per annum so that, by 1989, it stood at less than 16 percent.[43] In Canada, by contrast, union density rose steadily to its 1983 peak of 40 percent, fell to about 36 percent over the next few years and then stabilized at that level.[44]

Responding to the anti-union rhetoric and policy of the Reagan and Bush administrations, the intensification of international competitive pressures and declining union capacity to fight back effectively, most American employers adopted competitive strategies based on cost reductions through wage and benefit cuts, rather than through longer-term investment in better productive processes.[45] American employer violations of labour laws and regulations increased as union density and labour movement power fell.[46] Where unions could not be avoided or broken, dramatic wage and benefit concessions were demanded, often with success.[47] Where concessions could not be extracted—and frequently, even when they were—corporations moved from high union density, high wage regions of the United States to low union density, low wage states in the South and Southwest, or beyond to Third World countries in which labour rights were repressed.[48]

Canadian manufacturers were at least as exposed to intensifying international competition as their American counterparts, given the much more trade dependent character of the Canadian economy and Canada's inability to negotiate the kind of bilateral "voluntary export restriction" agreements secured by the Reagan and Bush administrations.[49] But the Canadian labour movement remained relatively strong, both in the economic bargaining power of its unions and in the influence exercised on public policy by the New Democratic Party. Consequently, employer labour law violations, while increasing in the 1970s and 1980s, remained at much lower levels than in the United States[50]and Canadian employer demands for wage and benefit concessions were not as successful, though they could not be entirely resisted.[51]Instead, employers sought to have Conservative provincial governments make changes to their labour laws.[52]

As a result, employers in Canada had to rely more on the threats of "exit" —relocation to the United States or Mexico—and high unemployment to push Canadian wages and benefits down to what they hoped would be more competitive levels. This threat was made easier to carry out, and hence more credible, when the Conservative government pushed through the FTA in the wake of the 1988 election. When an overvalued Canadian dollar[53] pushed Canadian wage costs above those in the United States in many industries, many American TNCs seeking to "rationalize" production decided to make good their threats and close their Canadian subsidiaries. Ontario Ministry of Labour data indicate that 65 percent of the factory jobs lost in that province in 1989-92 were the result of permanent plant closings, in contrast to the 1981-82 recession when only about 25 percent of lay-offs resulted from permanent plant closures. While the volume of manufacturing in the U.S. rose 1.6 percent from 1988 to 1991, it fell 11.4 percent in Canada in the same period.[54]

The impact of declining union bargaining power, wage concessions, rising unemployment and plant closures on income inequalities in the two countries was predictable. From the end of World War II to the late 1960s, American income inequality fell steadily so that, by 1968, the Gini coefficient for the United States was .348. Thereafter, however, American income inequality steadily increased so that, by 1986, the American Gini coefficient exceeded .390 for the first time since the Great Depression. The difference between the 1968 and 1986 Gini coefficients—.042— may seem small, but it amounted to a 17.9 percent decline in the average income of the poorest fifth of American families and a 7.9 percent increase in the average income of the richest fifth.[55] This trend was closely associated with the phenomena of the shrinking middle class and rising poverty levels. By one definition, the share of American families with middle-class incomes fell from 53 to 47.9 percent between 1973 and 1984.[56] By the late 1980s, 20.4 percent of American children and 10.9 percent of elderly Americans lived in poverty.

Canadian income inequality also grew in this period. Canada's Gini coefficient for personal income inequality rose from 0.39 in 1967 to 0.42 in 1986.[57] The share of middle-income *jobs* in Canada also shrank, falling from 27 percent in 1967 to 22 percent in 1986—paralleling the 5 percentage point decline in the American middle class.[58] However, the proportion of middle-income *families* in Canada remained constant at about 25 percent in this period, and the percentage of the population living in poverty actually decreased, owing to non-employment income, mostly in the form of government transfers. In the late 1980s, 9.3 percent of children and 2.2 percent of the elderly lived in poverty in Canada.[59] Thus, Canadian public policies were sufficient to offset the inequality and poverty increasing effects of market forces in the 1980s. However, recent cuts and the increased pressures associated with the recession of 1990-92 have probably dated this conclusion.[60]

Given the relative weakness of the American labour movement, the NAFTA is likely to reinforce growing income inequality and poverty in the United States primarily by inducing further reductions in the wages and benefits of "unskilled" workers, which comprise about 80 percent of the American workforce. The NAFTA will do this in at least three ways: first, by depressing the price of domestically produced manufactured goods and, with this, the wages and benefits of the American workers that produce them, without raising the wages of unskilled workers in other sectors;[61] second, by reducing the share of American employment in manufacturing, which will remain higher paying work than most unskilled service sector jobs; and third, if my projections of Mexican population growth and employment displacement are broadly correct, by increasing the number of legal and illegal Mexican workers entering the United States.[62]

In Canada, where greater labour movement power has resulted in more limited wage contraction and more extensive redistribution through government transfers, income inequality may continue to increase at a slower pace than in the United States. Given the relative "stickiness" of Canadian wages, a larger share of rising Canadian inequality is likely to be due to plant closings and unemployment, as more manufacturing firms close Canadian operations and set up in the United States and Mexico. It is difficult to predict the degree to which the NAFTA will contribute to this trend, but it will make Canadian and American investors contemplating relocation to Mexico feel more secure about their property rights in that country and about their prospects for exporting back to Canada and the United States without hindrance.

To sum up, if the NAFTA is implemented, it is likely that economic inequality and the erosion of labour rights will accelerate in both Mexico and the United States, even if aggregate economic growth is somewhat improved, owing to the type of economic growth that it will encourage. While the Canadian labour movement has resisted these trends more successfully to date, this has come at the price of higher levels of Canadian unemployment. Rising unemployment and falling government transfers result in growing income inequality as surely as falling wages. For Mexico, these trends mean that its chances of becoming a stable democracy are substantially reduced; for the United States and Canada, it means that the quality of democracy is deteriorating.

A PRO-DEMOCRACY TRADE POLICY

State protection of labour standards and rights is essential to promoting corporate competitive strategies that result in sustainable forms of productivity growth. Strong labour and environmental movements are usually necessary to obtain, improve upon and enforce these regulations. Strong labour movements also help to reduce income inequalities. High quality democracy makes governments more responsive to such social movements and more protective of their rights. There is, therefore, a virtuous circle between improving the quality of democracy and promoting sustainable economic development.

Trade policy—if it permits or facilitates corporate competitive strategies based upon externalizing social and environmental costs—can weaken some of the key links in this virtuous circle. A pro-democracy trade policy must instead strengthen them while promoting mutually beneficial exchanges of goods, services and investment. In this section, I first sketch a number of ways in which trade policy might contribute to the realization of these objectives. I then ask what such objectives imply for Canada's response to the NAFTA and the labour and environmental "side deals" which President Clinton proposes as supplements.

Four Objectives

A pro-democracy trade policy should do at least four things:

- promulgate and uphold high and rising labour and environmental standards that apply to unorganized as well as organized workers and firms. These measures will force corporations to internalize a growing share of the social and environmental costs flowing from their activities, thereby incorporating them into the price system;
- promote the organization of workers into independent, democratic unions in all of the countries that are parties to the trade agreement. This will help to reduce income inequalities within each trading country and to reduce the "social externalities" associated with labour exploitation.[63] It will not be sufficient, however, as long as many workers remain outside of unions;
- encourage governments to channel food, shelter, education and other basic resources to the poor; and

- ensure that the regulatory capacity of governments is protected.

How can trade policy advance each of these objectives?

Promoting High and Rising Labour and Environmental Standards. One way to promote high and rising standards is to include minimum international standards in trade agreements, together with processes for raising these standards as economic development and technological innovation permit. The European Community has developed EC-wide minimum environmental and labour standards as one element of what is called the "social dimension" of economic integration. Poorer member states are also provided with economic assistance to help them meet these standards through transfers, known as the "Structural Funds," from the richer community members.[64]

The minimum labour standards that constitute the EC's "social charter" are still being developed and remain very low in some cases. It is also too early to say how effective its enforcement mechanisms will be. The structural funds (with the exception of the Common Agricultural Policy) remain rather small.[65] Still, the EC's is a plausible *strategy* for responding to the problem; it should not be dismissed because its core ideas as yet have only been realized in a very imperfect form. Similar reasoning lies behind the positive review given by the congressional Office of Technology Assessment (OTA) in the United States to the option of a North American social and environmental charter.[66]

To adapt this model to trade agreements among countries exhibiting a greater range of economic development than the 12 EC countries will require either lower minimum standards—since poorer countries find it more difficult to realize higher standards—or larger scale "structural fund" transfers from rich to poor countries than those found in the EC.[67]

Two key Congressional Democrats—Max Baucus, Chairperson of the Senate Finance Committee's Subcommittee on Trade, and House Majority Leader Richard Gephardt—have proposed funding some transfers to Mexico to promote environmental clean-up in the U.S.-Mexico border region through a tax on goods and services moving across the border.[68] While the amount of the tax that they propose is inadequate to the larger purposes considered here, the idea of financing an equivalent of the EC's structural funds through a higher version of such a tax (with a Canada-U.S. border tax component as well) has two important merits. First, it ensures that economic integration is, in a sense, self-funding. The money needed to fund structural adjustments of various kinds comes directly out of the gains from freer trade. This is fair, because the beneficiaries of cheaper goods and services are the ones who pay the levy to help those who are harmed by the process. It is also politically smart, because it means that structural funds—which will come mostly from Canada and the U.S. and go mostly to Mexico—do not have to compete with a myriad of other powerful claims on the general revenues in an era when budget deficit concerns and spending cuts are widespread. The level of structural fund transfers could be linked to the pace at which recipient countries (and regions) move towards higher labour and environmental standards. This should increase the pace at which the poorest regions are willing and able to move up the scale and, hence, the rate at which minimum North American standards can be raised.

Trade agreements incorporating the above elements should be supplemented by domestic trade laws that use countervailing duties to enforce signatories' commitments and to prevent non-signatories from gaining cost advantages by denying labour rights and/or maintaining lax labour and environmental standards. Since 1984, U.S. trade law has made it a condition of eligibility for the Generalized System of Preferences that improvements in labour rights be made in countries where they have not been adequately protected.[69] There are now proposals for a similar Canadian law.[70] Ultimately, we should build such provisions into the GATT and create a new UN body to monitor and enforce such provisions at the global level.

But that day may be a long way off. In the meantime, domestic trade laws will constitute leverage for multilateral international minimum standards, because countries which would otherwise oppose such standards in principle will prefer a multilateral version of them to unilaterally imposed conditions interpreted, monitored and enforced by individual countries.

The approaches noted so far have focused on international standards and government obligations, but substantial progress could also be made by redesigning domestic tax laws pertaining to the overseas operations of Canadian and American TNCs. Taxes on the foreign earnings of these corporations could be varied in accordance with their level of compliance with labour and environmental standards. Several scales of rights and standards, with corresponding tax rates, could be established to increase the incentives for TNCs to move quickly to higher levels. If the governments of the United States, Germany and Japan alone could agree on the broad principles of such a corporate income tax regime, this would make it much easier for governments everywhere to develop and enforce worker rights and rapidly rising labour and environmental standards.

Promoting and Protecting Worker Organization. Protecting labour rights and standards by the means suggested above will facilitate worker organization into independent and democratic unions. However, this should be further encouraged by adapting another EC idea to North American needs in a legal requirement that TNCs in two or more North American countries form "works councils" which would regularly bring together elected worker representatives from their operations in these countries. For instance, the OTA study proposes the creation of North American works councils in firms employing more than 1,000 employees and more than 100 employees in two or more of the three countries.[71] Such councils will help to increase understanding and reduce trade tensions among workers from the three countries and, as is expected in the EC plan, may become the seeds of continental collective bargaining for that company.

A continental Auto Pact would strengthen key manufacturing unions in all three North American countries. It could also be expanded to include Japan.[72] Managed trade is already the rule in this sector—the only question is whether it will be managed in accordance with clear, fair, predictable rules, or in an ad hoc fashion as is the case with the "voluntary export restraints" negotiated between the United States and other countries in the 1980s. The Canada-U.S. Auto Pact of 1965, discussed above, represents a well-tried and highly successful example of the benefits of trade managed in accordance with fair, simple and transparent principles. This approach would result in less new auto company investment in Mexico, but it would get the incentives right: Mexico would increase its share of employment in this sector by increasing the incomes of its population sufficiently to consume more cars. The structural funds would provide some of the resources with which to do this and other reforms proposed here, such as the protection of labour rights, would help to ensure that workers get a larger and fairer share of the profits generated by auto plants which locate there, further contributing to Mexican auto consumption.[73] A parallel North American Steel Pact would make sense for the same reasons.

Encouraging State Redistribution to the Poor. In addition to helping governments meet the North American minimum standards proposed above, a substantial portion of the structural funds should be devoted to helping workers adjust to economic change and to providing basic food, shelter, health and education services to the poor in each of the countries signing the Agreement. Since these monies are not raised by income taxes on wealthy, powerful individuals or by corporate taxes, political resistance from these quarters is likely to be less substantial.

It may also be desirable to include a continental investment agreement—comprising rules and criteria designed to prevent national and subnational governments from bidding down taxes or spending scarce public monies on subsidies to attract or retain private investment. In principle, all governments lose in these competitions since each is forced to match the cuts of the others, leaving all of them worse off than before the round of cuts began. If this problem could be controlled, current budget deficits in rich and poor countries alike could be substantially reduced, making more substantial redistribution easier. A subsidies code might be a step in this direction, if it tackled the harmful subsidies and permitted helpful ones (e.g. for regional economic development and research and development) to continue. The failure of the FTA effort to develop such a code, the absence of such in the NAFTA and the bitter debates over the subsidies code proposed in the Dunkel draft of the current GATT negotiations reveal how difficult it is to develop a definition of undesirable and inefficient subsidies upon which all can agree.[74]

Protecting State Regulatory Capacity. Expansive definitions of "non-tariff barriers" designed to minimize impediments to trade must not be permitted to reduce the capacity of governments to develop and enforce effectively high and rising labour and environmental standards. In cases of conflict, the protection of these regulatory capabilities should take precedence over reductions in trade impediments for the reasons discussed earlier. Definitions of non-tariff barriers as they affect "technical standards" should be rewritten to reflect the normative priority of democracy. For the same reason, trade agreements should not reduce the autonomy of the State *vis-à-vis* TNCs—the latter already being by far the most powerful "special interest" in society—by assigning TNCs new property rights and powerful new legal procedures for enforcing those rights against democratic national and subnational governments. This will require either excising or substantially rewriting the NAFTA's Investment, Monopolies and State Enterprises, and Intellectual Property chapters.

What Next?

The foregoing analysis leads to the following conclusions: first, the NAFTA must either be reopened and fundamentally altered, or rejected; and second, whatever the NAFTA's fate, the three countries of North America must develop and implement a comprehensive continental social dimension, including the equivalent of the EC's structural funds. The current Canadian government opposes both of these prescriptions and has amply demonstrated its willingness—indeed, eagerness—to implement the current NAFTA without any social dimension whatever.[75] How can progress be made on one or both of these dimensions in this political context?

Some might place their hopes on the new American administration. The United States clearly has sufficient bargaining power to reopen the NAFTA and to insist upon the creation of a North American social dimension. The issue is how President Clinton and the Congress wish to use that power. Responding to the growing strength of congressional criticism of the NAFTA negotiated by the Bush administration, Clinton made an important campaign speech on October 4, 1992. He argued that the existing NAFTA would be beneficial, without any changes to the existing text, but only if supplemented by three "side deals" pertaining to minimum labour and environmental standards, and protection against import surges. This position received strong support from key Congressional Democrats such as Dick Gephardt and Max Baucus.[76]

Neither President Clinton nor the congressional leadership have wavered from this basic line since the elections of last November. Nor are they likely to want to reopen the Investment, Monopolies and State Enterprises, Intellectual Property, Technical Standards, Agriculture and other chapters in order to eliminate the new corporate property rights created there. The large American corporations that would be harmed by such changes are a key part of their political base, and most of these Democrats appear to believe that strengthening American corporations and increasing their access to foreign markets in these ways is a necessary if not sufficient condition for curing America's economic ills.

For some, American refusal to reopen the NAFTA is enough to merit rejection of whatever emerges from the labour and environmental side deal negotiations. They will argue that, however good they are, the side deals cannot redeem a bad agreement. Indeed, the better they are, the more they will facilitate the passage of the NAFTA by inducing support for the package as a whole in order to get the benefits of the side deals. They are the sugar coating on the poison pill. Strong side deals could split the opposition to the NAFTA in Canada (where it has a real chance of being stopped) or, if rammed through by a Conservative government that is subsequently defeated at the polls, reversed. In the United States, the side deals could fracture a strong, united opposition from the social movements and their congressional allies, which is the best hope we have for reopening and altering the NAFTA itself.

On the other hand, it could be argued that the United States and Mexico are likely to implement something close to the current NAFTA whatever Canada does, so that the only real issue is whether the Agreement is accompanied by strong or weak side deals. While Canada might gain by avoiding the restrictions that the NAFTA would impose, Canada also loses something if the side deals are weaker than they would have been with Canadian participation. After all, the process of continental economic integration will continue, as it has throughout the 1980s, whether or not Canada implements the NAFTA and, indeed, whether or not the NAFTA is implemented anywhere. In this context, it might be argued that it is worth accepting the NAFTA in return for strong side deals that form a solid base upon which to build a North American social dimension.

This counter-argument would be more persuasive if it were possible for Canada to participate in the side deal negotiations while rejecting the NAFTA, and if the Canadian government were strongly enough committed to the side deals to make a significant difference at the bargaining table. But, as noted above, the current Canadian government is not committed to the side deals, so it is not likely to push hard for stronger ones. If the negotiations are completed by mid-June, the current Clinton administration deadline, Canadians will have no opportunity to replace the Government before the side deal negotiations are finished. Nor is the Clinton administration likely to tolerate the bifurcation of the package that it wants to push through Congress. If Canada can take the good half and reject the bad, why shouldn't Americans do the same? This is not the kind of analysis that the Clinton administration wishes to encourage. Thus, even if we had a different Canadian government, it is unlikely that this "take it (social dimension) *and* leave it (NAFTA)" tactic would work at this time.

It therefore appears that Canadian participation in the side deal negotiations will entail significant costs (since we must accept the NAFTA to participate) without much likelihood (given the current Canadian government, the timing and the limited leverage of any Canadian government) of substantially increasing the scope and effectiveness of the side deals. Moreover, it appears that if the side deals amount to anything, Canada will benefit from them whether or not it participates in the negotiations or signs onto their outcome via the NAFTA.[77] Their most important benefit will be to strengthen Mexican (and, perhaps, American) worker rights and environmental and labour standards. This will make it easier to steer Canadian firms onto high wage, high productivity competitive strategies. It will also create a bigger Mexican market for Canadian goods than would exist without such protections, because it will distribute income more broadly within the Mexican population. Finally, it will reduce the scale of investment displacement from Canada to Mexico and the southern United States.

While it may be economically "rational," I am not arguing that Canada should be a perpetual "free-rider" on whatever social dimension emerges between the United States and Mexico in the coming months and years. Further down the road, Canada will be able to contribute to the creation of structural funds and to send committed people to the labour and environmental commissions. And Canada ought to make such contributions, both because our relations with our largest trade partner will be better if we bear a fair share of the burden of maintaining the social dimension from which we benefit and because it is a good way to contribute to genuine economic and political development in Mexico. At this juncture, however, when the social dimension is indissolubly linked to a bad trade deal, Canada must step back from both. That it is possible to do this without losing any of the benefits that will flow from the side deals is our good fortune.

At present, then, there is little to attract Canadians who might support the NAFTA if it were accompanied by strong labour and environmental side deals. This could change, however, because weak side deals will not do the job that the American administration wants them to do—getting American opposition forces on-side, or at least splitting off some of them.[78] Consequently, the American social movements and their congressional allies, the American administration, may be forced to strengthen its position. It is too early to know to what degree this is the case.[79] But it is my contention that even if the side deals that emerge from negotiations prove to be quite strong, this does not constitute a valid reason for Canadians to support a NAFTA that retains the features highlighted in this chapter.

CONCLUSION

In the 1980s, the three North American economies became more integrated than ever before under the impetus of the Tokyo round of the GATT, the FTA and unilateral deregulation initiatives in all three countries. This process of largely unregulated economic integration now has considerable momentum, whether or not the current NAFTA is implemented. But the NAFTA would increase the extent of this integration and the pace at which it takes place, thus reinforcing the economic, social and political trends of the 1980s. We cannot know exactly how much faster the NAFTA will propel us down the road we have been travelling for the last decade or so. Nor is it necessary that we know this in order to assess whether or not we ought to stay on this road.

I have tried to indicate why I believe we are on the wrong road, even if we are trying to get to no more exotic a destination than a restoration of high levels of productivity and sustainable economic development in Canada and beyond. My argument holds with even greater force if we accept the International Labour Office's premise that economic policy should ultimately serve "social" objectives such as the promotion of human rights and democracy. But the trends of the 1980s have not been encouraging for democracy in any of the three North American countries. In Mexico, genuine democracy is receding ever farther on the horizon, notwithstanding the rhetoric of the ruling party. In Canada and the United States, labour movement power has declined, labour rights have been diminished and income inequalities have widened.

The NAFTA, by intensifying the capital mobility and market pressures that generated these social trends—and equally important, by utterly failing to provide the kinds of institutions necessary to channel competition in socially productive ways—will further dim democratic prospects in all three countries. Hence, in its current form, the NAFTA must be rejected. But the alternative proposed here is not the status quo or a return to the protectionism of the 1930s. The status quo leads down the same undesirable road we travelled in the 1980s but at a somewhat slower pace. A significant move towards protectionism (as distinct from internationally managed trade in key sectors such as auto, steel, textiles and agriculture) would be massively disruptive in an economy as trade dependent as Canada's.

We must go forward, but on a different road, one that parallels the EC's efforts to build a strong, effective social dimension but diverges from the EC in not attempting to push for economic, much less political, union. This new road is only partially charted and is certainly uphill, but it leads out of the swamp into which we have been descending for more than a decade.

The success of efforts to stop the current NAFTA and replace it with such a North American social dimension is far from certain. But neither is the implementation of the current NAFTA the foregone conclusion that Prime Minister Mulroney and President Salinas would like us to believe. Opponents of the current deal in Canada and the United States have a fighting chance. If substantial progress can be made at the North American level, the chances of successfully projecting that progress to the GATT level are good. Ultimately, this is the level at which, and the form in which, we would be happiest to see the new principles embodied. At the Cold War's end, we must again summon the kind of long-range vision and institutional imagination exhibited at Bretton Woods. But our primary aim at such a "Bretton Woods II" should not be to promote "free markets" per se, or to defeat Communism, but to build democracy throughout the world and, upon that foundation, to promote economic development strategies compatible with social justice and environmental sustainability.

NOTES

I would like to thank Susan Phillips, Richard Simeon, Bruce Doern and Phil Ryan for their comments on earlier drafts of this chapter.

1   See, generally, Michael Piore and Charles Sabel, *The Second Industrial Divide* (New York: Basic Books, 1984). Government investment in training and "infrastructure" are necessary but not sufficient conditions of successfully promoting high productivity corporate competitive strategies. If some employers successfully achieve short-term competitive advantages by cutting labour costs, their competitors will be hard-pressed not to follow suit, even if they would otherwise prefer to invest in the longer term but potentially greater gains to be had from increasing worker skills and employer-union co-operation. On the need for well enforced labour rights and standards to prevent such "free riding," see Wolfgang Streeck, "The Social Dimension of the European Firm" (Discussion paper prepared for the 1989 Meeting of the Andrew Shonfield Association, Florence, Italy, September 14-15, 1989).

2   See Neil B. MacDonald, "Will the Free Trade Deal Drive a Gaping Hole through the Auto Pact?" *Policy Options* (Jan.-Feb. 1989): pp. 10-17.

3   See Charles E. Lindblom, *Politics and Markets* (New York: Basic Books, 1977).

4   Robert Dahl addresses the question of democratic decision making in the economic sphere in *A Preface to Economic Democracy* (Berkeley: University of California Press, 1985).

5   "Structural" factors affect the quality and stability of democracy independently of economic and political cycles, particular political personalities, changing international influences and so on. They do not explain the precise timing of Brazil's return to democracy, but they do help to explain why democracy was and still is much more fragile in Brazil than in Canada.

6   See Edward Muller, "Democracy, Economic Development and Income Equality," *American Sociological Review*, 53 (February 1988): pp. 50-68. Muller examined the 33 countries for which reliable income inequality data were available between 1960 and 1980. He found that nine countries which began the period as democracies had decayed into authoritarian regimes by its end. Democracy failed in all six of the countries in which the upper quintile's (i.e. the top 20 percent of the population's) income share was greater than 54 percent. By contrast, democracy survived in all 20 of the countries in which the upper quintile received less than 47 percent of all income. In the intermediate zone, where the top quintile's income share ranged between 54 and 47 percent, democratic regimes survived in four of seven cases. Regression analyses suggested that the level of income inequality accounted for over 60 percent of the variation in whether or not democracy endured. The top quintile's share of income in Finland, with the lowest inequality by this measure, was 36.8 percent in this period; in Japan, it was 38.2 percent; in Canada, 41 percent; in the U.S., 42.8 percent; in Italy, 46.5 percent; and in Mexico, above 60 percent.

7   On the historical contribution of labour movements to the construction and character of "the welfare state," see Gosta Esping-Anderson and Walter Korpi, "Social Policy as Class Politics in Post-War Capitalism: Scandinavia, Austria and Germany" in John H. Goldthorpe, (ed.), *Order and Conflict in Contemporary Capitalism* (Oxford: Clarendon Press, 1984), pp. 179-208. On the relationship between labour movement power and the economic and social roles of the State in the OECD countries, see

David Cameron, "Social Democracy, Corporatism, Labour Qui-
escence, and the Representation of Economic Interest in Advanced Capitalist Society" in Goldthorpe, *Order and Conflict*,
pp. 143-78.

8   Seymour Martin Lipset took the first position in his influential
essay, "Some Social Requisites of Democracy: Economic Development and Political Legitimacy," *American Political Science
Review*, 53 (1959): pp. 69-105, and in *Political Man*, expanded
edition (Baltimore: The Johns Hopkins Press, 1981). For an
advocate of the second proposition, see Frederic C. Deyo, "State
and Labor: Modes of Political Exclusion in East Asian Development" in Deyo, (ed.), *The Political Economy of the New Asian
Industrialism* (Ithaca: Cornell University Press, 1987).

9   See Dietrich Rueschemeyer, Evelyn Huber Stephens, and John D.
Stephens, *Capitalist Development and Democracy* (Cambridge,
England: Polity Press, 1992).

10   In the late 1960s, only 39.2 percent of Taiwan's national income
went to the top quintile, the same as for the United Kingdom. The
figure for South Korea's top quintile was 42.7 percent, about the
same as that in the United States. Taiwan's Gini coefficient is even
more striking; it was more egalitarian (0.28) than that of any First
World economy, the closest ones being Sweden (0.29), and
Norway and Japan (0.30). The South Korean Gini coefficient of
0.33 was the same as for Canada. The Gini coefficients summarize
the evenness of the distribution of income among the five
quintiles. The lower the score, the more equal the distribution. A
score of zero represents exactly equal shares of total national
income going to each of the quintiles. Data from Muller, "Economic Development and Income Inequality," p. 54.

11   See Article 904 of the NAFTA.

12   See "United States—Section 337, Report of the Panel (16.1.89),"
World Trade Materials, 2, 1 (January 1990): pp. 51-53.

13   Thanks to Frank Longo for this example.

14   The NAFTA's Investment chapter was the only one that American negotiators sought to protect with a clause guaranteeing that its provisions would continue to apply for a full decade after abrogation, should any party exercise its right to abrogate. This clause was dropped in the final round of negotiations and does not appear in the final text, but it indicates the unique importance attached to this chapter by American negotiators.

15   The Canadian government claims that it has secured a blanket exemption from the prohibition on technology transfer, but there is no such exemption for product mandating. With product mandating, TNC subsidiaries are mandated to develop and manufacture a few products for the continental or the world market. This contrasts with the "national mandate" that subsidiaries were originally given—to produce a much wider range of products exclusively for one national market—when the principal purpose of subsidiaries was to jump tariff barriers.

16   See Isaiah Litvak, "U.S. Multinationals: Repositioning the Canadian Subsidiary," *Business in the Contemporary World*, 3, 1 (Autumn 1990): pp. 111-19.

17   The U.S. Department of Commerce estimates that between 30 and 40 percent of all U.S. trade is the result of intra-firm transfers, *Left Business Observer*, 49 (November 4, 1991): p. 2.

18   See John Holmes, "The Globalization of Production and the Future of Canada's Mature Industries: The Case of the Automotive Industry" in Daniel Drache and Meric S. Gerther, (eds.), *The New Era of Global Competition* (Montreal: McGill-Queen's University Press, 1991), pp. 153-80.

19   Why, then, single out for prohibition seven particular performance requirements? Perhaps because the performance requirements so prohibited cannot be utilized by governments even if they are applied equally to domestic and foreign investors.

20   The Competition, Monopolies, and State Enterprises chapter can be considered as part of the Investment chapter for purposes of this

analysis. In earlier drafts, its key provisions were located in a larger Investment chapter.

21   Article 2021 of the NAFTA makes it clear that mere citizens will have no such standing in their courts to enforce NAFTA provisions.

22   See Jeff Faux and Thea Lea, "The Effect of George Bush's NAFTA on American Workers: Ladder Up or Ladder Down?" (Washington, D.C.: Economic Policy Institute, Fall 1992); United States, Congress, Office of Technology Assessment, *U.S.-Mexico Trade: Pulling Together or Pulling Apart?* (Washington, D.C., 1992), appendix to chap. 5, pp. 109-11.

23   Judith Adler Hellman, *Mexico in Crisis*, 2nd ed. (New York: Holmes and Meier, 1988), pp. 60-61.

24   World Bank, *World Development Report* (Washington, D.C., 1980), pp. 156-57.

25   Other countries, lying even further below the so-called Kuznets curve (i.e. with unusually high levels of inequality relative to per capita GNP) were Honduras, Peru, Brazil and Venezuela. See World Bank, *World Development Report*, pp. 40-41, 156-57.

26   The 1976 figure is from Adalberto Garcia-Rocha, "Mexico" in Stephen Herzenberg and Jorge F. Perez-Lopez, (eds.), *Labor Standards and Development in the Global Economy* (Washington, D.C.: U.S. Department of Labor, 1990), pp. 146-51; the 1987 figure is from Joan M. Nelson, "Poverty, Equity, and the Politics of Adjustment" in Stephen Haggard and Robert Kaufman, (eds.), *The Politics of Economic Adjustment* (Princeton: Princeton University Press, 1992), pp. 228-29; the 1992 figure is from David Barkin, "Salinastroika and Other Novel Ideas" (An unpublished manuscript kindly provided by the author, soon to be published in the second edition of Barkin's *Distorted Development: Mexico in the World Economy* (Boulder: Westview Press, 1990)). The Canadian wage share in the late 1980s was about 75 percent. See Alejandro Alvarez and Gabriel Mendoza, "Mexico: Neo-Liberal Disaster Zone" in Jim Sinclair, (ed.), *Crossing the Line: Canada*

and Free Trade with Mexico (Vancouver: New Star Books, 1992), p. 27.

27   See Gary S. Fields, "Labor Standards, Economic Development, and International Trade" in Herzenberg and Perez-Lopez, *Labor Standards and Development*; he is a strong proponent of "market" wage rates in developing countries and concedes that the wages of "unskilled" and "semi-skilled" workers are not likely to show significant increases—in the absence of state or union "intervention"—until close to the full employment threshold, p. 25.

28   Official Mexican statistics show unemployment at below 3 percent. However, given the always attenuated and currently shrinking character of the Mexican welfare state, Mexicans cannot survive on government transfers as an unemployed worker. Hence everyone who loses or fails to get a "formal" sector job works in the informal economy. Those who work more than one hour per week for income are counted as employed under the current Mexican definition of this term. See Office of Technology Assessment, *U.S.-Mexico Trade*, p. 69, n. 16. In this context, poverty statistics are more useful for assessing the economic condition of those without formal sector employment. Official Mexican poverty statistics indicate that the basket of goods deemed necessary to meet the basic nutritional needs of the typical worker's family costs about 4.78 times the official minimum wage in 1988. The 1990 Mexican census reports that 60 percent of Mexican households earn less than 2.72 times the minimum wage (and are thus classified as living in "extreme" poverty). More than 72 percent earn less than 4 times the minimum wage. These data are from Barkin, "Salinastroika."

29   Employment in the Mexican *maquila* sector has grown to just under 0.5 million since 1965, when foreign TNCs were first permitted to set up in a strip along the border with the United States. Thus, even if the size of Mexico's TNC/*maquila* manufacturing sector doubles in the next 10 years, it will create only about one million new jobs, assuming current productivity levels.

30   The U.S. International Trade Commission (ITC), an advocate of the NAFTA, predicts that the liberalization of the Mexican market

in basic grain, following from the NAFTA's reduction of Mexican agricultural tariffs, will induce a net migration off the land of between 0.5 and 1.5 million people over the next decade. See Center for Rural Affairs, "Special Report on the NAFTA" in *Trade Matters* (Walthill, Nebr., October 1992). The Mexican Undersecretary of Agricultural Planning places the figure at 13 million over the same period. Cited in David Barkin, "Agrarian Counter-Reform" in "Salinastroika." The Undersecretary may have had an incentive to exaggerate—to induce American trade negotiators to press less hard for reducing Mexican agricultural tariffs—just as the ITC had an incentive to downplay the scale of the rural exodus.

31   The NAFTA will eliminate the protective wall that previously prevented competition between the export oriented, TNC-owned *maquila* and the Mexican-owned, indigenously oriented manufacturing sector that is the legacy of Mexico's earlier Import Substitution Industrialization (ISI) strategy. Former *maquilas* and new TNC plants can be expected to win this new competition in most cases because they are much more productive and because, being largely non-union, they typically pay only about half the average wage in the ISI sector. Large manufacturing plants in the U.S. exhibit productivity levels that are 11 times the Mexican average. But in sectors such as auto, some U.S. *maquilas* are able to operate at 80 percent of U.S. productivity levels. See Alvarez and Mendoza, "Neo-Liberal Disaster," p. 34, for productivity data. The most recent wage data, for 1989, comes from the Bureau of Labor Statistics, Office of Productivity and Technology, "International Comparisons of Hourly Compensation Costs for Production Workers—Mexico" (April 1990).

As an indicator of what is to come, the experience in the Mexican auto sector in the last decade may be instructive. The exposure of Mexico's ISI auto sector to increased competition resulted in the loss of about 100,000 jobs between 1980 and 1987. In the same period, *maquilas* in the auto parts subsector alone increased from 53 plants and 6.3 percent of the total *maquila* workforce to 121 plants representing 21 percent of the workforce. Yet only about 90,000 jobs were created in the new *maquila* auto and auto parts plants, for a net auto manufacturing employment loss of about 10,000 jobs. See Jim Sinclair, "Cheap Labour,

Cheap Lives" in Sinclair, *Crossing the Line*, pp. 55-56.

32   Hellman, *Mexico in Crisis*, pp. 59, 70.

33   Mexican population growth fell from an average of 3.1 percent per annum between 1940 and 1980 to an average of 2.2 percent per annum in the early 1980s. But, unless the economic welfare of over 70 percent of Mexican families below the poverty line improves substantially, their economic incentives to invest in large families remain unchanged, and the fall in population growth is likely to flatten out. The World Bank's *World Development Report* (1988), pp. 274-75, predicts a 2.1 percent per annum Mexican population growth rate from 1986 to 2000. Frances Moore Lappe and Rachel Schurman, in *Taking Population Seriously* (San Francisco: The Institute for Food and Development Policy, 1990), pp. 54-65, note that the three poor countries with the lowest population growth rates between 1980 and 1986 were Sri Lanka, China and Cuba, with rates of 1.4, 1.2, and 0.8 percent per annum, respectively. Of the three, only China has an extensive government program to control family size, but all three had programs guaranteeing their poorest people unusually high levels of food security.

34   *Maquilas* in Mexico today are estimated to buy only about 2 percent of their inputs from Mexican suppliers. See Alvarez and Mendoza, "Neo-Liberal Disaster," p. 29.

35   Sinclair, *Crossing the Line*, p. 53.

36   This is not required by the NAFTA, but it is part of the same deregulation and privatization agenda that underpins President Salinas's support for the Agreement. See Dan LaBotz, *Mask of Democracy: Labor Suppression in Mexico Today* (Boston: South End Press, 1992), pp. 81-130.

37   Ford currently enjoys huge savings in labour costs in Mexico. Its Hermosillo plant, built in 1986 and employing 1,600 Mexican workers, is estimated to have an annual labour bill of about $7 million. In the United States, a plant of similar size and vintage would have a labour bill of about $100 million. See Alvarez and

Mendoza, "Neo-Liberal Disaster," p. 30. In spite of the scope for raising wages that such savings create, Ford is willing to resort to repression to prevent the formation of independent unions in its Mexican plants. In January 1990, unarmed workers involved in efforts to form an independent union in Ford's Cautitlan plant, near Mexico City, were attacked by armed thugs on the payroll of the "official" union. These thugs were permitted into the plant by Ford management. One worker was killed and several others were wounded. See LaBotz, *Mask of Democracy*, pp. 148-60. Ford is not alone among TNCs willing to use repressive tactics. Volkswagen of Mexico recently fired 14,200 workers from its huge complex and annulled the collective agreement that it had earlier signed with an independent union. See Office of Technology Assessment, *U.S.-Mexico Trade*, p. 85.

38   See Piore and Sabel, *Second Industrial Divide*, pp. 49-70, esp. 60-65.

39   The 1988 presidential election was the first in which a serious political challenge from the left was permitted. It is widely acknowledged that there was large-scale electoral fraud and that the candidate of the left, Cuatemoc Cardenas of the PRD, may have been the true winner. We are never likely to know because the Government suspended the count when the first 59 percent of the ballots revealed Cardenas leading Salinas by several percentage points. The remaining 41 percent were never made public, and a week later it was announced that Salinas had won an overall majority with 50.36 percent of the vote. All ballots were destroyed in December 1991. See Ken Traynor, "The Origins of Free Trade Mania" in Sinclair, *Crossing the Line*, pp. 2-7. The 1988 election was marred by many political assassinations, including the assassination of two close political advisers to Cardenas. Since the election, according to Mexican Federal Congressman Jorge Calderon, "more than 140 democratic social leaders have been murdered by paramilitary and repressive groups in various parts of the country." See Jorge Calderon, "Mexico 1992: Reflections about the Free Trade Agreement, Democracy, and National Sovereignty" (Paper presented in Toronto, November 1992).

40   For a brief history of Mexican labour relations, followed by a detailed look at labour repression under the Salinas regime, see LaBotz, *Mask of Democracy*. For data on recent trends in human rights violations more generally, see Ellen L. Lutz, *Unceasing Abuses: Human Rights in Mexico One Year after the Introduction of Reform* (New York: Americas Watch, 1991); Amnesty International, *Mexico: Torture with Impunity* (New York, 1991); Daniel Gerdts et al., *Paper Protection: Human Rights Violations and the Mexican Criminal Justice System* (Minneapolis: Minnesota Lawyers International Human Rights Committee, 1990).

41   In the fall of 1990, U.S. Commerce Secretary Mosbacher and Mexico Commerce Secretary Jaime Serra Puche conducted a series of day-long seminars promoting U.S. business investment in Mexico. Materials distributed to the executives claimed that "for every $10 per hour (fully burdened) job transferred to Mexico, the company will earn an additional $15,000 per year." The material went on to say that "because demand has hardly made a dent in supply, the direct [Mexican *maquila*] wage in 1994 should be only about $1.75 compared to $1.40 today.... And the gap between the U.S. minimum wage and the Mexican direct wage will in fact increase during this period as labor shortages in the U.S. increase demand." Quoted in Jeff Faux and Richard Rothstein, "Fast Track, Fast Shuffle: The Economic Consequences of the Administration's Proposed Trade Agreement with Mexico" (Washington, D.C.: Economic Policy Institute, May 1991), p. 12.

42   The most spectacular upsurge of democratic unionism in American history took place in the midst of the Great Depression, when official unemployment was above 20 percent, and real unemployment and underemployment were much higher. See David Brody, *Workers in Industrial America* (Oxford: Oxford University Press, 1980); Frances Fox Piven and Richard Cloward, *Poor People's Movements* (New York: Vintage, 1979), pp. 41-180.

43   Mary Lou Coates, David Arrowsmith, and Melanie Courchene, "The Labour Movement and Trade Unionism Reference Tables," *The Current Industrial Relations Scene* (Kingston: Industrial Relations Centre, Queen's University, 1989), p. 19.

44   Aggregate data are from Coates, Arrowsmith, and Courchene, "Labour Movement," p. 19. The stability in aggregate Canadian union density in the late 1980s and early 1990s masks declining private sector union density, which fell from 26 to 21 percent between 1975 and 1985. See John O'Grady, "Downhill all the Way: The Labour Movement, Wage Polarization, and the Wagner Act Model of Collective Bargaining" (Paper presented to the Centre for Research on Work and Society Conference on Broadening the Bargaining Structures in the New Social Order, York University, May 7-8, 1992), p. 3.

45   The Commission on the Skills of the American Workforce found that 90 percent of American corporations attempted to compete in the 1980s primarily on the basis of lower wages and Tayloristic work organization. In the six major competitors studied, a much larger share of companies adopted competitive strategies based on a high performance work organization. See Ray Marshall, "Work Organization, Unions and Economic Performance" in Lawrence Mishel and Paula Voos, (eds.), *Unions and Economic Competitiveness* (Armonk, N.Y.: M.E. Sharpe, 1992), p. 300.

46   On rising American employer "unfair labour practices," see Paul Weiler, "Promises to Keep: Securing Workers' Rights to Self-Organization under the NLRA," *Harvard Law Review*, 96, 8 (June 1983): pp. 1769-827. On the link between increasing international competition and the growing willingness of American employers to pursue anti-union strategies, see Joel Rogers, "Divide and Conquer: Further 'Reflections on the Distinctive Character of American Labor Laws,'" *Wisconsin Law Review*, 1 (1990): pp. 1-147.

47   See Bennett Harrison and Barry Bluestone, *The Great U-Turn: Corporate Restructuring and the Polarizing of America* (New York: Basic Books, 1990), pp. 21-52. By 1989, American "unit labour costs" (i.e. hourly compensation combined with output per person-hour) were more than 20 percent lower, relative to the United States's 12 major competitors (including South Korea and Taiwan), than they had been in 1973. This was not because American productivity was growing faster than elsewhere, but because wages were falling in the United States while rising in its

competitors. See Mishel and Voos, "Unions and American Economic Competitiveness" in Mishel and Voos, *Unions*, pp. 2-4.

48   For example, General Motors portrays the latest round of plant closings in Canada and the United States as rationalization to eliminate excess capacity, but it plans to build 27 plants in Mexico by 1995. GM currently has 30 Mexican plants employing 25,500 workers. See Sinclair, *Crossing the Line*, pp. 55-56.

49   On "voluntary export restraints" (VERs) and other trade restrictive policies adopted by American administrations in the 1980s, see I.M. Destler, *American Trade Politics*, 2nd ed. (Washington, D.C.: Institute for International Economics, 1992), chaps. 5, 6, 7.

50   For a comparison of rates of increase of "unfair labour practices" in Canada and the United States in the 1970s and early 1980s, see Weiler, "Promises to Keep." The trends he identifies intensified in the late 1980s and early 1990s.

51   For a comparison of concession bargaining outcomes in Canada and the United States in the 1980s, see Pradeep Kumar, "Industrial Relations in Canada and the United States: From Uniformity to Divergence" (Working paper, Industrial Relations Centre, Queen's University, Kingston, March 1991), pp. 60-80.

52   See Stuart Jamieson, "The Conservative Attack on Labour Unions" in Robert C. Allen and Gideon Rosenbluth, (eds.), *False Promises: The Failure of Conservative Economics* (Vancouver: New Star Books, 1992), pp. 163-78; Leo Panitch and Don Swartz, *The Assault on Trade Union Freedoms: From Consent to Coercion Revisited*, rev. ed. (Toronto: Garamond Press, 1988).

53   The Bank of Canada's rationale for the unprecedented gap between Canadian and American interest rates that produced the overvalued Canadian dollar was that inflation had to be vanquished no matter what the short-term cost in unemployment. For a summary and critique of the Bank of Canada's policies in the 1980s, see Clarence L. Barber, "Monetary and Fiscal Policy in the 1980s" in Allen and Rosenbluth, *False Promises*, pp. 101-20.

54   Johnathan Schlefer, "What Price Economic Growth?" *The Atlantic*, 270, 6 (December 1992): pp. 115-16.

55   Harrison and Bluestone, *Great U-Turn*, pp. 130-31 and, more generally, pp. 109-38.

56   Katherine L. Bradbury, "The Shrinking Middle Class," *New England Economic Review* (September-October 1986): pp. 41-55.

57   The American Gini coefficient is calculated using family income data, while the Canadian coefficient is based on personal income data, so the two figures are not strictly comparable. Family income data may show less of an increase in inequality than personal income data, owing to the increasing number of families in which both spouses worked full-time in the 1980s.

58   The Canadian and American data are not strictly comparable. Bradbury defined the American middle class as those families with incomes ranging between $20,000 and $50,000. The Canadian data define it as jobs with earnings ranging between 75 and 125 percent of the median income, which was $17,395 in 1986.

59   Canadian inequality data are from Economic Council of Canada, *Good Jobs, Bad Jobs: Employment in the Service Economy* (Ottawa, 1990), pp. 14-15. Canadian and American poverty data in this and the previous paragraph are from Maria Hanratty, "Social Welfare," *Social Policy*, 23, 1 (Summer 1992): pp. 32-37, and from the "Social Policy Index" on p. 7 of the same issue. See also National Bureau of Economic Research, *Small Differences That Matter: Labor Markets and Income Maintenance in Canada and the United States* (Chicago: Chicago University Press, forthcoming). See the chapter by N. Harvey Lithwick and Rebecca Coulthard, in this volume, for a discussion of the changing geographical distribution of poverty in Canada.

60   For example, in 1988, 70 percent of unemployed Canadians received insurance covering, on average, 60 percent of their wages. Only 32 percent of unemployed Americans qualified for unemployment assistance covering an average of 35 percent of their wages. U.S. benefits also last for a shorter period. The 1991

changes meant that Canadian workers had to be employed longer to be eligible for benefits. Those still qualifying received benefits for an average of 13 weeks less (reducing the portion of the unemployed covered to 58 percent). See Schlefer, "What Price," pp. 115-16.

61   Edward Leamer estimated trade-induced price changes for goods in 38 labour and capital intensive manufacturing industries in the United States between 1972 and 1985. He then estimated the impact of these price changes on the wages of professional and blue-collar employees in those sectors. He found that trade raised demand for higher-skilled work, so that the average annual pay of 17 million professionals was 9 percent or $1,900 higher than it would have been without trade growth. But annual pay for the more than 90 million "less skilled" workers in this sector was $465, or 3 percent, lower than it would have been otherwise. Leamer predicts that the NAFTA will exacerbate this polarization: "Indeed, if the reason for the expansion of international commerce is increased access to low-wage unskilled foreign labor it is virtually assured that our low-skilled workers will have their earnings reduced. Earnings reductions in the order of $1,000 per year ... seem very plausible." See Edward Leamer, "Wage Effects of a U.S.-Mexican Free Trade Agreement," NBER Working Paper no. 3991 (Cambridge, Mass.: National Bureau of Economic Research, February 1992), pp. 45-46. The quote is from "The global economy: Who gets hurt?" *Business Week* (August 10, 1992), pp. 51-52.

62   The total number of Mexicans currently in the United States illegally is estimated to be between two and three million, not counting the approximately three million whose status was legalized as a result of the Immigration Reform and Control Act of 1986. Their number is estimated to be increasing by about 200,000 per year at this time. See Office of Technology Assessment, *U.S.-Mexico Trade*, p. 117. The OTA notes, at p. 52, that this level of Mexico-U.S. labour migration is greater than that from Spain, Portugal or Greece to the rest of the European Community.

63 By "social externalities," I mean the costs of poverty, inequality and poor working conditions for the people who suffer their consequences—poor health, poor education, low quality work, wasted potential and so on—and their political consequences for the entire society, including higher levels of racism, violence, social instability and low quality democracy.

64 For a succinct discussion of the EC social dimension up to and including the Social Charter of 1988, see Valerio Lintner and Sonia Mazey, *The European Community* (London: McGraw-Hill, 1991), pp. 111-27. For a discussion of the ways in which the Maastricht Treaty of December 1991 will broaden and strengthen EC-level labour standards in the 11 signatories (the U.K. opted out of these provisions), see Brian Bercusson, "Maastricht: A Fundamental Change in European Labour Law," *Industrial Relations Journal*, 23, 3 (Autumn 1992).

65 Regional and social policy expenditures accounted for 7.3 and 6.5 percent, respectively, of the EC's total expenditures in 1988, as compared with the almost 66 percent that was allocated to agricultural policy expenditures. Total EC expenditures represent less than 4 percent of the combined expenditures of its 12 member states. See Lintner and Mazey, *European Community*, pp. 78-81. Still, if Mexico received regional fund transfers according to the old EC formula, it would be eligible for US$10 billion, equal to about 4 percent of the Mexican GDP. This is equal to the interest that Mexico currently pays on its foreign debt. The EC has pledged to double the size of its structural funds between 1993 and 1997. See Office of Technology Assessment, *U.S.-Mexico Free Trade*, p. 52. This would amount to US$68 billion over those four years. See Cuomo Commission on Competitiveness, *America's Agenda: Rebuilding Economic Strength* (Armonk, N.Y.: M.E. Sharpe, 1992), p. 234.

66 Office of Technology Assessment, *U.S.-Mexico Free Trade*, pp. 48-50.

67 For example, Spain's per capita income level in 1988 was 60 percent of the EC average, while Mexico's is less than 10 percent of the U.S. and Canadian average, a difference further magnified

by the more extensive character of Spain's social programs and the more equal distribution of income in that country. Cuomo Commission, *America's Agenda*, pp. 233-34. Moreover, Spain and Portugal combined represent only about 15 percent of the EC population, while Mexico represents 30 percent of the combined Canadian and American population. If Mexico is five times poorer and twice as big, relative to Canada and the United States, the "shock" of increasing Mexican economic integration can be crudely estimated as 10 times greater than that associated with the integration of Spain and Portugal into the EC.

68   To match the US$10 billion that would flow to Mexico under the EC formula, it would be necessary to hold Canadian, U.S. and Mexican tariffs on goods exchanged among them at about 5 percent and to transfer all proceeds into the structural adjustment fund.

69   See Peter Dorman, "Worker Rights and U.S. Trade Policy: An Evaluation of Worker Rights Conditionality under the General System of Preferences" (Washington, D.C.: Bureau of International Labor Affairs, U.S. Department of Labor, September 1989); Stephen Herzenberg, "Institutionalizing Constructive Competition: International Labor Standards and Trade," Economic Discussion Paper no. 32 (Washington, D.C.: Bureau of International Labor Affairs, U.S. Department of Labor, September 1988).

70   The theory and feasibility of such a trade law in Canada is discussed by Jim Stanford, "Cheap Labour as an Unfair Subsidy in North American Free Trade" (Ottawa: Canadian Centre for Policy Alternatives, 1992).

71   The Office of Technology Assessment considers a similar proposal. See *U.S.-Mexico Trade*, pp. 52-53.

72   In 1991, the U.S. deficit in auto trade was $60 billion, almost two thirds of the entire trade deficit. See U.S. Department of Commerce, *Survey of Current Business* (Washington, D.C.: Government Printing Office, June 1992).

73 Office of Technology Assessment, *U.S.-Mexico Trade*, pp. 50-51. The OTA study also discusses options of this sort.

74 For example, GATT Chairperson Arthur Dunkel's draft, the focal point of current Uruguay round negotiations, would render *all* subnational government subsidies subject to countervailing duties on the ground that they do not fall in the class of protected "general" subsidies, even if they are available to all businesses in the state or province. The Canadian government has stated that changing this provision is its top priority in the GATT negotiations. See *Inside U.S. Trade* (December 4, 1992), p. 3.

75 The Canadian government and its provincial allies find themselves in an embarrassing position. At the behest of several provinces—including Ontario, Saskatchewan and Manitoba—Ottawa asked for stronger labour and environmental provisions during the original NAFTA negotiations, secure in the knowledge that neither the Bush nor the Salinas administrations would support such demands. Ottawa then reported back to the provinces that, try as it might, it could make no headway. Now, however, the American demand for side deals starkly reveals Ottawa's lack of appetite for any such thing. Moreover, the current federal government's key provincial allies, Alberta and Quebec, are forced to plead openly with the federal government to resist the incursions into provincial jurisdiction that the side deals would represent, this, in spite of the fact that these same provincial governments have been the most stalwart defenders of the many incursions into provincial jurisdiction found in the main text of the current NAFTA.

76 Clinton's October 4 speech is reproduced in full in "Special Report: Clinton Calls for Supplementary NAFTA Pacts on Environment, Labor," *Inside U.S. Trade* (October 9, 1992), pp. S1-S3.

77 The benefits generated by a North American social dimension will be "public goods" in the technical sense of that term. That is why governments, rather than markets, must supply them in the first place by creating the institutions of the social dimension.

78   Representative Robert Matsui, a vocal supporter of the NAFTA, has stated, "My reading of the floor of the House is that the votes [to pass the NAFTA] are not there." See Peter Behr, "Free trade treaty in trouble, White House warned," *Washington Post*, March 12, 1993.

79   One key actor is, of course, the American labour movement. The AFL-CIO is reported to be signalling that it "would be satisfied with a NAFTA labor side pact that contained enforcement provisions identical to those provided for IPR rights-holders." See *Inside U.S. Trade* (March 5, 1993), p. S2. As in the ongoing American debate on health-care reform, the AFL-CIO's position may be more conservative than that of some of its major affiliates.

CHAPTER 11

Lowering the Safety Net and Weakening the Bonds of Nationhood: Social Policy in the Mulroney Years

James J. Rice

Michael J. Prince

Résumé : Ce chapitre est consacré aux réalisations du gouvernement Mulroney en matière de politique sociale. Alors que les Conservateurs semblaient envisager avec réticence la réforme de la politique sociale pendant leur mandat de 1984-1988, ils se sont montrés plus décisifs pendant celui de 1988-1993, coupant et restructurant les transferts et les programmes sociaux. Les Conservateurs menés par Mulroney ont fondamentalement modifié certains fondements de la politique sociale moderne du Canada, notamment en mettant fin au programme des allocations familiales, en abolissant l'universalité du programme de sécurité de la vieillesse et en coupant les contributions fédérales au régime d'assurance-chômage. Il est question, dans ce chapitre, de l'évolution des dépenses du gouvernement fédéral consacrées aux programmes sociaux ainsi que des grandes politiques mises en œuvre pendant les années Mulroney. Les auteurs concluent que les principales conséquences des réformes de la politique sociale faites par les Conservateurs sont la réduction du filet de sécurité et l'attrition de certains liens de cohésion nationale.

Abstract: The social policy record of the Mulroney government is examined in this chapter. While the Conservatives seemed fearful of social policy reforms in their 1984-88 mandate, they have been more decisive in their 1988-93 mandate in restraining and restructuring social transfers and programs. The Mulroney Conservatives have fundamentally changed some foundations of modern social policy in Canada, terminating the Family Allowances program, abolishing the universality of the Old Age Security plan and ending federal contributions to the unemployment insurance scheme. This chapter presents some federal social spending trends and major policy initiatives of the Mulroney period. The authors conclude that the most significant consequences of the Conservatives' social policy record have been a lowering of the safety net and a weakening of certain bonds of nationhood and citizenship.

Federal social policy has not been a dominant priority of the Mulroney government. The Conservatives have had other issues on their minds. Three general features of the Mulroney social policy record stand out. First, the recent history of federal social policy has been mainly a record of expenditure restraint and program restructuring. Since 1984, social policy making in Ottawa has operated within a neo-conservative agenda: program spending restraints, tax increases, deficit reduction, debt management and the encouragement of private sector competitiveness. The restraint of program spending, including social expenditures, has been the cornerstone of the Government's budgetary strategy. This restraint has been sustained over several years, with ongoing program reductions across a broad spectrum of social programs, client groups and government departments. Program spending has been constrained, frozen or reduced in social housing, legal aid, unemployment insurance, health care, social assistance and post-secondary education, among other areas. While the Conservatives seemed fearful of social policy reforms in their first mandate,[1] they have been much more decisive and active in their second mandate in altering the social safety net. Interestingly, the Conservative government did not concentrate their social policy restraints in just the early phase of their second mandate.[2] Policy changes that imposed losses (and also, perhaps, wins for some) were introduced throughout the 1988-93 mandate. In particular several key measures, such as cuts in grants to groups and in unemployment insurance, were undertaken in the final year of the Conservatives' mandate.

A second general feature of the Conservatives' social policy record is their central approach to making program changes. This approach has been called the "stealth style" of social policy formation, a process that "relies heavily on technical amendments to taxes and transfers that are as difficult to explain as they are to understand and thus largely escape media scrutiny and public attention."[3] The prominent federal institution involved in social policy by stealth is the Department of Finance, which has control over tax policy, intergovernmental fiscal transfers and expenditure restraint measures. Fundamental changes to federal social programs achieved by the stealth approach include the partial de-indexation of tax credits and certain transfers to individuals, cuts in federal social transfers to the provinces, changes in financing the unemployment insurance program, and the claw-back of Family Allowances and Old Age Security benefits. Such changes have typically been announced by the Finance Minister and were contained in budget documents. The Child Tax Benefit, introduced in January 1993, is one of the latest examples of social policy by stealth and is examined in detail in the following chapter.

Our third observation on the Conservatives' social policy record is that the overall structure and complexion of federal social spending have changed over the two mandates. For example, as a share of federal social expenditures, transfers to other levels of government and payments to major social Crown corporations (such as the CBC) have declined since 1984, while selective transfers to persons have increased. These trends are the result of a mix of fiscal restraint and program reform designed to respond to the needs of an ageing population, an economic recession and unemployment. In general, there has been a *selective* rather than a *universal* orientation in social budgeting and program development by the Conservatives. The preferred social policy instruments of the Mulroney era include tax credits, the targeting of transfer payments, and the contracting-out of research and advising. More than that, the Mulroney government has consciously made some fundamental shifts in the foundations of Canadian social policy laid down in the 1940s and early 1950s: the universal Family Allowances program was terminated at the end of 1992; the universality of the Old Age Security program was effectively abolished by 1991; and the federal government's direct contribution to financing the unemployment insurance scheme was ended in 1991. The 1992 budget announced the elimination of several independent government bodies engaged in social policy analysis and planning, most notably the Economic Council of Canada, the Law Reform Commission of Canada and the Science Council of Canada. Finally, the Conservatives abandoned their long-promised national child-care program.

The next section presents some trends in federal social spending. Against the backdrop of the Conservatives' agenda, we note some major initiatives in the social policy record of the Mulroney government, particularly the expenditure control and restraint measures. Since we cannot, of course, examine the entire social policy agenda of the Mulroney Conservatives here, we focus on the major income security programs and fiscal transfers to the provinces. Other social policy issues and domains are examined elsewhere in this volume as well as in past editions of *How Ottawa Spends*. In the third section, we consider the implications of this policy record for the economic and social security of Canadians.

In our view, the most significant consequences of the Conservatives' social policy record have been a lowering of the safety net and a weakening of the bonds of nationhood. Several Canadian social programs have become more like those of the United States: child benefits, drug patent legislation, elderly benefits and unemployment insurance. By restraining the social role of government, promoting market solutions to various social needs,[4] eliminating distinctive programs like Family Allowances, revamping old programs like unemployment insurance and introducing new policies like the Child Tax Benefit, the Mulroney government's policy agenda has moved Canadian social policy closer to the American system. Whether or not this policy pattern is due to the Free Trade Agreement, the results point to a trend towards harmonization between Canada and the United States in key elements of social policy. The final section concludes our analysis by exploring possible issues and directions in Canadian social policy for the next federal government.

THE GOVERNMENT'S AGENDA

The commitment to fiscal restraint and market solutions to social problems has led to many important decisions over the past eight years. The information presented in Table 11.1 places federal social spending in the context of Ottawa's expenditures and the Canadian economy over the 1981-82 to 1991-92 period.

There is no long-standing, consistent definition of social expenditures used by the federal government. Over the past 15 years, the social policy field in the federal budgeting system has been redefined three times, making it difficult to track trends and measure public spending in Canadian social programs.[5] As used here, federal social spending includes the following programs and activities: Old Age Security (OAS); the Guaranteed Income Supplement (GIS); Spouse's Allowances (SPA); unemployment insurance (UI); Family Allowances (FA); veterans' benefits; federal cost-sharing of provincial social assistance and social services under the Canada Assistance Plan (CAP); federal transfers

Table 11.1

Federal Social Spending in Context

| | Federal Social Spending[a] | | | Share of | |
| | Current | Constant 1992 | Program Spending | Total Budgetary Expend. | GDP |
	(millions of dollars)			(percentages)	
1981-82	36,371	56,062	59.9	48.0	10.2
1982-83	44,590	64,977	61.5	49.9	11.9
1983-84	49,698	69,401	63.1	51.3	12.3
1984-85	53,778	72,206	61.7	49.1	12.1
1985-86	55,733	71,891	64.7	50.0	11.7
1986-87	58,203	71,927	64.7	49.9	11.5
1987-88	62,305	73,998	64.4	49.5	11.3
1988-89	64,939	73,487	65.0	48.8	10.7
1989-90	68,083	73,477	65.5	47.7	10.5
1990-91	71,838	73,418	66.3	47.5	10.7
1991-92	78,509	78,509	67.8	49.4	11.6

Source: Public Accounts, Statistics Canada, Cat. no. 11-010; and authors' calculations.

Note: [a] Federal social spending includes transfers to persons, cash transfers to other levels of government, other major social transfers, and payments to Canada Mortgage and Housing Corporation and the CBC.

to the provinces through equalization payments and through the Established Programs Financing (EPF) arrangement for health care and post-secondary education; transfers to the territorial governments; other transfers for employment, Aboriginal peoples and farmers; and payments to the major social policy Crown corporations, notably the CBC and the Canada Mortgage and Housing Corporation (CMHC).

From 1984 until 1991, federal social spending did not increase significantly. In fact, social spending by Ottawa decreased slightly in real terms from 1987-88 to 1990-91, reflecting the Conservatives' emphasis on expenditure restraint. As Table 11.1 indicates, in current dollars social spending by the Mulroney government grew from $53.7 billion in 1984-85 to $78.5 billion in 1991-92. In constant 1992 dollars, which factors out the effect of inflation on the dollar, federal social spending grew modestly from $72.2 billion in 1984-85 to $73.4 billion in 1990-91 and then, reflecting the impact of the recession on unemployment insurance and social assistance, jumped to $78.5 billion in 1991-92. As a share of federal program spending, social expenditures have increased slightly over the Mulroney era. As a share of total budgetary expenditures (program spending plus public debt charges), social spending has declined marginally. In relation to Canada's overall economic activity as measured by the gross domestic product (GDP), federal social spending rose in the early 1980s due to the 1981-82 recession, peaked in 1983-84 at 12.3 percent of GDP, then—over the Mulroney years—declined from 12.1 percent in 1984-85 to 10.7 percent in 1990-91, indicating that social spending was growing more slowly than the Canadian economy. Federal social expenditures then rose as a share of GDP to 11.6 percent in 1991-92 as a result of the recession.

Table 11.2 reveals some indication of the priorities of the Mulroney period by calculating the rates of change in program spending organized into five functional areas: social programs, defence, transfers to businesses, payments to Crown corporations and government operations. In addition, the social programs category is divided into transfers to persons, transfers to other levels of government, other major social transfers and payments to major social Crown corporations. We see that total social spending and defence spending have been priorities, both growing at an average annual rate of 5.5 percent from 1984-85 to 1991-92

Table 11.2

Rates of Change in Program Spending,
1984-85 to 1991-92

	Average Annual Percentage Change, 1984-85 to 1991-92	Difference between Rate of Program Change and	
		Average Rate of Inflation (4.6)	Average Growth in GDP (6.3)
Social programs			
Transfers to persons	7.0	2.4	0.7
Transfers to other levels of government	2.9	-1.7	-3.4
Other major social transfers	9.6	5.0	3.3
Payments to major social Crown corporations	2.9	-1.7	-3.4
Total social spending	5.5	0.9	-0.8
Other programs			
Defence	5.5	0.9	-0.8
Other transfers	-1.9	-6.5	-8.2
Payments to other Crown corporations	-5.4	-10.0	-11.7
Government operations	2.8	-1.8	-3.5
Total program spending	4.2	-0.4	-2.1

Sources: Public Accounts, Statistics Canada; Department of Finance, *The Budget Papers* (February 25, 1992).

The growth in defence spending reflects the Conservatives' commitment to refurbish the armed forces. All other program areas were accorded less emphasis in budgetary terms. Spending on "other transfers," primarily direct subsidies to businesses, has been scaled back in absolute terms, and payments to commercial Crown corporations such as VIA Rail have been a major focus of expenditure restraint. Spending on government operations (that is, the cost of running the federal public service) has also declined in real terms. Within the social programs category, transfers to persons have grown at an average annual rate of 7.0 percent. These transfers include programs for the elderly, families, veterans and the unemployed. Transfers to other levels of government (under equalization, EPF and CAP) and payments to the social Crown corporations (CBC and CMHC) both grew at an average annual rate of only 2.9 percent and declined in real terms. By contrast, other social transfers to groups for education and cultural activities, and income assistance to the farming sector, grew at an average annual rate of 9.6 percent over the 1984-85 to 1991-92 period.

Over the Conservatives' two mandates, the structure of federal social spending has been altered. Shifts in the complexion of social expenditures have occurred because of societal trends like population ageing, economic events like the 1991-92 recession and policy choices like the fiscal restraint strategy.

The Mulroney Conservatives' fiscal record on social policy from 1984-85 to 1991-92 is summarized in Table 11.3. In 1991-92, Ottawa spent $40.8 billion on direct income support to individuals and families. In effect, more of the federal social policy budget in the 1990s is delivered through the statutory programs for the elderly and the unemployed. This shift happened in the late 1980s and early 1990s, mainly as a result of the recession and the rise in UI payments. A number of policy actions have been taken to restrain these transfer programs.

As shown in Table 11.4, the most notable change in the structure of federal social spending since 1984 has been the 6.1 percentage point decline in transfers to other levels of government as a share of social expenditures. These cuts illustrate the significant extent of the retrenchment of federal spending on provincial

Table 11.3

Spending by Major Social Program, 1984-85 to 1991-92

	1984-85	1991-92	Absolute Change	Annual Average
	(billions of dollars)		(percent)	
Transfers to persons	25.5	40.8	15.3	7.0
Elderly benefits	11.4	18.9	7.5	7.5
UI benefits	10.0	17.2	7.2	8.0
Family Allowances	2.4	2.8	0.4	2.1
Veterans' benefits	1.1	1.3	0.2	2.7
Transfers to other levels of government[a]	20.0	24.4	4.4	2.9
Equalization	5.4	8.4	3.0	6.7
Established Programs Financing	8.6	7.7	-0.9	-1.5
Canada Assistance Plan	3.7	5.7	1.9	6.2
Territories	0.5	1.0	0.5	11.3
Other major social transfers				9.6
Employment	1.6	1.6	-	-0.4
Aboriginal peoples	1.2	2.8	1.6	12.8
Agriculture	0.7	2.8	2.1	37.5
Other groups	2.1	3.0	0.9	5.8
Payments to major social Crown corporations				2.9
CMHC	1.7	2.0	0.3	3.6
CBC	0.9	1.0	0.1	1.9
Total social spending	53.8	78.5	24.7	5.5

Source: Public Accounts, Statistics Canada.

Notes: Figures may not add due to rounding and the exclusion of other smaller programs.

[a] Refers to the cash component of transfers to other levels of government.

Table 11.4

**The Restructuring of Federal
Social Spending**

	1981-82	1984-85	1991-92	Percentage Change 1984-85 to 1991-92
	(% of total social spending)			
Transfers to persons	47.5	47.5	52.0	4.6
Transfers to other levels of government	39.2	37.2	31.1	-6.1
Other major social transfers	8.9	10.5	13.0	2.5
Payments to major social Crown corporations	4.4	4.8	3.9	-0.9

Source: Public Accounts, Statistics Canada.

Note: Totals may not add to 100 due to rounding.

programs. The position of the Mulroney government, like that of the previous Trudeau government, has been that transfers to provinces are too large to be exempt from expenditure restraint. The Conservatives' objective has been to bring the growth of major transfers to other governments more into line with general federal program spending. Reductions in the growth of EPF cash transfers and limitations on federal CAP contributions, imposed unilaterally by the Mulroney government, have served to meet this objective. These measures have generated considerable intergovernmental acrimony and charges by provinces that Ottawa is offloading its financial responsibilities onto provincial administrations and services.

THE TRANSFER PROGRAMS

Transfers to Persons

Elderly benefits constitute the largest area of federal social spending and are among the fastest growing. Over three million seniors (those persons aged 65 years and over) received $18.9 billion through OAS, GIS and SPA in 1991-92. Over this period, transfers to seniors grew at an annual average of 7.5 percent, or about $1 billion a year, due to the full indexation of benefits to inflation and the growing number of seniors in Canada. In this sense, the increased expenditures in seniors' benefits represent a *de facto* priority area rather than a reallocation of resources to a government-designated priority.

The most significant action on elderly benefits was ending the universality of the OAS by introducing a special tax or claw-back on OAS benefits in 1989. In brief, the claw-back means that Canadian seniors repay 15 cents of their OAS pension for every dollar of net income above a threshold. In 1991, seniors with net incomes of $50,000 or less did not pay the claw-back; those with net incomes between $50,000 and $76,332 paid a graduated partial claw-back, keeping some of their old age pension; and seniors with net incomes above $76,332 paid the total claw-back, losing all of their OAS benefits. The claw-back ends the universal nature of the OAS because benefits are now subject to a special tax and are no longer taxed at the same rate as other income. Over time, a growing number of seniors will not retain any after-tax benefits from the program because the claw-back's threshold is only partially indexed to the inflation rate. With an initial 128,000 seniors estimated to be receiving no or less OAS benefits than before the claw-back, a concern voiced by social policy groups is that the claw-back's impact will weaken general public support for this and other social programs, rather than preserve the social safety net.[6]

The spending trends in this area of social policy are influenced not only by what the Mulroney government has done, but also by what it has not done. Seniors' benefits have been restrained by a number of non-decisions, that is, choices to do nothing new on certain issues and to confine actual reform to relatively inexpensive changes. The Conservatives have engaged in pension policy non-decision making by not raising the basic OAS benefit or GIS benefit and by not extending the SPA to include low-income couples or single individuals aged 60 to 64. During the Mulroney years, these policy options have been kept off the Government's agenda. With respect to the SPA, for instance, court challenges to broaden the program would, if successful, require the Government to spend substantial amounts of money. The 1992 *Budget Papers* caution that such a judgement would, "in the current fiscal circumstances, require a serious reconsideration of the program itself," to counter the serious financial effects on government spending.[7]

Unemployment insurance (UI) benefits were $17.2 billion in 1991-92 compared with $10 billion in 1984-85, an average annual growth rate of 8 percent. Prior to the 1991-92 recession, however, the growth of UI spending averaged only 3 percent a year from 1984-85 to 1989-90. The recent recession resulted in a rising unemployment rate, beginning in the second half of 1990, which increased UI payments by almost $1 billion relative to the February 1990 budget projection. In 1991-92, the impact of the recession resulted in a $3 billion increase in UI payments relative to the 1990 budget. From 1990-91 to 1991-92 then, the growth rate of UI spending was 21 percent.

The UI program perhaps best illustrates our propositions that the Conservatives have been more decisive in restructuring social programs in their second mandate than in their first; that social policy changes which imposed losses on Canadians were made late in the second mandate; and that some key Canadian social programs have become more like those in the United States. In 1985, in its first mandate, the Conservative government set up a commission of inquiry (the Forget Commission) on UI to review all elements of the program. The Commission's final recommendations, released in 1986, were not unanimous. The majority report proposed fundamental changes to the program including an annualization scheme designed to discourage people from getting UI after 10 weeks, limited regional-based benefits and reduced benefit levels. It was estimated that the changes would save the system $3 billion, which the majority report recommended be spent on job creation, income supplements and training programs. The minority report called for a return to benefit levels at two thirds of income, the restoration of coverage of workers over 65, the continuation of benefits for fishers and the extension of benefits to hunters and trappers. The report (or reports) generated considerable public debate among the commissioners and political exchange among the federal parties. The controversy and contradictory proposals led, in 1987, to the Mulroney government distancing itself from the report and taking a low posture regarding the recommendations.

Since their re-election in 1988, the Conservatives have implemented sweeping structural reforms to the UI program, which were announced in the April 1989 budget and December 1992 mini-budget. With a legislative change passed in November 1990, the federal government no longer contributes from general revenues to the UI Account for 1) regionally extended benefits, 2) extension benefits paid under job creation projects and training programs, and 3) fishers' benefits. The UI program is now funded entirely from employer and employee premiums. This change brought to an end an almost 50-year policy of tripartite funding of the UI program in Canada, moving the program's design away from European practice and more in line with practice in the United States. UI premiums for employees and employers were raised by 7 percent effective January 1990, and by 24 percent in July 1991, to offset the $2.9 billion loss of the federal government's contribution. Premiums were raised again in January 1992.

Other important changes to the UI program implemented in 1990 included increasing the maximum qualifying period from 14 to 20 weeks in some regions; reducing the maximum duration of benefits from a range of 46 to 50 weeks to a range of 35 to 50 weeks; increasing penalties for workers who quit their jobs voluntarily, and for claimants and employers who defraud the program; improving benefits for maternity, sickness and parental leave; and reintroducing coverage of workers over 65 to bring the UI program in line with recent court cases and the Canadian Charter of Rights and Freedoms. On these last two changes, a recent assessment of the Conservatives' record on social policy comments that

> these are laudable measures, but financing them through what amounts to cuts to benefits to unemployed Canadians is not. The changes to unemployment insurance are hitting lower-income unemployed Canadians hardest. Especially during a time of high

unemployment, some workers will no longer manage to qualify for unemployment insurance because they cannot work long enough and so have to turn to welfare if they lose their jobs. Shortening the duration of benefits for many UI recipients also swells the welfare rolls or forces unemployed workers into poorly-paid, often unstable jobs.[8]

Further restraint measures and cuts to the UI program were announced by the Finance Minister in a mini-budget statement in December 1992. Effective April 1993, people who voluntarily quit their jobs without just cause or who lose their jobs through misconduct will not be eligible for UI payments. Previously, people in these situations had to wait seven to 12 weeks for benefits and received less than other UI recipients. Also effective April 1993, benefits to new recipients will be cut to 57 percent of insurable earnings from the previous level of 60 percent. Furthermore, UI benefits will be frozen at current levels. It is estimated that these measures will save the government $2.5 billion by 1995.

The political fallout from these latest cuts to UI shows that not all social policy making by the Conservatives has exhibited the "stealth style" noted at the outset of this chapter. True, the cuts were announced by the Finance Minister in a budget statement that included $8 billion in spending cuts and about $1 billion in spending measures to stimulate the economy. It is also true that the Government relied on amendments to existing rules and procedures. But the UI cuts were quickly found and received media scrutiny, political debate (even within the Conservative caucus) and public attention by labour unions and women's groups.

Much criticism centres on denying benefits to people who leave a job without "just cause" and the risk of penalizing women who have been sexually harassed at work. These concerns have been expressed by two labour studies analysts:

The Unemployment Insurance Act lists sexual harassment as legitimate grounds for leaving a job. However, in order to qualify, women who have been sexually harassed on the job are required to make a formal statement and to have their charges formally reviewed.... Such formal exposure of sexual harassment can subject women to humiliation. Thus, a great many women never report sexual harassment when they quit their jobs.

Under the proposed changes to the UI Act, such women will be doubly penalized, first by sexual harassment, and second by denial of unemployment insurance benefits. In many cases, women will have to choose between welfare and putting up with sexual harassment on the job.[9]

These concerns raise larger questions about the equity of the changes and the policy obligations of the Department of Employment and Immigration. Who should assume the burden of proof in such cases—the claimant or those assessing the case? Do existing UI rules ensure administrative fairness? And to what extent, and in which ways, should the Department of Employment and Immigration be responsible for ensuring that safeguards exist in workplaces for individuals to report sexual and other forms of harassment?

As indicated in Table 11.3, spending on Family Allowances (FA) benefits in 1991-92 was $2.8 billion for 3.7 million families, representing an average yearly growth of 2.1 percent since 1984-85. However, in constant 1992 dollars, spending on this program declined steadily over the Mulroney period, from $3.3 billion in 1984-85 to $2.8 billion in 1991-92, then dropping to $2.2 billion in 1992-93. FA spending has been constrained through the partial de-indexation of benefits begun in 1986 and the claw-back of payments from middle- and high-income families implemented over the 1989-91 period. In January 1993, the FA program was eliminated and replaced by a Child Tax Benefit (CTB), which amalgamates the FA as well as refundable and non-refundable child tax credits. Announced in the February 1992 budget, the monthly CTB is targeted at about 3.1 million low- and middle-income families, and its cost is estimated at $2.1 billion over five years. As the CTB is delivered through the personal income tax system, it is netted against budgetary revenues and not reported as a direct expenditure. The effect of this is to lower program spending by about $750 million in 1992-93 and by about $3 billion in 1993-94 and each subsequent year.[10] This restructuring of the child benefits system followed the death of the Government's earlier commitment to establish a national child-care policy. In May 1992, the Minister of Health and Welfare announced the Child Development Initiative, with $500 million over five years, to reduce the risk of living in poverty that many children face. The initiatives concerning child benefits are fully examined in "The Politics of Stealth: Child Benefits under the Tories" in this volume.

Veterans' financial benefit programs are the smallest element in the federal transfers to persons category. In 1991-92, direct spending on veteran and civilian disability pensions, and veteran and civilian war allowances was $1.3 billion. These payments have grown at an annual average rate of 2.7 percent since 1984-85. In contrast to the FA and new CTB, the veterans' benefits have retained adequate indexation provisions. The war allowances are fully indexed to compensate for inflation and are adjusted quarterly, while the disability pensions are adjusted annually to the consumer price index or the increase in the average composite wage of a representative group of federal public servants, whichever is greater.

Transfers to Other Governments

The rate of growth of cash transfers to other levels of government, principally the provinces and territories, has been strictly curtailed by the Mulroney government. Overall, transfers to other governments have risen from $20 billion in 1984-85 to $24.4 billion in 1991-92, an average annual increase of only 2.9 percent, which is considerably below that of federal social spending or total program spending during the same period. This trend reflects Conservative policy to reduce the growth of federal transfers to the provincial governments. Two thirds of the increase is from growth in equalization payments, which help low-income provinces provide public services—including social programs—that are comparable with those in the richer provinces of Alberta, British Columbia and Ontario. Cash transfers for equalization have not been subject to expenditure restraint, and they grew by an average 6.7 percent a year over the 1984-85 to 1991-92 period. Through Established Programs Financing (EPF), the federal government provides equal per capita financial assistance to the provinces, intended to support health care and post-secondary education.[11] In 1991-92, the cash funding was $7.7 billion, a $900 million decline in absolute terms from 1984-85, and a 33 percent decline in real terms. Of all federal social programs over the two Mulroney mandates, EPF has been subject to the most significant restraint measures. In the 1986 budget, the indexation of EPF transfer payments was limited to the increase in GNP less two percentage points. The indexation provision was lowered again in the 1989 budget to the increase in GNP less three percentage points. In the 1990 budget, the Finance Minister announced that EPF transfers to the provinces would be frozen for 1990-91 and 1991-92; and in the 1991 budget the freeze was extended to the end of 1994-95, after which the GNP less three percentage points formula takes effect. As indicated in Table 11.5, the cumulative reductions in EPF from 1990-91 through 1995-96 are estimated at $38.4 billion.

The Canada Assistance Plan (CAP) is the social safety net of last resort. The federal government's CAP contributions support provincial and territorial programs in providing income assistance to single-parent families, unemployed people, and people with disabilities, as well as a range of social services to Canadians on low or modest incomes. Under the terms of the CAP, Ottawa's role has been to pay half the cost of all expenditures that qualify, with no ceiling on the amount of federal contributions. Federal spending on CAP grew from $3.7 billion in 1984-85 to $5.7 billion in 1990-91, an average growth rate of 6.2 percent a year. A closer look at the trend reveals that federal CAP contributions increased by 7.5 percent a year, on average, from 1984-85 through 1990-91 and then declined by 1 percent in 1991-92. This decline was the result of a cap on the CAP, first introduced in 1990 as part of the Expenditure Control Plan. With this cap, federal CAP transfers to the three richest provinces—Alberta, British Columbia and Ontario—are being limited to increases of 5 percent a year for five years. For the other seven provinces, Ottawa will continue to match all eligible social assistance spending on a dollar for dollar basis.

> The Finance Department's own figures put this loss [for the three provinces] at $2.3 billion in total, doubtless a very conservative estimate. These cuts mean that Ottawa has reneged on the principle of 50-50 cost-sharing that underlies the Canada Assistance Plan and hampered efforts at welfare reform in Ontario which has had to deal with enormous increases in its welfare rolls as a result of the [1991-92] recession.[12]

The Mulroney Conservatives had pledged in their first Speech from the Throne in November 1984 to inaugurate a new era of national reconciliation and consensus, based on a constant process of consultation with provincial governments at the ministerial level.[13] However, the dark cloud of fiscal restraint has rained heavily on this promised bright new day of co-operative federalism. The Conservatives' objectives of fiscal restraint and intergovernmental co-operation have been uneasy partners, if not contradictory values, in Canadian social policy. Moreover, the restraints applied to EPF and the CAP, as well as to the UI program, are producing a fiscally driven decentralization of Canada's federation. Thomas Courchene, a leading economist in Canadian policy studies, has outlined the mechanics and implications of the recent squeeze on intergovernmental transfers for social policy and the role of Ottawa.

> Leading the way is the current two-year freeze in established programmes' financing (EPF) after which growth in EPF payment will be pegged at the growth of gross national product (GNP) minus 3 percent. Since the financing of EPF is a combination of tax transfers and cash transfers, what this means is that the tax transfer component will progressively account for more of the total transfer. Indeed, estimates suggest that cash transfers to Quebec will fall to zero before the year 2000 and those for the rest of the provinces sometime before 2010. Thus the roughly $20 billion of federal transfers will eventually fall to zero. This can be viewed as decentralizing on three counts. First, if the provinces maintain service levels by increasing their taxes, the ratio of provincial to federal taxes will increase. Second, if the provinces react by cutting back these programs or redesigning them, this also would be decentralizing in the sense that these "national" programs will progressively be designed provincially. The third reason is closely related to the second: when the federal cash transfer falls to zero, how does or can Ottawa insist on any standards at all? Less dramatic, but nonetheless significant, are the selected freezes in the 1990 federal budget on the Canada Assistance Plan (for the "have" provinces) and the tightened regulations for unemployment insurance (which, for the poorer provinces, will transfer unfortunate citizens from "federally financed" UI to jointly financed welfare).[14]

Comparing the Mulroney period with the 1980-84 Trudeau period in the area of intergovernmental restraint, Courchene observes that

> whereas the 1980-84 squeeze on intergovernmental transfers was part of an overall framework to increase federal visibility and enhance national standards, the current squeeze is fiscally driven and, if anything, will lead in the direction of increased and/or enforced provincial autonomy over the design and delivery of the social envelope.[15]

In addition to being decentralizing, these restraints in federal social transfers will produce a weakening in the bonds of nationhood. A.W. Johnson, a major participant and keen observer on the development of Canadian social policy since the 1950s, has identified two essential elements of the bonds of Canada's nationhood. One is "the potential for Canadians to come to share certain common privileges and benefits of citizenship, wherever they live in Canada"; the second element is "the sense of affinity and association—even esteem—which Canadians feel, or may reasonably come to feel, for their national governmental institutions." Johnson suggests that nationwide programs or public services such as medicare, the CAP, Old Age Security pensions and accessibility to higher education, "while lying within provincial jurisdiction, have come to be seen by Canadians generally as being important to a decent and dignified life for all Canadians."[16] In a similar vein, Frances Abele, in the introduction to the 1991-92 edition of *How Ottawa Spends*, remarked that

> federal initiatives and federal spending are the traditional glue in the Canadian federation. When asked to identify key elements of what is distinctive about Canada, most Canadians will quickly mention Medicare and the social welfare system, as well as a civic culture relatively free of interpersonal violence. Deeper than this, there is the reality that Canada is largely the product of state initiatives.[17]

Other Major Social Transfers

The other major social transfers presented in Table 11.3 consist of grants and contributions for employment creation and training, transfers to Indians and Inuit, agricultural income stabilization programs, and funding for other groups such as educational loans. From 1984-85 to 1991-92, total spending on this category of federal social policy increased by 9.6 percent a year, well above inflation and the growth rate for social spending overall. Most of the increase in this category was concentrated in transfers to Aboriginal peoples and assistance to the agriculture sector. The specific programs in this category include

- funding for job creation and training, provided primarily through the Canadian Jobs Strategy over this period, was held constant and thus declined in real terms;
- Indian and Inuit programs funding grew 12.8 percent a year on average due in large part to increases in the eligible population;
- agriculture support reached $2.8 billion in 1991-92, reflecting assistance for grain farmers affected by depressed world markets (caused by the international grain subsidy battle). This represents yearly growth of 37.5 percent since 1984-85.

The Mulroney Conservatives have introduced at least a dozen major initiatives in agriculture, focused largely on Prairie farm income stabilization, credit problems of producers and the deficit position of certain agricultural safety net programs. In their first mandate, the Conservatives spent about $17 billion on agriculture, double the amount spent in the previous four-year period.[18] The Conservatives witnessed the farm safety net system put a heavy financial claim on the federal public purse. They also learned that Canada's major agriculture safety net programs did not provide farmers with adequate protection during extended periods of financial distress. In their second mandate, to assist farmers better, the Mulroney government introduced a new agricultural income support policy for the 1991 crop year. Made up of the Gross Revenue Insurance Program and the Net Income Stabilization Account, this policy replaced grain income support previously delivered through the Western Grain Stabilization Account and Agricultural Stabilization Account programs. These new programs are designed to be self-financing over time through premiums and are cost-shared with provinces and producers. Support to grain farmers has remained a priority area of the Conservatives and additional support was given to the farmers in 1991-92 and 1992-93.

The major Crown corporations in the federal social policy domain are the CMHC and the CBC. As shown in Table 11.3, payments to these agencies have been relatively constrained, growing less than the average rate for social spending and less than inflation. However, as Table 11.2 indicates, the social Crown corporations fared better in funding than did Crown corporations in the commercial sector such as Canada Post and VIA Rail.

The Conservatives' preoccupation with spending restraint has meant reductions in transfers to provinces for health care, higher education, social assistance, legal aid and social housing. These reductions almost certainly mean that much of social policy in Canada will become less national in perspective and in practice. The decentralization of program funding, design and delivery implies an erosion in nationwide levels of service and a move to "hodgepodge federalism" with respect to rights and benefits. By cutting back Ottawa's financial transfers for social programs—transfers that enable citizens across the country to share certain common public services—the Conservatives' restraint policy has weakened some important bonds of nationhood.

EXPENDITURE RESTRAINT

As part of its fiscal restraint strategy, the Mulroney government introduced the Expenditure Control Plan in the 1990 budget. Originally a two-year restraint program, this plan was extended to five years in the 1991 budget and was deepened by measures in the 1992 budget. The Expenditure Control Plan is the key framework in Conservative restraint budgeting. To date, the Plan has become a seven-year approach to spending control and reduction which has yielded substantial and ongoing fiscal savings. Under the Plan, program spending and activities are constrained, that is, limited in their growth, frozen, reduced, eliminated or subjected to management measures such as cost recovery. Table 11.5 provides an overview of expenditure control measures, with a focus on the projected fiscal impact on social programs—leaving aside other

Table 11.5

Fiscal Impact of Expenditure Control Measures
on Social Programs in the 1990s

	Cumulative Savings to 1995-96[b]	Cumulative Savings to 1996-97[c]
	(millions of dollars)	
Programs constrained		
Indian and Inuit	100	
Canada Assistance Plan	2,290	
CMHC Social Housing		622
Repayment of Old Age Security and Family Allowances benefits	1,795[d]	
Established Programs Financing	27,064	
Legal Aid Cost-sharing	7[d]	
Canada Student Loans (termination of six months' post-graduation interest-free period)		205
Programs frozen		
Established Programs Financing	11,429	
CBC	20	
Canadian Film Development Corporation	41	
Canadian Jobs Strategy		100
Legal Aid Cost-sharing	14[d]	
Programs reduced		
Grants and contributions from		
Secretary of State	92	10
Multiculturalism	21	6
Health and Welfare	44	
Communications		35
Indian and Northern Affairs		133
Programs/agencies/plans eliminated		
Federal financing of UI	6,500[d]	
CMHC Co-op Housing		25
Canada Child-care bill		1,145[d]
Court Challenges		12

Table 11.5

cont'd

	Cumulative Savings to 1995-96[b]	Cumulative Savings to 1996-97[c]
	(millions of dollars)	
Cost-sharing on services for victims of crime		11
Law Reform Commission, Economic Council, Science Council, etc.		45[a]
Management measures		
Dividends from cultural Crown corporations		55
Operating budget cuts in social policy portfolios	1,873[d]	462[d]
Cost recovery/user charges		
Veterans' programs	106	
Communications		111
Justice		7
Multiculturalism		13
Solicitor General		9
Total fiscal impact	51,305	2,873

Sources: Department of Finance, *The Budget Papers* (February 25, 1992), pp. 75, 81; President of the Treasury Board, *Managing Government Expenditures*, various years.

Notes: Unless otherwise noted, the fiscal impacts presented in this table are based on estimates presented in recent budgets. Actual fiscal impacts may be different.

[a] Based on measures announced in the 1990 and 1991 budgets except for a) the impact since 1990-91 of reductions in the EPF formula announced in the 1985 and 1989 budgets, b) the repayment of social transfers which was announced in the 1989 budget but did not take effect until 1990-91, and c) the termination of federal contributions to financing the unemployment insurance program announced in the 1989 budget, effective November 1990.

[b] Based on measures announced in the 1992 budget.

[c] Estimated by the authors.

programs such as science and technology, and defence—over the period 1990-91 to 1996-97. In addition, we present other spending restraint measures not officially included in the Plan but which have taken effect since 1990 and have significant fiscal consequences for social programs.

The Government states that, under the Plan, a limited number of programs are exempt from restraint in order that federal spending can be directed to the highest priorities. The exempted programs are all social policies and include the transfers to persons (elderly benefits, Family Allowances, unemployment insurance benefits and veterans' allowances) and certain major transfers to provinces (equalization and CAP transfers to the seven equalization-receiving provinces). However, the fact that these social programs are exempted areas in the Plan gives the misleading impression that federal social policy is largely shielded from expenditure control. Indeed, the Plan conceals the fact that most of these social programs are subject to reductions, which lie outside the Plan but are very much a part of the Mulroney government's restraint agenda and budgetary actions. In this regard, the Expenditure Control Plan is an example of the stealth style of policy making.

Social expenditure restraint is a main element in the Government's fiscal plan. This restraint has been, and will continue to be, sustained over many years, with reductions across a wide spectrum of social programs, government departments and client groups. We estimate the total fiscal impact from expenditure control measures on federal social spending at over $51 billion from 1990-91 through 1995-96, an average of $8.5 billion a year in cut-backs. This estimate includes the impact of the original and extended versions of the Expenditure Control Plan, along with other restraint actions announced in earlier budgets. The Plan contains no statement that the savings which result from these cut-backs will remain within the federal social policy sector. Rather, it appears that the Plan's intended purpose is to apply the bulk of these savings towards managing the federal deficit.

The 1992 budget broadened the Expenditure Control Plan, including plans for streamlining the federal government's organizational arrangements. The Conservatives' stated rationale was to eliminate waste created by duplication within government and duplication between government and the private sector; defer desirable initiatives that cannot be afforded in current fiscal circumstances; strengthen certain sectors by merging related organizations and their mandates; and privatize commercial functions that no longer serve a public policy purpose. Of the 46 government organizations affected by this streamlining initiative, at least 18 of these (listed in Table 11.6) are directly relevant to social policy in Canada.[19] Of these 18 organizations, half are to be eliminated. This unlucky half contains several policy research councils and ministerial advisory committees. Three new agencies that had been proposed—dealing with race relations, heritage languages and the corrections system—are now on hold indefinitely. Five federal organizations in the areas of justice and scholarship and research are being merged into two organizations; and one unit, which provides radiation monitoring services to workers, is being privatized. As indicated in Table 11.5, we estimate there will be about $45 million in savings from these streamlining measures over the next five years.

The most significant part of this streamlining from a social policy perspective is the elimination of the Law Reform Commission, Economic Council and Science Council. These prominent advisory agencies, each in existence for over 20 years and each with an arm's length relationship to the federal government, provided open and independent analysis and, at times, critical advice on important government initiatives. By eliminating these quasi-government sources of policy analysis, by contracting out for research and by reducing funding to non-governmental social policy research organizations such as the Canadian Council on Social Development, the Conservatives are altering the institutional context for social policy debate and public discussion in Canada.[20] These streamlining measures and other general restraints upon the federal bureaucracy over the past decade have undoubtedly affected the analytical capacities of the public service to generate and disseminate policy information. This, according to political scientist Sharon Sutherland, has been the Conservatives' intent, based on their ideological opposition to "big government" and lack of commitment to "building an in-house research capacity, preferring to buy the services from universities, the corporate sector, and think tanks."[21] For many in the social policy community, the message from the Conservatives' actions seems to be that independent research bodies are to be "lean and not heard."

Table 11.6

Streamlining Social Policy-Relevant
Organizations

Eliminated
>Law Reform Commission
>Veterans' Land Administration
>Demographic Review Secretariat
>Science Council
>Economic Council
>Pay Research Bureau
>Canada Employment and Immigration Advisory Council
>Advisory Committee on le Musée de la Nouvelle France
>Advisory Committee for le musée des arts et du spectacle
>>vivant

Deferred
>Canadian Race Relations Foundation
>Canadian Heritage Languages Institute
>Sentencing and Conditional Release Commission

Merged
>RCMP External Review Committee and RCMP Public
>>Complaints Commission
>Canada Council, the Social Sciences and Humanities
>>Research Council, and international cultural programs

Privatized
>Dosimetry Services Unit (Health and Welfare Canada)

Source: Adapted from Department of Finance, *The Budget Papers* (February 25, 1992), Table 3.5, p. 86.

THE IMPACT OF SOCIAL POLICY DECISIONS

The social policy decisions of governments have important consequences for Canadians. The decisions determine who is protected by society, the conditions under which protection is available and the level of benefits provided. The Conservatives have argued that Canadians can no longer afford the cost of providing the type of support that they are accustomed to receiving. They claim that social spending is draining the economy and slowing down economic growth. The following section examines the impact that government decisions, or non-decisions, have had on Canadians.

For the majority of Canadians, earnings from employment are their single most important source of income. An assessment of the distribution of earned income over the past eight years provides us with some understanding of how well Canadians have been able to meet their needs.[22] In 1991, average income earned from the sale of labour was $27,920 in constant 1986 dollars, it has not increased significantly from average income earned in 1981, which was $26,891 in constant 1986 dollars.[23] Between 1983 and 1986 there was a polarization of income, with more Canadians earning either high or low incomes and fewer earning middle incomes. The after-tax income share of the bottom and top third of income earners increased slightly while the middle third shrunk slightly. There has, however, been a slight shift back in the last few years.

The ability of middle-class Canadians to maintain or improve their share of income depends to a large extent on the structure of the labour force. During the seventies, the labour force grew at the rate of 3.2 percent per year; during the eighties, this rate fell to 1.9 percent.[24] When the Conservatives took power, the labour market was in poor shape—the unemployment rate was 11.2 percent and the 1981-82 recession had left many people unemployed. For six years, the unemployment rate slowly receded to 7.5 percent during a period of steady economic growth. However, the recession of the early 1990s has taken its toll, and in August 1992 unemployment was back up to 11.6 percent. There were many plant closures which resulted in people being permanently laid off and, in many cases, it took workers up to six months to find new employment, often at lower wage rates than they earned before. The average duration of unemployment increased significantly, beginning at a low of 15 weeks in 1981, rising during the recession of the early 1980s to a high of 22 weeks, falling to a low of 17 weeks in 1990 and rising to 23 weeks in 1992.[25] These long periods of unemployment force people to consume their reserve savings, increase their debt load and, when unemployment insurance benefits run out, turn to social assistance for help.

During this period, there have been significant changes in the types of persons who have become unemployed. In 1980, nearly half of the unemployed were between 15 and 24 years of age but, by the early 1990s, this age group accounted for less than one third of the total.[26] At present, the unemployment rate is 60 percent higher for those 25 to 44 years old than it was in 1980. Finally in the early 1980s, women were more likely to be unemployed than men; but during the past 10 years, the unemployment rates have become much closer.

The most disheartening aspect of the development of the economy during the Mulroney era was that many of the new jobs were part-time, and there was a dramatic shift from goods-producing industries and agriculture to the service sector. In 1984, when the Conservatives took power, 15.3 percent of those employed worked part-time and, of these, 30.1 percent were looking for full-time work. By July 1992, 17.3 percent of all employed Canadians worked part-time, the highest percentage on record. More than one third of these people said they could not find full-time employment and, therefore, had to work part-time. Part-time workers are mostly female (81 percent in 1992) and predominantly young (39 percent are between 15 and 24).

There has been a significant shift in the way governments bear the cost of helping the unemployed. The National Council of Welfare believes that the changes in the unemployment insurance system, which we discussed earlier, have forced people onto social welfare assistance. This shift has increased provincial expenditures while reducing the demands made on unemployment insurance. In part, the increase in the qualification period for unemployment benefits, in some regions, from 14 to 20 weeks and the reduction in the number of weeks that benefits can be collected have created increased demands on the welfare system. In 1984, there were approximately 1,742,706 people (7 percent of the total population) living on welfare in Canada. By 1987, the number had increased a little to an estimated 1,904,900 (7.4 percent); but between 1987 and 1991, the number had jumped to an estimated 2,282,200 (8.5 percent). Most of the increase was the result of single employable people being unable to find employment, although there was also an increase in the number of single parents receiving welfare.

One important indicator of how well a society is performing is changes in the standard of living. Canadians experienced a steady rise in the standard of living from the mid-1940s to the late 1970s. The standard of living then began to decline marginally, and it ended up in the early 1990s at a little less than the level achieved in 1977. This means that Canadians have not had an increase in their standard of living for 15 years. For those under 25 years of age, the standard of living has fallen by a staggering 20 percent. The impact of this has important implications for families who can now expect more young people of working age to remain at home and seek ongoing financial support from their parents. As a result, Canadians are becoming accustomed—for the first time—to the thought that their children can expect to live at a lower standard of living than they did at the same age. Older Canadians have been slightly more fortunate; their standard of living has increased by about 9.5 percent in this same period.

While the standard of living is an important indicator of how well the entire society is doing, it is of equal importance to examine how well the poorest section of the society is faring. Poverty can best be measured using Statistics Canada's "low income cut-off lines," which provide a constant measure that can be used to estimate the relative change between one time and another.[27] When the Conservatives took power, 18.1 percent of all persons in Canada were below the low income cut-off lines. This was a dramatic shift from the low of 15.3 percent in 1981. The rate fell from 1984 until 1989 when it reached a low of 13.6 percent, then it began to go up again.[28] By the first year of the current recession, the number of Canadians living in poverty had increased to 14.6 percent.[29]

The very poor are people who have little connection with labour markets. The economic system has passed them by. For the most part they live on the street, get food from food banks or hand-outs, have little money and live lives of desperation. In 1981, Canada had one food bank (in Edmonton); 10 years later, there are more than 350 across the country. Approximately 1.4 million people use food banks each year. At the same time, the Canadian Council on Social Development estimated that, on any given day, there were 10,000 Canadians staying in emergency shelters. Between 130,000 and 250,000 Canadians used these shelters in 1987. In 1984, it was estimated that there were 100,000 homeless people in Canada. This figure had grown to between 150,000 and 260,000 by 1991.

The dynamic structure of poverty means that people move in and out of poverty depending upon the availability of jobs, the nature of the job market and the background of the people who are looking for work. In its final report, *The New Face of Poverty*, the Economic Council of Canada described this dynamic dimension of poverty. The probability of becoming poor in any one year is 4.3 percent for all Canadian families. The risk is higher for single people with children (14.1 percent) and lower for married couples with children (3.1 percent). Two-earner families have the lowest rate of all at 2 percent.[30] The chances of becoming poor increase dramatically during periods of family breakup, particularly when children are involved. The odds of escaping poverty were highest for those where both people in the family found a job (53.4 percent) and lowest for single people with children (18.3 percent).

There has been a shift in the structure of poverty. Fewer elderly people are poor, and those who are face less desperation given income security programs. Other families have not done as well. Working families have found it increasingly difficult to make ends meet. Single-parent families have the most difficulty in obtaining the resources needed to raise children, and single people also find it difficult to make an adequate living.

While poverty has a powerful impact on Canadians in general, many analysts believe that the impact of poverty is felt most by children. In 1984, there were 1,209,000 children living in families with incomes below the low income cut-off lines. This number had declined to 913,000 by 1988, but had risen again to 1,105,000 by 1990.[31] A report by the National Youth in Care Network, called *Thursday's Child: Child Poverty in Canada*, states that poverty

> takes away the tools to build the blocks for the future—your "life chances." It steals away the opportunity to have a life unmarked

by sickness, a decent education, a secure home and a long retirement. It stops people being able to plan ahead. It stops people being able to take control of their lives.[32]

CONCLUSION

Over the past eight years, the Conservative government has been clearer about its economic agenda than its social policy agenda. In 1984, the Conservatives set a course to control the deficit and reduce government expenditures. *A New Direction for Canada: An Agenda for Economic Renewal* set out their strategy: to restore macroeconomic balance by reducing fiscal deficits and lowering inflation; and to reorient policies towards promotion of sustainable, medium-term growth by reducing the role of government, reforming the tax system, opening up trading relationships, and promoting investment in training, advanced education, research and development, and economic infrastructure. The overall strategy was to increase reliance on market instruments to solve the problems facing Canadians. The cost to Canadians has been a lowering of the safety net and a weakening of the bonds of nationhood. Budgets since 1984 have cut the growth of spending, limited program expenditures and reduced the deficit as a share of the GDP.

During this period, there has been a decline in the living conditions of many Canadians. Families are under greater economic pressure, more children are living in poverty, the unemployment rate is up, more young people have lost the will to look for work, there are fewer new, full-time jobs and housing is harder to find. The result is that more people are falling into and through the social safety net.

One of the costs of the changes that have taken place during the Conservative era has been a reduction in social integration. The stark differences between the "haves" and the "have nots" have been highlighted by the removal of universal programs. More and more, individuals have been made to feel like failures within the postindustrial society. Responsibility for their inability to compete in the workforce, or to find meaningful employment, is forced onto their shoulders. While this reinforces a neo-conservative agenda, it has long-term implications.

Canada can expect to face increasing social tensions as it undermines its welfare system. The collapse of the State in eastern Europe was not so much a repudiation of socialism as a repudiation of the inability of a government to solve social problems. By lowering the safety net and weakening Canada's nationhood, the Canadian government is taking one more step towards being unable to solve social problems in this country.

NOTES

1   James J. Rice, "Restitching the Safety Net: Altering the National Social Security System" in Michael J. Prince, (ed.), *How Ottawa Spends 1987-88: Restraining the State* (Toronto: Methuen, 1987), p. 228.

2   This is an alternative view to that of Carolyn Tuohy, "Social Policy: Two Worlds" in Michael M. Atkinson, (ed.), *Governing Canada* (Toronto: Harcourt Brace Jovanovich, 1993), p. 124.

3   Grattan Gray, "Social Policy by Stealth," *Policy Options*, 11, 2: p. 26.

4   See, for example, Michael J. Prince and James J. Rice, "The Canadian Jobs Strategy: Supply Side Social Policy" in Katherine A. Graham, (ed.), *How Ottawa Spends 1989-90: The Buck Stops Where?* (Ottawa: Carleton University Press, 1989), chap. 9. Ironically, the April 1989 Speech from the Throne of the second Mulroney government said, "Canada's social goals and programs will continue to be determined in Canada and by Canadians, in conformity and harmony with values they have historically nurtured." This statement seems intended to respond to concerns and charges raised during the 1988 election about the possible adverse impact of the Canada-U.S. Free Trade Agreement on Canadian social policies. Our argument is that certain value and policy shifts have happened that resemble patterns in the United States.

5   In brief, the recent history of the social policy field within federal budgeting systems is as follows: in 1979-80 with the creation of the Policy and Expenditure Management System (PEMS), a

Social Affairs envelope was established; in 1985-86, a Social Development envelope was created, comprising the former Social Affairs, and Justice and Legal Affairs envelopes; then, in 1989-90 (with the death of PEMS) Social Development was broken down into Social Programs, Communication and Cultural Programs, and Justice and Legal Programs. Since these changes in the budgetary concept of social policy have taken place with transitions in governments, perhaps the next alteration will be in 1994, after the next federal election.

6   For a review of the Mulroney government's policy actions in the pension field, see Michael J. Prince, "From Meech Lake to Golden Pond: The Elderly, Pension Reform and Federalism in the 1990s" in Frances Abele, (ed.), *How Ottawa Spends 1991-92: The Politics of Fragmentation* (Ottawa: Carleton University Press, 1991), chap. 10.

7   Department of Finance, *The Budget Papers* (Ottawa, February 25, 1992), p. 101. Established in 1975, the SPA program was designed to provide benefits to people in need aged 60 through 64 who were married to recipients of the Guaranteed Income Supplement, the income-tested program for people 65 and over with low incomes. In 1985, the Mulroney government expanded the SPA to include all widows and widowers aged 60 to 64. The SPA still does not cover low-income people aged 60 to 64 who never married, are divorced or separated, or where both spouses are under 65. These exclusions have provided the basis for court challenges on the grounds of unwarranted discrimination according to marital or family status.

8   Ken Battle, *The Tory Record on Social Policy* (Ottawa: Caledon Institute of Social Policy, August 1992), p. 5.

9   Belinda Leach and Donald Wells, "Proposed UI cuts will penalize workers," *The Globe and Mail* [Toronto], December 16, 1992.

10   Department of Finance, *The Budget Papers* (February 25, 1992), p. 99.

11   For a discussion of EPF, see Allan Maslove, "Reconstructing Fiscal Federalism" in Frances Abele, (ed.), *How Ottawa Spends 1992-93: The Politics of Competitiveness* (Ottawa: Carleton University Press, 1992), pp. 57-77.

12   Battle, *The Tory Record on Social Policy*, p. 6. See, also, National Council of Welfare, *The Canada Assistance Plan: No Time for Cuts* (Ottawa: Supply and Services Canada, Winter 1991).

13   On the social policy intentions of the first Mulroney government, see Michael J. Prince, "How Ottawa Decides Social Policy" in Jacqueline S. Ismael, (ed.), *The Canadian Welfare State* (Edmonton: University of Alberta Press, 1987), chap. 11.

14   Thomas J. Courchene, "Forever Amber" in David E. Smith, Peter MacKinnon, and John C. Courtney, (eds.), *After Meech Lake* (Saskatoon: Fifth House, 1991), p. 42.

15   Ibid., p. 42.

16   A.W. Johnson, "The Meech Lake Accord and the Bonds of Nationhood" in Katherine E. Swinton and Carol J. Rogerson, (eds.), *Competing Constitutional Visions* (Toronto: Carswell, 1988), p. 146. See also the valuable essay by Johnson, "Social Policy in Canada: The Past as It Conditions the Present" in Shirley B. Seward, (ed.), *The Future of Social Welfare Systems in Canada and the United Kingdom* (Halifax: Institute for Research on Public Policy, 1987), pp. 29-70.

17   Frances Abele, "The Politics of Fragmentation" in Frances Abele, (ed.), *How Ottawa Spends 1991-92: The Politics of Fragmentation* (Ottawa: Carleton University Press, 1991), pp. 23-24.

18   The Mulroney government's agriculture policy record for the 1984-88 period is examined in Michael J. Prince, "Little Help on the Prairie: Canadian Farm Income Programs and the Western Grain Economy" in Katherine A. Graham, (ed.), *How Ottawa Spends 1990-91: Tracking the Second Agenda* (Ottawa: Carleton University Press, 1990), chap. 6.

19   Department of Finance, *The Budget Papers* (February 25, 1992), p. 85. For a brief profile of the organizations being streamlined, see pp. 127-43 of *The Budget Papers*. On the dubious nature of the motives for, and savings from, this streamlining initiative, see Hugh Winsor, "Playing with politics instead of dollars," *The Globe and Mail* [Toronto], March 4, 1993, p. B1.

20   On the characteristics and incentives associated with different organizational contexts of policy analysis, see Leslie A. Pal, *Public Policy Analysis*, 2nd ed. (Toronto: Nelson, 1992), chaps. 4, 10. On the problems facing non-governmental social policy organizations in Canada, see Geoffrey York, "Defending the definition of poverty," *The Globe and Mail* [Toronto], July 16, 1992, p. A1; Patrick Johnston, "An open letter to CCSD members and supporters," *Perception*, nos. 2, 3, 1992, pp. 4, 6.

21   Sharon L. Sutherland, "The Public Service and Policy Development" in Atkinson, *Governing Canada*, p. 96. On the termination of the Economic Council and Science Council, see Larry Welsh, "Federal axing called political," *The Globe and Mail* [Toronto], March 4, 1993, p. B2.

22   In this chapter, a family refers to the economic concept of family. It is composed of all members who live together and are related by blood, marriage or adoption.

23   Statistics Canada, *Key Labour and Income Facts, 1992* (Ottawa, 1992), item 35.

24   Michel Cote, "The labour force: into the '90s," *Perspectives on Labour and Income*, Spring 1990, p. 9.

25   "The labour market: year-end review," Supplement,*Perspectives on Labour and Income*, Spring 1992, p. 7.

26   Gary Cohen, "Then and now: the changing face of unemployment," *Perspectives on Labour and Income*, Spring 1991, p. 37.

27   Low income cut-off lines are income levels used to identify families who spend a significantly higher proportion of their

income on necessities than other Canadian families. At present, the low income cut-off lines are established at a level where a family would need to spend more than 56.2 percent of income on food, shelter and clothing. The low income cut-off lines take into consideration family size, geography and the size of the community in which the family lives. Therefore, low income cut-off lines are relative and reflect the living standards of all Canadians. Christopher Sarlo's attack on this basic concept claims that the lines are too high and that poverty lines should be based on an absolute notion of poverty. Almost everyone else who writes about poverty rejects this notion, and Sarlo provides no new evidence upon which to build a better model. See Christopher Sarlo, *Poverty in Canada* (Vancouver: Fraser Institute, 1992); and David P. Ross and R. Shillington, *The Canadian Fact Book on Poverty—1989* (Ottawa: Canadian Council on Social Development, 1989).

28   National Council of Welfare, *Poverty Profile, 1980-1990* (Ottawa), Autumn 1992), p. 7.

29   David Ross, "Current and proposed measures of poverty, 1992," *Perception*, vols. 15-4, 16-1, p. 60.

30   "Basic poverty risk rates, Canada" in *The New Face of Poverty* (Ottawa: Economic Council of Canada, 1992), Table 7, p. 26.

31   National Council of Welfare, *Poverty Profile, 1980-1990*, Autumn 1992, p. 8.

32   National Youth in Care Network, *Thursday's Child—Child Poverty in Canada: A Review of the Effects of Poverty in Canada* (Ottawa, 1990), p. 1.

CHAPTER 12

The Politics of Stealth:
Child Benefits under the Tories

Ken Battle

Résumé : La réforme du crédit d'impôt pour enfants annoncé dans le budget de 1992 marquait l'étape finale du remaniement des programmes de sécurité du revenu pour les familles ayant des enfants entrepris par le gouvernement conservateur. Par le biais de ce remaniement, amorcé en 1985 sous forme d'une série de mesures complexes, le ministre des Finances a transformé le régime universel déficient institué par les Libéraux en un régime sélectif (assujetti à une évaluation du revenu) non moins inefficace, sinon davantage. Les changements propices, dont notamment les augmentations considérables du crédit d'impôt remboursable pour enfants et le regroupement des allocations familiales et des crédits d'impôt remboursables et non remboursables pour enfants en un seul régime subordonné au revenu, ont été infirmés par d'autres changements comme l'élimination de la protection intégrale contre l'inflation et l'augmentation de la déduction pour soins d'enfants régressive. L'analyse de ces mesures montre que celles-ci ont dans l'ensemble réduit l'efficacité avec laquelle les prestations pour enfants atteignent les objectifs visés et que le régime demeure compliqué, inéquitable et inadéquat. Dans ce chapitre, l'auteur avance que si le gouvernement Mulroney a pu apporter ces changements aux prestations pour enfants et à d'autres programmes d'aide sociale, c'est parce qu'il est passé maître dans «l'art de manœuvrer en douce», réussissant non seulement à sabrer à coup de milliards les dollars dépensés sur l'aide sociale, mais à le faire en neutralisant l'opposition des défenseurs des intérêts sociaux et en étouffant le débat public ouvert et informé qui est pourtant crucial alors que la politique sociale du Canada part à la dérive.

Abstract: The 1992 federal budget's announcement of a "new, integrated Child Tax Benefit" put the finishing touches on the Conservative government's transformation of income security programs for families with children. In a complex series of changes starting with the 1985 budget, the Minister of Finance has remoulded federal child benefits from the Liberals' flawed system with a universal base to an equally if not more flawed system with a selective (i.e. income-tested) base. Positive reforms, such as substantial increases to the refundable child tax credit and the rationalization of the trio of family allowances and the refundable and non-refundable child tax credits into a single income-tested program, have been negated by other changes such as the removal of full inflation protection and the enrichment of the regressive child-care expense deduction. Analysis shows that these measures have, on balance, weakened the capacity of child benefits to fulfil their objectives, and the system remains complex, inequitable and inadequate. This chapter argues that the Mulroney government accomplished its changes to child benefits and other social programs through the skilful exercise of "the politics of stealth" which has not only siphoned growing billions out of social spending at virtually no political cost, but also neutralized opposition from social advocates and stifled the informed and open public debate that is so badly needed as Canadian social policy wanders through the wilderness.

This chapter analyzes the Mulroney government's transformation of income security programs for families with children, which have seen more changes than any other area of federal social policy in recent years. It begins with a brief account of the objectives, characteristics and flaws of the old child benefits system as it stood under the Liberals in their last year of government, 1984. It then chronicles the Health and Welfare Minister's failed attempt to reform child benefits in the first year of the Tory mandate and the Finance Minister's numerous changes to the system in a succession of budgets, culminating in the new Child Tax Benefit announced in the 1992 budget and White Paper.

The chapter discusses the role of social policy and women's groups in the policy-making process. It also undertakes a detailed analysis of the impact of changes to child benefits programs and the tax system on families with children at different income levels, comparing them with childless couples.

The Tories' significant changes to child benefits and other social programs, as well as to the tax system, owe their success largely to "the politics of stealth," a fiscally potent and politically crafty strategy which has enabled Ottawa to impose its policies on the Canadian people without their understanding and without public debate. The politics of stealth has stifled exactly the kind of open, public debate on social programs that the Conservatives claimed they wanted to encourage when they took power in 1984, and which is so badly needed now.

THE OLD CHILD BENEFITS SYSTEM IN 1984

Canada's two oldest child benefits programs were born in wartime. The Children's Tax Exemption, created in 1918 as part of the "temporary" personal income tax system, provided a benefit—in the form of federal and provincial income tax savings—to taxpayers with dependent children. In support of the principle of "horizontal equity," the program was intended to help even out the unequal burden between taxpayers with equal incomes but unequal demands on those incomes as a result of the cost of raising children. Implicit was the belief that parents deserve some financial recognition from society for their child-rearing labours, although the design of the Children's Tax Exemption restricted it to parents who paid income taxes and awarded larger benefits to high-income beneficiaries.

The Family Allowances program was introduced in 1945 and provided a monthly cheque to every mother (later changed to lower-income parent, still usually the mother) on behalf of her children, regardless of the family's income. Starting in 1973, family allowances were counted as taxable income in the hands of the parent claiming the Children's Tax Exemption (i.e. the parent with the higher income), which means that after-tax benefits were largest for low-income families and smallest for high-income families. However, all families with children kept a substantial portion of their family allowances after federal and provincial income taxes—including the affluent, who ended up with about half of their gross payment. Family allowances were intended to serve two main purposes: recognize the contribution that parents make to society and the economy by raising future workers, taxpayers and citizens; and provide financial assistance to help low- and middle-income families fill the gap between their wages and their income needs, thereby helping ease poverty and supplement family incomes.

The refundable child tax credit was introduced in 1978. Designed to provide additional financial assistance to low- and middle-income parents and, thus, serve the anti-poverty and income supplementation objectives, the program was hailed as an important advance in Canadian social policy. For the first time, the federal income tax system was used to deliver a benefit which included, rather than excluded, poor parents below the taxpaying threshold. The refundable child tax credit allocated its largest payment to low- and modest-income families with children, a smaller and diminishing amount to middle-income families, and nothing to high-income parents.

The equivalent-to-married exemption allowed single parents an income tax exemption for one of their children equal to the exemption for married taxpayers supporting a spouse not in the labour force. It was almost five times larger than the Children's Tax Exemption and could be seen as providing horizontal equity between single-parent and two-parent families at the same earnings level. The equivalent-to-married exemption was a regressive social program, delivering its largest benefits to the well off, although in fact relatively few single parents had an income high enough to garner the maximum income tax savings from the program.

The child-care expense deduction provided an income tax deduction of up to $2,000 for each child aged 14 or under for whom receipts for child-care expenses were available. It went to the lower-income parent and was intended to provide a tax break to help ease the child-care costs of parents in the paid labour force, or taking training courses. The child-care expense deduction paid its largest benefits to high-income tax-filers and excluded the poorest families below the taxpaying threshold.

This multi-layered income security system paid out a substantial sum—$4 billion in 1984, or $5.7 billion in after-inflation 1993 dollars—and (through family allowances) served all 3.6 million Canadian families with dependent children. Nonetheless, social policy groups had long faulted the child benefits system for being inequitable, complex and inadequate.

The Liberals' child benefits system distributed its benefits in an irrational, inconsistent and unfair fashion. Family allowances and the refundable child tax credit were progressive programs that paid their largest benefits to low-income families, but the Children's Tax Exemption, equivalent-to-married exemption and child-care expense deduction were regressive programs that excluded poor families and benefited the affluent most. As a result, the pattern of child benefits bore no sensible relationship to income. This is illustrated in Figure 12.1, which shows benefits in 1984 for two-earner couples with two children (all figures are expressed in constant 1993 dollars). A system which paid $2,508 in child benefits to a $120,000 income family, yet only $2,073 ($435 less) to the poorest families struggling to get by on welfare, clearly gave more weight to the parental recognition/horizontal equity needs of affluent families than to the goal of fighting poverty.

Thus, the old child benefits system performed poorly in terms of its ability to meet the objective of vertical equity, which dictates that the amount of benefit be inversely related to the amount of income. In addition, because four of its five programs were based on individual income, the old system also imperfectly met its horizontal equity objective. Families with equal incomes ended up with different total benefits depending on the proportion of their income contributed by each of the two parents. For instance, a one-earner couple got larger income tax savings from the Children's Tax Exemption than a two-earner couple with the same income, because the parent in the one-earner family was in a higher marginal tax bracket. Only the refundable child tax credit avoided this problem because it was based on family income and so treated all families with the same income equally, no matter what proportion of that income came from each parent. Due to the profusion of programs with different rules, most families had little notion of how much they should get or, for that matter, even what they did get.

The old child benefits system also packed a pretty feeble anti-poverty punch. The maximum payment for poor families from family allowances and the refundable child tax credit totalled $1,036 per child (in 1993 dollars). Welcome as this money was, it could only close a small part of the poverty gap; low-income families with children fell, on average, $8,730 below the poverty line in 1984 even with their child benefits.[1] Nor did child benefits come close to offsetting the cost of raising a child, estimated at $5,000 to $6,000 per year.[2]

Another problem with the old child benefits system, which few of its critics recognized, was the potential conflict between its anti-poverty and parental recognition objectives. With existing resources, it is simply not possible to increase substantially the benefits for low-income families and maintain the same level of benefits for middle- and high-income families. This conflict was to loom larger as the fiscally strapped 1980s wore on and "new" money for social program improvements became increasingly scarce.

FROM 1985 TO 1992: "HONEY, I SHRUNK THE KIDS' BENEFITS"

Policy Proposed

Canada's oft-criticized child benefits system was the subject of the Conservatives' first dip in the treacherous waters of social policy reform. The outcome of that exercise surprised everyone but the Finance Minister.

Jake Epp, the Mulroney government's first minister of National Health and Welfare, released a *Consultation Paper on Child and Elderly Benefits* in January 1985. Nicknamed the "Blue Paper" for the colour of its cover—not for its political pedigree which, in fact, was more Tory red than true blue—the document affirmed three guiding principles for reform: "1) The concept of universality is a keystone of our social safety net. Its integrity must not and will not be called into question. 2) The concept of a means test to determine eligibility for selective benefit programs is not appropriate. Eligibility for these programs, such as the child tax credit and the Guaranteed Income Supplement, will continue to be determined on the basis of taxable income. 3) Any savings which may result from program changes will not be applied to a reduction of the deficit."[3] The first and third of these precepts were to fall at the hands of Finance Minister Michael Wilson. The second principle survived intact, although whoever edited the Blue Paper apparently did not know that the refundable child tax credit and Guaranteed Income Supplement do not use taxable income to determine eligibility.

The Blue Paper acknowledged one of the critics' key complaints—the irrational distribution of child benefits resulting from the incompatible mix of progressive and regressive programs—and agreed that the system must continue to rest on a solid foundation of universal family allowances. The possibility of a "special surtax" on the family allowances of high-income families was mentioned, but the income tax exemptions and deductions were seen as "the most regressive components of the existing system and are, therefore, those deserving most careful scrutiny"; in fact, a surtax did not even figure in the paper's policy options. Any changes to the system "should improve benefits for those most in need."[4]

The Blue Paper proffered two models for the reform of Canada's child benefits system. The "consultation option" would retain family allowances in their current form, eliminate the Children's Tax Exemption and re-deploy the resulting savings to increase the refundable child tax credit, although with a lower income threshold for maximum benefits. The "alternative option" would reduce both family allowances and the Children's Tax Exemption, and raise the refundable child tax credit. Conspicuous by its absence, in retrospect, was any mention of fiddling with the inflation protection afforded child benefits by their annual indexation to the cost of living.

The consultation option would achieve a more progressive child benefits system by abolishing the Children's Tax Exemption, but only low-income families would come out ahead; the majority of families, including many modest-income households, would lose benefits. The alternative option would produce a less redistributive, less progressive and, hence, politically safer child benefits reform. Low-income families would gain a modest increase in their annual child benefits; and most middle-income families would see little change in their benefits. High-income families would lose almost as much under the alternative option as under the consultation option, although they might well have preferred a smaller family allowance and Children's Tax Exemption to losing the latter altogether.

Children's advocates and social policy groups welcomed the public review of child benefits and agreed with the Blue Paper's criticisms of the existing child benefits system, but they found fault with the Government's two suggested options and put forward their own suggestions to create a more progressive child benefits system. The Social Policy Reform Group, a coalition of six national social policy and women's organizations, urged the Government to leave family allowances as is; eliminate the Children's Tax Exemption and redirect the savings to boost the refundable child tax credit; and convert the child-care expense deduction and equivalent-to-married exemption to credits. Their proposals would require no increase in the child benefits budget, so long as Ottawa managed to secure the provinces' agreement to leave their financial windfall (from abolishing the Children's Tax Exemption) in the federal child benefits system.[5]

The Government referred the Blue Paper to the House of Commons Standing Committee on Health, Welfare and Social Affairs, which held public hearings (19 groups testified and 92 briefs were submitted) and issued a report in April 1985. The report recommended a reform similar to that proposed by the Social Policy Reform Group.[6] But all this sound and fury turned out to signify nothing because the Finance Minister hijacked the process of reform.

Policy Imposed

Finance Minister Wilson's May 1985 budget announced some policy changes which it claimed would "ensure greater assistance to families with low incomes, thus making child benefits more progressive. The universality of family allowances will be pre-served and the tax system will continue to recognize the special needs of families with children."[7] In fact, the Conservatives' first budget undercut their modest, albeit progressive, amendments to child benefits with a momentous and far-reaching change that was to weaken seriously the system over the years. The 1985 budget also launched a new style of public policy change, which I have termed "social policy by stealth," that was to reap the federal treasury uncounted and unaccounted-for billions in reduced social expenditures and increased income tax revenues in the years to come.[8]

The 1985 budget announced a phased reduction in the Children's Tax Exemption from $710 per child in 1986 to $470 by 1988 and reduced to an amount equal to the family allowances from 1989 on. The refundable child tax credit was raised from $384 per child in 1985 to reach $549 in 1988, while its threshold was lowered from $26,330 to $23,500 in 1986.[9] These changes were significant but not unexpected, since they were in line with the Blue Paper's alternative option and, in fact, would have at least partly met advocacy groups' proposals for a more progressive child benefits system.

However, the 1985 budget also proclaimed a fundamental shift in social and tax policy because it abandoned full indexation of child benefits and the personal income tax system for partial indexation. Family allowances, the Children's Tax Exemption, the refundable child tax credit (including the income threshold for maximum benefits) and the income tax system's exemptions, deductions, credits and tax brackets would be adjusted each year only by the amount that inflation exceeded 3 percent, rather than by the full amount of inflation.

Partial indexation is deceptive, which is why it is so successful an instrument for cutting social programs. Each year that the inflation rate is more than 3 percent, child benefits increase in nominal terms, but they actually fall in real terms—what seems like more is really less. If inflation is 3 percent or more, child benefits decline in value by 3 percent. Even if inflation is less than 3 percent, benefits still fall in value by the rate of inflation. Partial indexation is also a regressive policy because child benefits make up a larger share of low-income families' limited income.

However, few people—most journalists and politicians included—understand the difference between nominal and real dollars, so the cuts set in place by the 1985 budget proved to be virtually invisible politically. Couple this with the fact that Ottawa raised the refundable child tax credit substantially between 1985 and 1988 (after which its value began to fall to inflation), and it is no wonder that social policy groups were so unsuccessful in their efforts to engender public protests, or even concern, about the damage wrought by partial indexation.

While seemingly small in the first few years, the cuts to benefits proved to be very lucrative over time; partial indexation siphoned about $4 billion on a cumulative basis out of the programs between 1986 and 1992, although the Finance Department understandably chose not to publish such figures. Partial indexation also allows governments to announce occasional "increases" in child benefits which do not make up for past erosion. This, in fact, happened in 1992 when the Tories announced their new Child Tax Benefit, discussed later in this chapter.

The Finance Minister took child benefits reform another step in 1988 as part of his sweeping reform of the personal income tax system. He converted the Children's Tax Exemption to a non-refundable credit of $65 for each of the first two children in a family and (at the suggestion of the House of Commons Standing Committee on Finance and Economic Affairs) $130 per child for the third and each additional child. The $3,740 equivalent-to-married exemption, which single parents can claim for one child only, was converted to a non-refundable credit of $850. He also raised the refundable child tax credit by $35, bringing it to $559 per child for 1988.

Women's and social groups reacted favourably to this part of the Government's tax reform (although certainly not to the whole package, which they found wanting) because they had long advocated the conversion of tax exemptions and deductions to credits.[10] However, they preferred to use the savings from abolishing the Children's Tax Exemption to increase the family allowances or refundable child tax credit instead of creating a non-refundable tax credit which did not help the poorest families, and they criticized the loss of protection from inflation for child benefits and the income tax system. The Health and Welfare Minister's own citizens' advisory body, the National Council of Welfare, concluded that "most families with children will lose child benefits as a result of tax reform" and families with children will fare worse than childless couples, thus weakening the tax/transfer system's ability to meet its objective of horizontal equity.[11]

As part of Ottawa's "national child care strategy," announced in December 1987, the Finance Minister doubled the maximum child-care expense deduction from $2,000 to $4,000 for children six years and younger (it remained at $2,000 for children aged seven to 14) and removed the $8,000 family limit for child-care expense deductions. He also added a $200 supplement to the refundable child tax credit (phased in by $100 in 1988 and the remaining $100 in 1989) for children six and under, bringing the maximum credit in 1988 to $659 for children under seven; the maximum credit for children seven and older was $559.[12] Child-care advocates and social policy groups argued that spending increasingly scarce public funds on bigger tax breaks for the well off and small increments to the refundable child tax credit was irresponsible and wrong-headed. This became all the more so since Ottawa subsequently abandoned its child-care strategy and, thus, saved in excess of $1.4 billion in new spending that had been allotted to increase the supply of child-care spaces.[13]

The 1989 budget introduced a special tax, or "claw-back" as it was popularly termed, on family allowances as well as on Old Age Security, even though four years earlier the Blue Paper had rejected just such a claw-back on the old age pension.[14] The family allowances claw-back was levied through the income tax system on families in which the higher-income parent's net income was $50,000 or more.

Social advocacy groups pointed out that, because the $50,000 threshold for the claw-back was only partially indexed, it would fall steadily every year and would catch more and more middle-income families over time. By the turn of the century, over one million families (or 29 percent of the 3.8 million total) would be hit by the claw-back, receiving less, and in many cases no, family allowances.[15]

The claw-back also discriminated against one-earner families because it was calculated on the basis of the higher-income parent's income, rather than on family income. For instance, a one-earner couple with two children and a net income of $56,000 paid back all of its family allowances to the full claw-back. In contrast, a couple with two children where the parents' earnings totalled $85,000 ($45,000 from one spouse and $40,000 from the other) paid nothing to the claw-back because the higher-income parent's net income was below the $50,000 threshold; instead, the higher-income parent paid only the normal federal and provincial income taxes on the family allowances and, thus, the family kept 60 percent of its gross payments.

The critics' main complaint was that the claw-back effectively converted Canada's two major universal income security programs to income-tested benefits that would exclude increasing numbers of middle-income Canadians. Not only was this a sea change in Canadian social policy that went against strong opinion voiced by seniors', women's and social groups, but the claw-back was imposed through a budget with no advance notice, no consultation and no opportunity for public debate. This policy change-by-fiat has proved to be characteristic of the federal Conservatives' social policy style.

The New Child Tax Benefit: The Bureaucrat's Gem

The 1992 budget and the White Paper that accompanied it announced a "New Integrated Child Tax Benefit" that would cap the Government's reform of the child benefits system. Finance Minister Don Mazankowski lauded his new scheme as "a streamlined, responsive and better-targeted program."[16] The Senior

Assistant Deputy Minister of the Tax Policy Branch pitched it as "such a gem from a bureaucrat's point of view," which is faint praise indeed.[17]

The Child Tax Benefit, as the Government christened the program, replaces family allowances and the refundable and non-refundable child tax credits. The maximum annual payment under the basic component is $1,020 for each child aged seven to 17 in 1993; children aged six and under are eligible for a $213 supplement, bringing their maximum credit to $1,233. Significantly, these benefits are equal to the sum of family allowances and the refundable child tax credit. The third and each additional child in a family get an extra $75, a feature similar to the supplement to the non-refundable child tax credit. The design of the new Child Tax Benefit is familiar. It is nothing more than a larger refundable child tax credit, but delivered every month like family allowances. The new Child Tax Benefit uses the same threshold as the refundable child tax credit ($25,921 for 1993).[18]

The Child Tax Benefit offers one novel feature. In addition to the basic benefits described above, the federal government will pay an American-inspired "earned-income supplement" which it claims will "reinforce the incentives for low-income parents to participate in the work force."[19] The earned-income supplement goes to working poor families with employment earnings of $3,750 or more. Over this earnings threshold, the earned-income supplement phases in at a rate of 8 percent (i.e. $8 for every $100 of additional earnings). This means that the maximum benefit—$500 per family in 1993—begins once family earnings reach $10,000 and will continue until net family income reaches $20,921. Above the $20,921 threshold, the earned-income supplement is reduced by 10 percent of net family income, disappearing when net family income reaches $25,921, which is the same threshold as for the basic credit. The supplement is delivered as part of the monthly Child Tax Benefit.

The new Child Tax Benefit is not the only change to child benefits. While the equivalent-to-married non-refundable credit for single-parent families remains as is (worth a maximum $1,416 in total federal and average provincial income tax savings in 1993), the child-care expense deduction got yet another boost. The maximum deduction increased from $4,000 to $5,000 for each child under age seven and from $2,000 to $3,000 for each child between the ages of seven and 14. The maximum $5,000 deduction saves a tax-filer in the bottom (17 percent) tax bracket $1,318 in combined federal and average provincial income tax; tax savings increase to $2,015 for a tax-filer in the middle (26 percent) tax bracket and to $2,248 for a tax-filer in the top (29 percent) tax bracket.

The new Child Tax Benefit lives up to some of the Government's claims and offers some advantages over the system it replaces. It simplifies and rationalizes the child benefits system to a certain extent. It combines three programs that had different design characteristics (e.g. definition of income, payment frequency) into one program which is based on family, rather than individual, income thus remedying the horizontal inequities we discussed earlier. Eligible families get a substantially larger benefit each month than they did from the old system's mix of (relatively small) monthly family allowances, annual or semi-annual refundable child tax credits and annual non-refundable child tax credits. This change in payment schedule ends the lamentable practice whereby some poor families paid high rates of interest to tax discounters in order to get their refundable child tax credit earlier than it was mailed out to them. The Government also announced that, in calculating the Child Tax Benefit, it will treat common-law couples the same as married couples. This change puts a stop to the unfair practice whereby some common-law couples pretend they are single parents in order to claim the equivalent-to-married tax credit. The earned-income supplement represents a small but significant step towards an income supplementation program for the working poor, which is a reform long advocated by many social policy organizations.

However, social policy organizations and children's advocates unanimously attacked the child benefit proposals as flawed and disappointing on several grounds. Their major criticisms concerned the new scheme's lack of protection from inflation, weak impact on family poverty, differential treatment of welfare and unemployed poor families, and lack of responsiveness to changes in family income, as well as its formal abolition of universal child benefits.

Like the system it replaces, the Child Tax Benefit is partially indexed, to inflation over 3 percent, which means that both its benefits and eligibility thresholds will fall steadily in real terms over time. Fewer and fewer low-income families will qualify for the maximum credit; more and more middle-income families will fail to qualify at all and the value of the benefits for those who do receive them will erode. The statistician Richard Shillington likened partial indexation to "putting child benefits on an escalator that is going down."[20] The Caledon Institute of Social Policy labelled partial indexation the "Achilles' heel of child benefits" and estimated that some $4 billion will be siphoned from the Child Tax Benefit between 1993 and the turn of the century, which certainly puts a different light on the Government's much-ballyhooed claim that it is infusing an additional $2.1 billion into the new system over its first five years.[21]

The critics also argued that the new child benefits system will do virtually nothing to improve the lot of low-income families. Poor families on welfare or unemployment insurance with one or two children (most families fall in this size category) receive not a penny more from the new Child Tax Benefit than they got from the combination of family allowances and the refundable child tax credit; larger families get a mere $75 more in 1993 for the third and each additional child. Working poor families are, at most, $500 ahead. Their child benefits are increased from $1,233 to $1,723 for a child under seven and from $1,020 to $1,520 for a child aged seven to 17—far below the estimated $5,000 cost of raising a nine-year-old—for a couple with income of just $15,000.[22]

Social, women's and labour groups assailed the Government for raising the ugly old head of the invidious distinction between the deserving and undeserving poor. They contend that the new Child Tax Benefit treats working poor families with children as deserving of extra assistance through the earned-income supplement and all other low-income Canadians as the undeserving poor. While by no means objecting to assistance to the working poor, the critics argue that the child benefits system is not the best vehicle for such aid, especially through a flawed program like the new Child Tax Benefit. Dick Martin of the Canadian Labour Congress stated that a "concept that sets aside the needs of one group of poor children based on the work force status of their parents is misguided, offensive and discriminatory."[23] Andy Mitchell of the Social Planning Council of Metropolitan Toronto observed that the earned-income supplement "wouldn't even cover the cost of a metro pass that would allow someone to get to work."[24] Several witnesses reminded the Legislative Committee on Bill C-80, the legislation creating the new benefits system, of the Government's failure to follow through on its commitment to increase the supply of child-care spaces—a policy failure that dwarfs the earned-income supplement.

The Child Tax Benefit cannot respond quickly to changes in income because there is a considerable lag between the period used to calculate eligibility for the program (earnings and income during the previous taxation year) and the period when benefits are paid (beginning in July of the current year). Families that experience a substantial rise or fall in their income during the course of one year are in for a surprise when their child benefits catch up and either decrease or increase substantially in July of the following year (by which time their income may even have changed again). Families will have little or no idea as to their entitlement and cannot readily ascertain if they have received what they are due. Indeed, the Child Tax Benefit is so complex that the Government will have to calculate families' benefits for them.

Some critics also pointed out that the new child benefits system not only still contains programs with quite different designs and distributional consequences, but has further exacerbated the problem. The Child Tax Benefit is a progressive program based on family income. Unfortunately, the Government not only kept the child-care expense deduction—a regressive program based on individual income—but also boosted it for a second time. In fact, some families with high incomes actually get a larger total benefit from the new system because their tax savings from the enriched child-care expense deduction more than make up for their lost non-refundable child tax credit.

What might appear to be the most significant change of all— replacing universal family allowances with an income-tested Child Tax Benefit—in fact was something of an anti-climax. The universal foundation of Canada's child benefits system already had begun to crumble with the 1989 budget's imposition of the claw-back; by 1991, when the claw-back was fully phased in, it had transformed Family Allowances from a universal to a selective program—even though the Government still pretended to uphold the supposedly sacred principle by continuing to mail out monthly cheques to all families with children. In their 1992 budget and White Paper, the Conservatives admitted openly that they had abandoned universal child benefits. However, that did not prevent Al Johnson, a prominent Conservative Member of Parliament in the so-called "family caucus," from refuting the social policy critics by concocting a wondrous new definition of universality drawn from the Alice in Wonderland school of social policy:

> One of the things that surprises me most about the criticism of this legislation is the accusation that it does away with universality, and I suppose in a limited type of definition it does do that. But I think the most powerful aspect of this legislation is the fact that for the first time we are delivering a social benefit according to income through the tax system and it is universally available to everyone.[25]

Not only has the tax system been used to deliver income-tested child benefits since 1918, but the notion that a social program that is restricted to families with incomes below a certain level can, at the same time, be deemed to be "universally available" defies logic and common sense.

Several witnesses appearing before the Legislative Committee on Bill C-80 raised a number of arguments made over the years in favour of universal family allowances. Universal child benefits, their supporters contend, recognize the contribution to society that all parents make by raising children. By delivering benefits to families at all income levels, universal programs foster broad public support for social programs in general, including those targeted to the poor. If middle-class Canadians perceive that they pay taxes for a welfare state that excludes them, they might be unwilling to support programs for the poor. Universal social programs are claimed to transcend social and economic barriers and help develop social solidarity. Micheline Lavoie, of the Quebec-based Reseau d'action et d'information pour les femmes, said that for an abused woman "family allowance is a life-saving buoy.... At least she will have the money for a taxi in which to escape with her children in case of assault, and she will be able to cover necessary minimum expenses."[26] The latter exemplified the "poor wives with rich husbands" argument of some feminists who argue that universal family allowances provide income directly to (usually) the mother who, in some cases, has no access to her spouse's income, even if he is affluent. Another advantage claimed of universal social programs like Family Allowances is that they are the simplest benefits to administer.

The Consultative Process: Ignoring Witnesses for the Social Policy Side

During its first term, the Mulroney government consulted both publicly and privately with social policy, women's and seniors' groups, but it ignored and rejected virtually everything they had to say on social policy. The Social Policy Reform Group coalition met regularly with the Finance Minister as part of the annual budgetary consultation process and occasionally with the Minister of Health and Welfare. Although the consultative process launched by the 1985 Blue Paper did not attract the broad spectrum of labour, business organizations, interest groups and provincial governments the paper called for (most of those that made representation were from the social policy sector), the Standing Committee on Health, Welfare and Social Affairs received 92 briefs. Most of the major social policy and women's groups submitted briefs, as did the Canadian Labour Congress, the United Church of Canada, the federal New Democratic Party, the Canadian Chamber of Commerce and two local chambers, the Life Underwriters Association and the Manitoba government. Much the same cast of characters took part in the House of Commons committee on Bill C-70, the legislation which partially indexed family allowances, and a wider range of organizations (including several Quebec groups) testified during the Senate Committee on Social Affairs' hearings on the legislation from December 1985 to March 1986.[27]

In the years that followed, social policy groups periodically and dutifully trotted up to Parliament Hill to voice their concerns to House of Commons and Senate committees which were considering child benefits and other social programs. As time went by, they came to view the consultative process as largely a waste of time and effort, even though most still take part because they feel they have a duty to make their views known to parliamentarians and the public.

Most of the social policy, women's and other groups which took part in the consultative process did more than just criticize the Government's changes to child benefits. They also put forward alternative proposals for reform.[28] Naturally, these suggestions differed somewhat in detail, but there was a remarkable degree of consensus on the principles and general design of a stronger, fairer child benefits system. This is perhaps best exemplified by the Social Policy Reform Group's proposal for a universal system that would provide larger benefits to low-income families by eliminating regressive exemptions and deductions, increasing the refundable child tax credit and retaining universal family allowances.

By the time of the 1992 budget and the White Paper on the new Child Tax Benefit, the federal government no longer bothered to keep up the pretence of consultation. The Legislative Committee on Bill C-80 heard only a handful of witnesses, hastily summoned at short notice, and refused to extend the deadline from summer to fall in spite of protests by social policy groups and the Liberal and New Democratic Party members of the Committee. The reason for the Government's haste was made clear when the Minister of Finance appeared before the Committee and urged it to proceed "with some dispatch if we are to have [the Child Tax Benefit] take effect on January 1, 1993."[29] Liberal members boycotted the Committee's final session to protest the Government's decision to cut off hearings after only 12 hours of testimony. And only nine out of some 40 potential witnesses had a chance to appear before the Senate Committee on Social Affairs when it examined the legislation.

One of the funniest and most telling moments in the recent history of Canadian social policy occurred on June 15, 1992, the second day of the Legislative Committee's hearings on the Child Tax Benefit legislation. A Conservative member asked the Chairperson, "Are we dealing with this mainly as a finance bill, a tax issue, or are we getting into social policy and planning?" On being assured by the Chairperson that, indeed, the Committee was looking at the legislation from the viewpoint of tax policy and not social policy, the Member of Parliament in question then said, "I have to ask you if some of these particular witnesses are not more on the social policy side. Is this something we agreed to at our last meeting?"[30]

GAUGING THE CHANGES TO CHILD BENEFITS

To assess the Conservatives' many changes to child benefits and the tax system, I analyzed their effects over a fairly long period, comparing child benefits in 1984 (the last year of the old system under the Liberals) with benefits in 1993 (the first year of the Tories' new Child Tax Benefit) and the year 2000 (when the no-longer new system would be worn down by seven years of inflation). I also examined changes in disposable income to see how childless couples fared compared with couples with children. The analysis assumes that both spouses work in the paid labour force, families with children have one child under and one child over age seven, and middle and high-income families claim a child-care expense deduction for the younger child. A series of graphs is used to illustrate the results of the analysis.[31]

Despite all the Government's changes and rhetoric about fairness, the new child benefits system in 1993 is not progressive overall. The new system under the Conservatives is, at best, only less regressive than the old one under the Liberals and surely just as irrational.

Figure 12.2 shows that families with incomes over $100,000 enjoy larger child benefits under the new system in 1993 than upper-middle income families earning between $70,000 and $90,000 (the $80,000 and $90,000 families get the least of all families shown). While modest-income families ($30,000 in our example) receive the biggest total child benefit in 1993—in 1984 this distinction belonged to the middle-income $50,000 families as seen in Figure 12.1—the new system still allocates less to welfare and working poor families than to lower-middle income families earning in the $30,000 to $40,000 range. Working poor families, earning between $10,000 and $20,000 in our example, get $500 more in child benefits than the welfare poor. Incredibly, families earning $100,000 or more get almost as much in child benefits ($2,015) as welfare families ($2,253).

While the "winners" under the new child benefits system in 1993 are families with modest incomes and below, and the "losers" are those with middle incomes and above, there is no rational or systematic pattern within each of the two groups. The biggest gainers are families earning $10,000 (not the poorest) and the biggest losers are those earning $90,000 (not the best off).

Figure 12.4 shows that families earning $45,000 or less receive about the same or (in most cases) more child benefits in 1993 than they did in 1984, ranging from virtually no change for the $45,000 and $25,000 families to a sizeable 28 percent increase for the $10,000 family. The poorest families—those on welfare—are only marginally better off in 1993 than they were in 1984, with $180 or 9 percent more in child benefits. Families earning $50,000 and up receive smaller child benefits in 1993 than in 1984, the losses ranging from 12 percent for those earning $50,000 to 43 percent for families earning $90,000.

The picture darkens considerably when we factor into account the corrosive effects of seven years of inflation on the new child benefits system. Almost all families will lose benefits between 1993 and 2000. The losses over this period range from 17 percent for welfare families and those earning $10,000 and $15,000 to 43 percent for families earning $60,000. The exceptions in our example are the $80,000 and $90,000 families, which will get a larger child benefit in 2000 than in 1993 ($1,608 in 2000 compared with $1,318 in 1993). This is because, ironically, partial indexation of the income tax system pushes the low-income parent into a higher tax bracket and so increases the value of the child-care expense deduction, the sole child benefit potentially available to high-income families.

The contrast between the child benefits system as it was in 1984 and as it will be in 2000 is even more stark. Almost all families will receive substantially smaller child benefits in 2000 than in 1984. Figure 12.5 presents the percentage change in child benefits between 1984 and 2000, with losses ranging (erratically, by earnings) to as much as 54 percent for those earning $60,000. Working poor families earning in the $10,000 to $15,000 range will get slightly more (5 to 6 percent) in 2000 than in 1984, but welfare families will get 10 percent less and working poor families earning $20,000 will lose a hefty 20 percent of their child benefit.

Child benefits contribute only a relatively small part of most families' income. What they get from the Government in child benefits is offset to a varying extent by what they pay in taxes. The tax system, like child benefits, has seen considerable change under the Tories, so it is important also to chart changes over time in disposable income, i.e. earnings plus child benefits and refundable GST credits minus federal and provincial income taxes and payroll taxes (unemployment insurance premiums and Canada Pension Plan contributions). In order to gauge the tax/transfer system's achievement of the horizontal equity objective, I compared families with children and families without children. Figure 12.6 shows changes in disposable income for two-earner couples with two children (the black bars) and for childless two-earner couples (the light bars).

All but the lowest-paid ($10,000) families will experience a significant drop in their disposable income from 1984 to 2000. Families with children in the lower-middle to middle-income range ($25,000 to $60,000) will suffer the largest loss in disposable income—between 9 and 10 percent. Those in the highest earnings group shown on the graph ($120,000) will see an 8 percent drop in their disposable income—less than the loss for families in the $20,000 to $110,000 range.

The majority of families with children will undergo a larger loss in disposable income from 1984 to 2000 than will childless couples with the same earnings; the only exception is the poorest families earning $10,000 and $15,000. This is dramatic evidence of the significant weakening of the horizontal equity objective of the federal tax/transfer system resulting from changes in child benefits and the partial indexation of GST credits. Moreover, the losses hit low-income families as well as the middle class and the well off.

CHILD BENEFITS REFORM: A SUMMARY

The Liberals willed the Conservatives a flawed collection of child benefit programs. While the Tories made some positive changes to the child benefits system, on balance their reforms have, in the immortal words of movie mogul Sam Goldwyn, "improved it worse."

Social policy under the Conservatives shows a distinctive pattern of progressive changes being undermined by regressive changes, which refutes their claims that they have created a simpler, fairer and more effective system of child benefits. The new system remains complex, inequitable and inadequate.

By far the most damaging change was the partial indexation of child benefit rates and thresholds, which is eroding the value of benefits and reducing both the number of low-income families eligible for maximum payments and the number of middle-income families eligible for partial payments. Fewer and fewer families will get less and less from the child benefits system as time goes by. Even with the infusion of an additional $500 million, the budget for the new Child Tax Benefit in 1993—$4.9 billion—is still $800 million short of what the Liberals spent on Family Allowances, the Children's Tax Exemption and the refundable child tax credit back in 1984.

These changes have, on balance, weakened the child benefits system's capacity to achieve all of its objectives. The parental recognition/horizontal equity objective is virtually extinct since high-income families no longer receive child benefits—except those that can claim the child-care expense deduction. Over time, families at all income levels will receive less and less recognition for their child-rearing contributions, as partial indexation eats away at their benefits. The child benefits system's anti-poverty power enjoyed a temporary boost from improvements to the refundable child tax credit during the Tories' first term and from the new Child Tax Benefit's earned-income supplement. However, partial indexation weakened the refundable child tax credit after its increases were phased in and will erode the new Child Tax Benefit in the same insidious manner.

THE POLITICS OF STEALTH

I have characterized the Tory style of public policy making as "policy by stealth" in order to dramatize its intent and effect:

> It relies heavily on technical amendments to taxes and transfers that are as difficult to explain as they are to understand and thus largely escape media scrutiny and public attention. It camouflages regressive changes in the rhetoric of equity in an attempt to convince Canadians that tax increases are tax cuts and that benefit cuts are benefit increases. By further complicating an already complex labyrinth of taxes and social programs, the stealth style of policy-making confuses the electorate and so insulates itself from criticism.[32]

Child benefits are a prime illustration of the successful practice of the politics of stealth, but they are merely one of several policy areas so affected. The Minister of Finance, who took decisive command over social policy under the Conservatives, played the politics of stealth with equal effect in other programs including Old Age Security; federal fiscal transfers to the provinces for health, post-secondary education, welfare and social services; and the income tax system and GST credits.[33] (The previous chapter by Jim Rice and Michael Prince also applies the concept of stealth to Tory social policy generally.) The politics of stealth has enabled the federal government to cut billions of dollars in social spending with virtually no political cost.

The politics of stealth has also crippled the public debate over social policy in this country. The main reason the Conservatives got away with their cuts to social programs and hidden income tax and GST increases is that most Canadians have no idea what has happened to them because the policy changes are so arcane and technical. This also makes the public more susceptible to government propaganda, which has become more bold and blatant in recent years. The same applies to journalists, politicians and pundits who, with a few fortunate exceptions, have little understanding of even the most basic workings of social programs, let alone the subtleties of the machinations of stealth.

The opposition parties joined the social policy groups in opposing the Tories' changes, but a majority government does not need or want to pay its opponents much mind, especially when it is scrambling to gear up for a new delivery system for child benefits, as was the case after the 1992 budget and White Paper. Most of the Tories' social policy changes were propounded, not in the two election campaigns or in public discussion papers where they would be subject to scrutiny and debate, but rather in successive budgets as part of a long list of policy measures that were imposed largely without amendment.

Social policy groups were vocal and analytically sophisticated in their criticisms, but they were ineffective in communicating their concerns to the media and the public, and powerless to alter the course of social policy under the Tories. They cast no fear into a government which believed (with good reason) that social advocates have little or no capacity to mobilize significant numbers of voters.

The politics of stealth has stifled the public debate over social programs called for by the Conservatives' 1984 manifesto,

A New Direction for Canada: An Agenda for Economic Renewal.
Such a debate is all the more necessary in the 1990s when social
policy seems to be wandering in the desert. There are tough and
controversial issues that neither governments nor social policy and
women's groups have faced squarely. One obvious issue is
universality, which the federal government killed off in child and
elderly benefits without any public discussion to speak of, let alone
any mandate from the voters. There are credible arguments both
for and against universal child benefits which should have been
debated openly. Perhaps the case will be reopened by a future
government, though I would not count on it.

A far more important issue in my view is the competition
between the anti-poverty and parental recognition/horizontal
equity objectives of the child benefits system. Larger child benefits
for low-income families cannot possibly eliminate child poverty
on their own, but they can significantly reduce the depth and extent
of poverty. Unfortunately, boosting benefits for poor families
means reducing benefits for middle-income families and so poses
thorny equity and political problems, particularly during these
times of scarce resources. It is possible to design targeted-but-
universal options which manage to improve significantly benefits
for the poor and restore a universal base to the system. Ironically,
however, middle-income families lose benefits while high-income
families gain from this approach.[34] Without a massive infusion of
new funds, which seems highly unlikely these days, it is simply not
possible to strengthen substantially the child benefits system's
anti-poverty capacity and still maintain the same level of benefits
for the middle-income majority of families.

The politics of stealth should be replaced by informed, open
public discourse on the present and future course of social policy
in this country. That debate should begin with a clear understanding of the substance, process and implications of the profound
changes that have been made since 1985 to child benefits, old age
pensions, unemployment insurance, social transfers to the provinces and the tax system. It should tackle tough but critical issues
involving the purposes, scope, potential and limits of social policy
in an economy and society that would be barely recognizable to the
founders of the Canadian welfare state.

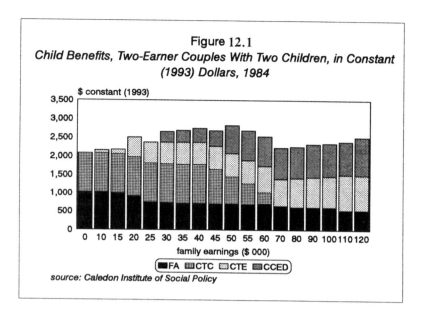

Figure 12.1
Child Benefits, Two-Earner Couples With Two Children, in Constant (1993) Dollars, 1984

source: Caledon Institute of Social Policy

FA = family allowance　　　　　*CTC = child tax credit*
CTE = children's tax exemption　　*CCED = child-care expense deduction*

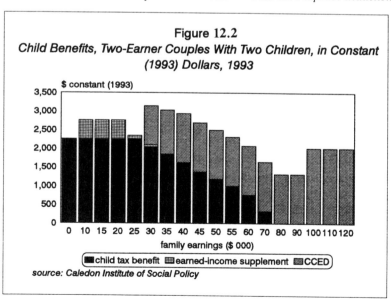

Figure 12.2
Child Benefits, Two-Earner Couples With Two Children, in Constant (1993) Dollars, 1993

source: Caledon Institute of Social Policy

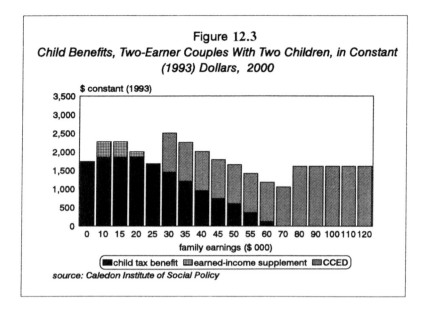

Figure 12.3
Child Benefits, Two-Earner Couples With Two Children, in Constant (1993) Dollars, 2000

source: Caledon Institute of Social Policy

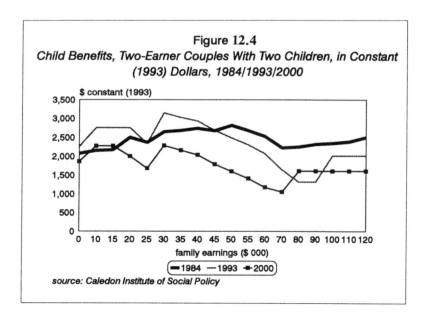

Figure 12.4
Child Benefits, Two-Earner Couples With Two Children, in Constant (1993) Dollars, 1984/1993/2000

source: Caledon Institute of Social Policy

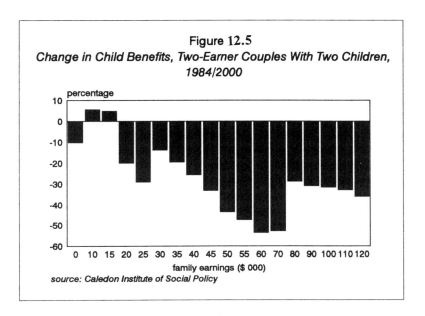

Figure 12.5

Change in Child Benefits, Two-Earner Couples With Two Children, 1984/2000

source: Caledon Institute of Social Policy

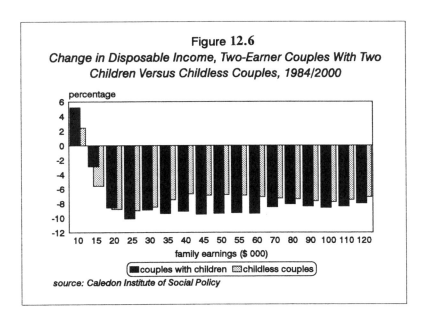

Figure 12.6

Change in Disposable Income, Two-Earner Couples With Two Children Versus Childless Couples, 1984/2000

source: Caledon Institute of Social Policy

NOTES

1   Statistics Canada, *LICO/LIM Income Deficiency/Surplus Tables, 1980-1990* (Ottawa, May 1992), Table 3. I converted the 1984 figure to 1993 constant dollars.

2   See Health and Welfare Canada, *The Basic Cost of Raising a Child in Canada in 1982* (Ottawa: Program Evaluation Directorate, July 1985), p. 8. I used the results for a two-child family and converted them to constant 1993 dollars.

3   Jake Epp, *Child and Elderly Benefits Consultation Paper* (Ottawa: Government of Canada, January 1985), pp. 5-6.

4   Ibid., p. 9.

5   Social Policy Reform Group, *Child Benefit Reform* (Ottawa, March 1985). The group's members were the Canadian Advisory Council on the Status of Women, the Canadian Association of Social Workers, the Canadian Council on Social Development, the National Action Committee on the Status of Women, the National Anti-Poverty Organization and the National Council of Welfare. See also National Council of Welfare, *Opportunity for Reform* (Ottawa: Supply and Services Canada, March 1985).

6   House of Commons, Standing Committee on Health, Welfare and Social Affairs, *Report on Child and Elderly Benefits* (Ottawa, April 1985), pp. 22-25.

7   Michael Wilson, *Securing Economic Renewal: Budget Papers* (Ottawa: Department of Finance, May 23, 1985), p. 42.

8   Grattan Gray (a pseudonym for Ken Battle), "Social Policy by Stealth," *Policy Options*, 11, 2 (1990).

9   Wilson, *Securing Economic Renewal* (May 23, 1985), pp. 42-45.

10   For a fuller account of child tax benefit changes from 1985 through 1989, see Allan Moscovitch, "Slowing the Steamroller: The Federal Conservatives, the Social Sector and Child Benefits

Reform" in Katherine A. Graham, (ed.), *How Ottawa Spends 1990-91: Tracking the Second Agenda* (Ottawa: Carleton University Press, 1990). See also Ken Battle, "Clawback: The Demise of Universality in the Canadian Welfare State" in Ian Taylor, (ed.), *The Social Effects of Free Market Policies* (New York: Harvester Wheatsheaf, 1990).

11   National Council of Welfare, *Testing Tax Reform* (Ottawa: Supply and Services Canada, September 1987), p. 14.

12   Michael Wilson, *Securing Economic Renewal: Budget Papers* (Ottawa: Department of Finance, February 10, 1988), p. 9.

13   Child care was another chapter in the politics of stealth. See Susan Phillips' insightful study, "Rock-a-Bye Brian: The National Child Care Strategy" in Katherine A. Graham, (ed.),*How Ottawa Spends 1989-90: The Buck Stops Where?* (Ottawa: Carleton University Press, 1989), pp. 165-208.

14   The Blue Paper argues that a claw-back on Old Age Security "would seriously disrupt our retirement income system, both for current pensioners and those now planning for retirement, and would unduly penalize those most affected by reason of retirement income resulting from private savings in earlier years." See Epp, *Child and Elderly Benefits*, p. 9.

15   National Council of Welfare, *The 1989 Budget and Social Policy* (Ottawa: Supply and Services Canada, September 1989), p. 10.

16   Donald Mazankowski, testimony to the Legislative Committee on Bill C-80, *Proceedings*, June 15, 1992.

17   Ian Bennett, testimony to the Committee, *Proceedings*, June 15, 1992, p. 29.

18   The Child Tax Benefit has two reduction rates (2.5 percent for families with one child, 5 percent for families with two or more children) rather than the refundable child tax credit's single 5 percent rate.

19   Benoît Bouchard, *The Child Tax Benefit: A White Paper on Canada's New Integrated Child Tax Benefit* (Ottawa: Government of Canada, 1992), p. 9.

20   Richard Shillington, testimony to the Committee, *Proceedings*, July 16, 1992, p. 13.

21   Ken Battle, testimony to the Committee, *Proceedings*, June 16, 1992, p. 10.

22   Shelley Phipps, testimony to the Committee, *Proceedings*, June 23, 1992, p. 8.

23   Dick Martin, testimony to the Committee, *Proceedings*, July 14, 1992, p. 63.

24   Andy Mitchell, testimony to the committee, *Proceedings*, June 23, 1992, p. 31.

25   Al Johnson, testimony to the Committee, *Proceedings*, June 15, 1992, p. 32.

26   Micheline Lavoie, testimony to the Committee, *Proceedings*, July 16, 1992, p. 46.

27   Moscovitch, "Slowing the Steamroller," pp. 178-83.

28   Other interesting ideas were put forward by the Child Poverty Action Group, which advocated a "universal child income credit" generous enough to cover the cost of raising a child; see Brigitte Kitchen, *A Fair Chance for Children* (Toronto: Child Poverty Action Group, 1986), p. 13. The Ontario Social Assistance Review Committee suggested a joint federal-provincial child benefit radically targeted to poor families; see *Transitions* (Toronto: Queen's Printer for Ontario, 1988), pp. 115-18. The Senate Committee on Social Affairs developed both universal and selective options that would substantially boost child benefits to low-income families; see *Children in Poverty: Toward a New Future* (Ottawa: Supply and Services Canada, 1991), pp. 27-31

and Appendix II. See also Moscovitch's summary of various alternative proposals in "Slowing the Steamroller," pp. 196-98.

29   Mazankowski, *Proceedings*, June 15, 1992, pp. 18-19.

30   Barbara Sparrow, testimony to the Committee, *Proceedings*, June 15, 1992, p. 39.

31   My analysis also looked at one-earner couples with and without children. Because they cannot claim a child-care expense deduction since one parent works in the home, the child benefits system in 1984 was more rational for one-earner than for two-earner couples, and, in 1993, becomes entirely income-tested and more progressive than it is for two-earner couples (although working poor families earning between $10,000 and $25,000 get the largest child benefits because they qualify for the earned-income supplement). However, as with two-earner couples, most one-earner couples will lose child benefits and disposable income between 1984 and 2000, and families with children generally will lose more disposable income than childless couples.

32   See Gray, "Social Policy by Stealth," p. 17. The thesis of policy by stealth is not meant to suggest that the Tories are the first—or will be the last—government to make changes to public policy through technical means or to make changes without first putting them to the test of the voter or engaging in a genuine process of public consultation and debate. I am grateful to Bruce Doern for bringing this to my attention. However, I would argue that the Tories have made much more use of such methods than previous governments and have done so in a deliberate, calculated manner that defines their style.

33   See ibid.; also Allan Maslove, "Reconstructing Fiscal Federalism" in Frances Abele, (ed.), *How Ottawa Spends 1992-93: The Politics of Competitiveness,* (Ottawa: Carleton University Press, 1992); National Council of Welfare, *Funding Health and Higher Education: Danger Looming* (Ottawa: Supply and Services Canada, Spring 1991); National Council of Welfare, *The Canada Assistance Plan: No Time for Cuts* (Ottawa: Supply and Services Canada, Winter 1991).

34   See, for example, the various "targeted" and "mixed" child
      benefit options which Richard Shillington and I prepared for the
      Senate Standing Committee on Social Affairs, *Children in Pov-
      erty: Toward a New Future* (Ottawa: Supply and Services Canada,
      1991), pp. 27-31 and Appendix II. I explored updated versions of
      these options as well as less sharply targeted models and compared
      them with the new child tax benefit; all my options produced
      significant improvements in child benefits for low-income fami-
      lies, though with varying degrees of loss for middle-income
      families.

CHAPTER 13

Accountability, Back-to-Basics and Choice: An ABC for Educational Change?

Saul Schwartz

Résumé : Le besoin d'aligner les études primaires et secondaires sur les exigences économiques apparentes est l'un des arguments qui a été invoqué le plus souvent pour justifier la nécessité d'une réforme du système scolaire. Les propositions formulées en vue d'opérer cet alignement sont généralement fondées sur trois principes simples de réforme scolaire : l'obligation de rendre compte, le retour aux principes fondamentaux et le choix. Cette théorie comporte deux écueils. D'une part, tous ne conviennent pas que le but premier de l'instruction est de préparer les enfants au travail. D'autre part, si les réformes sont opérées de manière simpliste, il pourrait fort bien arriver que les élèves n'acquièrent pas les compétences qui, selon les experts, augmenteront la «compétitivité» nationale. Le gouvernement fédéral s'est engagé dans la foulée de «l'instruction pour la compétitivité». Malheureusement, son influence à ce chapitre est limitée puisque l'entière responsabilité des régimes scolaires repose sur les provinces.

Abstract: One persistent element in the press for educational reform has been the call to align elementary and secondary education more closely with the perceived needs of the economy. Proposals to achieve that realignment usually involve a simple ABC of educational reform—accountability, back-to-basics and choice. There are two problems with that ABC. First, not everyone believes that the primary function of education is to prepare children to be workers. Second, if the reforms are implemented in a simplistic fashion, they may actually make it less likely that students will obtain the skills that advocates assert will promote "competitiveness." The federal government has put its weight behind "education for competitiveness." Unfortunately, the Government cannot bring very much weight to bear since responsibility for education lies entirely with the provinces.

Real problems plague Canadian elementary and secondary schools. Despite unceasing advice from adults about the need for more education, 28 percent of boys and 19 percent of girls drop out of high school before graduating.[1] A large proportion of Canadians are unable to read, or work with numbers, well enough to undertake relatively common tasks.[2]

Over the past three years, the federal government has worked hard to convince Canadians that education is an issue of national concern. Speaking to a general meeting of the Progressive Conservative Party in late August 1989, Prime Minister Brian Mulroney promised to make education a central item on his government's agenda. Citing the rates of functional illiteracy and the low Canadian ranking on international science tests, Mulroney said that the Canadian education system was "shortchanging many Canadians and imposing a severe burden on our national competitiveness."[3]

As William Johnson wrote a few days later in *The Gazette*, Mulroney seemed

> for all the world like the federal minister of education. Only trouble is, there is no federal minister of education. Education is a provincial responsibility, and the most jealously guarded of all the provinces prerogatives.[4]

But the Prime Minister proposed no interference with provincial authority to set educational policy. He suggested only that Canada undertake a collective study of its entire education system and the relationship of that system to economic competitiveness.[5] By the end of 1992, the federal part of that collective study had resulted in several documents. The now defunct Economic Council of Canada published *A Lot to Learn*, the "first ever comprehensive examination of the way primary and secondary schools and the training system in Canada prepare young people for employment." The departments of Industry, Science and Technology (ISTC) and Employment and Immigration (EIC) sponsored a series of consultations that are summarized in *Learning Well, Living Well* and in *Inventing Our Future*.[6]

The federal government's interest in education had a very clear source. The Government has often stated its belief in the theory that economic competitiveness depends on a highly educated and well trained labour force.[7] Through its efforts to analyze and publicize the perceived weaknesses of Canadian schools, the federal government has put its weight behind one vision of education—that of education as preparation for future employment—and behind one vision of educational reform—accountability, back-to-basics and choice.[8]

The vision of education as preparation for future employment sees children primarily as future *workers*, whose efficient training will assure their own prosperity and that of Canada. There is, however, a competing vision of children as future *citizens*, whose education should be driven by their individual interests and abilities, rather than by uncertain future labour market conditions.

In practice, the vision of children as future workers implies a set of school reforms that Michael Fullan has labelled "intensification," while the vision of children as future citizens is associated with the set of school reforms known as "restructuring."[9] Where the underlying thrust of intensification has been accountability, back-to-basics and choice, that of restructuring has been the comprehensive reorganization of schooling.

Intensification and restructuring advocates often have different political biases. Supporters of intensification seem to tend towards a kind of "conservative populism," characterized by a distrust of large bureaucracies and a belief in individual responsibility.[10] Supporters of restructuring tend to view government authority (though not necessarily large bureaucracies) as essential to the assurance of equal opportunity. Allowing children to exploit their individual talents and interests is, at least in principle, a central element of restructuring efforts.

In recent years, as most Canadian provinces have tried to rethink and reorganize their elementary and secondary school systems, they have picked their way among the precepts of these two broad strategies.[11] As a result, reforms associated with *both* intensification and restructuring are being implemented at the provincial level. By contrast, the federal government has supported, at least rhetorically, the reforms associated with intensification. For that reason, this chapter critically evaluates those reforms.

The push for intensification has come from parents, employers, taxpayers and the federal government. But parents, taxpayers, employers and government departments do not actually do any teaching. Teachers teach. Realizing the difficulty of directly changing what teachers teach, outside reformers must push for "reform at a distance," a set of indirect changes which they hope will eventually alter what is learned within the walls of the classroom. The three "reforms at a distance" that will be discussed here are the expansion of parents' choice among schools, curricula that place greater emphasis on "basic" skills and the use of testing as a means of holding the education system accountable.

The ABC of intensification—accountability, back-to-basics and choice—suffers from an important drawback. The ideal forms that these reforms might take are not the same as their likely reality. If only oversimplified versions of the reforms can be implemented, there may be unintended side-effects that are worse than the original problem. For example, one of the important trade-offs in educational reform may be between a greater emphasis on reading, writing and arithmetic, and higher drop-out rates.

Criticism of the intensification reforms should not be confused with criticism of their goals. Accountability is favoured by all, including teachers themselves; no large enterprise can function efficiently without monitoring the performance of its employees. All of us hope that all children can graduate from high school, not only with a command of basic skills but also with a command of the "new" basics of problem-solving and critical thinking. And who could object to school choice, if equality of opportunity and social cohesion were guaranteed?

But I believe that the practical implementation of intensification is unlikely to lead to a rapid change for the better in Canadian education. In fact, I believe that it may well lead to change for the worse. Perhaps the most likely scenario, however, is that (like the many reforms that have gone before it) intensification will have little effect either on what children learn behind classroom doors or on the culture of learning in Canada.

BACK-TO-BASICS

The high school drop-out rate in Canada and the high rate of functional illiteracy and innumeracy among those who do graduate are real problems. The ability to read, write and work with numbers is essential to fulfilling one's role as a Canadian citizen. And no one doubts that, in the coming decades, the number of jobs available to those without these fundamental skills will be increasingly limited.

A conceptually separate issue, though, is the potential mismatch between the skills thought to be necessary to assure Canada's prosperity in a "competitive global economy" and the skills thought to be possessed by Canadian workers. For the federal government, the lack of "employability" skills is problematic because such skills are seen as fundamental to the quality of the Canadian labour force. Moreover, the quality of the labour force is seen as essential to the future prosperity of Canada.

> There is a growing consensus among educators, business people and policy makers that Canada's learning performance is simply not good enough to prepare us for the future. If we are to continue enjoying a high standard of living, we must improve greatly the level of basic skills of all Canadians and ensure that many more Canadians acquire advanced and specialized skills. [12]

The skills that are seen as "basic" by the federal government go well beyond the "old" basics of literacy and numeracy.

> In an effort to define goals for education and to pinpoint critical skills and abilities, provincial governments, business-education groups like the Conference Board of Canada and other educational organizations like the Canadian School Board Association have reached remarkably similar conclusions. Generally considered to be essential are the ability to read, write and work effectively with numbers, as well as the knowledge of core subjects. Also found to be critical are creativity, self-esteem, communication skills, self-management and interpersonal relations. [13]

In truth, these lists of "employability" or "foundation" skills more closely resemble the New Year's resolutions of the particularly penitent than a pragmatic set of goals for Canadian education. Few of us, much less all of us, can hope to possess any large proportion of these "essential" skills.

The Economic Council of Canada was much more forthright and realistic in its appraisal of essential skills. Highlighting the possibility that one million more illiterate Canadians would enter the labour force before the year 2000, the Council's first target for the education and training system was that all 16-year-olds be literate and numerate.[14] This emphasis coincides with the call of supporters of intensification for the back-to-basics reform of elementary and secondary education, where the relevant "basics" are the old ones of reading, writing and arithmetic.

Because the federal government has no authority to set educational policies, its studies of education and training shy away from recommending specific curriculum guidelines and specific teaching methods. But if schools are to give greater emphasis to reading, writing and arithmetic, teachers are going to have to do something in their classrooms that they are not doing now. What teachers do in their classrooms is called "teaching practice," a subject that has been much studied by researchers and by teachers themselves. As a result, innovative methods for teaching virtually anything—and certainly for teaching reading, writing and arithmetic—can be found. The fear aroused by a simplistic back-to-basics strategy is that back-to-basics could mean back to the rote learning and memorization that characterized education before 1960. If that is indeed the practical implication of a back-to-basics movement, there are several unintended side-effects that must be considered.

First, efforts to ensure that all children acquire the basics may lead to higher school drop-out rates. If students are bored by the basics or if they are unable to meet new, higher standards, they may simply leave school at age 16.[15]

Second, rote learning and memorization are antithetical to critical thinking and creative problem-solving. If schools re-emphasize reading, writing and arithmetic by re-emphasizing rote learning and memorization, efforts to teach creative problem-solving and critical thinking will be blunted.

Third, the range of abilities and interests in today's classrooms is much greater than it was before 1960. Today, 75 percent of Canadians graduate from high school, whereas only 35 percent graduated from high school in 1960.[16] Because of the greater heterogeneity among today's students, methods that worked with the more homogeneous student population of 1960 may not work as well today.

Despite disagreements about teaching practices, there is consensus that basic literacy and numeracy skills, of the sort measured by the literacy survey of Statistics Canada, are important.

The activities of daily life—reading the instructions on packages of medicine, deciphering bus schedules and dealing with routine banking transactions—require greater levels of literacy and numeracy than were required years ago. And more and more jobs require at least basic literacy and numeracy: to read instruction manuals, to operate and maintain production equipment, or to understand workplace reorganizations.

But even if all Canadians were literate and numerate, the federal government would still see a need for educational reform. As illustrated in the earlier quotation from *Inventing Our Future*, the federal government believes that Canadians must acquire an additional and lengthy list of employability skills.[17]

The Government's assessment of the skills needed to assure economic competitiveness is grounded in a particular view, and a controversial one at that, of the evolution of the world economy. That view is based on three assumptions about the future, that 1) firms will be increasingly able to move from nation to nation in search of the highest possible profits; 2) unlike firms, workers will remain rooted, by and large, in their own countries; and 3) goods and services will be able to move from country to country without facing major trade barriers.[18] The implication of these assumptions is that low-skilled Canadian workers will face competition from the rest of the world, competition that will certainly drive down their wages. No nation will be able to raise wages unilaterally because any attempt to do so will simply induce firms to move to other countries. Under these conditions, if Canada continues to have large numbers of unskilled and semi-skilled workers, these workers will have to accept either very low wages or unemployment. No public policy, short of generous social assistance, will be able to prevent their impoverishment. The only "solution," according to this perspective, is to raise the skill levels of every person in Canada. However, even Robert Reich, whose optimism knows few bounds, concedes that "the task of transforming a majority of the ... work force into symbolic analysts would be daunting."[19]

Such theories of competitiveness, however plausible, are just that—theories.[20] Even if we accept that basic literacy and numeracy skills are essential in today's world, no one really knows what other skills future jobs might require. One possibility is that the new technologies might lead to skill "upgrading," to the general increase in skill levels (and thus wage levels) required of production workers. Alternatively, it is entirely possible that the economy of the future will require fewer skills for most workers, even as it requires greater skills for a small élite. If new manufacturing technologies lead to "deskilling" (the general reduction in skill levels required of production workers), then the workforce may be polarized. One group, the managers, would need very high skill levels, while the other group, the workers, would need only rudimentary skills (and would receive only basic wages).

An emerging consensus seems to be that the effect of the new technologies on skill levels will be contingent not just on the nature of the new technologies themselves, but on how they are used.[21] For example, computer-controlled machine tools are now commonly used in machine shops in place of hand-controlled equipment. The computer-controlled equipment can be programmed to machine pieces of metal more consistently and more quickly than the hand-controlled equipment. But the programming itself can be done either by management or by the machine tool operator. An operator who does not do any programming uses fewer skills than the operator of a hand-controlled machine tool. In contrast, an operator who both programs and operates uses more skills.

Even if we accept the necessity of providing children with skills for the job market, we need not accept the notion that job requirements should determine what we teach. This is a two-way street; the skills that people possess can drive the skill requirements of jobs. Indeed, the federal notion of education is that if we create a workforce that is highly skilled, we will be creating a national resource that multinational firms would flock to Canada to exploit.

In summary, if one believes that education is primarily a way of preparing children to fit into the labour market, there is consensus that literacy and numeracy are essential. But, there remains uncertainty about the necessity and the possibility of making sure that *all* workers have the higher levels of other skills.

The provinces are less concerned than is the federal government with these vocational aspects of education.[22] Teaching the basics, both old and new, is assumed to be part of the task of education, regardless of their relevance to the job market. For example, restructuring blueprints in British Columbia, Ontario and New Brunswick all assume that the skills to be taught include creative problem-solving and critical thinking, as well as literacy and numeracy.

In contrast to the simpler back-to-basics approach, restructuring is an attempt at the comprehensive reorganization of many aspects of education, including grade levels, curricula and the interconnections between levels of the education system.

> School systems need to rethink their purposes, structures and processes in order ... to develop new "forms" of schooling that are more appropriate for enabling diverse student populations to function successfully in a knowledge-based society.[23]

Both Ontario and British Columbia are in the midst of major school restructuring programs which antedate the more recent interest of the federal government in education. In Ontario, restructuring means a new curriculum for the newly created "Transition Years" (grades 7-9), new diploma requirements for the "Specialization Years" and, the most visible reform to date, the elimination of streaming in Grade 9.[24]

In British Columbia, the "Year 2000" reforms involve a reorganization of grades (four years of ungraded primary education, seven years of "intermediate" grades and a two-year "graduation" program). The curriculum will be organized into four "strands"—humanities, sciences, fine arts and practical arts— which will subsume the more traditional subjects.

> For example, study of the early history of Canada might lead to discussion of the geographical factors that affected the location of major towns and cities; that in turn could be related to the geographic and economic factors that influence the location of modern towns in B.C.... In this way, students acquire knowledge that is relevant to their everyday lives.[25]

The restructuring efforts of these provinces are a radical departure from past organizational structures, but the underlying philosophy of education is still closely tied to the "child-centred" philosophy that has heavily influenced school practices for the past 20 or 30 years. This "developmental" perspective on childhood education, especially for children in the elementary grades, is quite a distance from the vision of education as preparation for future work.

> Educators of young children have long believed that children learn in many different ways, demonstrating in the process that they have multiple patterns of growth and achievement. This belief has given direction to programs with diversified aims and goals. In these programs, children are respected, regardless of racial background or socioeconomic class. Their interests become basic starting points for learning. Such developmental programs tend to support more formal instruction in reading, for example, only when children are ready and not simply because they are 6 years of age.[26]

It might seem that a simplistic back-to-basics agenda is unlikely to succeed, given the broad vision of provincial restructuring plans. But there is a considerable gap between the expressed aims of provincial ministries and what goes on in the classroom. In discussing attempts by provincial governments to narrow that gap by giving more specific instructions to school boards, Fullan writes,

> the latest curriculum guidelines and documents are not in "implementable" form. Goal statements are more clear, content to be covered is set down more specifically and reference to expected learning outcomes is tighter but the *means* of implementation (e.g. teaching strategies and activities) are not well developed or integrated.[27]

The opening for those who support increased emphasis on literacy and numeracy is through this gap between bureaucratic intent and classroom practice. And the vehicle for exploiting that gap is accountability. Virtually all provinces, especially British Columbia, Alberta and New Brunswick, are increasing the intensity and frequency of standardized testing. Unless considerable attention is paid to test construction (and perhaps *despite* the attention paid to test construction) "he who measures the outcomes calls the tune.... As more and more emphasis is placed on standardized tests, less and less will be given to teaching students real skills like writing, thinking and creating."[28]

ACCOUNTABILITY

> Please follow the instructions in your test booklet carefully. Be
> sure to use a Number 2 pencil.

For most Canadians, these are familiar phrases, heralding an hour
or two spent puzzling over whether a cactus needs more or less
water than a cabbage, or whether Switzerland is bordered by Italy,
France, Germany, all of the above or none of the above.

In the past 10 years, standardized testing has emerged as a
central element in Canadian educational reform. In the mid-1980s,
Alberta began to require that 50 percent of each student's Grade
12 mark be based on a standardized test; the province also
introduced standardized achievement tests in earlier grades.
British Columbia has reintroduced public school-leaving examinations, which will count as 40 percent of a student's Grade 12
mark.[29] Similar testing is planned as part of the New Brunswick
educational reforms. At lower grade levels, standardized tests
(such as the Canadian Test of Basic Skills) are also common,
although they do not play a role in establishing student grades. In
the spring of 1993, the Council of Ministers of Education, Canada
(CMEC) plans to administer the first Canada-wide standardized
test as part of its School Achievement Indicators Program (SAIP),
a program that has been four years in development.[30]

The current enthusiasm for standardized tests is an attempt
to hold the education sector *accountable* for educational outcomes.
Canada spends about $7 billion annually for elementary and
secondary education; as a percentage of national income, this is
more than any other Western country. In return for that investment, parents, taxpayers and employers expect schools to teach
children how to read and understand fairly simple prose. They
expect schools to teach children how to do basic arithmetic and to
teach them a minimal set of facts about history, geography and
politics.

But learning is a private process, unfolding silently within
the minds of individual learners. The efforts of teachers are only
slightly less private, contained as they are within classroom walls.
Standardized testing gives parents, taxpayers and employers a
method of overseeing and directing the work of teachers and their
administrative support staff.

In this light, standardized testing is a management tool, intended to align the objectives of "management" (parents, taxpayers and employers) with the incentives faced by the "production workers" (teachers and education administrators), in a setting (classrooms) in which the productive process is not entirely visible to management. Among economists, it is almost axiomatic that firms that do not monitor the productive process will find themselves without any production.

The desire for accountability crosses the ideological divide before those favouring intensification and those favouring restructuring. But that divide reappears when the test must actually be designed. What form should the test take? What subject areas should it cover? To what other uses will the test be put?

Multiple-choice tests—tests that ask students to choose one answer from a short list of possible answers—are the least expensive and most frequently administered standardized tests. Standardized multiple-choice tests are designed to provide only a partial measure of a child's skills, often those skills that are easily measured such as arithmetic and vocabulary. When such tests are used as designed, as one of a number of assessment tools, this is not problematic. Teacher evaluations can be used to supplement the narrow assessment provided by the multiple-choice test.

But as a means of holding schools and, thus, teachers accountable for the achievement of students, standardized multiple-choice tests have several well-known drawbacks. First, the "window" provided by standardized multiple-choice tests overlooks only a narrow corner of the classroom. Schools try to teach much more than the literacy and numeracy skills that most tests are designed to measure; children are also supposed to learn to solve problems, think critically and work co-operatively. Mistaking multiple-choice tests for an indicator of the cumulative effect of education is "akin to mistaking pulse rate for the total effect of a healthful regime."[31]

Second, the skills that a student possesses at any one time are a function of that child's lifelong experience in a wide range of settings. Many outside factors impinge on the achievement of students. As just one example, Canadian children spend more time, on average, watching television (about 1,000 hours per year) than they do in school. Judging schools and teachers by the performance of their students, attractive as that may be, risks attributing responsibility to them that may rightly belong elsewhere.

Third, achievement tests are not very reliable indicators of future success. This is true for college admission tests as predictors of first year university grades and for employment tests as predictors of job performance. As the U.S. National Commission on Testing and Public Policy noted, "the general finding that tests predict less than one-quarter of the variance in actual on-the-job or in-school performance is clear from research literature dating back to the 1920s."[32] Because they are unreliable indicators of future performance, students may be misclassified if the tests are used to place them in academic tracks or are used as a criterion for promotion or high school graduation. Such misclassification is bad enough, but there is some evidence that misclassification is especially likely among the poor and among ethnic minorities.[33]

Multiple-choice tests are often worse than no testing at all. The partial coverage of standardized multiple-choice tests forces teachers to "focus time, energy, and attention on the simpler skills that are easily tested and away from higher-order thinking skills and creative endeavors."[34] For supporters of intensification, however, the limitations of multiple-choice testing are not compelling. They *want* teachers to focus time, energy and attention on the simpler skills. Therefore, the fact that teachers teach to the test, when the test measures basic skills, is not at all disturbing for such supporters.

Educators have developed numerous ways of overcoming the limitations of multiple-choice testing but, as will be seen, their solutions come at a cost. "Authentic" testing, "testing that requires students to perform a task rather than select an answer from a ready-made list,"[35] is a response to the objection that standardized multiple-choice tests measure only part of what is taught and only the most easily measured part at that.

> Do we judge our students to be deficient in writing, speaking, listening, artistic creation, finding and citing evidence, and problem solving? Then let the tests ask them to write, speak, listen, create, do original research, and solve problems.[36]

But authentic testing requires that the test-makers agree on the tasks to be performed. Since the tests are intended to influence the activities of teachers, agreement on the content of the test will be difficult if there is no agreement on the desired activities of the teachers. Those who want teachers to place more emphasis on basic literacy and numeracy skills will want the test to require more tasks involving those skills. Those who want teachers to place more emphasis on problem-solving and creativity will want the test to require more problem-solving and more creativity. Compromise will not come easily. Furthermore, evaluating problem-solving skills and creativity is inevitably subjective and would require hours of careful and costly examination.

Because the *level* of a child's academic achievement depends on many factors besides the effectiveness of a teacher in any one year, the *gain* in a child's achievement over the course of a year would be a better, though still imperfect, measure of a teacher's effectiveness. Of course, measuring the gain in achievement would require testing every student every year.

Finally, if testing is to serve as a means of holding schools and teachers accountable, tests must be cheap as well as accurate. Firms need to oversee the activities of their employees, but not at any cost, not if the cost of supervision does not justify its benefits. Frequent testing of all students, using authentic tests that can more accurately assess their knowledge and ability, is simply too costly.

The testing now being undertaken by the School Achievement Indicators Program (SAIP) of the Council of Ministers of Education, Canada (CMEC) is an example of how we can begin to use testing as a way of holding the education system accountable.[37] Tests will be administered to a relatively small, randomly chosen, sample of 13- and 16-year-olds from all provinces (except Saskatchewan).[38] Rather than asking only multiple-choice questions, the SAIP tests will also ask students to show what they can do. The mathematics test will require explicit problem-solving; the writing assessment will include, for some students, an evaluation of a "collection of a sample of their favourite classroom work."[39] Thus, these tests, which were developed in consultation with teachers' groups, are intended to measure a wider range of skills in a more authentic way than could be measured using only a multiple-choice format.

Random sampling avoids two of the problems of standardized testing in a single stroke. First, the results of the SAIP assessment will not be used to make any decisions about individual students, so unfair misclassification is not an issue.

More importantly, assessing the effectiveness of individual teachers, of individual schools or of individual school boards will not be attempted. Only provincial comparisons will be possible. More widespread testing—testing every student every year in order to measure the average achievement gain for each teacher and school—would not only have been prohibitively expensive but would have plunged the Council directly into the controversy over the extent to which schools and teachers should be held responsible for the achievement gains of their students.

The CMEC program is only a beginning. While it does not seem to be cost-effective to use tests in every school as a means of holding schools and teachers accountable, there is no reason why future SAIP results cannot be reported at the school board level, especially for the large, urban boards. Further, the CMEC will not be collecting demographic information on the tested students, so that no analysis of the relationships between test scores and socio-economic status, race, ethnicity and family status can be attempted. Without such information, it will be impossible to know if differences among provinces are due to differences in provincial educational policies or to differences in student characteristics. As of this writing, the Council is planning to administer the mathematics part of the SAIP in the spring of 1993 and the reading and writing parts in 1994.

Given the amount of resources devoted to education, and the common feeling that the resulting outcomes are not all that we would like them to be, it seems only prudent to develop a method of holding the education system accountable for its activities. But the simple and relatively cheap accountability that comes in the form of standardized multiple-choice tests administered to every student may be worse than no accountability at all. By contrast, authentic tests administered to a randomly drawn sample of students offer the promise of a higher quality, if more limited, accountability.

CHOICE

The push for more emphasis on basic skills, enforced by standardized testing, has not yet been realized. Provinces have not repudiated the developmental philosophies and practices that have guided Canadian educational policy over the past 25 years. Provincial restructuring plans do not call for more emphasis on reading, writing and arithmetic at the expense of problem-solving and critical thinking. Teachers are not visibly returning to rote learning and memorization in their classrooms. Simplistic standardized multiple-choice tests of basic skills have not yet been widely administered in the name of accountability.

However, supporters of intensification have another weapon in their arsenal—school choice. In Canada, the vast majority of students attend publicly funded schools that charge no tuition. Such schools are organized and administered by locally elected school boards that operate under the control of provincial ministries of education. Two avenues are open to Canadian parents (including supporters of intensification reforms) who want to choose schools for their children.[40]

First, school boards now allow parents considerable latitude to choose among the schools operated by the local school board. For example, Vancouver and Edmonton have "open enrolment" schemes that allow parents to choose, at least in principle, among all publicly funded schools in the city. That ability to choose would mean little if the schools within a board were homogeneous. But the past decade has also seen a rapid expansion in the diversity of publicly funded schools (and in distinct programs within schools). French immersion schools, "alternative" child-centred schools, schools for gifted children and speciality high schools all compete with more traditional public schools for students.

Second, parents who can afford to pay tuition for their children's education can opt for a limited number of private, or independent, schools. In 1990-91, just under 5 percent of Canadian students attended such schools.[41] Private schools are free of the administrative control of school boards but must still comply with provincial regulations.

The latter form of choice—private or independent schools— is controversial because the extent to which such schools receive public funds has increased in recent years. Some provinces, notably Quebec, have always used public funds to support Roman Catholic schools. But in 1987, Ontario also extended full public funding to Roman Catholic schools, which now operate much as do secular schools with publicly elected school boards operating under the control of the provincial ministries. Another recent extension of public financial support for private schools came when British Columbia increased the subsidy that it gives to its independent schools. As of 1989, each independent school could receive, for each enrolled student, up to 50 percent of the average per capita cost of educating a child in the public sector. Five provinces—British Columbia, Quebec, Alberta, Manitoba and Saskatchewan—subsidize private schools in this way (see Appendix 13.1).[42] Private school subsidies do not mean that these schools no longer charge tuition; the effect of the subsidies is to make tuition lower than it would otherwise be. As always, parents who cannot pay the tuition cannot send their children to the private schools.

The extension of the range of choice, through greater subsidies to private schools and through more choice and diversity within the public sector, does not give parents an unlimited ability to pick and choose among alternative curricula. All schools receiving public funds must comply with provincial regulations regarding curricula, admission requirements, teacher certification and school building codes.

Ironically, the effect of greater public subsidies to private schools may be to *limit* choice, as the private schools alter their practices to conform to heavy provincial regulation. In her analysis of the effects of the greater subsidies in British Columbia, Jean Barman writes,

> Government funding, intended to expand the boundaries of choice for parents, did bring higher enrolments and new schools. This in turn encouraged greater public oversight which then constrained the boundaries of choice.[43]

In Quebec, where receiving government subsidies means complying with government language laws, some private schools simply avoid that prospect by refusing the subsidies.

So the level of choice in Canada is far from the choice that would prevail if free and open competition were allowed in education. The current policy, perhaps best described as "diversity within limits," is a way of accommodating the many different aspirations of various subgroups of parents.[44] It would seem to give parents the schools they want while allowing provinces to maintain at least a modicum of control over school practices. While this is not the place for a comprehensive discussion of the pros and cons of school choice,[45] I will make three points that bear specifically on the desire for a greater linkage between education and the job market.

The first point is that allowing parents and children a wider range of choice among schools is likely to lead to a set of schools that, taken as a whole, places more emphasis on skills that will be rewarded in the job market. Mainstream economists have long argued that schooling produces two general kinds of skills in children. One set of skills is directly related to their future employment—the "employability" skills that the federal government is so anxious to encourage. The other set of skills does not yield any financial reward to the student but instead benefits the public at large; these skills constitute what economists call "public goods." For example, schools try to teach students to be sensitive to issues of race and gender in an effort to foster attitudes that will make Canada a better place to live for all Canadians. This "sensitivity to difference" benefits everyone, but will not lead to financial reward for any one individual.

On a broader level, schools try to create social cohesion. There is a large and growing gap between the incomes of the poorly educated and those of the highly educated. In the United States, some argue that this gap has led to the "secession" of the upper middle class, who have responded to the misfortunes of their fellow citizens by withdrawing into suburban enclaves and by resisting the taxation necessary to subsidize the long-term poor and the unemployed.[46] But as Milton Friedman wrote in *Capitalism and Freedom*, "a stable and democratic society is impossible without a minimum degree of literacy and knowledge on the part of most citizens, and without widespread acceptance of some common set of values."[47] Promoting that "common set of values" is one of the primary goals of public schooling.

The view that schooling must teach subjects that will not be rewarded by higher wages creates an economic problem. If families are free to choose among schools, many will opt for ones that focus more narrowly on basic skills at the expense of skills that might be socially relevant, but which are not privately profitable.

The result will be that not enough attention will be paid to areas such as social cohesion or sensitivity to race and gender issues.[48]

The second point about school choice concerns the relationship between equality of opportunity and some forms of school choice. In the absence of strong regulation, the provision of public funds to private schools might lead to the "balkanization" of Canadian schools. If allowed to do so, parents may segregate their children from other, dissimilar, children. Certainly, high-income parents will be able to segregate their children from the children of low-income parents. Even with public funding, tuition at private schools can be quite high. Thus, in the five provinces that allow such funding, public funds are now used to subsidize expensive private schools that remain out of the financial reach of most Canadians. Similarly, parents whose children have high intellectual ability will be able to keep their children apart from children with lower ability; school choice can be a radical form of streaming. More importantly, perhaps, school choice generally allows parents to choose their children's classmates. Just as Roman Catholics can now choose to send their children to schools attended primarily by other Roman Catholics, more choice might mean that Ukrainians could choose Ukrainian schools, Jamaicans could choose Jamaican schools and so on.[49]

School choice will not *necessarily* result in schools that are more homogeneous. Because place of residence will always be important in determining the schools children attend, and because people tend to live in neighbourhoods with other people like themselves, schools are already fairly homogeneous. To the extent that school choice weakens the link between residence and school, it could foster less homogeneity within schools.

If school choice does lead to a greater balkanization of Canadian schools, children who might have benefited from interacting with their more fortunate peers will be made worse off. For example, a "back-to-basics" school is unlikely to attract children with learning disabilities or children whose parents cannot or will not provide the educational support that such schools demand. If no school exists that can provide comparable education to such students, they will have been denied equality of opportunity.

The third point about school choice is that, paradoxically, it can be a way of *enhancing* equality of opportunity. All across

North America the poor, non-white groups who feel so ill-served by formal schooling look to school choice as a way of escaping the inappropriate and failed curricula imposed upon their children. In some American inner cities, school choice means the ability to send Baptist children to Roman Catholic schools where discipline will be maintained and basic skills will be taught. For others, including Aboriginal groups in Canada, school choice means the ability to make education conform more closely to their own culture.

From a more academic perspective, schools are seen to be wanting because they are run by education bureaucrats who are trying to maintain their own privileged positions rather than trying to serve the public interest. According to this view, the current structure of schools is "symptomatic of the successful lobbying for monopoly power by organized suppliers,"[50] where the "organized suppliers" are those directing the public education system. Expanded school choice is a weapon that can be used by the public to break the monopoly power of the education bureaucracy.

The reality in Canada is that school choice is here to stay. Given the uncertainty surrounding what is best for children, apart from literacy and numeracy, expanded choice is a way of giving parents the right and the responsibility to choose a path for their children. But expanded choice is not without serious dangers. The primary danger is that some of the most treasured values of public education—among them the equality of opportunity fostered by providing a "common ground" for all students and instruction that is not guided exclusively by vocational considerations—might be threatened by allowing parents greater choice.

Because of these considerations, the policy problem facing provinces is how to regulate the further extension of school choice. The provincial governments still have enormous, though not unlimited, power to determine what is taught in classrooms, both through curricular guidelines and through standardized testing. Furthermore, the provinces can make sure that equality of opportunity is maintained by regulating the admission requirements of schools. As yet, there is no sign that provinces are willing to give up these regulatory powers.

CONCLUSION

According to virtually all popular authors writing on "competitiveness," successful contemporary economies must be linked to exemplary education systems. Given the current state of Canadian education, this logic implies that our elementary and secondary schools must become better than they ever have been. They must first ensure that every student, not just the university-bound student, has a firm grasp of basic skills—reading, writing and arithmetic. Furthermore, the economy demands that education be extended so that more students learn more about more subjects. All the while, however, the creative spirits and the critical faculties of the students must be kept alive, so that they can create new products and solve new economic and social problems.

This is a noble vision and a worthy challenge to education. In truth, however, those in the education system know more about the nobility of the vision and the nature of the challenge than any expert on competitiveness. Take away the requirement that schools be exclusively linked to jobs and add in the desire that each child reach his or her own potential, and we have a pretty fair description of what teachers are now trying to accomplish. Few complaints about elementary and secondary education would be heard if schools actually accomplished what they already aim to accomplish.

The yawning chasm between the stated goals of contemporary education and what actually happens has generated any number of pleas for educational reform. In this chapter, I have tried to identify parts of an agenda for educational reform that would alter educational policy in order to align it more closely with the perceived needs of the economy. That agenda is accountability, back-to-basics and choice, *implemented in a particular fashion*, which includes the mass administration of standardized multiple-choice tests for accountability, "basics" defined as literacy and numeracy, and the widest possible latitude for parental choice among schools.

In my view, the adoption of this simplistic ABC would have serious unintended side-effects. It would give insufficient attention to the "new basics" of problem-solving and critical thinking and, in the case of expanded school choice, might generate the possibility (though not the certainty) of diminished equality of opportunity and increased social segregation. It might also have an opportunity cost, a missed chance to give all workers (and not just the highly skilled workers) more control over their work. Many years ago, long before education reports started referring to "creative problem-solving" and "critical thinking," John Dewey looked for

> the development of such intelligent initiative, ingenuity and executive capacity as shall make workers as far as may be possible, the masters of their own industrial fate.... The kind of vocational education in which I am interested is not one which will "adapt" workers to the existing regime; I am not sufficiently in love with the regime for that. It seems to me that the business of all who would not be educational time-servers is ... to strive for a kind of vocational education which will alter the existing industrial system and ultimately transform it.[51]

The existing industrial system is being altered right now, towards a system in which many workers (though still far from all) *might* acquire greater autonomy and greater responsibility in the workplace. If we continue to try to make workers what they have always been, only with a bit more reading and arithmetic, we will have missed the opportunity to give the nation not only greater income but also greater democracy.

The provincial ministries that control Canadian education have actually adopted accountability, back-to-basics and choice, but not in a highly simplistic form and not with the sole goal of aligning education with the economy. The provinces are placing more emphasis on the "basics" but with the wider definition of "basics," one that includes creative problem-solving and critical thinking. Testing for the purpose of assessment is more widespread than previously but, in many provinces, the tendency is towards authentic tests that measure more than the basics and ask students to show what they can do. Finally, parents have quite a choice among schools, including a diversity of publicly funded schools and (in some provinces) private schools that are partially subsidized by public funds. Thus, the question is not whether accountability, back-to-basics and choice will prevail; the question is which version of them will prevail.

The differences between restructuring and intensification may be less than they seem. One could argue that *both* view children as future workers, the only difference being that supporters of restructuring believe that children need "new" and "old" basics, while supporters of intensification believe they need only the old basics. But where is it that we teach children their rights and responsibilities as citizens of a democracy? How do we prevent the more fortunate minority from "seceding" from the less fortunate majority if we do not teach our children that, as Canadians, they have a responsibility to use their good fortune to aid their less fortunate fellow citizens? We cannot ignore the economy as we redesign schools, but it behooves us to remember that children must be citizens as well as workers.

One of the painful lessons of the 20th century is that, when we reach into complicated social systems to fix their obvious flaws, our solutions are often worse than the problems. Mass education is one such system, slowly evolving and highly complicated. Proposals to "fix" it, whether they be proposals for vastly expanded school choice, for radically higher standards or for dramatic restructuring, may well be worse than what we have.

Whatever the direction we might want to take our education system, two features will certainly constrain the extent of educational change. The first is the obvious fact that, roughly speaking, the 300,000 teachers we have now are the teachers we will have for the foreseeable future; the practical impact of any changes in rules and regulations must hinge on the co-operation of the existing group of teachers. The second is that, roughly speaking, the five million children we have now are the children we will have for the foreseeable future. Unless we figure out how to redirect some of their efforts towards more scholastic pursuits than Nintendo, and how to induce hard-pressed parents to support that redirection with more than just words (or votes), any reform efforts will be doomed.

In fact, the various reforms-at-a-distance that outsiders propose depend on the conjunction of so many unlikely events that rapid and radical change is quite unlikely. Instead, the current furore over educational reform will likely pass, especially as baby boomers turn their attention from their children's education to their own retirement years.

This is not to say that educational change is *not needed*. The future of the Canadian economy probably *does* depend on the quality of the Canadian labour force. But we must respect the apparent reality that change will be slow and take solace in the knowledge that the existing education system has not been built capriciously.

Appendix 13.1

Provincial Policies regarding Public Funding
for Independent Schools

Newfoundland -	"a partnership between denominational education boards and the province ... [and three] types of boards exist: 21 Integrated Boards represent Anglican, United Church, Salvation Army and Presbyterian churches; 12 Roman Catholic Boards; and one Pentecostal Board plus one Seventh Day Adventist."
Nova Scotia - New Brunswick. P.E.I.	No funding for independent schools.
Quebec -	Full public funding for the Roman Catholic and Protestant schools. Substantial funding is provided to independent schools; all such schools receive 46% of the average public school grant; schools deemed to be "in the public interest" receive 66%.
Ontario -	Full public funding to non-denominational schools and to Roman Catholic and French language boards No funding to other independent schools.
Manitoba -	Roman Catholic schools, other denominational schools and independent schools receive 55% of the average public school grant.
Saskatchewan -	Independent high schools in operation for more than five years receive two thirds of average grant to provincial high schools. No support to independent elementary schools.
Alberta -	Qualifying independent schools receive 72% of provincial support levels for all schools.
British Columbia -	All schools other than non-denominational schools receive 50% of average per pupil funding of provincial schools.

Source: Tim Sale, *Financing of Elementary and Secondary Education in Canada*, Working Paper no. 29 (Ottawa: Economic Council of Canada, 1992).

NOTES

1   In 1991, Statistics Canada surveyed a cohort of 20-year-old Canadians. Of these 20-year-olds, 24 percent reported that they had dropped out of high school at some point in the past. A substantial minority later returned to school. These "ever dropped out" rates, by province and gender, are as follows:

	Male (percent)	Female (percent)	Total (percent)
Newfoundland	32	20	26
P.E.I.	36	18	27
Nova Scotia	33	15	25
New Brunswick	30	19	25
Quebec	32	22	27
Ontario	31	18	25
Manitoba	26	21	24
Saskatchewan	18	17	17
Alberta	18	14	16
British Columbia	20	19	24
Canada	28	19	24

Source: Statistics Canada, *Survey of School Leavers* (Ottawa, December 1991), p. 7.

2   In 1989, Statistics Canada surveyed a large sample of Canadians, aged 16-69, in an effort to measure their literacy and numeracy skills. In the sampled group, 16 percent could not read well enough to decipher even rudimentary texts (Reading Levels 1 and 2), while an additional 22 percent read only well enough "to carry out simple reading tasks within familiar contexts" (Level 3). The corresponding percentages with comparable numeracy problems were 14 percent and 24 percent. Younger people and those with more schooling were considerably less likely to have literacy or numeracy problems. See Statistics Canada, *Adult Literacy in Canada: Results of a National Study* (Ottawa, 1991).

3   In fact, Canadian 10- and 14-year-olds ranked in the middle of the 16 countries participating in the Second International Science

Study. In his analysis of this set of tests, Robert Crocker suggests that "scores for students in Canada ... may be considered satisfactory," although he goes on to say that this finding "gives little reason for complacency, when one considers that other countries ... perform at substantially higher levels." Among senior secondary students, Canada's students *were* close to the bottom of the rankings but this comparison is muddied by differing criteria for selecting students to be tested. See Robert Crocker, "Science Achievement in Canadian Schools: National and International Comparisons," Working Paper no. 7 (Ottawa: Economic Council of Canada, 1991), p. 56-57.

4   "Mulroney dips his federal toe into education," *The Gazette* [Montreal], August 29, 1989, p. B3.

5   "Better education, scientific research PM's top priorities," *The Globe and Mail* [Toronto], August 26, 1989, pp. A-1 to A-2.

6   See *A Lot to Learn: Education and Training in Canada* (Ottawa: Economic Council of Canada, 1992), p. vii. *Learning Well, Living Well* is a 1991 report published under the name of the Prosperity Secretariat while *Inventing Our Future: An Action Plan for Canada's Prosperity* is a 1992 report published under the name of the Steering Group on Prosperity.

7   Richard Harris and William Watson discuss the various theories about "competitiveness" in their lucid and entertaining paper entitled, "Three Visions of Competitiveness: Porter, Reich and Thurow on Economic Growth and Policy" (Kingston: John Deutsch Institute for the Study of Economic Policy, 1992).

8   The federal government has a *political* interest in education to the extent that all parties seem to believe that the state of elementary and secondary education is both interesting and important to the electorate. We can expect education to be an important topic in the upcoming federal elections, despite the federal government's lack of formal authority in this policy area.

9   Michael Fullan describes the two reform "waves" as follows in *The New Meaning of Educational Change* (Toronto: OISE Press,

1991), p. 7: "One wave of reform ... I have called 'intensification.' Increased definition of curriculum, mandated textbooks, standardized tests tightly aligned with curriculum, specification of teaching and administrative methods backed up by evaluation, and monitoring all serve to intensify ... the what and how of teaching.... The other wave ... goes by the label of 'restructuring': it takes many forms, but usually involves school-based management; enhanced roles for teachers in instruction and decision making; integration of multiple innovations; restructured timetables supporting collaborative work cultures; radical reorganization of teacher education; new roles such as mentors, coaches, and other teacher leadership arrangements; and revamping and developing the shared mission and goals of the school."

10   My colleague Leslie Pal suggested this definition of "conservative populism" and also suggested the label itself.

11   New Brunswick Commission on Excellence in Education, *Schools for a New Century* (Fredericton, 1992); British Columbia Royal Commission on Education, *Legacy for Learners: Report of the Royal Commission on Education* (Victoria, 1988); George Radwanski, *Ontario Study of the Relevance of Education and the Issue of Dropout* (Toronto: Ontario Ministry of Education, 1987).

12   Prosperity Secretariat, *Learning Well, Living Well*, p. vii.

13   Steering Group on Prosperity, *Inventing Our Future*, p. 37.

14   Economic Council, *A Lot to Learn*, p. 50.

15   The Economic Council finesses this point by calling for literacy and numeracy for all *16-year-olds* so that, if students leave school at age 16, they will at least have the basics in hand.

16   These graduation figures are cited in Brian Titley and Kas Mazurek, "Back to the Basics? Forward to the Fundamentals?" in Brian Titley, (ed.), *Canadian Education: Historical Themes and Contemporary Issues* (Calgary: Detselig, 1990), p. 115.

17   The belief that some Canadians have weak literacy and numeracy skills is supported by the empirical evidence in Statistics Canada's literacy survey. But there is no comparable empirical basis for the Government's belief that Canadians are not good enough at solving problems creatively, at thinking critically or at working co-operatively.

18   In terms of economic theory, these assumptions (plus the assumption that wages and prices can move freely) imply "factor price equalization"; i.e. that the wage of a certain kind of worker is the same everywhere in the world. They imply, for example, that an unskilled worker in Canada will tend to be offered the same wage as an unskilled worker in Mexico.

19   Robert Reich, *The Work of Nations* (New York: Knopf, 1991), p. 247. To Reich, "symbolic analyst" is a synonym for the highly skilled "knowledge" workers, who occupy and will continue to occupy the top of the income distribution.

20   While most analysts argue for better education (who would argue for less?), they differ in their visions of the future. Lester Thurow, for example, argues that the world will come to be divided into three trading blocs, led by the United States, Japan and the European Community, respectively. In that setting, wages and profits would be equalized within in each bloc but not necessarily across blocs. See Lester Thurow, *Head to Head* (New York: Morrow, 1992). Michael Porter argues that national firms, "loyal" to their country of origin, will remain important. See Michael Porter, *The Competitive Advantage of Nations* (New York: The Free Press, 1990).

21   See Ruth Milkman and Cydney Pullman, "Technological Change in an Auto Assembly Plant: The Impact on Workers' Tasks and Skills," *Work and Occupations*, 18, 2 (May 1991): pp. 123-47; William Form, Robert L. Kaufman, Toby L. Parcel, and Michael Wallace, "The Impact of Technology on Work Organization and Work Outcomes: A Conceptual Framework and Research Agenda" in George Farkas and Paula England, (eds.), *Industries, Firms and Jobs: Sociological and Economic Approaches* (New York: Plenum Press, 1988); Kenneth I. Spenner, "Technological Change,

Skill Requirements and Education: The Case for Uncertainty" in Richard Cyert and D.C. Mowery, (eds.), *The Impact of Technological Change on Employment and Economic Growth* (Cambridge, Mass.: Ballinger, 1988); Kenneth I. Spenner, "Skill: Meanings, Methods, and Measures," *Work and Occupations*, 17, 4 (1990).

22   In a chapter on "Significant Changes and Innovations" in Canadian education, the Council of Ministers of Education, Canada (CMEC) puts the federal government efforts in a section called "Education and the world of work," apart from previous sections concerning provincial policy initiatives. See Council of Ministers of Education, Canada, *Education in Canada, 1988-1992* (Toronto, 1992).

23   H. Dickson Corbett and Bruce L. Wilson, *Testing, Reform and Rebellion* (Norwood, N.J.: Ablex Publishing, 1991), p. 128.

24   "Streaming" or "tracking" is the practice of assigning students to different classes based on an assessment of their ability. Students perceived to be weak academically might be assigned to a "basic" track, the bulk of students might be in a "general" track, and those perceived to be "gifted" might be in an "enriched" stream. The exact nature of the tracks varies among school systems. Tracking is common at the secondary school level but relatively uncommon at the elementary level. In Ontario, students in grades 1 to 8 have *not* been assigned to tracks in recent years. Students in grades 9 to 13 are grouped or "streamed" according to their perceived ability. The current controversy is about the "destreaming" of Grade 9.

25   British Columbia Ministry of Education, *Changes in Education: A Guide for Parents* (Victoria, 1987), p. 12.

26   Vito Perrone, "On Standardized Testing," *Childhood Education*, (Spring 1991): pp. 132-42.

27   Michael Fullan, *New Meaning*, p. 230.

28   Arthur E. Wise, "A look ahead: Education and the new decade," *Education Week*, January 10, 1990, p. 30, cited in Corbett and Wilson, *Reform and Rebellion*, p. ix.

29   School leaving examinations have long been administered in Newfoundland and Quebec. Ontario discontinued such exams after 1967, soon followed by Manitoba. After first reducing the weight of its exams from 100 percent to 50 percent in 1971, Alberta discontinued them in 1973. See Titley and Mazurek, "Back to Basics?" p. 117.

30   The CMEC is an organization funded by the provinces. It has published a series of bulletins and short background papers that describe its School Achievement Indicators Program. My discussion of the CMEC testing programs, here and later in the chapter, is based on CMEC Bulletins 1-4 and Background Papers 1-2 (Toronto, 1991-93).

31   Grant Wiggins, "A True Test: Toward a More Authentic and Equitable Assessment," *Phi Delta Kappan* (May 1989): p. 704.

32   National Commission on Testing and Public Policy, *From Gatekeeper to Gateway: Transforming Testing in America* (Chestnut Hill, Mass.: Boston College, 1990), p. 20.

33   Ibid., pp. 10-14.

34   Walter Haney and George Madaus, "Searching for Alternatives to Standardized Tests: Whys, Whats, and Whithers," *Phi Delta Kappan* (May 1989): p. 684.

35   U.S. Department of Education, "Education Research Consumer Guide," Number 2 (Office of Educational Research and Improvement, November 1992), p. 1.

36   Wiggins, "A True Test," p. 705.

37   The Council's stated objectives are to provide data that will help provinces design educational policy and help the public assess educational effectiveness across Canada; see CMEC (Toronto,

December 1991), Background Paper no. 1, pp. 1-2.

38   Saskatchewan has chosen, for now, to take an observer's role in the SAIP program. For a time Ontario also took an observer's role, but when Ontario's concerns were addressed by negotiations between Ontario and the CMEC, Ontario returned to active participation.

39   CMEC, School Achievement Indicators Program, Background Paper no. 2 (Toronto, July 1992), p. 2.

40   Actually, the most common way for parents to choose schools for their children is to choose a neighbourhood in which to live. The quality of the local school is often quite relevant to parents' choice of residence.

41   According to Statistics Canada, *Elementary-Secondary School Enrolment 1990-91* (Ottawa, 1992), 4.7 percent of Canadian students attended private schools in 1990-91. This compares with 2.4 percent in 1970-71. "Private" schools are defined as schools that "operate outside the public system.... Some receive provincial support but they are managed privately by individuals, associations or corporations."

42   See Tim Sale, *Financing of Elementary and Secondary Education in Canada*, Working Paper no. 29 (Ottawa: Economic Council of Canada, 1992).

43   According to Barman, "Deprivatizing Private Education: The British Columbia Experience," *Canadian Journal of Education*, 16, 1 (1991), the provision of public funds to private schools in British Columbia began in 1977, when subsidy levels ranged from 10 to 30 percent, depending on the degree to which private schools were willing to obey provincial regulations. The maximum funding percentage was increased to 50 percent in 1989. Barman writes that "today ... the overwhelming majority of non-public schools receive 50 percent of the funding accorded local public schools." The public funding of private schools has led to an expansion in their enrolments in British Columbia from 4.3 percent in 1977-78 to 7.3 percent in 1990-91.

44   A policy of limited diversity is characteristic of contemporary educational policy in a number of countries other than Canada. As ably described by Edwin West, other Western countries are also loosening the ties between individual schools and education bureaucracies while maintaining significant government regulation of the curriculum. See Edwin West, "Education and Competitiveness" (Carleton University, Ottawa, 1992, photocopy). For example, in the United Kingdom individual schools can now choose to operate independently of the local school system while receiving funding directly from the central government. That increased autonomy is coupled, however, by the requirement that all schools adhere to a national curriculum, backed up by national testing. See United Kingdom, Department for Education, "Choice and Diversity: A New Framework for Schools" (London, 1992).

45   For a review of these arguments, see Edwin West, "Education and Competitiveness," and Henry M. Levin, "The Economics of Educational Choice," *Economics of Education Review*, 10, 2 (1991).

46   See Reich, *Work of Nations*.

47   Milton Friedman, *Capitalism and Freedom* (Chicago: University of Chicago Press, 1962), p. 86.

48   The extent to which the current set of private or independent schools actually avoids the production of these "public goods" is unknown. The most reasonable presumption is that while private schools would produce some of the public goods, the public schools would produce the public goods more effectively. At the same time, the private schools would produce the private goods more effectively.

      Furthermore, the same bias towards skills that will be rewarded in the job market exists if choice is expanded within the public sector. The problem created by a public good is that private parties have little incentive to use resources to produce the public goods because they cannot increase their own private gain by doing so. As long as parents can influence the curriculum of schools—private or public—there will be pressure to emphasize basic skills at the expense of abilities that the market does not reward directly.

49   In writing about the consequences of the 1977 decision to extend funding to formerly private schools, Barman ("Deprivatizing Private Education," pp. 20-21) writes that the number of Christian schools increased dramatically. Other private schools "fared variously" but "among the groups newly establishing schools in the 1980s in British Columbia were Mormons, Sikhs and Muslims."

50   Edwin West, "Public Education via Exclusive Territories," *Public Finance Quarterly*, 18, 4 (October 1990): p. 374.

51   Cited in Albo, "What Comes Next? Canadian Employment Policies After Fordism" (Toronto: York University, 1991), p. 41.

FISCAL FACTS AND TRENDS

This appendix presents an overview of the federal government's fiscal position and includes certain major economic policy indicators for the 1982-91 period, as well as some international comparisons.

Facts and trends are presented for federal revenue sources, federal expenditures by policy sector, the Government's share of the economy, interest and inflation rates, Canadian balance of payments in total and with the United States in particular, and other national economic indicators. In addition, international comparisons on real growth, unemployment, inflation and productivity are reported for Canada, the United States, Japan, Germany and the United Kingdom.

The figures and time series are updated each year, providing readers with an ongoing current record of major budgetary and economic variables.

Federal Tax Revenue By Source

Legend: Other, Indirect, Corporate, Personal

Fiscal year: 1983, 1984, 1985, 1986, 1987, 1988, 1989, 1990, 1991, 1992

($ Billions): $0, $20, $40, $60, $80, $100, $120, $140

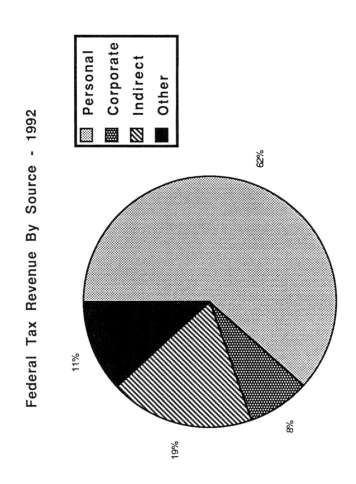

Federal Tax Revenue By Source - 1992

Personal
Corporate
Indirect
Other

62%

8%

19%

11%

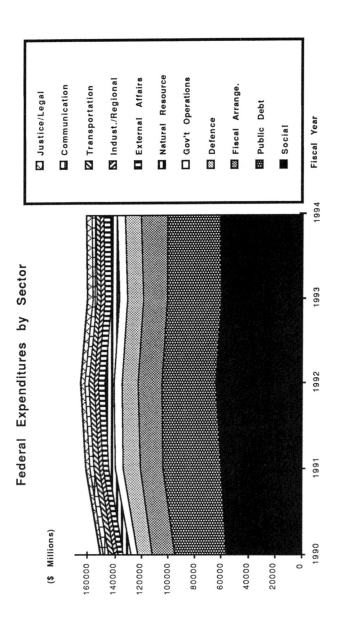

Federal Expenditures by Sector

Projected Federal Expenditures by Sector - 1994

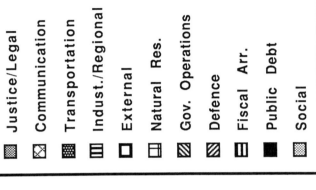

Justice/Legal

Communication

Transportation

Indust./Regional

External

Natural Res.

Gov. Operations

Defence

Fiscal Arr.

Public Debt

Social

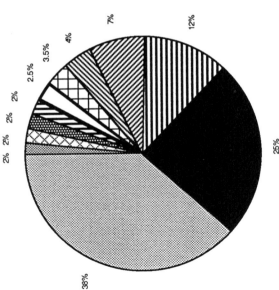

7%

12%

4%

3.5%

2.5%

2%

2%

2%

25%

38%

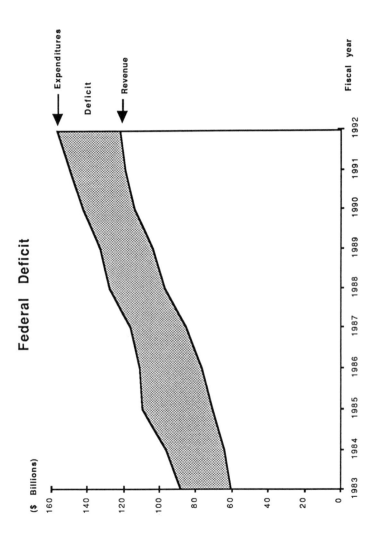

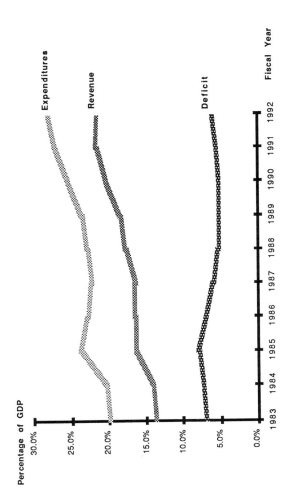

Revenue, Expenditures, and Deficit as
Percentages of Gross Domestic Product

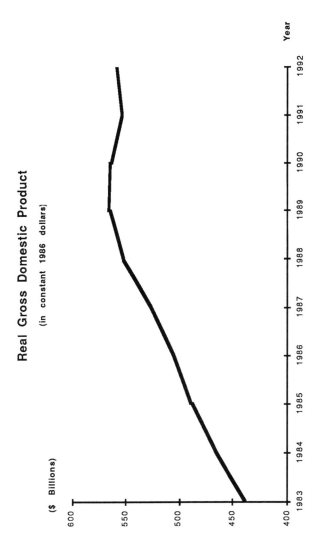

Real Gross Domestic Product

(in constant 1986 dollars)

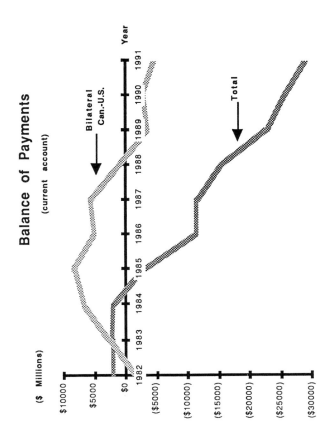

Balance of Payments
(current account)

($ Millions)

Year

Bilateral
Can.-U.S.

Total

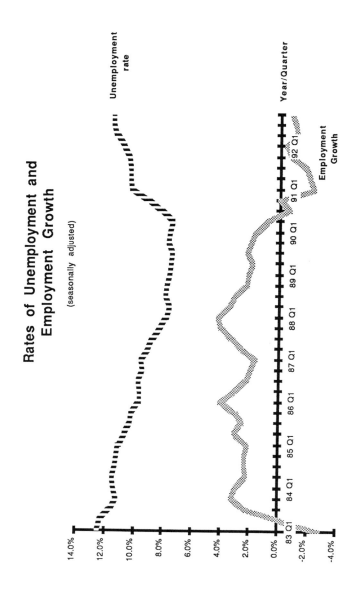

Rates of Unemployment and
Employment Growth

(seasonally adjusted)

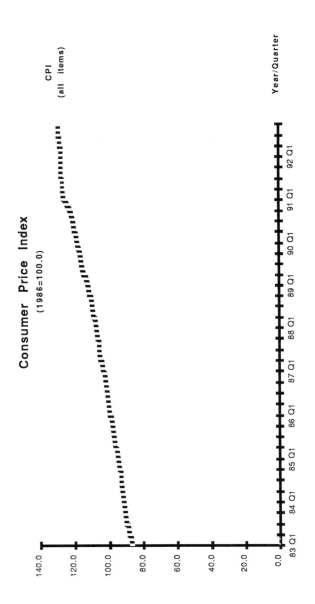

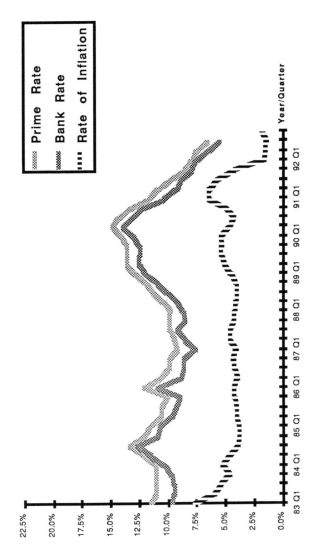

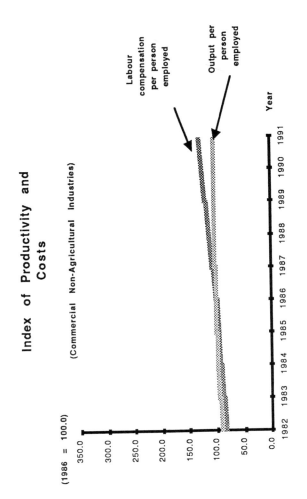

Index of Productivity and Costs

(Commercial Non-Agricultural Industries)

(1986 = 100.0)

Labour compensation per person employed

Output per person employed

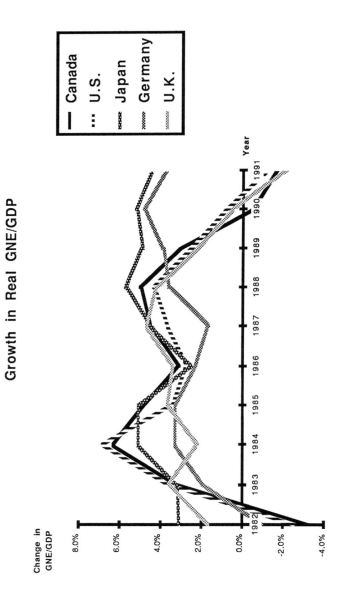

Growth in Real GNE/GDP

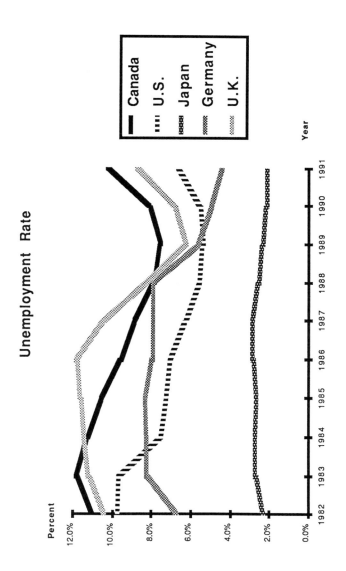

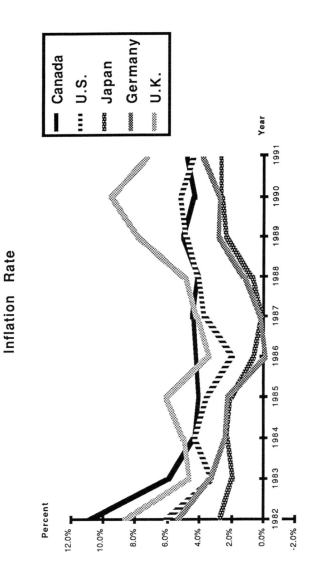

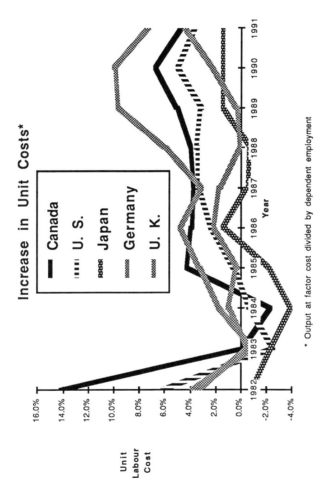

Federal Revenue by Source*
(% of Total)

Fiscal Year	Personal Tax (a)	Corporate Tax	Indirect Taxes (b)	Other Revenue (c)	Total Revenue	% Change Prev. Yr.
1983	47.8	13.0	23.1	16.1	100.0	2.0
1984	43.5	11.7	24.6	20.2	100.0	12.5
1985	47.1	12.0	23.3	17.6	100.0	25.9
1986	50.3	11.1	22.8	15.8	100.0	6.3
1987	54.1	11.3	23.9	10.7	100.0	5.6
1988	55.8	10.9	23.6	9.7	100.0	13.7
1989	54.0	11.0	24.6	10.4	100.0	6.6
1990	52.4	10.9	26.0	10.7	100.0	12.7
1991	57.4	11.2	21.8	9.6	100.0	2.3
1992	61.9	7.6	19.1	11.4	100.0	1.1

SOURCE: Dept. of Finance, Public Accounts (Ottawa: Supply and Services Canada), Various Years

(a) For the years 1985-88 unemployment insurance contributions are included in the total.

(b) Consists of sales taxes, energy taxes (except for petroleum & gas revenue tax and incremental oil revenue tax), excise duties, custom imports, and other excise duties and taxes.

(c) Consists of non-resident income tax, petroleum and gas revenue tax, incremental oil revenue tax, miscellaneous other taxes, and non-tax revenue.

Federal Deficit*
(millions of dollars)

Fiscal Year	Total Revenue	Total Expenditures	Budgetary Deficit	Percentage Change	As a % of GDP
1982	60,001	74,873	14,872	10.0	4.0
1983	60,705	88,521	27,816	87.0	6.9
1984	64,216	96,615	32,399	16.5	7.3
1985	70,891	109,222	38,324	18.3	8.0
1986	76,833	111,237	34,404	-10.2	6.8
1987	85,784	116,389	30,605	-11.0	5.6
1988	97,452	125,535	28,083	-8.2	4.7
1989	103,981	132,715	28,734	2.3	4.4
1990	113,707	142,703	28,966	0.0	4.4
1991	119,353	149,971	30,618	5.7	5.4
1992	122,032	156,675	34,643	13.1	5.1

SOURCE: Canada. Dept. of Finance, Public Accounts (Ottawa: Supply and Services Canada), 1991-92, Table 1.2.

* Revenues are calculated on a net basis.

Federal Expenditure by Sector
(% of Total Outlays)

Fiscal Year	Social	Fiscal Arrang.	Gov't Operation	Defence	Indust./ Regional	External Affairs	Justice Legal	Natural Resources	Transport.	Commun.	Public Debt	Total Outlays
1990	37.4	10.9	3.5	7.3	2.0	2.8	1.8	3.7	2.7	2.1	25.8	100.0
1991	37.7	10.8	3.7	7.5	1.9	2.3	1.9	3.4	2.3	2.0	26.5	100.0
1992	38.6	10.7	3.6	7.1	1.8	2.5	1.9	4.4	2.5	2.0	24.9	100.0
1993	37.8	11.0	3.8*	7.7	2.1	2.6	2.0	3.9	1.8	2.2	25.0	100.0
1994	38.0	11.9	3.8*	7.3	2.1	2.5	2.1	3.5	1.9	2.1	24.7	100.0

SOURCE: Canada. Dept. of Finance, Public Accounts (Ottawa: Supply and Services Canada), 1990-92; Canada. Dept. of Finance, 1993-94 Estimates (Ottawa: Supply and Services Canada, 1993).

* Excludes Government Contingency Vote (TB Vote 5); contingency amounts included in Total Outlays.

International Economic Comparisons*

(percentage changes)

	1982	1983	1984	1985	1986	1987	1988	1989	1990	1991
Growth in Real GDP (1)										
Canada	-3.2	3.2	6.3	4.8	3.1	4.5	5.0	3	-0.5	-1.7
U.S.	-2.5	3.6	6.8	3.4	2.7	3.7	4.4	2.5	0.8	-1.2
Japan	3.1	3.2	5.1	5.1	2.5	4.5	5.7	4.9	5.2	4.4
Germany	-1.0	1.9	3.3	3.3	2.3	1.7	3.6	3.9	4.8	3.7
U.K.	1.7	3.6	2.2	3.7	3.4	4.7	4.2	2.2	0.5	-2.2
Unemployment rate (2)										
Canada	11.0	11.8	11.2	10.5	9.5	8.8	7.8	7.5	8.1	10.2
U.S.	9.7	9.6	7.5	7.2	7.0	6.2	5.5	5.3	5.4	6.6
Japan	2.3	2.7	2.7	2.6	2.8	2.8	2.5	2.3	2.1	2.1
Germany	6.7	8.2	8.2	8.3	7.9	7.9	7.9	5.6	4.9	4.3
U.K.	10.4	11.2	11.4	11.6	11.8	10.4	8.2	6.2	6.8	8.7
Inflation (3)										
Canada	10.8	5.9	4.3	4.0	4.2	4.4	4.0	5	4.3	4.8
U.S.	6.1	3.2	4.3	3.5	1.9	3.7	4.1	4.8	5.2	4.3
Japan	2.7	1.9	2.3	2.0	0.6	0.1	0.7	2.3	2.6	2.6
Germany	5.3	3.3	2.4	2.2	-0.2	0.2	1.2	2.8	2.7	3.8
U.K.	8.6	4.6	5.0	6.1	3.4	4.2	4.9	7.8	5.3	7.2
Unit labour costs in manufacturing(4)										
Canada	14.2	-0.1	-2.3	4.3	3.9	3.7	4.0	5.1	6.8	4.7
U.S.	6.1	-2.5	-0.6	0.6	2.4	3.3	3.4	3.1	5	3.6
Japan	-0.8	-2.3	-3.9	-2.2	1.4	-0.5	-0.7	1.5	1.5	1.5
Germany	3.3	-0.5	1.0	0.3	2.2	1.7	0.1	0.4	2.3	4.5
U.K.	3.9	-1.0	1.8	3.3	4.8	3.1	6.0	9.7	10	7.2

SOURCES: OECD, Economic Outlook: Historical Statistics 1960-1986 (Paris: OECD) ; OECD, Economic Outlook (Paris: OECD), 1982-91.

* According to figures compiled by the OECD.

1. GNE data are reported for the U.S., Japan, Germany, and Canada, while GDP data are reported for the U.K.

2. Unemployment rates are on the basis of national definitions.

3. As measured by the year-to-year variation in the Consumer Price Index.

4. Defined as output at factor cost divided by dependent employment.

THE AUTHORS

Ken Battle is the President of the Caledon Institute of Social Policy in Ottawa.

Paul L.A.H. Chartrand is an Associate Professor in the Department of Native Studies, University of Manitoba.

Rebecca Coulthard is a masters student in the School of Public Administration, Carleton University.

Alexandra Dobrowolsky is a doctoral student in the Department of Political Science, Carleton University.

G. Bruce Doern is a Professor in the School of Public Administration, Carleton University.

Jane Jenson is a Professor in the Department of Political Science, Carleton University.

N. Harvey Lithwick is a Professor in the School of Public Administration, Carleton University.

Leslie A. Pal is a Professor in the School of Public Administration, Carleton University.

Susan D. Phillips is an Assistant Professor in the School of Public Administration, Carleton University.

Michael J. Prince holds the Lansdowne Chair in Social Policy, University of Victoria.

A. Paul Pross is a Professor in the School of Public Administration, Dalhousie University.

James J. Rice is an Associate Professor in the School of Social Work, McMaster University.

Ian Robinson is a Post-Doctoral Fellow at the Institute of Labor and Industrial Relations and a Visiting Assistant Professor in the Department of Political Science at the University of Michigan, Ann Arbor.

Saul Schwartz is an Associate Professor in the School of Public Administration, Carleton University.

F. Leslie Seidle is the Director of Research at the Institute for Research on Public Policy in Montreal.

Miriam Smith is an Assistant Professor in the Department of Political Science, Carleton University.

Iain S. Stewart is a masters student in the School of Public Administration, Dalhousie University.

Bruce W. Wilkinson is a Professor in the Department of Economics, University of Alberta.

THE SCHOOL OF PUBLIC ADMINISTRATION
at Carleton University is a national centre for the
study of public policy and public management
in Canada.

The School's Centre for Policy and Program Assessment provides research services and courses to interest groups, businesses, unions, and governments in the evaluation of public policies, programs, and activities.